POLITICAL
COMMUNICATION
and
DELIBERATION

Dedicated to Janet and Gordon Gastil.
If all else fails, run for Congress.

POLITICAL COMMUNICATION *and* DELIBERATION

JOHN GASTIL

University of Washington

SAGE Publications

Los Angeles • London • New Delhi • Singapore

Copyright © 2008 by Sage Publications, Inc.

All rights reserved. No part of this book may be reproduced or utilized in any form or by any means, electronic or mechanical, including photocopying, recording, or by any information storage and retrieval system, without permission in writing from the publisher.

For information:

Sage Publications, Inc.
2455 Teller Road
Thousand Oaks,
  California 91320
E-mail: order@sagepub.com

Sage Publications India Pvt. Ltd.
B 1/I 1 Mohan Cooperative
  Industrial Area
Mathura Road, New Delhi 110 044
India

Sage Publications Ltd.
1 Oliver's Yard
55 City Road
London EC1Y 1SP
United Kingdom

Sage Publications Asia-Pacific Pte. Ltd.
33 Pekin Street #02-01
Far East Square
Singapore 048763

Printed in the United States of America

Library of Congress Cataloging-in-Publication Data

Gastil, John.
Political communication and deliberation/John Gastil.
     p. cm.
Includes bibliographical references and index.
ISBN 978-1-4129-1627-1 (cloth)—
ISBN 978-1-4129-1628-8 (pbk.)
    1. Communication in politics. 2. Discussion. 3. Democracy.
I. Title.

JA85.G384 2008
320.01′4—dc22   2007025410

This book is printed on acid-free paper.

07   08   09   10   11   10 9 8 7 6 5 4 3 2 1

Acquisitions Editor:	Todd R. Armstrong
Editorial Assistant:	Sarah K. Quesenberry and Katie Grim
Production Editor:	Catherine M. Chilton
Copy Editor:	Cheryl Duksta
Typesetter:	C&M Digitals
Proofreader:	Doris Hus
Indexer:	Jeanne Busemeyer
Cover Designer:	Candice Harman
Front Cover Design:	Michael Briand
Marketing Manager:	Carmel Withers

Brief Contents

Detailed Contents

Preface

This book simultaneously introduces two subjects—the larger field of political communication and the more specialized topic of public deliberation.[1] When understood in broad terms, deliberation is the central concept underlying a range of empirical research topics and moral questions raised in political communication scholarship—from how media framing can constrain public discussion to how partisan pressures warp congressional debates. Deliberation provides a unifying conceptual and critical framework within which one can better organize and understand the large array of political communication topics.[2]

New Topics in Political Communication

I refer to this as a broad deliberative framework because I advance a more flexible yet precise definition of deliberation than scholars have used in the past.[3] This book unfolds that definition in detail, but in shorthand terms, people deliberate when they carefully examine a problem and a range of solutions through an open, inclusive exchange that incorporates and respects diverse points of view.

This definition is adaptive enough to encompass a wide range of activities. If, by contrast, deliberation is defined solely as a formal public process of face-to-face discussion, that would exclude more informal activities and mediated processes that do not necessarily entail interpersonal interaction.[4] Working from a broader definition of deliberation, in each political communication context I specify a distinct and precise meaning that makes deliberation a more concrete concept. This specificity avoids the problem that arises when one uses only a generic meaning that encompasses both face-to-face discussion and mediated deliberation, such as "reasoning and discussion about the merits of public policy."[5]

Working within this flexible deliberative framework, it is easy to identify some topics that have been overlooked by conventional political communication handbooks, textbooks, and reviews. For instance, there exists a growing body of research on political conversation and discussion. These topics elude many observers of political communication, except insofar as talk among citizens serves as a conduit for media influence. Jury deliberation has been construed as a nonpolitical process, despite the fact that jury service is a uniquely valuable and political experience in public deliberation for many citizens. Public meetings are another important venue in which citizens step into the public sphere, and new research is helping us understand how those meetings unfold and what impact they have on larger political processes. Synthetic analyses of political discourse and communication systems spanning communities and nations often remain disconnected from other political communication research, yet such work can help us theorize public talk at the highest levels of abstraction. All of these subjects can fall outside conventional boundaries of the field of political communication, and this book integrates these overlooked subjects with more familiar ones, such as media messages, campaign behavior, and public opinion.

Organization of the Book

The first chapter of the book sets the stage for studying political communication across a range of contexts. Chapter 1 introduces the broader concept of deliberation by showing its central role in the democratic process. An overview shows how the meaning of deliberation effectively adapts to different contexts, from face-to-face conversations to macrolevel political systems.

Conversations and discussions are the simplest and most familiar forms of deliberation. Accordingly, Chapter 2 introduces a more detailed conception of deliberation in this context, talking about deliberative experiences to which any reader can relate. A theme running through Chapter 2 is how deliberation shapes participants' opinions, and Chapter 3 continues this thread by examining how the mass media shape public opinion. Chapter 4 moves from public opinion to voting choices in elections, and this chapter shows how conversations, public discussions, and media can combine to facilitate a large-scale deliberative electoral process. Chapter 5 then asks whether those who win public elections—along with those whom elected officials appoint—deliberate once they take office.

Taken together, Chapters 2 through 5 describe the role of deliberation in a representative democracy—from opinion formation to elite decision making. Given the condition of modern society, the deliberative framework is more of a critical lens than it is an apt description of this process, but as a lens it shows how the various defects in existing practices and institutions add up to serious systemwide deficiencies. This is not to say that there are not deliberative features or moments in modern public life, but the deliberative project is more often about effective criticism of the status quo than it is about self-congratulation.

Chapter 6 returns to the small-group level of analysis introduced in Chapter 2, this time focusing on the jury to consider how well citizens deliberate within this unique institution. The deliberative framework highlights the considerable value of jury service as an archetype of deliberation and a means of teaching everyday citizens the basic skills of deliberation. As it happens, the jury is also the model for some recent attempts to incorporate citizens more directly in public policy discussions. Chapter 7 introduces these ideas by reviewing the range of public meeting methods in use—from conventional public hearings, to deliberative polls, to innovative citizen juries.

Chapters 8 and 9 pull together the practices and institutions from Chapters 2 through 7 to consider what deliberation might look like in a larger system. Chapter 8 asks what it would mean to be a deliberative community. How can a town or city integrate ongoing public discussions, media, and public meetings to foster a deliberative spirit not just during elections but throughout its public decision-making processes? Chapter 9 considers the potential for deliberative practices that cross national borders. How deliberative are bodies such as the United Nations or the World Trade Organization, and can new institutions provide a common space in which the world might deliberate?

Historical, Theoretical, and Empirical Questions

Chapters 2 through 9 follow deliberation through distinct contexts, but in each case the same four kinds of questions are addressed. These questions give each chapter a parallel structure that helps students navigate across a variety of topics.

First, each chapter briefly considers the historical context of a given practice or institution, such as the mass media or the jury system. For instance, where did the idea of a jury originate, and how have jury systems evolved over time? Answers to these questions give the reader a greater sense for how political communication practices and systems change over time.

Second, broad theoretical questions frame the research reviewed in each chapter. As a starting point, each chapter poses a conceptual question: What does deliberation mean in this context, such as in the case of mediated deliberation? Each chapter then raises a moral philosophical question: When is deliberation appropriate in this setting? Answers to these questions give the reader a clear understanding of what deliberation would look like in this context and when one might hope to see it happen.

Attention then turns to research on the modern practice of political communication. How often, for instance, do individual citizens actually participate in public meetings, and are those meetings typically deliberative? What are the consequences of this deliberation, or the lack thereof? Looking carefully at current practices shows the ways in which modern political communication is (or is not) deliberative and what that means for our society. This constitutes the main portion of each chapter, and the goal is not so much to provide comprehensive coverage of topics and studies as much as it is to incorporate the most significant, sustained political communication research programs, along with some of the most striking recent findings in the field.

Each chapter also considers the potential for change toward ever more deliberative practices. Just as current practices grew out of previous ones, so will the future bring changes, for better or for worse. What forces promote or obstruct deliberation in the modern context? What reforms are most likely to improve the frequency and quality of deliberation? Answers to questions such as these help readers imagine more deliberative conversations, media, public meetings, and more.

A Note for Instructors

This book was written to be appropriate not only for general and academic readers but also for students in a course on political communication or deliberation. When used as a primary text, this book should help students learn in four ways. First, students should develop a critical theoretical framework through which they can appraise the deliberative democratic quality of media, meetings, and even conversations. Second, students should learn general facts about historical and contemporary political communication practices. Third, students should acquire the skills, habits, and motivation they need to be effective deliberators in public life. Finally, students should gain a better sense for what can be done to promote a more deliberative democratic system in their own communities and the world.

Instructors using this book as a primary text should log on to this book's Web site, which describes activities students can do inside and outside of class to learn the concepts and skills of deliberation. From conducting media content analyses to participating in a jury deliberation exercise, students can see through their own work what deliberation looks like and what habits and practices stand in its way.

Companion Web Site

A dedicated Web site, www.ideliberate.org, will inventory anything else that might be useful for instructors using *Political Communication and Deliberation* in their courses. Syllabus suggestions will show how to use the book when teaching a semester- or quarter-long course, and there is a set of classroom exercises and larger projects that have been used in previous courses. Also, a wiki and a forum will let instructors exchange teaching ideas, links, and new content to supplement each chapter.

Acknowledgments

Deliberation made this book possible. This book builds on fifteen years of lively exchanges with colleagues and students in classrooms, conferences, coffee houses, and cyberspace. At the same time, it draws on decades of conversations (and arguments) with family, friends, and neighbors about democracy and American politics. Perhaps most of all it incorporates insights codiscovered with undergraduates and graduate students in seminar rooms and lecture halls. Weaving all these threads together has been a delight, and were the following list complete, I would thank almost everyone I have known (and many persons I have never met off the printed page).

For extensive comment on drafts of this manuscript, thanks go to Simone Chambers, Lew Friedland, Jamie Moshin, and David Ryfe, along with Todd Armstrong, Catherine Chilton, Katie Grim, Cheryl Duksta, and Sarah Quesenberry at SAGE. Among those colleagues I must thank by name for their thoughts and suggestions on deliberation, I count Ted Becker, Lance Bennett, Laura Black, Don Braman, Michael Briand, Stephanie Burkhalter, Martin Carcasson, John Dedrick, Perry Deess, Jim Fishkin, Sue John, Bill Keith, Jay Leighter, Peter Levine, Bob Luskin, Dan Kahan, Todd Kelshaw, Jay Leighter, Matt Leighninger, Stephen Littlejohn, Carolyn Lukensmeyer, Patricia Moy, Gerry Phillipsen, Hank Jenkins-Smith, Jenny Mansbridge, David Mathews, Walter Parker, Pat Scully, Mark Smith, Phil Weiser, Mark West, and Mike Xenos. In addition, I heartily thank the reviewers of the proposal and draft manuscript for their thoughtful and helpful insights: Robert Asen (Department of Communication Arts, University of Wisconsin–Madison), Simone Chambers (Department of Political Science, University of Toronto), Lew Friedland (School of Journalism & Mass Communication, University of Wisconsin–Madison), Francesca Polletta (Sociology Department, Boston College), David Ryfe (Donald W. Reynolds School of Journalism and Center for Advanced Media Studies, University of Nevada–Reno), and Katherine Cramer Walsh (Department of Political Science, University of Wisconsin–Madison). Friends and family who have shared more insights than I dare credit in the endnotes include Ned Crosby, Bob Kraig, Ralph Shelton, Cindy Simmons, James Webb, Uncle Ray, and Todd Wynward.

Finally, in lieu of the obligatory greatest thanks of all, let me note that Claude Bart has been with me always as I wrote this book, yet he offered no concrete assistance whatsoever. He has his reasons but—he would insist—no excuses. Apology accepted, Claude.

Notes

1. For reviews of the theoretical and empirical literature on deliberation, see Chambers (2003); Delli Carpini, Cook, and Jacobs (2004); Mendelberg (2002), and Ryfe (2005). The field of political communication is too diffuse to be summarized in this way, but one gets a sense of the breadth of work in the field by perusing the journal *Political Communication* or Kaid (2004).

2. Besley and McComas (2005) made a similar effort to frame much political communication research in relation to the concept of procedural justice. In effect, I am making the same argument but with greater specificity, arguing that the deliberative democratic procedure is the primary justice frame through which scholars carry out their research and both scholars and citizens evaluate their political communication system and practices.

3. I count myself among those who have worked from more restrictive definitions of deliberation in previous work. A good example of my previous attempts to define the term are Gastil (1993), Gastil (2000), and Burkhalter, Gastil, and Kelshaw (2002). Dahlgren (2002) struggled with this problem of trying to reconcile abstract theoretical conceptions of deliberation with broader notions of political talk. Ultimately, he concluded that *deliberation* is a "specialised, formal mode of discourse, and thus we would do better, in the empirical world, to think about 'discussion' or 'talk,' which can encompass many different kinds of communicative interaction" (p. 10). *Civic discussion,* in this scheme, is one of the five dimensions of "civic culture," yet he then added, "This dimension is in some way an overarching one, one that embodies the others. Yet, I think it will prove productive to see it as a distinct dimension, functioning in reciprocity with the other dimensions of the circuit, being both shaped by and impacting on the other five" (p. 18). An "overarching" yet "distinct" conception of deliberation (or "discussion") is precisely what I aim for in presenting a general definition of deliberation that articulates itself differently in Chapters 2 through 9. In addition, staying with the word *deliberation,* rather than *discussion,* facilitates the creation of a critical (as well as conceptual) framework, as deliberation has more straightforward normative implications than do "discussion" or "talk."

4. Walsh (2004) made this observation when juxtaposing her work on informal, community-building conversations with more formal conceptions of deliberation. Definitions of deliberation that conceptualize deliberation as a small group activity include Mendelberg (2002) and Burkhalter et al. (2002).

5. Page (1996, p. 2). Similarly, Kim, Wyatt, and Katz (1999, pp. 361–62) come close to defining deliberation in a way that would exclude non-interactive deliberative processes, such as mediated deliberation.

SOURCE: iStockphoto. Used by permission.

1

Democracy and Deliberation

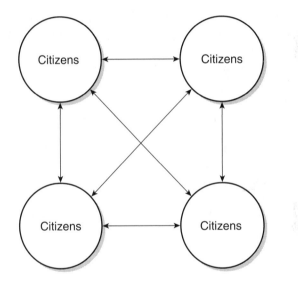

If liberty and equality, as is thought by some, are chiefly to be found in democracy, they will be best attained when all persons alike share in the government to the utmost.

—Aristotle[1]

Voting is a sacred act in a democracy. Whatever its virtues, a political system cannot begin to call itself democratic unless its citizens, one and all, have the right to vote. By degrees, many societies have met this basic standard, with each of their citizens empowered to elect representatives or vote directly on policy. But is that enough?

Imagine a country in which all citizens could vote but they could not express themselves, save through marking a ballot. Would it be enough for people to go about their lives in quiet isolation, periodically appearing in public to punch holes next to candidates' names? Or, even worse, what if citizens could communicate but lacked the ability to think, to reason, to judge for themselves? What kinds of results would elections yield if voters had no concept of whom they were voting for or what a "yes" or "no" vote really meant on a ballot initiative?

This hypothetical nation of zombie-citizens, more likely to eat brains than use them, may sound like a made-for-television science-fiction movie, but the living dead have more in common with the living than we might care to notice. Most U.S. citizens shy away from political conversation and rarely attend public meetings of any sort.[2] Even then, only about half of Americans choose to express themselves by voting for their president, with far fewer choosing to vote during other elections.[3] Moreover, we often know precious little about whom or what we are voting for. In 2004, for example, a survey shortly before the presidential election found that two thirds of those voting to reelect George W. Bush believed he supported banning nuclear weapons testing and participating in the Kyoto treaty on global warming—two policies he openly opposed.[4] A 2003 study of voters in Washington State just a week before Election Day found that very few even knew what issues would appear on their ballot. On most issues, fewer than one in five Washington voters could make a pro or con argument.[5] A few days later, these people cast their ballots, endorsing or rejecting laws to which they had given precious little thought.

The lesson here is not that your long-lost neighbor has risen from the grave and may soon develop an appetite for human flesh. Rather, the point is that we may want to ask more of our political system than merely granting us the right to vote. More fundamentally, we might even say that democracy requires more than just voting rights and "rule by all." But what, then, does democracy mean? If we want to expect more of our fellow citizens, and perhaps our public officials and our media as well, what exactly should we expect? Beyond allowing the vote, how do we know when a system is democratic?

Three Criteria for the Democratic Process

Anyone can call his or her country a democracy. It is quite fashionable for American politicians to refer to the United States as "the world's greatest democracy," despite remarkably high numbers of citizens declining to vote in each election. Indians refer to their country as "the world's largest democracy," despite its maintenance of a rigid caste system. Greeks call their nation "the world's oldest democracy," though the ancient Athenian system consciously excluded women and endorsed slavery throughout its existence. Cubans now proclaim their system a "true democracy," though the Cuban government pro-foundly limits dissent.[6]

Vernacular understandings of democracy are also inadequate. One careful study of what democracy means to average Americans found that, despite their devotion to it as a principle, most people lack a firm grasp of the concept. "You mean freedom?" one respondent asked. Another suggested that democracy means "freedom of choice in anything you want to do, short of killing some-body or kidnapping or stuff like that." A third respondent expressed a senti-ment many of us might share: "I feel so stupid. People come around and say, 'Oh, you live in a democracy,' [but] I don't know exactly what they are talking about when they say that."[7]

At its core, democracy means self-rule, rule by all. When Aristotle wrote *Politics*, he construed democracy as a set of institutions that make the will of the majority into the law of the land:

> Such being our foundation and such the principle from which we start, the characteristics of democracy are as follows: the election of officers by all out of all; and that all should rule over each, and each in his turn over all; that the appointment to all offices, or to all but those which require experience and skill, should be made by lot; that no property qualification should be required for offices, or only a very low one.[8]

What is noteworthy about Aristotle's conception of democracy is its emphasis on holding regular elections, giving persons an equal chance to hold offices, and limiting the constraints on full citizenship. Those are, indeed, foundational ideas in democracy, but in the modern context it takes more than these minimal characteristics to count as a full-fledged democracy.

There is no consensus on what democracy means, but political scientist Robert Dahl developed a useful way of understanding the term.[9] In his view, just as no human being is perfect, no nation is a pure democracy. Instead, each country is more or less democratic by degrees. The way you can tell them apart is by asking how well a system sizes up when measured by specific criteria: inclusion, effective participation, and enlightened understanding.[10] These cri-teria work equally well for large nations, small groups, or any association that hopes to call itself democratic.

INCLUSION

First, a system (country, organization, group) must satisfy the criterion of inclusion by welcoming into its political process all adults who exist within its boundaries. To the extent that a system counts people as adult members but excludes them from its decision-making process, the system cannot call itself democratic.

This definition presumes that children are incapable of creating a self-governing society, *Lord of the Flies* notwithstanding, but any parent will agree that, at least at early ages, children are ill-equipped to make judgments on behalf of the larger public. Left open to question is the precise age marking the end of childhood. After all, the voting age was lowered in the United States from 21 to 18 with the passage of the Twenty-sixth Amendment in 1971, and it may eventually fall to 16. Even advocates of lowering the voting age, however, are comfortable stopping at 16, for fear of the ramifications of handing over ballots to roaming packs of middle schoolers.[11] In addition to children, a democratic system can exclude those who are just passing through, such as tourists or visiting guests, as well as those who are severely mentally incapacitated to the point of being unable to care for themselves.

PARTICIPATION OPPORTUNITIES

Once you are recognized as a member of a democracy, you must then have equal and adequate opportunities to participate in three related ways—putting issues on the agenda, expressing your views on those issues, and voting on those issues, directly or indirectly. What these processes mean depends, in part, on whether you belong to a representative or direct democracy.

In a direct democracy, such as a small group that elects no leaders and makes all its decisions by consensus, democracy requires that you have the same chance as anyone else in your group to put items on the group's meeting agendas, express your views on those items when they come up for discussion, and vote for or against an idea, presuming it garners enough support to even come up for a vote.

More common are systems that elect representatives. From fraternities and sororities to cities and nations, democratic systems rely on the election of representatives to carry out the business of making policies and laws. In these cases, it is critical that you and your fellow association members have an equal opportunity to nominate candidates, cheer some and boo others, and then vote for or against them. Those elected representatives then must have equal say in placing issues on their agenda, debating them, and voting on them.

Even in a system with elected representatives, however, democracy requires that all citizens have an equal chance to raise issues for discussion—either by fellow citizens or by their elected representatives. Citizens must also have the chance to articulate their positions and attempt to persuade one another and their public officials.

Moreover, many systems offer a mix of direct democracy with the election of representatives. If you live in a city or state that puts questions on ballots in the form of referenda, initiatives, or ballot measures, for instance, you are participating directly in the lawmaking process. A democratic process requires that in such elections, you have an equal chance to put issues on the ballot (by gathering signatures or by other means), discuss and debate the issues with fellow citizens, and vote yea or nay on each issue.[12]

Note that your opportunities to participate—directly and through the election of representatives—must not only be equal to that of your neighbors but also must be adequate. This means that a system fails to be democratic if it divides up the opportunity pie evenly but fails to make enough pie to satisfy. Nobody likes getting shortchanged on pie, even if it's known that everybody else also got half a teaspoon. Thus democracy requires that all people have sufficient opportunities to set the agenda, speak their minds, and complete their ballots.

ENLIGHTENED UNDERSTANDING

Finally, all members of a democracy must have the chance to figure out which issues concern them, what they think about those issues, and how they should vote when given the chance to do so. Enlightened understanding, the third and final criterion, is critical because, frankly speaking, it separates a deliberative system from an unreflective one. An inclusive system that gives everyone the opportunity to speak but does not grant the time (or tools) to think will be a dismal one indeed, full of empty speeches and reckless voting. Only when members of the public become accustomed to figuring out what's important will the issues of the day be of consequence. And only when people learn how to study issues and reflect carefully on their values—as well as those of their fellow citizens—will the public become well informed enough to speak, act, and vote in accordance with their enlightened self-interest, let alone for the greater public good.

This is not to say that I, you, or anyone else knows what is in everybody else's best interest. If we did, then who would need a democracy? No, what this means is that people need to have enough of a chance to work through issues to say with confidence that they understand which issues are important and to explain what their own views are on those issues. One clear sign of enlightened understanding, for instance, is when people can explain not only their own views on these subjects but also the views of others with whom they disagree. A person with an enlightened point of view incorporates relevant facts to arrive at informed judgments. Enlightened persons also can empathize with the emotional experiences of people on all sides of an issue, genuinely understanding the hopes and fears of others with views different from their own.

It may seem remarkable for a democracy to require such enlightened understanding from its citizens, but this is no different from expecting elected representatives to listen to competing points of view and to gather and weigh important facts. The only difference is the level of technical detail representatives must gather and the sheer volume of issues they must weigh in a given year. At a minimum, average citizens must become sufficiently enlightened to cast meaningful ballots in elections; ideally, democratic citizens must learn much more if they are to participate effectively in setting the system's agenda and persuading policy makers.

How Deliberation Makes Democracy Work

Because democracies large and small require coordination among their members, democracy cannot long survive without communication. A democracy must be inclusive, and therefore its communication infrastructure must be able to accommodate diverse voices and ways of speaking. Because a democracy must ensure adequate opportunities to participate, its public must have the capacity to hear from thousands or even millions of fellow citizens at the same time. And because a democracy must cultivate an enlightened understanding of each citizen's interests, it must have a sophisticated means of collecting, processing, and distributing information and experiences among its diverse, large membership. Some of this communication infrastructure is inevitably centralized in government agencies, but the bulk of the political speaking, broadcasting, and publishing takes place in private institutions, such as newspapers and nonprofit organizations, and in informal encounters.

The character of centralized and decentralized political communication varies tremendously from one society to the next and even within a given system. Political communication likely includes every form of speech, such as explaining, arguing, refuting, criticizing, pleading, and so on. Deliberating is a particularly important way of communicating but not because it is most common, most popular, or most powerful. Instead, deliberation is valuable because it is the standard by which one can judge the wider array of political communication practices. The more often a system deliberates, the more readily it can meet the three criteria for the democratic process.

WHAT DELIBERATION MEANS

When people deliberate, they carefully examine a problem and arrive at a well-reasoned solution after a period of inclusive, respectful consideration of diverse points of view.[13] That shorthand definition packs a set of discrete considerations into a single statement, but it is helpful to break the term down into separate parts. Each of these parts takes on a more precise meaning depending on the context in which we are deliberating, and each chapter in this book introduces a distinct meaning for deliberation. Nonetheless, as in the previous statement, deliberation has a general significance that transcends a variety of political communication settings.

Deliberation begins when we create a solid information base to make sure we understand the nature of the problem at hand, such as air pollution. Second, we identify and prioritize the key values at stake in an issue. In the case of controlling pollution, for instance, we might weigh values as diverse as maintaining public health, protecting endangered species, permitting free enterprise, and preserving the pleasant view of a blue sky. Third, we identify a broad range of solutions that might address the problem, including everything from enacting a system of voluntary self-regulation by polluters to prohibiting the emission of certain industrial pollutants to exhorting the public to change its consumption habits. Fourth, we weigh the pros, cons, and trade-offs of the solutions by systematically applying our knowledge and values to each alternative. Thus, a deliberating group might eliminate one solution as too costly, despite its profound health benefits. A group will have deliberated in this respect if it faces the trade-offs among different alternatives, recognizes that no solution is perfect, and tries to grapple with conflicting values and information. If it takes place within a decision-making body, deliberation ends with the group making the best decision possible, in light of what has been learned through discussion; otherwise, the deliberation may end with each individual participant arriving at an independent judgment on the matter.[14]

Deliberation, however, is not just about the substance of an exchange. Deliberation also refers to the social process of communicating. Foremost among these considerations is ensuring all participants an adequate opportunity to speak. If, for instance, our hypothetical pollution debate involves two people out of twenty monopolizing the discussion, the process would be less deliberative due to this domineering behavior.[15]

We are all familiar with this notion of speaking rights, which is taught to most people in early childhood ("You'll get your turn to speak, Stewie"). Less intuitive is the idea that you also have a right to comprehend what others are saying, albeit within limits. If another person explains a problem to you in terms you cannot understand, it may be that you lack the technical training necessary to comprehend the complexity of the issue. It is more likely, though, that the speaker has not made an effort (or simply failed) to communicate in a way that you can understand. After all, if Stephen Hawking can make a small fortune by explaining intricate astrophysical principles in terms a general audience can grasp, it is likely that in most political discussions a speaker can help you follow what he or she is saying.

Just as deliberative speakers give you the chance to understand them, so do you have the obligation to consider carefully the words that you hear others utter. Consideration begins with careful listening that is attentive both to the content of a speaker's words and to the speaker's larger perspective or experience. You can consider what someone says about pollution by processing the raw content. Thus, the statement "I grew up in a city where our schools had to close due to 'smog days'" tells you that some cities have such bad pollution that the air is unsafe for children—something you may not have known. In addition, though, you can consider the lived experience of the speaker, who is telling the group that he or she has personally breathed air so foul that the speaker can probably remember its smell and taste. Considering people's words, then, means both reasoning through their words and taking them to heart.

Finally, the deliberative process requires maintaining a degree of respect for yourself and your fellow participants, unlike the all-too-common type of exchange shown in Figure 1.1. Respect is a complex concept, but at this point it is enough to say that deliberation asks you to remember that each participant is simultaneously a private individual with unique hopes and fears and a member of the larger group or society to which you belong. Respect also means treating all others as sincere, competent participants, as long as they do not themselves reject these principles.[16] When other deliberators begin to recklessly disregard the principle of respect, it is hoped that you can at least be congenial or neighborly, even if they make you want to scream (or worse).

Figure 1.1   What the World Looks Like Without Deliberation

DELIBERATION ACROSS DIFFERENT
SETTINGS AND LEVELS OF ANALYSIS

One of the challenges of studying deliberation and political communication is that they happen in so many different places—from street corners to legislatures. But even more difficult is tracking them across different levels of analysis. The smallest social unit of analysis is the dyad, a pairing of two people, such as in a one-on-one political conversation. At this level, we look at the utterances of two people and examine how the people take turns speaking, how they listen and respond to each other, and so forth. The next largest unit is the group meeting, such as a deliberating jury, in which multiple people are speaking and listening. At this level, things can happen that don't occur in a dyad, such as a few group members breaking off into a side conversation or one set of members forming a coalition against others. The organizational level of analysis, which applies to legislatures, adds the extra complexity of group members not always being copresent (in the same room at the same time) and communicating with each other in a variety of settings (committee hearings, floor debates, conversations in the hall, confidential e-mails, etc.).

One can keep moving up to even higher levels of abstraction. When we talk about how the media facilitates deliberation, we must look at how independent groups of individuals (reporters, editors, bloggers, etc.) create a complex web of media that is then read, watched, or otherwise processed by a diffuse public. At the largest level of analysis, we can ask whether an entire election campaign is a deliberative process or whether a community, nation, or international community is deliberating effectively on a given issue.

The challenge of studying communication across these different political settings and levels is keeping a steady frame of reference. What the deliberative perspective offers is both a broad conceptual framework and a philosophical point of view. First, each of the facets of the deliberative process, such as the development of an information base to aid decision making, is a key concept that organizes a considerable amount of research in the field. Second, each facet of deliberation also identifies a key ethical principle in communication research, such as the idea that different persons, with their own points of view, should have equal voice. Deliberation is powerful because we can use its different components to organize research across the diversity of settings and levels of analysis in the field of political communication. For example, some media consolidation researchers worry about the exclusion of certain voices as media outlets become part of an ever-smaller number of parent companies. Research on public meetings often asks whether social or political minorities are likely to feel welcome to speak up during meetings. Despite the difference in scale and setting, both of these research areas are asking a question about equality of access—essentially, opportunities to speak.

Using deliberation as a consistent set of concepts and ethical concerns, we examine in succession eight different political communication contexts. We begin in Chapter 2 with the simplest and most familiar form of deliberation, the political conversation or group discussion. The development of new communication technology now makes it possible to look at both face-to-face and online interactions, but in either case the number of participants is small and the interaction is relatively finite. Chapter 3 moves to a much higher level of analysis to look at the larger conversation that takes place when the public deliberates—or fails to deliberate—through the mass media. Chapter 4 moves to an even higher level of abstraction by asking whether elections are ever deliberative. This involves looking at not only media and public conversations but also strategic campaign communication through advertising, candidate debates, and other political activities.

The next two chapters return to a more focused setting for analysis. Chapter 5 examines whether those elected or appointed to government positions actually deliberate while serving as public officials. Chapter 6 looks at citizens who are temporarily in a kind of public office when they are sworn in as jurors and asked to deliberate on civil and criminal cases. Juries have been largely overlooked in political communication research, but as the most widely recognized form of public deliberation they merit careful study. Chapter 7 adds to the two previous chapters by looking at how public officials and citizens can work together in public meetings. This chapter considers a range of public meeting processes where citizens and officials meet, from conventional public hearings to citizen juries.

All of the processes in Chapters 2–7 come together in Chapters 8 and 9, which look at deliberation from the highest levels of analysis. These chapters consider what an entire political communication system might look like in terms of deliberation. Chapter 8 asks how a larger community could blend public discussions, media, and public meetings to foster a continuously deliberative process of solving its larger problems. Chapter 9 asks a similar question, but of international problems rather than local ones: How deliberative are international bodies such as the United Nations or the World Trade Organization, and how can we improve those institutions?

Conclusion

Across all of the subjects covered in this book, the core questions remain the same: Are we deliberating? If not, how can we make the process more deliberative? Behind those questions is that same aspiration with which we started—a hope that we can make our society more democratic. In a modern society, even after we settle legal issues about who is included in our political process, we continue to struggle with questions about equal participation and how well the public understands the questions we must confront. In the end, it is deliberation that helps us decide which issues to place on our nation's agenda, and it is deliberation that helps us work through those issues as we speak our minds before casting our votes. From the casual conversation to the congressional debate, we are nearer or farther from the democratic ideal depending on how well we learn to deliberate.

Notes

1. Aristotle (1988, book 4).
2. See Huckfeldt and Sprague (1995) and Jacobs, Delli-Carpini, and Cook (2004).
3. Even then, only about half of Americans choose to express themselves by voting for their president, with far fewer choosing to vote during the more common varieties of elections.
4. See Ivins (2004).
5. These data were reported in Gastil and Crosby (2003).
6. Instances of these and similar phrases abound in the self-congratulatory texts and pronouncements of many nations. See Holt (2006).
7. Rosenberg, Ward, and Chilton (1988, pp. 70–71).
8. Aristotle (1988, book 6:2).
9. Dahl (1989).
10. Dahl (1989) has a total of five criteria, including the three listed herein plus "voting equality at the decisive stage" and "control of the agenda." To simplify his model, I have collapsed those two criteria under effective participation by counting agenda setting and voting as critical forms of participation. Dahl defines voting equality thusly: "At the decisive stage of collective decisions, each citizen must be ensured an equal opportunity to express a choice that will be counted as equal in weight to the choice expressed by any other citizen. In determining outcomes at the decisive stage, these choices, and only these choices, must be taken into account" (p. 109). Control of the agenda means that "the demos must have the exclusive opportunity to decide how matters are to be placed on the agenda of matters that are to be decided by means of the democratic process" (p. 113).
11. See http://www.youthrights.org/vote10.shtml.
12. On the mechanics and impact of the initiative process in the United States, see Matsusaka (2004).
13. Burkhalter, Gastil, and Kelshaw (2002).
14. This model can be traced back to Dewey's (1910) analysis of how people think through problems. Gouran and Hirokawa (1996) extended Dewey's ideas to small groups.
15. Later, I stress that within a larger social context it can be important to have debates, polemics, and other "nondeliberative" modes of expression rounding out a larger systematic deliberative process. Thus, a deliberative media environment might include each of these modes, with the sum of the parts adding up to a lively, inclusive mass process of deliberation.
16. This definition of respect incorporates all of the elements of democratic relationship, which I outlined in *Democracy in Small Groups* (Gastil, 1993). At the time, I did not think of these as part of a group's "deliberation," but I have come to view them as being integral not only to democracy but to deliberation itself.

SOURCE: FIMA.

2

Conversation and Discussion

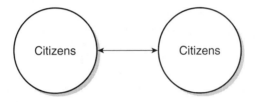

Conversation is the soul of democracy.

—Joohan Kim, Robert Wyatt, and Elihu Katz[1]

L et's join an online conversation already in progress. And, yes, the following
exchange is real. . . .

Eric shouts in frustration. He has just read a newspaper headline about New
Jersey's troops that have died in the Iraq War: "Jersey's share of a somber toll:
53 who won't see home again." So he puts his fingers on his keyboard and
writes his 1,997th post at conservative-talk.com. The point of that headline,
he surmises, "was that, even if it had been worth it to end the rule of Saddam
Hussein, there didn't seem to be a good reason why troops remain to secure
a democratic Iraq. The subtler message was that their lives had been wasted."
After comparing the Iraq coverage to reporting from World War II, he calls
out to his fellow conservatives, "I think in order to get the [conservative/pro-war]
movement some more momentum, we will have to eventually deal with the
media. Thoughts?"

   The first reply comes from a sympathetic reader going by the handle Mobile
Vulgus: "I think Americans ARE 'dealing with the media,'" he says wryly.
"Newspapers are falling apart in readership. The Network News is a shadow of
its former self in viewership, and news magazines have lower subscription
rates every year."

The next reply, however, challenges Eric's main points. Ken's posting offers historical perspective by way of his own experience. "Eric," he writes, "I remember sitting at the radio listening to the grim facts of war. 'Today we lost a hundred and twenty aircraft over Germany' was typical. The movie news reels showed Tarawa beaches awash with Marine dead. [World War II] was started because we were attacked; we knew who was responsible." By contrast, Ken argues, the Iraq War is now officially being waged "to remove a dictator (who we placed in power, just as we did to Pinochet and Noriega). We have lost two thousand people for what, to establish democracy? Why don't we go after Malaysia—there you can get five years for not being Muslim but being Christian or Jewish. I think they need democracy, too, don't you? Let's invade them."

WIRichie1971 quickly comes to Eric's aid and offers this challenge to Ken: "Okay Kenny [sic], I call bs: where are your links supporting the claim the CIA installed Saddam in power? Every biography I have ever read about him claimed he murdered his way to the top."

As I write, Ken has not yet taken up that challenge.[2] I briefly consider whether to jump into the fray or maintain my professional distance. A quick search on Google confirms my recollection that the PBS program *Frontline* explored early links between Saddam and the Central Intelligence Agency (CIA),[3] but I don't want to register at conservative-talk.com to make that point. I have enough junk e-mail as it is. Instead of posting, I return to my day job—writing this book.

Conversations like these happen every day, more likely every minute, in the online community, just as they have happened face to face for millennia. In a democratic society, informal discussions make up a large percentage of the universe of political communication messages that people produce. Though political talk itself is ancient, how we talk, whom we talk with, and what we discuss has varied considerably. Like most of our other basic social practices, from standing quietly in elevators to wearing black at funerals, talking about politics is a cultural accomplishment that requires a set of general rules that we learn through childhood socialization and have come to take for granted as adults. Our knowledge of those rules is tacit in that we cannot always articulate them, but they are real, whether or not we can see them at work.[4] To understand the hows and whys of modern political discussions, such as the one that took place between Eric, Mobile Vulgus, Ken(ny?), and WIRichie1971, it is useful to begin with a bit of history.

Historical Notes on Political Chatter

If the early political history of human civilization was one of repression and intolerance, it is fair to say that deliberative political conversation is on the upswing since those ages. As Susan Herbst has observed, "The hallmark of an oppressive society is the absence of a rich and varied public sphere where citizens can convene to debate vital questions of the day."[5]

Where open, unfettered political conversation first became the norm remains unclear, but we do know some early forerunners of modern conversational practices. As early as 1617, the French developed salons in Paris, not for haircuts and spa treatments but for conversation among the social elite outside of the palace or other places of government. In this setting, conversation was refined as an art, purposeful in its ends but open in its structure. Satisfying and effective conversation required the advance planning and graceful facilitation of a hostess, or salonnière, typically a woman of high social standing.

Herbst offers us this quick peek into one such conversation, culled from the notes of Mademoiselle Quinault, who was leading a group though reflections on religion. At one point, Monsieur Duclos asked the group, "Where does this nation keep its reasoning capacity? It scoffs at people of other lands, and yet is more credulous [ready to believe] than they." Monsieur Rousseau replied, "I can pardon its credulity, but not its condemnation of those whose credulity differs from its own." Mademoiselle Quinault interjected that "in religious matters, everyone was right," but "all people should stick to the religion in which they were born." Rousseau countered that they should certainly not stay with their inherited faith "if it is a bad religion, for then it can only do much harm." In the exchanges that followed, Mademoiselle Quinault decided that her own point of view lacked merit. The others, she recalled, "refuted me with arguments which did, as a matter of fact, appear to be better than mine."[6] These conversations were not trivial intellectual or theological exercises because they provided at least a thin slice of French society the space in which they could explore new ideas that would, ultimately, challenge the power of not only the church but of the king himself.

Appropriately enough, it would be the Frenchman Alexis de Tocqueville, who would come to recognize a new kind of civic discourse taking place in the still-young United States. Americans had discovered their own brand of spirited exchange, but what made it particularly remarkable in de Tocqueville's eyes was how far the Americans had gone toward overcoming the stiff reserve of the English:

> If two Englishmen chance to meet where they are surrounded by strangers whose language and manners are almost unknown to them, they will first stare at each other with much curiosity and a kind of secret uneasiness; they will then turn away, or if one accosts the other, they will take care to converse only with a constrained and absent air, upon very unimportant subjects. Yet there is no enmity between these men; they have never seen each other before, and each believes the other to be a respectable person.
>
> In America where the privileges of birth never existed and where riches confer no peculiar rights on their possessors, men unacquainted with one another are very ready to frequent the same places and find neither peril nor advantage in the free interchange of their thoughts. If they meet by accident,

they neither seek nor avoid intercourse; their manner is therefore natural, frank, and open. . . .

What made white American men different from their English counterparts, whom most counted as their ancestors? The answer, de Tocqueville reasoned, was "their social condition"—the relative indifference to social rank and class.[7]

The cultural contours of conversation have ebbed and flowed in the United States, as elsewhere. One particularly important trend was the early 19th century movement from informal, one-on-one conversation to structured group discussion. Roughly one hundred years ago, it became fashionable to debate and discuss ideas in large groups, such as a debate club, an open forum, or a town hall.[8]

As the popular affection for discussion grew, educators adapted their pedagogy away from lecture toward a more interactive method of instruction. In 1928, two influential books appeared, *Public Discussion and Debate* and *The Process of Group Thinking*.[9] These works helped to formalize emerging practices into a set of rules and procedures for effective discussion.

As recounted by communication scholar Ernest Bormann, discussion advocates insisted that "the individual citizen has an innate worth and dignity," which means that they are not to be manipulated for the state's purposes. Thus, each citizen should be free to discover his or her own opinions, and "public discussion gives citizens a chance to hear all sides of important public questions." Specifically, discussion should deploy "the scientific method" to conduct a rational analysis after discussants have "purged themselves of all emotional prejudices, interests, and biases." In the end, this process would benefit not only the individual but also the society, for "in the long run the majority of informed citizens would make the right decision."[10]

This rational model of discussion is still with us today, and it shapes the way many Americans think about conversation and discussion. Most of all, it has a profound influence on modern conceptions of what it means to have a deliberative conversation.

Imagining a Deliberative Conversation

THE IDEAL SPEECH SITUATION

Modern deliberative democratic theory comes directly from the cultural tradition that Bormann calls the public discussion model. Among the most influential works setting the stage for modern theories of deliberation are two works by German philosopher Jürgen Habermas, the *Structural Transformation of the Public Sphere* and *Communication and the Evolution of Society*.[11] In these works, Habermas tried to conceptualize an "ideal speech situation," in which two or more persons could infinitely question one another's beliefs about the world until each perspective had been fully scrutinized, leaving only a limited set of valid statements on which to base one's conclusions about an issue. Behind the abstract, at times impenetrable, philosophical language of Habermas's theory was none other than the public discussion model—the ideal of a rational exchange of views resulting in enlightened understanding.

There is no question but that this is part of what ideal deliberative conversation entails. In fact, the analytic process described in the left-hand column of Figure 2.1 conforms to this rational ideal to a degree. After all, gathering data and analyzing it systematically using consistent criteria is a relatively rigid way of deducing a solution.

DEMOCRATIC CONVERSATION

Deliberation, however, is more than this. Around the same time that Habermas was shaping his political theory, Benjamin Barber was capturing the imagination of scholars and citizens alike with his popular polemic *Strong Democracy*. Barber's book was an indictment of thin democracy, a bland soup of legal rights and institutions lacking in human connection and any tangible sense of a public. "At the heart of strong democracy," Barber insisted, "is talk."[12] By *talk*, Barber was not referring to the cold exchange and aggregation of individuals' predefined interests into a majority preference; rather, he imagined a more complex mix of imagining, wondering aloud, listening, and understanding. If thin democracy reduced talk to "the hedonistic speech of bargaining," then strong democracy would celebrate conversation.[13]

By *conversation* Barber meant a more open-ended process that was as much about mutual discovery as problem solving. In Barber's more florid prose, "A conversation follows an informal dialectic in which talk is used not to chart distinctions in the typical analytic fashion but to explore and create commonalities."[14] Talk of this sort must be open, inclusive, and free flowing: "Because conversation responds to the endless variety of human experience and respects the initial legitimacy of every human perspective, it is served by many voices rather than by one and achieves a rich ambiguity rather than a narrow clarity."[15]

With that in mind, look at the right-hand column in Figure 2.1 and notice that the analytic process includes personal and emotional experiences as well as facts. It involves introspection on subjective values, rather than merely objective analysis. It also includes open-ended brainstorming, holding more than one perspective at a time, and possibly never reaching a decision. In other words, it may be enough to just talk and listen for a while.

The social process in Figure 2.1 draws on both the Habermasian and Barberic conceptions of talk. Equal access, comprehension, and consideration have a rationalist side, but the social process of deliberation also speaks directly to Barber's interest in mutual respect and the consideration of "the other" as a

General Definition of Deliberation	Specific Meaning for Conversation/Discussion
Analytic Process	
Create a solid information base.	Discuss personal and emotional experiences, as well as known facts.
Prioritize the key values at stake.	Reflect on your own values, as well as those of others present.
Identify a broad range of solutions.	Brainstorm a wide variety of ways to address the problem.
Weigh the pros, cons, and trade-offs among solutions.	Recognize the limitations of your own preferred solution and the advantages of others.
Make the best decision possible.	Update your own opinion in light of what you have learned. No joint decision need be reached.
Social Process	
Adequately distribute speaking opportunities.	Take turns in conversation or take other action to ensure a balanced discussion.
Ensure mutual comprehension.	Speak plainly to each other and ask for clarification when confused.
Consider other ideas and experiences.	Listen carefully to what others say, especially when you disagree.
Respect other participants.	Presume that other participants are honest and well intentioned. Acknowledge their unique life experiences and perspectives.

Figure 2.1   Key Features of Deliberative Conversation and Discussion

whole person—more than just a source of ideas and information that happens to be human. Philosopher John Weithman describes this process as follows:

> Citizens taking part in public deliberation should be willing to offer considerations in favor of their positions that will enable others to see what reasons they have for them. They must be appropriately responsive to the reactions and replies those considerations evoke. They must be appropriately responsive

to the considerations put forward by others in favor of their positions. And they must respect at least those other participants who show that they are willing to comply with the norms of well-conducted deliberation.[16]

GRICEAN MAXIMS

Lest the deliberative model of conversation sound like a political philosopher's ungrounded abstraction, we should notice the many ways in which it corresponds to the universally taken-for-granted assumptions of human conversation. Linguist H. Paul Grice posited a series of rules or maxims that we all unconsciously follow as listeners to make sense of everyday conversation.[17] Figure 2.2 transposes each of the maxims into common expressions used in vernacular English. They can be summarized even more succinctly in the statement "Briefly tell me the complete truth I need to hear." The deliberative variant could be similarly summarized as "Let's briefly exchange the truths we need to share."

One of the ways we have confirmed that these maxims are at the core of our rules of speech is by watching the linguistic behavior of autistic children. Children with a specific language impairment have difficulty recognizing the

---

Maxim of Quality: Truth

- Do not say what you believe to be false ("Don't lie").
- Do not say that for which you lack adequate evidence ("Don't go out on a limb").

Maxim of Quantity: Information

- Make your contribution as informative as is required for the current purposes of the exchange ("Let's hear the facts").
- Do not make your contribution more informative than is required ("Too much information!").

Maxim of Relation: Relevance

- Be relevant ("Stay on topic").

Maxim of Manner: Clarity

- Avoid obscurity of expression ("Make some sense").
- Avoid ambiguity ("Don't waffle or be vague").
- Be brief ("Keep it short").
- Be orderly ("Keep it organized").

Figure 2.2   Gricean Maxims in Plain English

violation of maxims, and this makes normal conversation tremendously difficult for them, both as speakers and listeners.[18]

In practice, we frequently violate the maxims to varying degrees. Normally, their violation simply prompts the listener to make an inference, such as when a truncated comment ("I'm tired") prompts the listener to construct a more complete thought, based on the context ("I'm too tired to go out to a movie"). Other times, though, the accidental or careless violation of the maxims results in confusion, misunderstanding, and frustration. Their willful and malicious violation can result in manipulation or deception. And, more happily, their intentional, playful violation can result in comic genius.

For our purposes, not only do the maxims parallel some of the principles of deliberative conversation, they also provide another illustration of what a conversational ideal looks like. It is important to remember, as we read about how people talk about politics in everyday life, that the deliberative ideal of conversation and discussion is just that—an ideal. Like democracy, the conversational ideal is something that we can use as a critical standard for judging the quality of actual talk, but it is not something humans can live up to, at least not all the time. Moreover, the deliberative ideal is something that—even if not always clearly articulated—is widely recognized, as shown in a pair of inductive studies on how professional facilitators or lay jurors understand the term.[19]

Informal Conversation

In this chapter, we consider two kinds of talk—casual political conversations and more organized group discussions. Both are informal processes, and neither has a direct link to official decisions. Conversation, however, has less structure and, more rarely, an orientation toward formal problem solving. We begin by studying the flow and content of conversation, but when we turn to look at the process of discussion, we examine a slightly different kind of deliberation.

DRAWING ON MEDIA AND PERSONAL EXPERIENCE

Sociologist William Gamson broke new ground in 1992 with *Talking Politics*, a careful account of how small groups of friends and acquaintances discuss political issues in informal chats. He used a modified focus group research method to bring together not strangers but small peer groups to participate in loosely moderated conversations on a variety of current affairs. He transcribed thirty-seven discussions involving 188 diverse working-class participants. Afterward, he concluded, "Listening to their conversations over a period of an hour or more, one is struck by the deliberative quality of their construction of meaning about these complex issues." He saw the participants in the peer-group conversations "achieve considerable coherence in spite of a great many handicaps, some flowing from limitations in the media discourse that they find available and others from their own lack of experience with the task."[20]

The first point Gamson made in *Talking Politics* is that the conversations were deliberative. At the time he wrote his book, Gamson did not make an explicit link to work on deliberative democracy; rather, he used the term in its vernacular meaning. Nonetheless, it is striking how many of Gamson's specific findings highlight aspects of the definition of deliberative conversation in Figure 2.1. For example, Gamson's research often explores the development of opposition—how dissent can congeal into organized resistance to dominant ideas and institutions. In the study detailed in his book, he explored the balance between themes and counterthemes. For example, two contrasting technology themes are making "progress through technology" and maintaining "harmony with nature."[21] In the deliberative framework, discussing themes and counterthemes constitutes weighing alternative evaluative criteria or reflecting on your own values, as well as those of others present. Gamson found that groups readily drew on opposing themes or values in their discussions, implicitly considering each and weighing them against one another. In other words, Gamson's research showed evidence that everyday political conversation is, indeed, often deliberative.[22]

Gamson's second point was that the quality of a group's conversation comes from drawing on its available resources, no matter how limited. Two principal sources of information and ideas in peer conversations are media content and personal experience. Probably the most common interpretation of Gamson's work is that he found out how, in more concrete detail, media content frames how citizens talk about issues.[23]

For example, the citizens Gamson observed drew on media coverage to inform their discussions of nuclear power. Participants discussed the catastrophic 1986 accident at the Chernobyl nuclear power plant, in which a nuclear reactor collapsed and deadly amounts of radioactivity spread into the surrounding environment.[24] That they mentioned the topic is unremarkable, as it was a gripping current event. What was more noteworthy was that participants latched on to particular facts or arguments presented in the media to frame their understanding of nuclear power. For instance, one fact that had come up in media discussions of Chernobyl came into a conversation in this way: Ida, a bookkeeper in her late sixties, argued that Chernobyl should not make Americans worry about our own power plants. "You see," she explained, "our plants are built better than that one." She then added that "it didn't have the safety features that our plants already have." In a separate conversation, Joe, a firefighter in his fifties, interjected, "Look at Chernobyl. They're comparing it to the nuclear power plants in the United States. They can't do that! . . . That plant's antiquated. Know what I mean?"[25]

The plant comparison Ida and Joe heard in the media was not just an idle bit of trivia. Rather, it was an important piece of information that helped them understand a problem and, ultimately, judge the value of maintaining the nuclear power program in the United States. In the next chapter, we consider whether media coverage of issues such as these is "fair and balanced." For now, it is important only to notice how conversations can help citizens broaden their base of information by facilitating the exchange of information they learn through the media.

A less widely recognized finding in Gamson's work is that people's conversations draw on personal experience as much as they do on media content. This is particularly true for certain issues, such as affirmative action, which directly touch on people's daily lives. But personal knowledge came into discussions of every issue Gamson studied. Returning to the issue of nuclear safety, Gamson admitted, "Initially, I thought that the issues of nuclear power . . . were so far removed from people's daily lives that it surprised me to find a substantial minority introducing experiential knowledge. . . ."[26] In one such conversation, two discussants in their early twenties had this exchange:

Rich: From my window at school, I could see the Yankee—no, what was it? What was the one in Vermont? Vernon, the Vernon power plant.
Pat: You could see that?
Rich: Yeah.
Pat: You could see the lights of the plant?
Rich: You can see the lights—about eighteen miles down the river. And they were busted every three or four months for venting off the steam, which is really illegal. You're supposed to cool it with the water tanks and everything. But it cost a lot of money, and they didn't care. I mean, they're run so lax.[27]

As this example illustrates, referring back to the definition of deliberation in Figure 2.1, political conversations like these touch on "personal and emotional experiences," as well as "known facts." In Gamson's terms, conversations like these pull together personal and cultural knowledge to understand or "frame" issues. Gamson observes that "there is a special robustness to frames that are held together with a full combination of resources"—when conversants effectively marshal all their experiences and recollections.[28] In this way, conversation can help people analyze problems and arrive at judgments. By talking with others, they broaden their information base and the range of arguments they can consider; however, as we will see later, there is no guarantee that the conversation will include a diverse set of participants.

COMMUNITY BONDING THROUGH CONVERSATION

Whatever its merits as an analytic process, political conversation serves other functions. Foremost among these is developing a sense of community, what

Barber calls "exploring and creating commonalities."[29] The recent research of political scientist Katherine Cramer Walsh helps us understand this process. She spent three years with "the Old Timers," a group of politically conservative, retired white men at a corner store in Ann Arbor, Michigan. Her goal was to better understand what informal political conversation accomplishes for its participants. At the conclusion of her study, she wrote a personal letter to the Old Timers. She explained her research to the corner store gang in these words:

> Many political scientists believe conversation is the soul of democracy. . . . The idea is that by talking to each other, Americans can create a "better" society and learn to get along with many different kinds of people. By spending time with you (as well as a group of women who get together every week at a local church), I came to a different conclusion. When most people talk informally about politics, they aren't doing it to solve the world's problems. Their intent is not to improve democracy or foster brotherly love. Instead, their conversations are a way of sharing time, figuring out the world together, and feeling like part of a community.[30]

Walsh acknowledged that she, along with many others, read that finding as a "pessimistic conclusion" because it implies that conversation reinforces borders between social groups rather than bridging them. The men at the corner store provide each other with a palpable sense of community, and that alone is valuable. To the extent that conversation builds strong, isolated communities, however, it cannot function to bring a diverse society together into a coherent public.[31]

DIVERSITY IN CONVERSATION

Turning away from her detailed case study, Walsh looked to survey data to find out whether other voluntary associations were as homogenous as the Old Timers. To her chagrin (but not surprise), she found that men tend to affiliate with men—not women—when they join senior groups, fraternal or service organizations, book clubs, civic groups, and the like. Women are even more likely to seek out fellow women. Moreover, racial or ethnic homogeneity in such groups is even greater. Thus, for example, sixty-one percent of women reported that their most important and active voluntary group had no racial diversity, and forty-one percent said their groups included no men. Even in the many associations with diverse memberships, the problem is that all too often, people tend to affiliate with members more like themselves and then place greater value on those particular affiliations.

Political communication researchers Diana Mutz and Paul Martin addressed this question more precisely.[32] Their survey data focused on conversations, per se, rather than the voluntary associations in which such exchanges take place. They also focused not on the diversity of participants' backgrounds but on the diversity of their political viewpoints. Their survey asked respondents to report their own political point of view and then compare that view with those they hear in a range of communication settings. Results showed that the setting in which participants were least likely to hear different views was in talking with their "primary discussant." Others' views begin to diverge significantly from one's own only after leaving discussants and voluntary associations and entering the workplace setting. Ultimately, it is the media sources that offer contrary points of view, and this underscores the importance of considering the potential value of mediated deliberation, which we do in Chapter 3.

Conversations and voluntary associations, however, are more politically homogenous for some than for others. Mutz and Martin found that Republicans tended to talk with Republicans to an even greater degree than Democrats kept to their own, and this was true both for individual discussants and voluntary associations to which respondents belonged. Independents, by contrast, had a harder time finding like-minded voices anywhere: primary conversation partners tended, on balance, to share their views, but in every other setting, independents found contrary points of view to be the norm.[33]

DISAGREEMENT AND PERSUASION

If conversations are so often among like-minded persons, can they really be deliberative? This was one of the questions motivating the research of Robert Huckfeldt, Paul Johnson, and John Sprague. They reasoned that "the benefits of deliberation," such as promoting tolerance, compromising, and increasing political engagement, "depend on disagreement, which is defined in terms of interaction among citizens who hold divergent viewpoints and perspectives regarding politics." If we only talked with like-minded citizens, deliberation would become difficult because we would miss important information; misconstrue, forget, or overlook important alternatives; or never know others' value priorities. Even if people chatted with people whose views differed from their own, there is no guarantee that they would, in fact, deliberate. After all, "individuals may ignore, avoid, or dismiss politically disagreeable viewpoints."[34]

Huckfeldt and his colleagues set out to understand what gives rise to "effective" political conversation (mutual "comprehension," when phrased in deliberative terms) and "persuasive" conversation, which results when people change their mind on an issue. A key consideration in studying conversation is an individual's partisanship. Strong partisans are those who hold the firm conviction that their political party is best. One variety of a strong partisan, for example, is the "yellow dog Democrat." The term comes from the 1928 presidential election, in which a prominent Democratic senator from Alabama broke with his party to support Republican Herbert Hoover. Angry Alabama Democrats showed their party loyalty by boasting, "I'd vote for a yellow dog if he ran on the Democratic ticket."[35]

Let's imagine that you are alternately conversing with Susan, with the "S" signifying a strong partisan, and Wendy, with the "W" representing her relatively weak partisanship. With regard to mutual comprehension, you might guess that relative to Wendy, Susan is a poor conversational partner because she tends to be bombastic, stubborn, and unwilling to listen to you. Quite to the contrary, Huckfeldt and his colleagues found that people are no more likely to avoid or misjudge people like Susan than they are anyone else. Susan is just as likely to be a good listener as Wendy, and Susan is more likely to be an effective communicator in that she will make more clear, memorable statements about her own views. Moreover, if you and Susan disagree, this is unlikely to upset or disturb you, because you come away from conversations with Susan more clear in your own views than if you had just spoken with Wendy.[36]

Another important difference between weak and strong partisans is in their susceptibility to influence through political conversation. If you are trying to persuade Susan to change her vote, you are unlikely to make any progress. If you then try to persuade Wendy, you will be successful, so long as Wendy has other discussants who share your view. In other words, weak partisans might change their mind if numerous people in their social network try to convince them to change their vote to a rival candidate. One nudge is not enough, but when people get strong signals from different corners of their social network, the individual nudges add up to a sufficiently powerful push.[37]

Huckfeldt's research team also found that both weak and strong partisans, along with independents, typically converse in interlocking networks. For example, Susan and Wendy might be the two people you most often turn to when you want to talk about politics, but you are not the only one they seek. Susan has two other friends and a co-worker with whom she frequently converses on public issues, and Wendy has a classmate she talks to, in addition to you and Susan.

This pattern of small, interlocking political conversation networks can make deliberative conversations a powerful force for changing attitudes. Figure 2.3 illustrates this process in the case of three connected conversation networks—A, B, and C. Imagine a series of conversations happening over the course of three years. In Year 1, the person who participates in networks A and B (person A3/B1) is influenced by the three Democratic partisans because this person's network consists of two strong Democrats (A1, B2), one weak Democrat (A2), and one independent (B3). During this same year, there are no other strong influences: the other independent (B3/C1), in particular, has a more mixed network consisting of two strong Democrats (B2, C2), one strong Republican (C3), and a fellow independent.

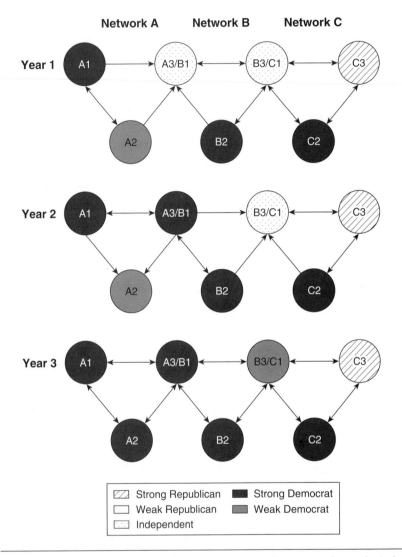

Figure 2.3   Changing Patterns of Partisanship Over Three Years of Hypothetical Conversations

Turning to Year 2, person A3/B1 has become a strong Democratic partisan as a result of Year 1 influences. Now the remaining independent is getting more consistent pressure to swing to the left because his or her former independent ally (A3/B1) is now a strong Democrat. Three-quarters of the person's conversants are Democratic, and that is enough to convert him or her to a weak Democrat by the beginning of Year 3. This former independent may never become a strong Democrat, owing to the steady counterarguments coming from C3, but without a change in the size or composition of the individual's network, he or she is likely to remain a Democrat indefinitely.

Something else is happening in Year 2 as well. The weak partisan Democrat A2 is now being persuaded by A1 and A3/B1 to firm up his or her convictions. By Year 3, A2 has moved from weak to strong Democrat.

At this point, all three networks in this diagram stabilize, with no further shifts to the left or the right. Notice, though, that even this diagram is a simplification of the interlocking nature of conversation networks. For instance, it is likely that persons A1 and A2, along with B2, C2, and C3, have additional conversational partners not shown in Figure 2.3. In other words, the effects of shifts in these three networks could radiate out even farther. As Huckfeldt and his colleagues concluded, "The conversion of any single individual to a particular candidate's cause is not only important in terms of a single vote or a single unit of social influence. It is also important in terms of the enhancement and attenuation effects that it creates throughout the networks of relationships within which the individual is imbedded, quite literally transforming entire patterns of social influence."[38]

This is not to say that it is conversations alone that change people's attitudes. Quite to the contrary, recall from the work of Gamson that the ideas and information people receive from the media constitute much of the meat in their conversations. Add to this a separate study's finding that people who get issue-specific news from the media are also the most likely to engage in issue-specific and general political discussions and one can see more clearly the media–conversation connection.[39] As Huckfeldt and his fellow researchers concluded, "Political interdependence among citizens might actually *magnify* the importance of events in the external political environment."[40]

As a final note, it appears that the conversational influence Huckfeldt and others found in the United States is common in European nations. A study of Britain, Germany, Spain, and the United States found that spouses, relatives, and friends influenced voting choices in each country during elections in 1990–1993, with the strongest influence coming from persons in the communication network who were closest to the respondent (e.g., spouses and close personal friends).[41]

Moving From Conversation to Discussion

To this point, we have examined the informal political conversations that occur among family, friends, and acquaintances. One of those conversational settings included the Old Timers, who met each morning over coffee in Ann Arbor.

Their conversational ritual was unusual in that it occurred regularly in a public setting. Most political conversations occur spontaneously in more private settings, such as the home, work site, or office.[42] Even in a public venue, however, it was still a closed conversation among friends.

Public discussions are a bit different. Participants in these discussions can include complete strangers, their occurrence is more programmed, and sometimes their process is managed by a facilitator or otherwise governed by a set of explicit ground rules. Discussions are important forms of political talk, but they are so varied that it is useful to look at discussions one setting at a time. We begin with one that is half conversation, half discussion—the online chat room or discussion board.

CYBERCHATTING

Let's return to the exchange that began this chapter, the exchanges about Iraq involving Eric, Mobile Vulgus, Ken, and WIRichie1971. That conversation could be categorized as many things—socializing, seeking information, debating, or venting frustration, among others. These things can take place during both conversations and discussions, but what gives us the first glimpse of a discussion is a stricter requirement of topical coherence and the presumption that the exchange is "public." In the opening excerpt, Eric was not sure who would reply to his initial post, but he was reasonably sure his suggested topic would generate discussion. In fact, he could not be sure anyone would reply. Not every topic posted on a discussion board or offered in a chat room has takers because there is no social sanction against lurking silently or ignoring other visitors in cyberspace.

Because the Internet is a relatively new communication medium, extensive research on its use as a means of generating discussion does not exist. It is common knowledge that Internet users are disproportionately younger, as is typical of any new communication technology. A representative telephone survey of Americans' Internet use patterns suggests a less obvious finding—that the Internet may be drawing young people into politics and civic affairs who would otherwise be unlikely to engage in such activities.[43] Though it is clear that the Internet is yet another medium for politically active persons to express themselves and obtain political information, it appears that the Internet may draw in some of the nonvoting, politically disaffected younger demographic, which includes anyone less than thirty years of age.

Another indirect piece of evidence for the impact of Internet use is how information exchange online sparks social capital—the network of personal associations and mutual trust that are essential for democratic society.[44] A national survey found that casual Internet use for entertainment and socializing had no connection to one's social capital or political participation, but the use of the Internet for information exchange did have such a relationship.[45]

What about the content of online discussion? Little research has investigated the subject, but at least one finding is very encouraging. A concern addressed in more detail in the next chapter is the spiral of silence, whereby people choose not to express their opinions when they perceive that theirs is the minority or dissenting point of view. A comparison of face-to-face and online groups found that in both cases persons in the minority were willing to speak their minds on the controversial subject of abortion.[46]

Even if one person in the minority is reluctant to speak, so long as another speaks up, the view is brought into the discussion; in an online discussion, it is not always easy to see how many people are present, so it is even more ambiguous whether one view or another is being underrepresented in the discussion. Moreover, members of the majority, more so than those in the minority, may choose not to speak up simply because they have already had their view articulated by others.[47] From the standpoint of deliberation, what is more important than hearing every person's voice is hearing every perspective, and in this sense it appears that online discussions are at least as valuable as those that occur offline.

That is good news because there are a growing number of sites appearing on the Internet devoted to promoting online discussion. One of those is e-thePeople.org, which first appeared online in August of 2000. Every day, hundreds of new articles and comments are posted on this site, and the subjects range from longstanding political debates to issues of the day, such as hurricanes, international crises, and political scandals. A study of the site conducted in 2002 found that the most common reasons for participating in the e-thePeople discussions were "to voice my opinion" and "to influence policy makers," specifically the elected officials who sometimes take part in e-thePeople's discussions. In addition, more than a third of users reported coming to the site "to listen to others," which is encouraging from the standpoint of deliberation. More than a quarter of the regular users of the site, in fact, reported that participating in online discussions gave them greater "awareness of viewpoints" and helped them follow the news and current events. Those are central purposes for traditional political conversation, so e-thePeople is likely extending the same habits and benefits of political talk to its users.[48]

From the standpoint of the organizers of e-thePeople, there are also some disappointing findings about their site. More often than not, it is replicating the offline reality of homogenous conversation: fifty-seven percent of its users rate the other users whom they interact with as "like-minded" people. More discouraging is the finding that only seven percent of the thousands of conversations begun in the past year were "successful," as measured by a decent popularity rating and at least twenty or more replies.[49] Thus, most of the conversations are like the Iraq thread that Eric began at conservative-talk.com, a perfectly interesting topic that attracts some attention but then essentially ends, often in what would seem to be the middle of a discussion.[50]

NATIONAL ISSUES FORUMS

From the most critical standpoint, cyberchatting is a glorified form of political conversation, and as such it is usually unqualified to call itself a true discussion. Michael Schudson takes the position that public discussion distinguishes itself from mere political conversation by being more strictly rule governed and goal directed (i.e., oriented toward solving public problems, choosing policies, or arguing on behalf of one's principles, rights, or interests). In his view, conversation is not the soul of democracy because it is too often aimless, unstructured, and inconsequential, and it typically fails to bring together sufficiently divergent views to really call it an inclusive, public activity.[51]

Fortunately, there exist a wide range of public discussion projects active in the United States.[52] Each provides a glimpse of the kind of power that discussion can have, even when it is not strictly oriented toward decision making. The best contemporary political discussion programs address public issues of immediate local or national relevance. Since 1990, the number of modern discussion programs has proliferated, and two of the most widely used and influential are the programs developed by the National Issues Forums (NIF) Institute.

The NIF is a decentralized public discussion program for which thousands of conveners have received training. Political deliberation is the central concern of NIF, which promotes the idea that citizens must make hard choices and take responsibility for the public judgments at which they arrive through deliberation. All of the national issues that NIF addresses, such as health care and criminal justice, are those that "engage our most deeply held convictions about what we value." On these issues, "policy options pull and tug on our values." Real "choice work" forces us to acknowledge the negative implications of our favored choices and the positive value of alternatives; we must see the effects of policies on ourselves as well as others. Through careful and empathic listening, we force ourselves to come to understand and respect other people's perspectives, and we combine diverse viewpoints to create "a sense of the whole." When we engage in this kind of deliberation, political "conflict is not only among us, it is within us."[53]

NIF presumes that the best context for doing this kind of work is face-to-face deliberation among fellow citizens. In NIF parlance, deliberation is "the act of weighing carefully. . . . It's a process for determining what action is in the best interest of the public as a whole." During a forum, we have the opportunity to "talk through" an issue with peers; we begin "talking to understand our options, face up to our limitations, and put ourselves in a position to make a serious choice." After a forum, citizens continue talking and thinking about both facts and values, further developing their views on the issues they discussed in the forums. Eventually, preferences evolve into choices and private opinions become "public judgments." Judgment is distinct from mere opinion because it "rests on what we think the second time—after we have talked with others, considered the consequence of our options, and worked through the conflicts that arise."[54]

Does NIF, in fact, teach participants how to develop more informed and reflective opinions on current policy issues? More broadly, does it achieve its goal of educating citizens in the art of public deliberation? Considerable research has been done on NIF, and the balance suggests that it does, indeed, have some of the anticipated impacts on the people who take part in the forums. Among its effects are broadening participants' outlooks, causing them to think beyond their narrowly defined self-interests to arrive at more well-conceived judgments on public issues. In addition, NIF appears to teach participants new ways of participating in groups and talking about politics. Though NIF may not make people ideal deliberators, it does appear to reduce the likelihood that they will be domineering or unwilling to listen when talking about politics with fellow citizens.[55]

So many people want to improve the quality of discussion in their communities that NIF has become remarkably popular. During 1993, for example, by NIF's best estimate, forums were convened by approximately 1,440 adult literacy programs, 2,600 high schools, and 1,360 civic organizations.[56] Given the success of NIF's book publishing, the number of forums has likely grown in the years since.

In the end, even the NIF forums are like political conversations in that they often involve like-minded, self-selected participants exchanging information and ideas in a way that arrives at no final conclusion. Moreover, there is evidence that people leave NIF forums more convinced of their original views than newly aware of a publicly shared common ground.[57] Even in these cases, though, it is clear that participants learned something about themselves, their own views, and deliberation itself. There is also evidence that participants can then apply those lessons outside the forums to change how they talk about and address public problems.[58]

Dialogue and Deliberation

Before you reach the back cover, this book will provide many examples of deliberative innovations that aim to improve how we talk to one another—conversationally, in more formal discussions, and in official meetings. Almost always I emphasize decision making, which is appropriate given the decision-oriented meaning of deliberation. At the level of conversation and discussion, though, this decision requirement can be relaxed somewhat, and participants can orient themselves more toward an open-ended dialogue.

This idea of having a dialogue holds great appeal for many civic reformers and citizens, many of whom worry that focusing exclusively on policy debate could cause us to overlook the important work that must be done before we can deliberate effectively. In their book *Moral Conflict*, communication scholars Barnett Pearce and Stephen Littlejohn argued that there are many instances where people come to public meetings unprepared to deliberate because they do not yet understand how other parties in a conflict reason and talk, let alone what views these other participants might have on the issue at hand. In these situations, dialogue might help to develop a kind of "creole language in which one side can communicate with the other."[59]

THE PUBLIC CONVERSATIONS PROJECT

To get an idea of the power of dialogue, consider the case of the Public Conversations Project, an entity that weaves together the virtues of conversation and discussion into a single process. Since 1989, the project has tried to help apply the principles of family therapy and alternative dispute resolution to public conflicts. In their official materials, project staff define dialogue as "any conversation animated by a search for understanding rather than for agreements or solutions. It is not debate, and it is not mediation."[60]

Though they advocate an exploratory, open-ended conversation, one should not get the impression, however, that the project's approach to dialogue is loose. On the contrary, dialogues set up by the project follow a complex sequence of steps, as dialogue can be difficult to generate in the midst of bitter personal, partisan, and often moral or ideological conflict. Though each instance is unique in one or more respects, the project generally begins with these steps:

1. In response to an initial request, project organizers assess whether the participants in the conflict have the time and resources necessary to engage in dialogue.

2. Project staff research the issue and speak with conflict participants to learn the contours of the debate they are stuck inside, as well as those moments—if any—when they appeared to be having more fruitful exchanges.

3. Staff then create a meeting design and clear meeting objective, which is then communicated to the invitees from all parties involved in the conflict. Only those who agree to abide by the meeting's ground rules—or at least try to do so—are encouraged to attend.

4. The dialogue occurs in one meeting or a series of meetings, which always begin with a reiteration of the meeting's goals and rules. Thereafter, the structure of the conversations varies considerably, but there is always emphasis on asking questions, listening carefully, and taking turns speaking—the basics of an open-ended, exploratory conversation. Professional facilitators help participants stick to the rules and purpose of the meeting, but participants do the hard work of speaking frankly and listening attentively, even when hearing words that hurt or offend them.

Consider the case of abortion—the issue that sparked the Public Conversations Project.[61] The idea of bringing together prochoice advocates and pro-life activists may sound crazy to anyone who has seen these factions clash outside an abortion clinic or at a public rally. One side stands for personal liberty, grounded in the principles of liberal political philosophy and the principle of sexual equality advanced through the women's rights movement, whereas the other is led by its understanding of biblical scripture to oppose all threats to the life of the unborn and to challenge the spiritual health and morality of abortionists and the women who turn to them. Not fertile ground for dialogue, it would seem.

Since 1990, the project has used its approach to address this issue in Massachusetts and elsewhere. The questions posed to participants are deceptively simple:

> (1) How did you get involved with this issue? What's your personal relationship, or personal history with it? (2) We'd like to hear a little more about your particular beliefs and perspectives about the issues surrounding abortion. What is at the heart of the matter for you? (3) Many people we've talked to have told us that within their approach to this issue they find some gray areas, some dilemmas about their own beliefs or even some conflicts. Do you experience any pockets of uncertainty or lesser certainty, any concerns, value conflicts, or mixed feelings that you may have and wish to share?[62]

Questions such as these can get a conversation started, which invariably leads to both parties in the conversation acknowledging the issue's complexity and the difficulty they have talking constructively with their respective opponents. Consider how this comment from an online conversation moves from expressing hurt at being personally attacked to seeing some basis for common understanding:

> I certainly have felt stereotyped over the years. The pro-life community is very aggressive; I've had friends called "baby killer" and been told that we are "damned by God." Many people on both sides of the issue see it in very black and white terms—which, of course, is the ultimate silliness, since all reality is merely shades of gray.[63]

In moments like these, speakers move from reciting their own experience of being stereotyped and misunderstood to acknowledging, even if only fleetingly at first, the problems created by "people on both sides of the issue."

Once again, the purpose of such dialogue is not to resolve the abortion debate. Dialogue, instead, aims to promote understanding, appreciation, and respect. Instead of debating the issue of abortion, participants in these dialogues have—sometimes for the first time in their public lives—the experience of listening to the other side. As a result, common ground can be found on occasion, such as in improving prenatal care for low-income pregnant mothers or in providing women with birth control to prevent unwanted pregnancies. If the parties in the debate continue to debate, but more deliberatively and honestly, with a newfound respect for one another's views and commitments, the project has done its job.

NARRATIVES AND STORYTELLING

One of the most striking effects of dialogue is the personal stories that emerge. These stories, which sometimes include very detailed narratives about people's lives and their policy-relevant experiences, can arise in any number of deliberative settings, but processes that are too solution oriented and heavily facilitated tend to snuff them out.

For instance, when communications scholar David Ryfe conducted a study of the NIF, he was struck by participants' eagerness to tell stories, as well as the way forum facilitators cut stories short. "Strong facilitators," Ryfe concluded, "tend to short-circuit the storytelling process." They control the flow of conversation "by asking questions like, 'What bothers you about that?' and, 'What is your reaction to that?'" Seemingly helpful summarizing can also strip stories of their power. When facilitators continue to interject themselves into conversations, "forums tend to have a rapid-fire, scattershot quality. Participants tend to say less, to tell fewer stories, and to talk more directly to the facilitator . . . and there is less of the thinking-out-loud."[64]

By contrast, many stories emerge in a series of online forums about what to build at the site of the former World Trade Center in New York City. Ryfe found the NIF stories helpful in getting participants down to the business of deliberating, and communications scholar Laura Black found that this was also the case in the online forums. Black distinguished among Introductory, Adversarial, Unitary, and Transformation story types.[65] Introductory stories served to engage participants in the task of deliberation by connecting abstract issues with their lived experiences. The two most common story types (Adversarial and Unitary), however, served as relatively straightforward means of argumentation. The Adversarial story amounts to an often emotional narrative argument for one side of an issue, whereas the Unitary story argues more tentatively and in a way that aims to includes all participants. Consistent with Ryfe's findings, Black found that these stories can serve as a kind of evidence, furthering the deliberation on the policy question at hand.

Black also theorized that narratives can help groups work through values conflicts and form a shared identity—larger tasks that address the problem. Qualitative and quantitative analyses of the stories participants told showed that each of these types of story serve a powerful purpose for online discussion groups. Black found that the Unitary stories "can be useful to help group members move beyond the limitations of seeing their differences as simply a two-sided debate."[66] Though told from one person's own experience, these stories had the power to evoke a shared experience—in this case, that of a great sense of loss in the collapse of the Trade Center buildings. That, Black explains, can serve to bring participants together and lead them to "find areas for compromise or consensus within the group."[67]

A more uncommon variety of narrative Black encountered earned the label of Transformation stories. These stories are characterized by "mixed, contradictory, or changing emotions" entailed in "personal and social transformation." A typical Transformation story tells how a person "has changed his or her perspective" on the matter at hand, and it invites other participants to consider the fluidity of their own positions. Consider this example of a participant who changed her own sense of what would be an appropriate replacement for the Twin Towers:

> In the days after nine eleven I put up pictures of the Towers in my apartment. Coffee table books were returned to the coffee table and opened to those glorious pictures of downtown. . . . And then, after several weeks, the Towers— my beautiful Towers—began to look like two giant tombstones. It took a while for this to sink in, but it happened. A pair of tombstones standing over a soon-to-be cemetery. How ironic. And again I cried because I knew I would never be able to look at them the same way again. Yes, I'd love my Towers rebuilt. I'd love to go back to nine ten. But it can't happen. Everything is different. The terrorists "win" if we live in the past. Our spirit will not be broken. We will turn adversity into strengths. We will move on. [68]

Typical of this genre of story, the teller moves toward an inspirational tone, asking listeners to understand the transformation as a positive move to a place of greater serenity and clarity. It is not a smooth argument for a particular position because the teller is able to empathize with conflicting points of view. The telling of such a story makes it safe for other participants to express uncertainty. It provides others with the freedom to openly explore their own doubts and shifts in their thinking. And that, in the end, is one of the points of a dialogue—helping participants move from fixed positions in a tense debate to more flexible reflections open to discovery.

Conclusion

There is no inevitability to the occurrence of such dialogue, let alone more conventional political conversation and discussion. Though we can take discussion for granted as a common practice in a free society, it is just that—a practice, an activity that is socially constructed to be done a certain way, with certain people, at certain times, and in certain places. The historical record shows that modern political discussions, study circles, and issues forums are something that a culture invents and practices over the years, sometimes abandoning old practices in favor of new ones. National Issues Forums take us back to past ways of holding public discussions, and online chats are likely a sign of how we will discuss politics in the future, for better or worse.

Whatever form conversation and discussion take in the future, it is certain that they will both remain connected to other communication channels, particularly mass media. Whether in coffee shops, chat rooms, or issues forums, participants bring to their discussions things they have picked up from television, newspapers, radio, Web sites, and other media. In the next chapter, we consider just what those mediated messages add up to. If conversations and discussions can sometimes sustain one kind of deliberation, can the media produce another?

Notes

1. Kim, Wyatt, and Katz (1999, p. 362).
2. This conversation is posted online at http://forums.conservative-talk.com/t1764-treacherous-journalism.html. To protect the innocent, the grammar has been changed (a little).
3. See *Frontline* (http://www.pbs.org/wgbh/pages/frontline/shows/saddam/interviews/aburish.html).
4. This conception of tacit knowledge comes from Giddens (1984).
5. Herbst (1999, p. 187).
6. Quoted in Herbst (1999, pp. 192–93).
7. Tocqueville (1835/1961, book III, Chapter 2). There is no doubt that in many respects, de Tocqueville idealized American society. If Americans of today seem more guarded and class conscious than these romanticized cultural pioneers, it is partly because the past is routinely lionized as a period of great civic spirit. Thus, Michael Schudson (1998) observed that "intellectuals have complained that 'we no longer have citizens' since at least 1750," when French political philosopher Jean-Jacques Rousseau lodged this very complaint about his own era (p. 295). There is little hard evidence tracking political conversational habits over long periods of time, so the question remains unsettled. As one exception, Huckfeldt, Johnson, and Sprague (2004, p. 44) cite a 1972–1990 longitudinal data set that shows decreasing correspondence between social networks and political preference. That might signal an increase in disagreement within conversations, but in the United States, increasingly sharp partisanship could signal the opposite trend (Abramowitz and Saunders, 1998).
8. See Mattson (1998), Levine (1990), and Gastil and Keith (2005).
9. Baird (1928) and Harrison (1928), respectively.
10. Bormann (1996, pp. 101–3).

11. Habermas (1979, 1989).
12. Barber (1984, p. 173).
13. Ibid., p. 179.
14. Ibid., p. 183.
15. Ibid., p. 185.
16. Weithman (2005, pp. 282–83). In Weithman's view, these are aspects of democratic character. I prefer to describe these as behaviors enacted during deliberation, not requiring that they reflect an ongoing disposition toward particular interactive norms. As long as one behaves in this way during a discussion, we can say deliberation took place without having to judge the underlying character of the participants.
17. Grice (1975).
18. Surian (1996).
19. On forum facilitators, see Mansbridge et al. (2006); on jurors, see Sprain and Gastil (2007).
20. Gamson (1992, p. 175).
21. Ibid., p. 136.
22. On the link between media use and deliberative conversational habits, see Moy and Gastil (2006).
23. Scheufele (1999, p. 106).
24. For background on this incident, see http://www.nrc.gov/reading-rm/doc-collections/fact-sheets/chernobyl-bg.html.
25. Gamson (1992, pp. 120–21).
26. Ibid., p. 131.
27. Ibid., p. 132.
28. Ibid., p. 128.
29. Barber (1984, p. 183).
30. Walsh (2004, p. 233).
31. Ibid., p. 234.
32. Mutz and Martin (2001). The authors also validate the accuracy of self-reported estimates of other points of view by comparing independent ratings of other sources (newspapers, discussants) with self-reported ratings and finding a remarkably good fit.
33. Ibid., pp. 101–2. Similar research on presidential voting in 2000 found that, on average, forty-eight percent of those who voted for Bush had conversation networks consisting exclusively of Bush voters, whereas forty-two percent of Gore voters had exclusively Gore-voting networks (Huckfeldt, Johnson, and Sprague, 2004, pp. 38–39).
34. Huckfeldt, Johnson, and Sprague (2004, pp. 13–14). See also Huckfeldt, Mendez, and Osborn (2004). On the benefits of conversational network diversity, and disagreement, for democracy, see Mutz (2006) and Scheufele et al. (2006).
35. Modern yellow dog Democrats are celebrated at http://www.yellowdogdemocrat.com.
36. Huckfeldt, Johnson, and Sprague (2004, pp. 68–97).
37. Ibid., pp. 54–60.
38. Ibid., pp. 121–2.
39. Kim, Wyatt, and Katz (1999, pp. 371–73).
40. Huckfeldt, Johnson, and Sprague (2004, p. 122).

41. Schmitt-Beck (2004).
42. Wyatt, Katz, and Kim (2000).
43. Krueger (2002).
44. On social capital, see Putnam (2000).
45. Shah, Kwak, and Holbert (2001).
46. McDevitt, Kiousis, and Wahl-Jorgensen (2003).
47. Ibid., p. 466.
48. Weiksner (2005, pp. 220–25).
49. Ibid., pp. 220–21, 225.
50. For research on organized online deliberation, see Muhlberger and Weber (2006) and Price and David (2005).
51. Schudson (1997).
52. For overlapping reviews of public discussion programs, see Button and Mattson (1999), Button and Ryfe (2005), and Ryfe (2002).
53. McAfee, McKenzie, and Mathews (1990, pp. 10–15).
54. Ibid., pp. 17–22.
55. Melville, Willingham, and Dedrick (2005). See also Gastil and Dillard (1999a), Gastil (2004), and Gastil, Black, and Moscovitz (forthcoming). A study of the deliberative poll used methods similar to the Gastil and Dillard study and did not find evidence of increased sophistication (Sturgis, Roberts, and Allum, 2005). For more on deliberation and thinking in terms of the public good, see the discussion of the general will in Chapter 7.
56. National Issues Forums (1990, 1992).
57. Gastil and Dillard (1999b). Schkade, Sunstein, and Hastie (2006) also found evidence of polarization, which Sunstein (2002) views as a common result of deliberation. My own research suggests that polarization occurs only in a limited range of circumstances (Gastil, Black, and Moscovitz, forthcoming); for a critique of Sunstein's view, see Kahan, Slovic, Braman, and Gastil (2006).
58. Daugherty and Williams (2007).
59. Pearce and Littlejohn (1997, p. 123).
60. This and other material come from the project's Internet archive at http://www.publicconversations.org. Those interested in reading more about the project's work should refer to Chasin et al. (1996). On how the project's work fits into the larger dialogic approach to conflict, see Gergen, McNamee, and Barrett (2001), Pearce and Littlejohn (1997), and Tonn (2005).
61. On this particular aspect of the project's work, see http://www.publicconversations .org/pcp/resources/resource_detail.asp?ref_id=97.
62. Gergen et al. (2001, p. 687).
63. Excerpt from project online dialogue available at http://www.publicconversations. org/pcp/index.asp?page_id=194&catid=66#Q2response.
64. Ryfe (2006, p. 88).
65. Black (2006) also identified Introductory stories, which are similar to some of the stories Ryfe (2006) identified as serving to get participants engaged in the task of deliberation. Note that Black refined her story typology in the second of two qualitative case studies (see Chapter 5 of her study).
66. Black (2006, p. 252).

67. Ibid. McBride (2005) points out a logical implication of deliberation's tendency to promote a shared civic identity—its threat to more group-specific identities. Thus, deliberation may threaten politically salient identities, which entitle minority groups to special recognition as underrepresented constituencies or voices.

68. Black (2006, p. 130).

SOURCE: iStock. Used by permission.

3

Mediated Deliberation and Public Opinion

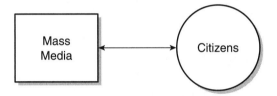

I'm not going to be your monkey.

—Jon Stewart, anchor of *The Daily Show*

On October 15, 2004, CNN's political talk show *Crossfire* brought into its studio Jon Stewart, the host of Comedy Central's *The Daily Show with Jon Stewart*. The next thirty minutes were among the most important in the history of live television:[1]

Co-host Tucker Carlson: Well, he's been called the most trusted name in fake news. Next, we're joined by Jon Stewart for his one-of-a-kind take on politics, the press, and America. . . .

Stewart: Thank you very much. That was very kind of you to say. Can I say something very quickly? Why do we have to fight? [Laughter] . . . [In pitying voice] Why do you argue, the two of you? [Laughter] I hate to see it.

Carlson: We enjoy it. . . . Let me ask you a question. . . . Is John Kerry really the best the Democrats can do?

Stewart: I thought Al Sharpton was very impressive. I enjoyed his way of speaking. I think, oftentimes, the person that knows they can't win is allowed to speak the most freely, because, otherwise, shows with titles such as *Crossfire* . . . or *Hardball* or "I'm Going to Kick Your Ass" will jump on it. In many ways, it's funny. I made a special effort to come on the show today because I have privately, amongst my friends and also in occasional newspapers and television shows, mentioned this show as being bad.

Co-host
Begala: We have noticed.

Stewart: And I wanted to—I felt that that wasn't fair and I should come here and tell you that I don't—it's not so much that it's bad, as it's hurting America. But I wanted to come here today and say . . . stop, stop, stop, stop hurting America.

Begala: OK now.

Stewart: And come work for us. . . . See, the thing is, we need your help. Right now, you're helping the politicians and the corporations. And we're left out there to mow our lawns.

Begala: By beating up on them? You just said we're too rough on them when they make mistakes.

Stewart: No, no, no, you're not too rough on them. You're part of their strategies. You are partisan, what do you call it, hacks. . . .

             [Carlson critiques Stewart for not asking presidential candidate John Kerry tough questions when Kerry appeared on his program.]

Stewart: I didn't realize that—and maybe this explains quite a bit—the news organizations look to Comedy Central for their cues on integrity. [Laughter] So what I would suggest is, when you talk about holding politicians' feet to fire, I think that's disingenuous. . . .

Carlson: We're here to love you, not confront you. . . .

Stewart: No, no, no, but what I'm saying is this. I'm not. I'm here to confront you, because we need help from the media, and they're hurting us.

Begala: *Crossfire* reduces everything, as I said in the intro, to left, right, black, white . . . because, see, we're a debate show.

Stewart: No, no, no, no, that would be great. . . . I would love to see a debate show.

Begala: We're 30 minutes in a 24-hour day where we have each side on, as best we can get them, and have them fight it out.

Stewart: No, no, no, no, that would be great. To do a debate would be great. But that's like saying pro wrestling is a show about athletic competition. [Laughter]

Carlson: Jon, Jon, Jon, I'm sorry. I think you're a good comedian. I think your lectures are boring. . . .

Stewart: But the thing is that this—you're doing theater, when you should be doing debate, which would be great. It's not honest. What you do is not honest. What you do is partisan hackery. And I will tell you why I know it.

Carlson: You had John Kerry on your show and you sniff his throne and you're accusing us of partisan hackery?

Stewart: Absolutely. . . . You're on CNN. The show that leads into me is puppets making crank phone calls. [Laughter] What is wrong with you? . . . You know, the interesting thing I have is, you have a responsibility to the public discourse, and you fail miserably.

Carlson: You need to get a job at a journalism school, I think.

Stewart: You need to go to one. The thing that I want to say is, when you have people on for just knee-jerk, reactionary talk. . . .

Carlson: Wait. I thought you were going to be funny. Come on. Be funny.

Stewart: No. No. I'm not going to be your monkey. [Laughter] I watch your show every day. And it kills me.

Carlson: I can tell you love it.

Stewart: It's so—oh, it's so painful to watch. [Laughter] You know, because we need what you do. This is such a great opportunity you have here to actually get politicians off of their marketing and strategy.

Carlson: Is this really Jon Stewart? What is this, anyway?

Stewart: Yes, it's someone who watches your show and cannot take it anymore. [Laughter] I just can't.

SOURCE: CNN.com, *Crossfire* (transcript pp. 57–59). Used by permission.

In a nutshell, Stewart argued that the media has "a responsibility to the public discourse" and *Crossfire* "fails miserably" at performing that duty. Stewart asked for substantive debate, not political theater. Because *Crossfire* presented itself as part of the deliberative process yet engaged in "partisan hackery," Stewart concluded that what it does "is not honest."

The charge stuck. Three months later, CNN cancelled *Crossfire.* CNN Chief Executive Jonathan Klein commented, "I guess I come down more firmly in the Jon Stewart camp." He added, "I doubt that when the president sits down with his advisers they scream at him to bring him up to date on all of the issues," Klein said. "I don't know why we don't treat the audience with the same respect." Stewart's reaction was only to acknowledge his bewilderment: "I had no idea that if you wanted a show canceled, all you had to do was say it out loud."[2]

Though *Crossfire* may be off the air, the media continue to play a range of roles in public life, and deliberative theory provides precisely the lens through which Stewart and other critics can continue to identify the media's triumphs and failures. In this chapter, we grind and polish that critical lens, then look through it to survey the modern media landscape. We begin, however, by considering how we came to be in the mediated world we inhabit today.

Expressing Ourselves Through the Ages

A few things have changed in the course of the past few centuries. There are many more people, and there are many more ways to communicate. Conversation and discussion have always been a source of deliberative activity, from the dawn of civilization to the present day. People do not need a computer or phone to chat with their neighbor about the weather, their children's school, a recent burglary, or any other issue. But as our communities have grown in size and number over time, so have our communication media.

MEDIA TECHNOLOGY

Table 3.1 offers a whirlwind historical tour that shows an acceleration in both the number of people to communicate with and the ways we can do it. Every advance offers new expressive media, distribution systems, or recording devices. Whether it's clay tablets, the pony express, or the home computer, each of these is augmenting an ever-growing set of communication tools. One can compare the gaps between major media advances and notice that from the initiation of writing to the creation of paper took roughly 3,000 years, from paper to Gutenberg's printing press took half as long (roughly 1,500 years); the leap to the electric telegraph took just another 500 years, with the computer coming just 150 years later. One can hopscotch along this historical timeline many different ways, but all show the acceleration in media innovations, leading one to wonder what will come next—and how quickly? Today's Weblogs and podcasts will seem, sooner than we might think, as primitive as the first awkward, clunky home computer, the pony express, or the earliest clay printing presses.

Table 3.1   Mass Communication and Population 3500 BCE–2012 CE

Year	Technology	World Population	U.S. Census[a]
3500–2900 BCE	Writing (Phoenicians, Sumerians, Egyptians)	15 m	? m
1700 BCE	Postal service (Persia)	50 m	
530 BCE	Library (Greece)	100 m	
200–100 BCE	Human message relay systems (Egypt and China)	150 m	
105 BCE	Paper (Tsai Lun)	175 m	
305 CE	Wooden printing press (China)	200 m	
1048	Movable type (Pi Sheng)	250 m	
1450	Metal movable type (Johannes Gutenberg)	400 m	
1714	Typewriter (Henry Mill)	600 m	
1793	Long-distance telegraph (Claude Chappe)	850 m	4 m
1814	Photographic image (Joseph Nicéphore Niépce)	900 m	9 m
1831	Electric telegraph (Joseph Henry)	1 b	13 m
1860	Pony Express relay system (US)	1.2 b	30 m
1877	Phonograph (Thomas Edison)	1.3 b	50 m
1889	Direct dial telephone (Almon Strowger)	1.5 b	60 m
1910	Motion pictures with sound (Thomas Edison)	1.8 b	90 m
1930	"Golden Age" of radio	2.1 b	120 m
1949	Network television in US	2.5 b	150 m
1958	Photocopier (Chester Carlson)	3 b	180 m
1966	Fax machine (Xerox)	3.4 b	190 m
1972	Cable television (HBO)	3.9 b	200 m
1976	Home computer (Apple)	4.2 b	210 m
1979	Cell phones (Japan)	4.4 b	230 m
1991	Global release of Internet (US)	5.4 b	250 m
2012	What's next?	7.0 b	315 m

SOURCE: Technology timeline is from Mary Bellis, "The History of Communication," http://inventors.about.com/library/inventors/bl_history_of_communication.htm. Population estimates are from http://www.census.gov. For a history of the mass media in the United States, in particular, see Blanchard (1998).

a. There is no solid estimate of how many people inhabited what is now the United States before the official U.S. Census began in the 1700s. Even the lowest estimates assume that there were millions of people, but whether it was five, ten, fifteen—or even many more million—remains unclear. See, for example, Thornton (1987).

Even more fundamentally, these advances in media reflect an aspiration to communicate in the most profound sense of the term. In his historical review of the idea of communication, John Durham Peters explained that "'communication' is a registry of modern longings. The term evokes a utopia where nothing is misunderstood, ears are open, and expression is uninhibited."[3] Each new communication technology or method promises to bring us closer together. Electricity's earliest media offspring, such as the telegraph and radio, transformed the term communication "into a new kind of quasi-physical connection across the obstacles of time and space."[4]

The idea that mass media could solve our communication problems sounds quaint today. As we shall see in this chapter, most political communication research on mass media reflects serious doubts about the potential for mass media to facilitate deliberation. The deliberative ideal still lingers in the background as a critical standpoint but not as a societal achievement.

MEASURING PUBLIC OPINION

Before turning to contemporary media, however, it is important to note that while mass media technologies proliferated in step with the growing global population, we have also witnessed an expansion in the variety of means for expressing and recording public opinion. Table 3.2 shows how new modes of public expression coincide with significant moments in political history. With the emergence of classical Athens came a clarification of the role of oratory and discussion in democracy. With the gradual development of self-government in Europe came a wave of political communication methods—from pamphleteering to petitioning. Revolutionary protest became a powerful mode of public expression, but postrevolutionary governments eventually ushered in a variety of mass electoral methods and worker strikes. Finally, with the expansion of mass media and the enfranchisement of women and minorities, came modern democratic social movements and new deliberative processes.

Some of these historical modes of public expression intertwine with modern political processes that we examine in detail in this book, such as discussion (Chapter 2), general elections (Chapter 4), jury deliberation (Chapter 6), and modern forms of public meetings (Chapter 7). In this chapter, however, we focus on modes of public opinion expression tied to the modern mass media, including public opinion polling and interactive media, from call-in radio to Internet microjournalism and blogging.

It would be a mistake, however, to say that all of these changes in media and public opinion expression mediums amount to an evolution in society toward evermore democratic modes of talk. As sociologist Anthony Giddens cautioned, "Human history does not have an evolutionary 'shape', and . . . harm can be done by attempting to compress it into one."[5] This review of historical context

Table 3.2   Expressing and Recording Public Opinion in Historical Context

Year	Mode of Public Expression	Historical Events and Writings
500 BCE	Public rhetoric and discussion	Athenian democracy (500–300 BCE)
1200s	Jury of peers	Magna Carta (1215)
1500s	Political publishing and pamphleteering	• European Renaissance • Protestant Reformation
1600-1700s	Crowds, petitions, salons, and coffeehouses	• Age of Reason/Enlightenment • *Two Treatises of Government* (1689)
Late 1700s	Revolutionary movements	• American Revolution (1776) • French Revolution (1789)
Early 1800s	General elections, strikes, and straw polls	• *Communist Manifesto* (1848) • *On Liberty* (1859)
Mid 1800s	Modern newspapers and letters to editors/officials	• *New York Times* founded (1851) • Australian secret ballot (1850s)
Late 1800s	Initiative and referenda	• Swiss Federal Constitution (1848) • Women's suffrage in New Zealand (1893)
Early 1900s	Mass media political programs and random sample surveys	• Franklin D. Roosevelt's fireside chats begin (1933)[a] • Gallup Poll established (1935)
Mid 1900s	Modern social movements	• Gandhi's salt march to Dandi (1930) • Montgomery bus boycott (1955)
Late 1900s	Modern deliberative processes and global social movements	• Citizen juries developed (1974)[b] • Seattle World Trade Organization protests (1999)

SOURCE: Adapted and expanded from Herbst (1993), p. 48.

a. Ryfe (1999).

b. Crosby and Nethercutt (2005).

simply serves as a reminder that what it means for the mass public to deliberate today depends critically on how we conceptualize mass media and public opinion in the modern world.

What Is Mediated Deliberation?

This brings us to the question, what does mediated deliberation mean, exactly? Benjamin Page advanced this conception of deliberation in *Who Deliberates? Mass Media in Modern Democracy.* Page argued that the sheer size of the mass public, along with the complexity of modern public problems, makes it impossible to rely on only face-to-face conversation and discussion. It would also be a mistake to rely solely on elected officials to deliberate on the public's behalf, as this would make the public too weak to hold its leaders accountable. Somehow, for the public to "actively control what its government does, the public, collectively, must be well informed. Some kind of effective public deliberation is required that involves the citizenry of the whole."[6]

What Page proposes is a "division of labor" between the mass public and the "professional communicators," including "reporters, writers, commentators, and television pundits, as well as public officials and selected experts from academia or think tanks."[7] Through the elaborate communication technology and industry of the mass media, these communication professionals convey information, values, and diverse points of view to the mass public, which then deliberates vicariously through the give-and-take and to-and-fro of these various professionals.

This view of deliberation fits with the conception of deliberation advanced by Jurgen Habermas, whose "ideal speech situation" (described in Chapter 2) laid the foundation for modern deliberative theory. In a 2006 essay on media and democracy, Habermas argued that "only across the system as a whole can deliberation be expected to operate as a cleansing mechanism that filters out the 'muddy' elements from a discursively structured legitimation process."[8] Paralleling Page's view, Habermas argued that no modern political process could function effectively without the "professionals of the media system" and the various elites who produce mediated political communication. Ideally, this mass-mediated deliberation serves the following functions:

> to mobilize and pool relevant issues and required information, and to specify interpretations; to process such contributions discursively by means of proper arguments for and against; and to generate rationally motivated *yes* and *no* attitudes [i.e., public opinions] that are expected to determine the outcome of procedurally correct decisions.[9]

In its ideal form, this mediated deliberation prominently features the very kind of programming that Jon Stewart pleaded for in his *Crossfire* appearance—a debate show that honestly presents conflicting points of view in a way that helps viewers work through the issues for themselves. In this perfect world, mass communication media would promote public knowledge and enlightened public opinion through engaging, substantive programming that goes beyond mere "theater" and "partisan hackery," to use Stewart's phrasing.

The middle column of Figure 3.1 formalizes this conception of the collective responsibility of media producers, which prominently includes television newscasters, newspaper editors, and information Web site managers. An important point here is that this responsibility is best understood as applying to the media system as a whole, rather than an individual producer, let alone an individual piece of reporting or a single program. For instance, consider criterion B2: "Present the broadest possible range of solutions to problems, including nongovernmental and unpopular ones." It makes more sense to think of this as a collective responsibility of the media than to expect such breadth of every single story or telecast on the subject. By analogy, a healthy diet includes fruits, vegetables, grains, and protein-rich foods, but nobody wants to subsist on a multivitamin-style glop that blends all these nutrients together into a nasty-tasting gruel. So all we should ask is that content producers provide nutritious and delicious content that contributes to a media diet that is, on the whole, deliberative.

Another important point is to broaden our conception of media, at least momentarily. The focus in this chapter is on public affairs news media—the sort of programming Jon Stewart produces and critiques—from the evening news to talk shows to newspapers, magazines, and Web sites on current affairs. But it is important to recognize that the process of mediated deliberation can also include entertainment media, such as films, novels, and theater. In reality, many people learn about historical events or other life experiences through these media, whether it's a drama about World War II, a novel about growing up poor in the South, or a play that addresses child abuse. Australian philosopher Robert Goodin explained this point:

> It is not just that fiction (and art more generally) might, and often does, contain allusions to social, economic, political and historical facts, and in that way might serve certain didactic purposes. The larger point is that those lessons come packed with more emotional punch and engage our imagination in more effective ways than do historical narratives or reflective essays of a less stylized sort.[10]

Because political communication—and deliberation—literature focuses more on news media than it does on the larger world of art, fiction, and other cultural or entertainment media, this chapter has a similar focus. Nonetheless, it is important to recognize that there is more to the deliberative media diet than news alone. Beyond the more obvious examples are works and performances that stretch one's perception of reality. Comedian Richard Pryor accomplished this, and when he passed away in 2005, fellow comic Jerry Seinfeld described Pryor in this way: "He started with what he knew and brought you to it. He made you fall in love with him. And he did it so that you would relate to things you didn't think you could relate to."[11]

Goodin's philosophical writings also draw attention to the deliberation that takes place inside an individual's mind—what he calls "deliberation within."[12] The point in having a deliberative media process is for individuals to hear conflicting considerations and weigh them to arrive at their own judgments. Even

	Media Producers	Media Users
Analytic Process		
Create a solid information base.	Present media users with a broad base of background information by reporting extensively on important issues.	Seek out opportunities to learn of others' experiences and relevant expert analyses.
Prioritize the key values at stake.	Explore the underlying public concerns behind the surface facts and events that define an issue.	Consider the diverse concerns underlying issues and how others prioritize issues differently.
Identify a broad range of solutions.	Present the broadest possible range of solutions to problems, including nongovernmental and unpopular ones.	Learn about how people like or unlike yourself think about addressing a problem.
Weigh the pros, cons, and trade-offs among solutions.	Report different viewpoints but do more than juxtapose them; subject them to careful scrutiny.	Reassess your biases favoring or opposing different solutions by seeing how others weigh pros and cons.
Make the best decision possible.	Make recommendations but keep editorial content distinct from news; leave the decision to the media user.	Take responsibility for making up your own mind after listening to the advice of experts, partisans, and others.
Social Process		
Adequately distribute speaking opportunities.	Use diverse sourcing, invite diverse guests with different ways of speaking, and reach beyond conventional debates (left/right).	Make time to listen to sources with views different from your own. Add your own voice when appropriate.
Ensure mutual comprehension.	Make news and information understandable for readers; prose should be accessible to the audience.	When you cannot understand an issue or argument, seek clarification from others.
Consider other ideas and experiences.	Take arguments from all perspectives seriously.	When hearing different views, avoid tuning out or ruminating on counterarguments before considering what is said.
Respect other participants.	Model respect for different views; treat readers with respect by making news serious but engaging.	Give the benefit of the doubt to sources but demand better behavior from those who violate your trust.

Figure 3.1   Key Features of Mediated Deliberation

when people ultimately choose to attend deliberative forums, they have likely viewed, read, and heard considerable media information and engaged in a process of internal reflection.

Thus, the right-hand column of Figure 3.1 shows the criteria by which we can judge whether an individual has engaged in mediated deliberation on a public issue. For example, whereas the media's responsibility for identifying a broad range of solutions is to present such breadth, as the media user, your responsibility is to "learn about how people like or unlike yourself think about addressing a problem." The media provides diverse perspectives and you should use enough of these media opportunities to learn about these different perspectives.

To take another example, criterion B1 assesses the adequacy of speaking opportunities. For the media producers, this requires that they "use diverse sourcing, invite diverse guests to speak in different voices, and reach beyond conventional debates." For you as a media consumer, this means that you must "make time to listen to sources with views different from your own" and "add your own voice when appropriate."

The point of creating a detailed definition of mediated deliberation is to have a critical yardstick against which we can measure the behavior of actual media producers and users. To what extent do media practices approximate the deliberative ideal, and in what ways are they less than deliberative? More specifically, the remainder of this chapter asks how the media functions in the United States.

Do We Have a Deliberative Media System?

Studies of the media fill volumes, and we cannot hope to even glimpse the full breadth of such work in this chapter's review of current research. Instead, we will on questions about how the media cover important public issues, with emphasis on the practice of reporting and the interplay of mass media and public opinion.

INVESTIGATIVE JOURNALISM

Perhaps the most important question about media coverage of important public events is, did they get the story right? How in-depth is the reporting, and did they miss the story altogether? One simple indicator of how well news organizations are doing is the frequency of original investigative reporting. Most often, a news outlet responds to external events—crises, public events, crime reports, or even press releases. Sometimes, however, the media do original research and investigation, whether on a reporter's hunch or in response to an outside source— as with the famous "Deep Throat," who helped spur the *Washington Post*'s articles on the Watergate coverup, which brought down President Nixon.

On the bright side, a recent survey of 103 local television news directors around the United States found that seventy-five percent of "local news stations are still doing investigative reporting," with twenty-five percent employing full-time investigative staff. Also, "half of those doing it say they are willing to investigate their sponsors."[13] From a more pessimistic viewpoint, however, one can see that these figures also mean that a majority of newsrooms either do no investigative reporting or are unwilling to investigate those who advertise on their station.

Worse still, the trend over time is not encouraging. The frequency of original watchdog reporting has declined steadily: such reportage accounted for fewer than one of every one hundred fifty stories in 2002, compared to one in sixty in 1998. According to the survey's authors, "Serious investigative work takes resources and time, two things news directors increasingly say are in short supply."[14]

The decline in the frequency of such reporting has many causes, including the ever-stronger profit motive and the perception that investigative reporting does not pay for itself in increased audience size or loyalty. Other causes include successful libel suits against newsmakers, along with the humbling public ridicule following flawed investigations, such as the flawed story on George Bush's military service that forced Dan Rather to step down as anchor at CBS.[15] The increased emphasis on light, entertaining news programming also discourages spending resources on the kinds of investigations that result in grim (and often quite complex) reports.[16]

Lest we conclude that the mass media had a golden age that is now lost, the historical record is replete with serious errors and blunders in past reporting, even by the most venerated news organizations. Consider the *New York Times*'s coverage of the early months of Hitler's term as German chancellor in 1933. Even though other media were reporting on the violence and civil unrest taking place in the country as Hitler consolidated the Nazi regime, a March 20 editorial reassured readers that the new regime was "not contemplating anything startling or wild in foreign policy." And a February 26 editorial compared the Storm Troopers to "a gang of sophomores trying to break up the freshman dinner."[17]

FAIRNESS AND BALANCE

When a story is covered by the media, is the coverage balanced and fair-minded? Benjamin Page asked this question of a more recent story covered by the *New York Times*, the 1991 U.S. war against Iraq. Page focused on the editorial pages of the *Times* from November 9, 1990, to January 15, 1991, to see if the paper incorporated a diversity of views on the war from a variety of sources. As for the voices represented on the editorial pages, the editors and regular columnists writing for the *Times* accounted for sixty-nine percent of the significant discussions of the issue, with another ten percent coming from current and former government officials, nine percent from "think tanks," and the rest from various writers and advocates. Beyond the dominance of the usual voices heard in the *Times*, Page noted that there were relatively few columns by experts on the Middle East, prominent religious or philosophical voices, or peace groups. Ordinary citizens got the chance to express their voices on these pages of the *Times*, though they did so exclusively in the Letters section.[18]

What was said is more important than who said it. The *Times*'s editors took a consistent stance in their unsigned editorials: all of these writings favored sanctions. The columnists, by contrast, were evenly divided among three views of the conflict with Iraq: thirty-three percent favored an entirely peaceful solution; thirty-five percent thought the United States should continue to use economic sanctions followed by military intervention, if necessary; and thirty-two percent advocated the immediate use of force. The letters from regular readers of the *Times*, however, overwhelmingly supported the peaceful option, with two-thirds of the letters taking that position. Another twenty-seven percent favored sanctions, with just seven percent calling for immediate military intervention. This more peaceful stance represented in the Letters section was roughly consistent with public opinion at the time.[19]

Page concluded his investigation by clarifying his understanding of balance in mediated deliberation: "Although there was indeed 'balance' (rather precise balance) among the three sets of policy stands, other major viewpoints were not included." Not only were ordinary citizens' voices relegated to the Letters section, but also their views on the conflict "were not presented in proportion to their adherents among the general public."[20]

Following the definition of mediated deliberation in Figure 3.1, however, the absolutely equal balance of views is less important than the adequacy of each view's expression. In this sense, the most important point is that prominent and serious views were shut out of the *Times* debate. As Page noted, very little writing on the editorial pages took seriously the idea of negotiations or concessions, let alone the possibility that Iraq had a legitimate grievance with Kuwait. Instead of offering a sufficient broad range of views, the *Times* arranged its columns "in a balanced and symmetrical fashion, so that they flanked—on the hawkish and the mildly dovish sides—numerous 'centrist' editorials and columns that called for continued sanctions, and force if necessary later," which was precisely the position favored by the *Times* editors.[21]

A team of researchers led by Lance Bennett found more recent evidence that the media often fail to present a balanced account of current events when such balance is most needed. When a powerful executive governs without a strong opposition party, such as in the wake of September 11, 2001, the media have a tendency to mirror the one-sided political terrain with relatively uncritical coverage of a popular administration.[22] Following the logic of Page's analysis, if the mass media convey the elite debate to the public so that citizens can deliberate, then it should be no surprise that when there exists an elite consensus—or at least only a weak voice of dissent—the media carry that message, uncritically, to the public.

OBJECTIVITY, EXPERTISE, AND BIAS

Looking beyond the editorial page, a deliberative media system more generally aims to provide not only a balanced mix of viewpoints but also a relatively objective accounting of the relevant facts on an issue. All too often, media coverage of events provides a lazy kind of balance by simply juxtaposing conflicting accounts and views of a controversy without regard to the veracity or implications of either side. When media stop doing investigative reporting and trim their staff while continuing to produce the same volume of news, their already frazzled reporters naturally resort to simplistic "balance" in their stories to avoid inappropriately discounting one or another point of view.

The *Maine Sunday Telegram* illustrates an alternative approach that often better serves the purposes of mediated deliberation. This paper, and others like it, decided to report on local events—from changing workers' compensation policy to protecting endangered songbirds—from the standpoint of an objective observer who can reach conclusions and pass independent judgment. The *Telegram* called it expert reporting.

Telegram Executive Editor Lou Ureneck gave clear instructions to reporter Eric Blom when he developed their first "expert" story: "We told him to get beyond the whipsaw of competing quotes that are often put into a story for 'balance,'" Ureneck explained. "We told him to avoid bogging down in excessive attribution, weasel words and hedging phrases. We told him to support his conclusions with facts and to write forcefully in plain language."[23]

Following these guidelines, the first piece in Blom's four-part series began, "The Maine workers' compensation system is a disaster. It wastes millions of dollars each year. It destroys employer-employee relationships. . . . It crushes businesses with outrageous premiums. It mires thousands of injured workers in unproductive lives that spiral ever downward."[24]

Critics view such reportage not as expert but as advocacy journalism. They argue that this sort of opinionated reporting is precisely what has undermined public trust in the media. The evidence suggests otherwise, in that declining public trust in news organizations flows more from a general civic malaise than from particular practices of the media. Survey research has found that conservative Republicans—especially those who choose to listen to political talk radio—have the least trust in the media, but their complaint targets "liberal bias," not a general decline in journalistic standards.[25]

Well, is there such a bias? Ink has spilled like blood in the popular battle on this question, including Bernard Goldberg's *Bias: A CBS Insider Exposes How the Media Distort the News* and Eric Alterman's *What Liberal Media? The Truth About Bias and the News*. Such competing titles sell well and elicit hundreds of angry or fawning reviews on Amazon.com, which, at the time of this writing, offers its own tribute to balance by offering to sell the eager reader these two mutually incompatible books together, at a modest discount.

Academic research on the subject, fortunately, offers a relatively clear picture of where the "bias" lies. In a nutshell, it is the case that reporters are disproportionately liberal and tend to vote for Democrats, but there is no consistent partisan bias in the content of the mass media.[26] As for the partisanship of the rank-and-file reporter, one much-traveled radio and print correspondent has quipped, half-seriously, that "no conservative would work for what the average news job pays."[27] The antiauthority stance of liberals may also explain their appetite for media jobs, which still offer the chance to question authorities and hold powerful officials and corporations accountable.

If the content of media is, on balance, well, balanced, what then explains the growing perception of liberal bias, a view held by only twelve percent of Americans in 1988 but espoused by forty-three percent in 1996. One explanation is that conservative cultural and political leaders have marshaled this critique as an effective means of inoculating conservative Americans against media critiques of Republican candidates and policies. A second reason is that increasing news coverage of the media itself, including hand-wringing about the charge of liberal bias, reinforces the credibility of the charge in the public's mind.[28] The latter explanation offers a delicious irony: If one came to believe that the media were biased, owing to their own accounts of such bias, can one believe the accounts, given their source?

In any case, there is surely room in the larger media environment for explicitly liberal, conservative, and objective media outlets. The problem of bias only arises when a network, newspaper, or other entity poses as neutral but practices a decidedly partisan form of reporting. The clearest case of such an entity in the present media environment is Fox News Channel (FNC), which has successfully captured a conservative audience by framing news with a partisan point of view that is, despite occasional protestations to the contrary, obvious to even many of the network's most devoted viewers. One media observer made the following comment in a comparison of FNC and the older Cable News Network (CNN):

> Cable news networks appeal to two distinct audiences: highly ideological so-called news junkies whose daily entertainment derives from the overheated debates of the political class and a less-committed group who rely on experienced news gathering when a global crisis hits the headlines. CNN's operation is designed as a resource for the latter; FNC's for the former.[29]

Broadcasting (and Shaping) the Public's Voice

Even if the media, taken as a whole, lack a comprehensive partisan bias, they may still have a variety of effects on public opinion as a result of the issues they choose to cover and how they report on it. Political communication researchers have found a variety of connections between the media and the public, from how the media set the public's agenda to how reporting on public opinion polls shape opinion itself.

AGENDA SETTING AND FRAMING

The simple premise of the agenda setting research program is that the media may not shape the public's views as much as they shape the public's agenda. Maxwell McCombs and Donald Shaw's study of the 1968 presidential election showed that when the media focused on an issue, media influenced the issues that appeared on the agendas of undecided voters.[30] After three decades of research, McCombs and Shaw concluded that the agenda setting theory holds true, and it is most clearly observed for those issues that "do not directly impact the lives of the majority of the public, such as foreign policy or government scandal."[31] (Other actors, prominently including the government, shape the media's own agenda, but we save this important detail for Chapter 4.)

Researchers have made many significant modifications to the original model since its introduction. One such change is to distinguish between first level and second level agenda setting.[32] A first level effect draws the public's attention to a particular issue or subject, such as when the media, following the lead of the Bush administration, put Afghanistan's rulers (the Taliban) on the American public's agenda following the September 11, 2001, terrorist attacks. After the U.S. military removed the Taliban from power, the media then shifted the public's attention to Iraq, in another instance of a first level effect. Once focused on Iraq, however, the media also spurred a series of second level effects (influencing the public's attitudes on an issue) from "the Iraqi government supports terror" to "the Iraqi government is a threat to the security of the United States" to "the Iraqi government restricts the freedom of its citizens." In these ways, the media can not only put an issue on the public's agenda but also shape how we think about it. When this second level effect is understood as synonymous with a framing effect, it means the same thing as the media framing effects William Gamson found when studying political conversations, as described in the previous chapter.

One of the more powerful examples of agenda setting comes from Salma Ghanem's research on crime in Texas. From 1992–1994, crime went from being the principal concern of one in fifty Texans to more than one in three residents of the Lone Star State. As in most of the United States at that time, actual crime rates were dropping, but crime coverage in the news aired with increasing frequency. Looking at these trends over time, the increase in coverage appears to have spurred the increasing concern for a clear example of a first-level agenda-setting effect. In addition, however, news coverage of crime also had a second level effect by providing principally local coverage of robberies, murders, and the like in a way that focused Texans' attention on those crimes that directly threaten the average person, as opposed to national or international criminal activity or crimes committed against governments or corporations.[33]

Another helpful contribution to this literature comes from communication scholar Dietram Scheufele, who persuasively distinguished between media frames from individual frames. Journalists use media frames to organize and make sense of events, such as when a kidnapping is framed as part of the war on terror. Individuals also have frames, including global, cultural, or ideological ones and more issue-specific short-term ones. These cognitive frames help people process and make sense of media content, and they are often triggered by a parallel media frame.[34]

Key influences on journalists' choice of media frames include the prevailing social norms of their society, pressures and constraints within their media organization, interest group pressures (such as the flak reporters often get from organized critics for using certain frames), the journalistic habits or routines they have developed over the years, and, finally, their own ideological or political orientations—or, at least as often, those of their editors.[35] In turn, the frames the media select can influence what readers, viewers, and listeners judge to be the most important aspects of a story, determine who they should credit or blame for events, and suggest who they should view as the victims or victors. Depending on how one frames a proposed tax cut, for instance, the proposal can sound like a fiscal windfall for the rich or a popular uprising to lighten the working family's tax burden. In the end, these media frames have the potential to shape even individual frames, as the repetition of a particular framing of a story (such as welfare reform) gradually leads individuals to spontaneously deploy the same frame when they try to make sense of related events in other media or in their personal experiences.

MIRROR MIRROR: POLLS AND IMPERSONAL INFLUENCE

Thus far, it would seem that the media determine—to a degree—which issues the public thinks about and how it thinks about them. But what happens when the media report the public's own voice through polling data? Political communication scholar Diana Mutz views this mediated interaction as a kind of mass society discussion: "Much of the deliberation that may once have occurred in face-to-face meetings of people with differing views may now occur in an individual's internalized conversation with generalized others."[36]

Pre-election polls are one of the most common forms of survey data found in the media. These polls, among other things, can determine which candidates the public perceives as viable—capable of potentially winning an election. Mutz looked at the 1988 Democratic and Republican primaries to see whether a candidate's rising poll trends affected the candidate's fundraising fortunes. She found that favorable polling results could, indeed, boost contributions to a candidate. The same results could reduce the flow of funds into a falling candidate's campaign coffers. Survey data suggest, however, that the changes in contributions reflected not the influence of the polls on readers' own preferences but rather an influence on the perceived value of making a donation to a candidate one already preferred. In other words, what I learn about fellow citizens' candidate preferences affects my strategic choices but not my own candidate preferences.[37]

In an experimental study during the 1992 Democratic primary, Mutz found evidence of polls shaping opinions, but the impact was not of the kind one might expect. Participants in the study heard about recent polling data (the content of which was experimentally manipulated) and were then asked to state their candidate preference. Had you shown up in Mutz's laboratory, the following statements might have appeared on your questionnaire: "As you may have heard, some recent polls show that a large number of Democrats support Bill Clinton for the presidential nominee of the Democratic Party. How about you? Which of the candidates now in the running for the Democratic presidential nomination do you like best?" You would then choose your preference from a list of candidates and answer this follow-up question: "As you were thinking about your choice of candidate, what kinds of thoughts occurred to you?"

What predicted survey respondents' candidate preference was not just the nudge of the poll results but the combination of that information and their own thought processes. If a respondent had been leaning toward Clinton before hearing he was popular, then the poll numbers made the person even more likely to reflect on the reasons why others preferred Clinton. This in turn made the respondents that much more likely to express support for Clinton. If they initially leaned toward another candidate, such as Tom Harkin or Jerry Brown, the poll made them more likely to argue with the pro-Clinton poll results and reaffirm their initial leanings. This complex process was even stronger for those who were previously less concerned about the primary. In other words, the polling information did not serve as a consensus heuristic, whereby people blindly follow the lead of those surveyed to join what they perceive as a growing consensus view. Rather, the poll results prompted more reflection on one's own preferences, generally reinforcing previous inclinations.

After reviewing many findings of this sort, from both classroom experiments and national surveys, Mutz concluded that exposure to contrary points of view and different life experiences "does not automatically compel" people "to change their views." On the other hand, "when multiple others endorse a particular view, it is more likely to prompt a reassessment of their own positions in light of this new information. Thus, contrary to the conventional wisdom, impersonal influence need not be synonymous with empty-headed, sheeplike behavior or mass susceptibility to media influence." It could well result in "more reflective public opinion."[38]

A SPIRAL OF SILENCE

A more dismal view of the effects of polling comes from the "spiral of silence" theory advanced by Elisabeth Noelle-Neumann. This theory assumes that society functions as a collective, with individual members craving cohesion through a broad consensus on values and goals—what we commonly call public opinion.[39] Those who publicly "deviate from the consensus risk being ostracized by society—cast out as an unwelcome non-conformist." This results in the following consequence:

> If people believe that their opinions are shared in a consensus of public opinion, they have the confidence to speak out—whether in public or in private—displaying their convictions with buttons and bumper stickers, for instance, but also through the clothes they wear and other publicly visible symbols. When people feel they are in the minority, they become cautious and silent, thus further reinforcing the impression in public of their side's weakness, until the apparently weaker side disappears completely except for a small hard core that clings to values from the past, or until the opinion becomes taboo.[40]

Noelle-Neumann's observations of the 1965 German federal elections inspired this theory of how polls can promote conformity. The two leading parties—the Christian Democrats and the Social Democrats—were in a deadheat in the months leading up to the election, but voters began to believe that the Christian Democrats were pulling away, though this was a misperception. In the final weeks before the election, this became a self-fulfilling prophecy, as voter preference, in fact, swung in the direction that voters mistakenly believed it had already swung, and the Christian Democrats won by nine percent.

A more contemporary example comes from a study of public discussion on a controversial ballot initiative on affirmative action that Washington voters considered in 1998. Researchers surveyed more than two hundred randomly selected passengers aboard the ferry across Puget Sound to and from Seattle. A careful analysis of the results found that, consistent with the spiral of silence theory, people were a bit less willing to discuss the affirmative action initiative if they had a more pronounced fear of isolation and if they perceived their view as unpopular. Contrary to the theory, however, what concerned the ferry passengers most was the fear of dissenting from the views of friends and family, not the larger collective of Washington voters.[41]

The balance of research on the spiral of silence produced results like those obtained on the ferry—general corroboration of the theory's broadest claims but only weak effects and some contradictory findings, when one scrutinizes the details. A review of such studies by Dietram Scheufele and Patricia Moy suggested the need for many refinements and continued research.[42] Two themes in their critique are the need to distinguish among individuals and among larger cultures.

First, we know that individuals differ in their fear of isolation, their tendency to conform, and the strength of their convictions. It is likely that the effects of the spiral are quite strong for the person who is most fearful, most conformist, and least confident of his or her own views. Cultures that host a disproportionate number of such people are most likely to experience spirals of silence.

Second, one is most likely to see the spiral occur when issues with a moral dimension arise. This likely reflects the fact that individuals identify themselves with culturally like-minded people who principally share a set of values or core beliefs about how society should organize itself.[43] It follows that for people with a strong cultural identity, the relevant reference group is their cultural group—not society as a whole or, necessarily, their friends and acquaintances. We may overlook the spiral of silence's effect within a given political-cultural group, such as passionate libertarians, because we presume them to hold identical views. Such within-group similarity, however, is likely not just a consequence of like-minded people finding one another but also a result of group members choosing to conform to what they perceive as the view of their peers. After all, when a new issue arises, such as the limits on civil liberties in the Patriot Act or the ethics of regulating stem cell research funding, members of a culture arrive at a policy consensus that ensures its continued existence as a cohesive reference group.

A SPIRAL OF CYNICISM

If the media can contribute to a spiral of silence, ultimately foreclosing public deliberation on an issue, it follows that media could have other cascading effects. One particular impact that has received scholarly attention is the potential for the media to erode the public's willingness to trust public officials, government institutions, and even each other.

Communication researchers Patricia Moy and Michael Pfau addressed this issue in their book *With Malice Toward All? The Media and Public Confidence in Democratic Institutions.*[44] This work included a review of diverse literatures bearing on the link between trust in public institutions and exposure to different media sources. Their original research combined a content analysis of media with survey data from 1995 to 1997, and their conclusions contradicted the view that declining public trust is a straightforward consequence of negative media coverage. On the contrary, Moy and Pfau presented evidence supporting their theory that media can, under specific circumstances, actually bolster the public's confidence in its institutions. For instance, television news viewing had a positive impact on the public's views of the news media and public schools. Reading newspapers contributed to relatively favorable assessments of the much-maligned criminal justice and public school systems.

More disappointing findings, however, come from Joseph Cappella and Kathleen Hall Jamieson's *Spiral of Cynicism: The Press and the Public Good.*[45] Like

Moy and Pfau, they were concerned with the media's effect on how the public sees people and institutions, and their work returns us to the earlier discussion of framing. What they contrasted were substantive versus "strategic" news frames on issues and candidates. A substantive framing on a story about Bill Clinton's health care proposal, for example, would emphasize the details of the policy, its likely consequences, and the alternatives. In other words, such a story would be *endnote* designed to promote the very deliberative process detailed at the start of this chapter. A strategic frame, by contrast, would emphasize how the health proposal fits into the larger political contest between Democrats and Republicans. The story does not help the reader understand the proposal so much as grasp its political costs and benefits for partisan interests. Similarly, during an election, a strategic frame emphasizes the "horse race" among the candidates, rather than the substantive, philosophical, and relevant character differences between them.

Cappella and Jamieson conducted a series of experiments and surveys to assess the effects of strategic news frames on public attitudes, and they found that even a single news story can cause a reader to attribute cynical motives to the public officials in a news story. The cumulative effect of such strategic stories is additive, in that each adds an increment of cynicism to the reader's own understanding (and retelling) of current events. Moreover, such cynicism can do real harm to the deliberative process. In the case of Clinton's health care proposal, its demise can be explained partly due to a chain of effects starting with strategic media coverage. The cynical framing led citizens to attribute negative traits to the proposal's sponsors, which triggered broader cynicism and mistrust, which then led to a rejection of the plan—not on its merits as a policy solution but owing to a media-amplified distrust of public officials.

Strategic frames can also have a beneficial effect by making the substantive issues of a policy debate more interesting and engaging, helping media users understand the political process, and increasing political sophistication overall. Nonetheless, to the extent that media make people unwilling to consider public officials' arguments, unable to conceive of public-spirited behavior, and uninterested in the deeper substance of political conflicts, they undermine the potential for mediated deliberation.

TALK RADIO AND PUBLIC VOICE

Not all media, however, speak *to* the public. Long before the advent of interactive online media, call-in radio programs popularized the practice of speaking *with* the public. Political talk radio has won a large and devoted listenership. Although a 2000 review of top-rated programs found the medium overwhelmed by the conservative voices of Rush Limbaugh and his imitators,[46] Al Franken and investors created the Air America radio network in 2004 in an attempt to create a space for liberals to hear liberals on the air.

To some extent, political talk radio programs do nothing more than recycle the news and information already circulating in the mainstream media. Listening to one or another of these programs, one gets to hear headlines read from the morning paper, extended quotes from op-eds and opinionated Web sites, and interviews with guests who have just arrived in the studio after appearing earlier that morning on the television.

What makes talk radio worthy of special mention, however, is its open broadcast of interaction between the host and the listener—something talk radio foregrounds but other media, by contrast, only occasionally feature (or mimic in the more controlled output of a public opinion survey). This creates the potential for the mass public to hear itself, via the talk radio broadcast. In effect, talk radio permits the rabble to rouse itself.

This function is important because even advocates of representative deliberation acknowledge that professional communicators, no matter how well intentioned, often fail to fulfill their responsibilities to produce a deliberative media system. More radical critics have pointed out that the mass media, intellectual elites, and public officials often pursue agendas that conflict with the public's interest.[47] Benjamin Page, who popularized the notion of mediated deliberation, recognized one problem in particular:

> The most prominent journalists, television commentators, and public officials tend to have much higher incomes than the average American and to live in very different circumstances. On certain class-related issues, it seems possible that these professional communicators may interpret events in ways that do not take the public's values into account and may recommend policies contrary to those values.[48]

When elites share such similar orientations and backgrounds, mass deliberation often fails, such as when the United States has a "bipartisan foreign policy." Under these circumstances, the public often remains unaware of an important issue or its ramifications for the general population.[49]

Even in these situations, the mass media might solve their own problems by providing alternative communication outlets, such as the talk radio medium mentioned earlier. To illustrate the importance of this form of public voice, Page offered the example of the Zoe Baird nomination. President Clinton nominated Baird for U.S. attorney general, and her confirmation appeared likely, despite the revelation that she and her husband had hired two illegal aliens to help with driving and baby-sitting. The criticisms of Baird flowed through call-in radio programs that encouraged discussion of current issues. Callers to programs across the country were outraged that a lawbreaker would serve as the highest-ranking law-enforcement official. Though elites sympathetically sided with Baird's decision, the general public did not. As one Boston talk show host remarked, "I don't think the average schmo says, 'Hey, I know 15 people who have Peruvian live-in nannies.'" Baird's bipartisan support thus eroded, and

Clinton withdrew his nomination after a firestorm of public opposition. Though some might have suspected a behind-the-scenes orchestration of public outcry, evidence suggests that the criticism of Baird was a case of genuine popular backlash.[50]

If talk radio is an important forum for the expression of the public's voice, the next question concerns who takes part in this form of discussion. Though the overwhelming majority of its hosts are conservative, talk radio's listeners appear to be somewhat more diverse. Long before the arrival of the liberal talk radio network Air America, one comprehensive survey of national talk radio audiences found a profile that defies the stereotype of the white, male, and conservative "ditto-head."[51] A survey of radio listeners in San Diego, California, found that the listening frequency of talk radio was unrelated to every major demographic variable.[52] In other words, talk radio listeners come from all bands of the demographic and political spectrum, even though talk radio listenership certainly over-represents conservatives. Research also suggests that those listeners who call talk radio programs come from diverse backgrounds, though callers typically have exceptional levels of political self-confidence.[53]

Regardless of the host or the audience, the talk radio format that has taken hold in American political culture does not permit the kind of deliberative discussion described in Chapter 2. No popular program currently attracts listeners through the to-and-fro of honest political debate between intellectual equals. More common is the sort of staged or false debate decried by Jon Stewart in the opening of this chapter. Even then, talk radio may serve a function in a larger deliberative media system by giving the public a venue to vent frustrations overlooked even by the ever-watchful political parties and pundits, who make it their job to anticipate public opinion trends. The more emotionally charged talk shows, including even the outrageous antics on *The Jerry Springer Show*, can also permit frank public testimony and moral debate that otherwise do not occur in an overly polite public debate.[54]

Visions of a More Deliberative Media

It is possible to imagine a more unambiguously deliberative media process, whereby the media produce richer content and citizens play a less passive role in consuming it. This chapter concludes with a glimpse at three promising ideas and practices—public journalism, watchdogs and blogs, and microjournalism.

PUBLIC JOURNALISM

When Jay Rosen wrote "Public Journalism: First Principles" in 1994, the public journalism movement had already begun to take off. This new form of journalism (sometimes called civic journalism) includes a wide range of goals and purposes, but, in essence, it "tries to place the journalist within the political community as a responsible member with a full stake in public life. . . . In a word, public journalists want public life to work," and they are no longer neutral on basic democratic questions, such as whether people participate in public life, "whether a genuine debate takes place when needed," and "whether a community comes to grips with its problems."[55]

Among the early successes of public journalism, Rosen counted the following:

- Three newspapers had "redesigned their coverage to emphasize the concerns of citizens rather than the maneuvers of candidates or the machinations of insiders" (Wichita Eagle, Charlotte Observer, and Tallahassee Democrat).

- Some had played the role of community organizer by sponsoring "neighborhood roundtables that encourage citizens to meet in private homes to discuss public issues" (Portland Herald Press, Minneapolis Star-Tribune).

- Others "convened discussions among local leaders in communities where there was no movement or momentum" (Daily Oklahoman, Boulder Daily Camera).[56]

The movement has had considerable success in the years since. Many observers share the view of political scientist Albert Dzur, who declared in 2002 that "public journalism is arguably the most significant reform movement in American journalism since the Progressive era."[57] Dzur added that public journalism, from its inception, was "influenced by the ideals of deliberative democracy" and principally "advocates changes in techniques of newsgathering and reporting to foster more public deliberation."[58]

One of the many examples of public journalism is the efforts undertaken by the *Tallahassee Democrat*. The State of Florida has been the butt of many jokes since it bungled the 2000 presidential election, but this Tallahassee paper has been a source of pride for its readers. The *Democrat*, working with a TV station and two local universities, initiated the Public Agenda project, which began with a series of surveys and focus groups to learn which issues most concerned the wider Tallahassee community. The *Democrat* then used the results of these studies to frame a series of professionally moderated public meetings that included community leaders, civic organization members, and the general public. These general meetings led to the formation of subgroups focusing on key issue clusters, such as "Jobs and the Economy" and "Children, Values, and Education." In parallel, the *Democrat* created the Public Agenda Page, an online forum that collected citizen comments, hosted open discussions and question-and-answer periods with public officials, and created a progress report on each issue.[59]

Today, the Public Journalism Network brings together a diverse group of print and electronic media organizations that share the same general goal of connecting with the public they serve and promoting not just media deliberation but also the kinds of conversations, discussions, and public meetings described throughout this book. Figure 3.2 shows the declaration of the network's charter members, and the language of that document makes it clear that these journalists believe they can maintain objectivity on the substance of the issues they cover (e.g., "journalists should stand apart in making sound professional judgments about how to cover communities"), but they also believe that they must "adhere to democratic discipline" in their reporting and editing.

A declaration written by the Charter Members of the Public Journalism Network in Kennesaw, Georgia, January 25, 2003.

The Public Journalism Network is a global professional association of journalists and educators interested in exploring and strengthening the relationship between journalism and democracy.

We believe journalism and democracy work best when news, information and ideas flow freely; when news fairly portrays the full range and variety of life and culture of all communities; when public deliberation is encouraged and amplified; and when news helps people function as political actors and not just as political consumers.

We believe journalists should stand apart in making sound professional judgments about how to cover communities, but cannot stand apart in learning about and understanding these communities.

We believe the diversity and fragmentation of society call for new techniques for storytelling and information-sharing to help individual communities define themselves singularly and as part of the whole set of communities.

We believe the stories and images journalists produce can help or hinder as people struggle to reach sound judgments about their personal lives and their common well-being.

We believe we must articulate a public philosophy for journalism that helps journalists reach deeper into the communities they serve and that helps communities work more closely with the journalists who serve them.

We believe democracy benefits when journalists listen to the people.

We believe we can learn and grow as practitioners, educators and scholars—and strengthen practice, education and scholarship—by examining, experimenting with and enhancing the theory and practice of journalism in relation to the theory and practice of democracy.

We believe in the value of studying the dynamics of communities and the complexity of public life. Just as journalists need to adhere to professional and financial discipline to succeed, we believe they must adhere to democratic discipline.

We believe the best journalism helps people see the world as a whole and helps them take responsibility for what they see.

Figure 3.2   A Declaration for Public Journalism

SOURCE: Public Journalism Network.(Charter available online at www.pjnet.org/charter.shtml.) Used by permission.

Critics of the public journalism movement worry that it threatens the independence or freedom of the media. Part of what makes private media so valuable in a democracy is that they exist apart from the government and the public. Reporters cherish their "autonomy" or "detachment" because it gives them the freedom to report candidly on issues, no matter how uncomfortable they might make power holders, or the lay public for that matter. As journalism professor Michael McDevitt explained, it is one thing to make a "valid criticism of conventional detachment"—the tendency of journalists to become disengaged from the public's concerns—but this does not "constitute a rationale for questioning the basis of journalistic authority itself."[60]

This, like many critiques of public journalism, is really more of a warning to not take the idea too far—beyond a renewed concern for sustaining deliberation to becoming a public servant, catering to the whims and prejudices of a community rather than challenging it to meet the same standards one sets for one's own newsroom. Public journalism, in this sense, asks that if the media meet their deliberative obligations as media producers, as described in the central column of Figure 3.1, then the public too must meet its own responsibilities, shown in the right-hand column of the same figure.

In an ideal community, focusing on one's role as a deliberative media producer may mean relinquishing some of the more secondary responsibilities that media like the *Tallahassee Democrat* have accepted. The media must play the role of "deliberative-democratic watchdog"—an outside critic not only of public officials but also of citizens and the very kinds of discussions and meetings that the *Democrat* has promoted. After all, in a mature, deliberative community, like those envisioned in Chapter 8 of this book, the media would have responsibility for determining "what and who is left out of public discussions and official decisions."[61]

WATCHDOGS AND BLOGS

The metaphor of media as watchdog is an old one, but some media have given new life to this cliché by suggesting ways in which they can keep a watchful eye on themselves. One of the means they have deployed is the Weblog or blog, which is nothing more than a diary-style Web site with commentary and links concerning a stream of topics or current events.

Along these very lines, in 2005 CBS News launched PublicEye, the self-proclaimed aim of which is to "bring transparency to the editorial operations of CBS News."[62] To be transparent in this context means to make one's newsmaking processes visible, subject to outside scrutiny, and, ultimately, more accountable. If PublicEye makes CBS truly transparent, CBS news will make its activities visible for anyone who cares to watch.

What prompted CBS to launch PublicEye was the effectiveness of independent blogs—the public's own unappointed (and unleashed) watchdogs. Just two months before the 2004 presidential election, the CBS News program *60 Minutes II* presented an in-depth report alleging that President George W. Bush received "preferential treatment" while serving light duty in the Texas Air National Guard. The story was an old one, but what made this news was the presence of four previously unseen memos, including the one shown in Figure 3.3.

Shortly after the story aired, the memos were proved to be forged. The first attack on the CBS story appeared on the blog FreeRepublic.com, authored by an active Air Force officer. A succession of other blogs picked up and elaborated the story, including Republican sites such as rathergate.com, a blog registered to the Republican consultant Richard Viguerie. As recounted by journalist Corey Pein in the *Columbia Journalism Review,* the ensuing fracas was not entirely deliberative. It is not clear, in the end, whether the blogs helped CBS News get the story right. For instance, one of the principal arguments establishing the memos as inauthentic was the presence of the superscript characters "th," which numerous blogs alleged could not be produced on typewriters in the 1970s (when the memos were allegedly typed). Though others knowledgeable of that era's technology refuted that claim, it stuck. All the blogging in the world could not undo the power of this and similar "definitive" evidence of fraud. Moreover, the debate over the memos distracted the public's attention from the point of the story, which was that a preponderance of evidence suggests that President Bush did not fulfill the full requirements of his service in the National Guard.[63]

01 August 1972

MEMORANDUM FOR RECORD

SUBJECT: Bush, George W. 1st Lt.3244754FG
         Suspension of Flight status

1. On this date I ordered that 1st Lt. Bush be suspended from flight status due to failure to perform to USAF/TexANG standards/and failure to meet annual physical examination (flight) as ordered.

2. I conveyed my verbal orders to commander, 147th Ftr Intrcp Gp with request for orders for suspension and convening of a flight review board IAW AFM 35-13.

3. I recommended transfer of this officer to the 9921st Air Reserve Squadron in May and forwarded his AF Form 1288 to 147th Ftr Intrcp Gp headquarters. The transfer was not allowed. Officer has made no attempt to meet his training certification or flight physical. Officer expresses desire to transfer out of state including assignment to non-flying billets.

4. On recommendation of Harris, I also suggested that we fill this critical billet with a more seasoned pilot from the list of qualified Vietnam pilots that have rotated. Recommendations were received but not confirmed.

JERRY B. KILLIAN
Lt. Colonel

Figure 3.3   The Memo That Brought Down Dan Rather

The high political stakes of this particular episode may have resulted in a more muddled outcome than is commonly the case. A recent study of those who read blogs found that many Internet users have become devoted to regularly reading blogs "devoted to critiquing media coverage." Bloggers in this tradition "routinely fact check stories in traditional media and gleefully point out errors." An irony of these Web sites is that "because most bloggers are not independent newsgatherers, they must rely heavily on the Web for their content." Consequently, "much of that comes from the traditional media"—the very same outlets that bloggers critique. Moreover, bloggers seeking credibility "often try to lend authority to their sites by providing links to traditional media sites."[64] Even those who regularly read blogs can recognize the limits of a Weblog: although seventy-two percent rated the blogs they read as moderately or very in-depth in their coverage, only fifty percent gave them such a rating on accuracy, and only thirty-eight percent gave a similar rating on fairness.[65]

Though it may be stretching the metaphor too far, we might view blogs as true watchdogs of the deliberative scrap yard, in that they do, indeed, keep a keen eye out for intruders who wish to do our democracy harm, but they are also often junkyard dogs—mean-spirited, free-roaming, likely feral canines who thirst for a bite of leg or arm, regardless of the virtue of those who cross their path. In the larger media system, there is a place for such reportage, but blogs are largely dependent on mainstream media and old-fashioned investigative reporting. In the end, blogs are more likely to complement media than replace them.

MICROJOURNALISM AND THE RESURGENCE OF LOCALISM

One of the irreplaceable features of mainstream media is their coverage of daily events. In particular, while the wire services and national media cover our nation and the world, it is the local newspapers and television that keep us current on the events in our cities and towns. The simple act of reading the local newspaper on a regular basis makes a citizen more likely to participate in local politics, remain aware of local issues, and develop passionate convictions about local issues.[66]

The notion that local media matter has deep roots in the media system. Localism is one of the values that the Federal Communications Commission (FCC) is chartered to uphold. The deregulation of the media system to permit greater concentration of ownership, however, has reduced the amount of local control and programming at many media outlets. Even the highly regarded system of National Public Radio (NPR) stations has reconceptualized "local" as a notion that transcends geographic borders, with local stations offering national programming that speaks to the issues and concerns of national communities rather than local ones.[67]

An alternative media tradition persists, however, and stridently local "community" or "grassroots" radio stations (along with some NPR affiliates) continue to produce locally grown programs that focus on the lives of people within their broadcast coverage. These stations can stimulate and enliven current public debates, along the lines of public journalism, and they can also serve an educational function by giving their numerous volunteers the chance to hone their own reporting and broadcasting skills.[68]

If local journalism is good for the local community, would neighborhood journalism be good for the neighborhood? One enterprising team of journalists presumed the answer was yes, and they set out to report on their block. From 1995–1997, Albuquerque residents Cindy Simmons, Todd Wynward, Peg Bartlett, and I put out *The Truman Trumpet*, a very irregular newspaper devoted to covering the news and events that happened on our block. A stray cat, a stolen car, a new shed—nothing was too small to cover—and much of the coverage was done in the same hard news tradition of the *New York Times*. The results were sometimes hilarious, but the paper had the effect of making the block feel real and alive to its residents, many of whom had lived there for decades but had fallen out of the habit of conversing with their next-door neighbors.

When Cindy Simmons moved to Seattle in 1998, she continued this experiment by starting the *Wallingford Word*, a free newspaper that she circulated quasi-monthly for four years. The *Word* reached out to a wider community—an urban Seattle neighborhood with a mix of residences and businesses covering perhaps a single square mile—than did *The Truman Trumpet*. The goal remained the same—to help a neighborhood take itself seriously by looking very closely at its local problems and successes. Figure 3.4 shows the front page from one of the final issues of the *Word*. The feature stories examine three of the transportation options Wallingford residents have when trying to get to downtown Seattle during rush hour. The subject is serious, but the writing is lighthearted and accessible.[69] The other cover story addresses an upcoming election for the Wallingford Community Council, a quasi-governmental organization that often has great difficulty inspiring enough people to run for its offices, let alone enough participants to spark a lively debate on neighborhood issues.

Simmons refers to efforts like these as microjournalism. If the future of deliberative media includes public journalism and bloggers, it is also likely to include many microjournalists in the tradition of *The Truman Trumpet* and the *Wallingford Word*. As more people go online, neighborhood news sites become an increasingly viable option for those who wish to reach their readers at minimum expense. Nonetheless, there will likely always be a place for the hand-distributed newsletter because the periodic doorstep meetings between oneself and one's neighbor promote a kind of connection that is unique to the face-to-face encounter.

Taken to its extreme, in fact, microjournalism draws a connection from the practices of mass media institutions all the way down to informal news networks among friends, coworkers, and community members. Sociologist Herbert Gans observed that even when "neighbors pass along the latest block gossip" through

$\mathcal{T}_{he}$ **Wallingford Word**

Switchblade Suzy
Takes on Energy Crisis
Profiteers
page 3

Within Walking
Distance
page 4

Volume 4 Issue 3   FREE   April, 2001

The Great Wallingford Bus Race

What's the fastest way to get downtown at rush hour? Enquiring minds need to know. So five intrepid Wallingford Word reporters met at 8 a.m. one Thursday at the intersection of 45th and Wallingford to race to Pioneer Square. Did the tortoise Metro beat the swift-but-time-wasting hare of a station wagon? Read on to find out.

Riding the 26 Bus
By Cindy Simmons

It's 8 a.m. on a rainy Thursday. Too early for a telecommuter like me to be outside, but if hundreds of thousands of downtown workers have to wake up early to fight through traffic every weekday, I can do it once in the name of science.

John and I hop around on the corner of Wallingford and 45th to keep warm. Tracy and her reporter-in-training kids drive up.

Our goal is to determine the fastest way to get downtown from Wallingford. Since Tracy's kids didn't bring coats, they get to take their station wagon. It's raining, so none of our bicyclists show up. I draw the short straw and have to walk five blocks to get the 26.

It's 8:13 when we split up. I can actually see John's 16 pulling up in front of Bartell's. But I'm not jealous. This is science. And besides, I've got a secret weapon.

The walk down Wallingford is undoubtedly the most beautiful view of the Seattle skyline. At 43rd, a man is standing on his front walk, transfixed by the rain clouds moving over the city. I admire the gardens as I speed along. On the east side of the street, someone has cemented a Barbie doll into the sidewalk. I love

(Continued on page 2)

The 16 bus returns to base, defeated by traffic.

Trapped on the 16
By John Gastil

Victory was surely mine. All I had to do to win the Great Wallingford Bus Race was walk twenty yards to a waiting 16 bus, sit peacefully for a few minutes, then disembark and walk a few blocks to Pioneer Square.

The 16 glides through Wallingford with ease, picking up grateful commuters at the usual

(Continued on page 2)

Driving the Kids
By Tracy Romoser

I arrive 8:05 a.m. with my two coatless children at Wallingford and 45th. We're given the task to drive downtown to Pioneer Square and rendezvous at the desecrated Pergola. I accept with great gusto, knowing full well that I can now return home immediately to grab my children's coats or risk being turned into the Department for Underdressed, Grossly Abused and Neglected Children.

Driving allows for more flexibility with timing and scheduling, which in turn allows more time for forgetting important items and lollygagging around. I spend 20 minutes driving back to the house, ushering children into the bathroom and grabbing coats.

We pass the starting point again at 8:35 a.m. and drive west to 99. Turn left onto the southbound lane and soon learn why traffic is so Quixotic in this lovely town of ours. We make great time over the bridge until we hit the slowdown midway past Westlake. While in the far left lane I notice the flashing lights above the Battery Tunnel. Too late to get over to the Seattle Center exit, I turn on NPR for the traffic report 11 minutes before the hour (Why don't they just wait one minute for 10 till?) and

(Continued on page 2)

This Ain't Sleepy Hollow, But Wallingford Has a Headless Council Slate
By Cindy Simmons

Wallingford Community Council terms are set to expire next month, but at the April 4 board meeting, the nominating committee had no candidates for president or first vice president.

"Having people volunteer and having people participate in the community council has become progressively more difficult," said Bar-

bara Reine, who was elected first vice president last year, but moved up to president after Karen Buschow had to resign.

Reine said she would prefer not to take on another term at the top.

"I just retired," she said. "I'm hoping for a short time to have a window of less responsibility."

Steve Cyr, who is currently third vice president, said the presidency takes 15 to 20 hours per week. Cyr said he doesn't have that much time, but he, Reine and Buschow are negotiating some type of shared power arrangement.

While the Community Council has a vampiric need for new blood, the slate makers feel

(Continued on page 3)

Figure 3.4   A Front Page From the *Wallingford Word*

SOURCE: Cindy Simmons. Used by permission.

everyday conversations, they are acting as unpaid reporters. "If journalism is defined as the gathering and reporting of new information to an audience," Gans pointed out, "we are all journalists."[70] Of course, the average person has neither the tools nor reach of media professionals who work within vast media organizations. The point here is simply to recognize the potential for lay citizens to informally distribute and analyze their own news outside of the larger media system.

Conclusion

There is no national scorecard on how well the media promote a kind of mass deliberation, nor is there an inventory of how often individual citizens, as a result of media consumption, have conversations within their head that might look like deliberation. We do know that the public remains largely ignorant or confused about many important facts about their political—and larger—world.[71] We also know that most citizens do not feel sufficiently aroused by the issues in their community, nation, and world to engage in ongoing political action.[72]

This suggests that we can do better. A more public-oriented journalism, coupled with a diverse proliferation of bloggers and microjournalists, would likely improve the deliberative quality of the larger media system. For professional media organizations leery of a full commitment to the credo of public journalism or the lawlessness of the blogosphere, a middle way may be simply demanding that public institutions give satisfactory reasons for their actions that comport with basic social values, such as justice and fairness. Communication professor James Ettema proposed this approach in his essay "Journalism as Reason Giving." A single media organization can combine objective reporting on an issue with uncovering the issue's moral dimensions and, through its editorial capacity, staking out a position in light of the findings of its investigations. Ettema wrote:

> [Journalism] must itself be a reasoning institution that aggressively pursues, rigorously tests, and compellingly renders reasons that satisfy the key criterion of deliberative democracy. If journalism ought to encourage debate . . . and hold governors accountable . . . , then we must ask journalism to not merely record the processes of deliberation but also to act as a reasoning participant in those processes. We must ask journalism to embrace a further paradox: to function as both a fair-minded moderator and a committed speaker.[73]

Taking this, or any other more deliberative orientation, could engender profound changes. Whether deliberative or not, our media frame the issues we think about and how we think about them. Of particular importance, the media prove a critical conduit through which we debate the issues and candidates that come before us each election cycle. It is this issue that captures our attention in the following chapter.

Notes

1. Scholars have begun to look at *The Daily Show* as signaling a new form of political reporting, blending news and entertainment in a way that holds the attention of younger viewers while delivering real substance and even complex understandings of news and current events (Baym, 2005). The program also inspired a spirited discussion panel at the National Communication Association annual conference in 2006.
2. Grossberg (2005).
3. Peters (2001, p. 2).
4. Ibid., p. 5.

5. Giddens (1984, p. 236).
6. Page (1996, p. 5).
7. Ibid., p. 6.
8. Habermas (2006, p. 416).
9. Ibid.
10. Goodin (2000, p. 96).
11. Quoted in McKinley (2005, p. B1).
12. Goodin and Niemeyer (2003) found evidence of such internal reflection in the case of citizen juries held in Australia.
13. Just, Levine, and Regan (2002, p. 102).
14. Ibid., p. 102.
15. For CBS's own admission of error, see http://www.cbsnews.com/stories/2004/09/08/60II/main641984.shtml.
16. For more on the fate of investigative reporting, see Greenwald and Bernt (2000).
17. Klein (2001, p. 134).
18. Page (1996, pp. 21–26).
19. Ibid., pp. 26–35.
20. Ibid., p. 35.
21. Ibid., p. 36.
22. Bennett, Lawrence, and Livingston (forthcoming).
23. Newman (1993, pp. 12–13).
24. Ibid.
25. Jones (2004). See also Lee (2005).
26. Lee (2005, pp. 43–44) summarized a long list of such studies.
27. Cindy Simmons, quoted in personal correspondence.
28. Watts, Domke, Shah, and Fan (1999) and Domke, Watts, Fan, and Shah (1999).
29. Farhi (2003, pp. 32–33).
30. McCombs and Shaw (1972).
31. Weaver, McCombs, and Shaw (2004, p. 258).
32. Ibid., p. 259.
33. Ibid., p. 262.
34. Scheufele (1999, pp. 106–7).
35. Ibid., p. 109.
36. Mutz (1998, p. 295).
37. Ibid., pp. 246–58.
38. Ibid., p. 24.
39. Habermas (2006) aptly noted that the phrase *public opinion* is a "singular phrase" that "only refers to the prevailing one among several public opinions" (p. 417).
40. Noelle-Neumann (1991, p. 259).
41. Moy, Domke, and Stamm (2001).
42. Scheufele and Moy (2000).
43. Gastil, Kahan, and Braman (2005).
44. Moy and Pfau (2000).
45. Cappella and Jamieson (1997).
46. Gastil (2000, pp. 103–5). Much of the text in this section is adapted from Gastil (2000, pp. 101–6).
47. Herman and Chomsky (1988) demonstrated how different "news filters" can result in biased coverage, even when reporters intend to report faithfully on world affairs.
48. Page (1996, p. 10).

49. Ibid., p. 119. See also Bennett et al. (in press).
50. Quotation and observations are from Page (1996, p. 89). He drew on stories written in the *Boston Globe, Los Angeles Times, New York Times,* and *Washington Post.*
51. The survey was conducted by *Talkers Magazine* (Longmeadow, Massachusetts), which updates the survey every six months online at http://www.talkers.com/talkaud.html. The term *ditto-head* comes from Rush Limbaugh, who uses the term without irony to refer to his listeners, who often offer "dittos" to Limbaugh. After listening to the Rush Limbaugh radio show, this begins to sound like a devoted incantation, recited by the most loyal listeners.
52. Hofstetter et al. (1994, pp. 474–76).
53. Newhagen (1994). The study did not suggest a single causal direction, and it is plausible that calling shows may heighten self-efficacy, as well as vice versa. Hofstetter et al. (1994) found the same relationship. Also see Hollander (1997), who found that talk radio has likely helped to mobilize conservative voters in the United States.
54. Lunt and Stenner (2005) provided just such an analysis of *Springer,* pointing out the less-than-obvious ways in which the show embodies the Habermasian ideal of a deliberative public sphere. When evaluating programs such as this, it is important to distinguish between requiring a particular program to model deliberation, per se, and asking that a program contribute to a larger societal-level debate—a deliberative media system, in which there is always room for the occasional polemic or extreme emotional outburst. As a side note, on the Air America radio network, Jerry Springer currently hosts a radio program that sounds more reflective and dialogic than most talk radio. In other words, it appears that Springer can consciously craft a variety of discursive spaces—not just the spectacle that is his infamous television program. Current information on the program is available at http://www.airamerica.com.
55. Rosen and Merritt (1994, p. 11).
56. Ibid., p. 9. Rosen (2001) updated this optimistic view of public journalism and explained the movement more fully.
57. Dzur (2002, p. 313).
58. Ibid.
59. Ibid., pp. 317–18.
60. McDevitt (2003, p. 162).
61. Dzur (2002, p. 335).
62. Dorroh (2005, p. 14).
63. Pein (2005). Note that Pein can embrace the irony of having his own blog, coreypein.com. He wrote, "I know the site looks like a blog. This sort of annoys me, because ninety-eight percent of blogs are crap. So, I guess, is ninety-eight percent of what's published anywhere, but blogs, to an extent heretofore unseen, encourage self-obsession and useless rambling. Before I go too far down that road, I must stop typing" (http://coreypein.com/2004/06/introduction.html).
64. Johnson and Kaye (2004, p. 625).
65. Ibid., p. 629.
66. Scheufele, Shanahan, and Kim (2002). See also McLeod et al. (1996). These impacts have limits, however. McLeod, Scheufele, and Moy (1999) found that the effect of local newspaper and television use extended to conventional, institutionalized participation (only indirectly for television) but not to participation in local forums, such as those described in Chapter 2.

67. Stavistsky (1994).
68. Forde, Meadows, and Foxwell (2003).
69. An earlier *Word* story on the potential elimination of Bus 26 may have helped save that bus line, whose riders spoke up after reading the story.
70. Gans (2007, p. 161).
71. Delli Carpini and Keeter (1996).
72. Verba, Schlozman, and Brady (1995).
73. Ettema (2007, p. 145).

SOURCE: Associated Press. Used by permission.

4

Deliberative Elections

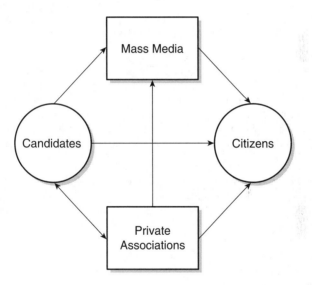

Our primary electoral act, voting, is rather like using a public toilet: we wait in line with a crowd in order to close ourselves up in a small compartment where we can relieve ourselves in solitude and in privacy of our burden, pull a level, and then, yielding to the next in line, go silently home.

—Benjamin Barber[1]

If raising money is the most important activity for a candidate seeking public office in the United States, the second most important activity is spending money. Most of the money spent on a campaign pays for communication, which includes television, radio, print ads, brochures, and direct mail. The distinct advantage of direct mail is that a candidate can send a tailored message to a specific set of targeted households. Thus it remains one of the most popular methods of communicating with voters, especially in state, local, and low-profile contests, which make up the vast majority of all elections. Thus, the life history of a piece of direct mail gives us a good first glimpse of the state of deliberation in modern elections.

The Story of Maily, the Bulk Rate Direct Mail Piece

Day 1: A piece of direct mail—we'll call it Maily—is conceived in the mind of a campaign manager who works for a mayoral candidate. The idea is to label an opponent as an outsider who doesn't understand local people and their concerns. Maily will help plant this idea in voters' minds.

Day 2: The campaign manager passes the idea of Maily to a hired public relations expert, who decides that Maily will be an oversized card—a colorful two-sided piece of mail that requires no envelope and can be sent with minimal postage. The expert asks the campaign's opposition researcher to look for photos of the opponent stepping onto or off of an airplane. The expert also gives Maily a headline: "The People of Smallville Want Leaders From Smallville." Maily likes that the headline is in big letters so everyone can see it.

Day 6: The opposition researcher has come back with the perfect photo for Maily, taken of the opponent while returning from a trade mission. Not only is the opponent stepping out of the door of an airplane, but also the plane is an expensive-looking executive jet. To the delight of everyone on the campaign staff who has seen the photo, the opponent is pictured with the worst case of bedhead they have seen, presumably from sleeping on the nonstop flight back from Tokyo. Maily wishes the photo had better resolution but is glad everyone seems to like it.

Day 10: Maily gets laid out by the campaign's volunteer graphic designer, who puts the color photo on one side and the pithy headline on the other. Beneath the headline is a cliché-ridden paragraph explaining that the opponent is a newcomer to Smallville, with big city ideas that don't play well with locals. The incumbent mayor, who is paying for Maily, is portrayed as a small town hero who will continue to work for jobs, parks, and the things local people cherish. Maily does not know that the opponent was actually born in Smallville but moved away at thirteen, when her mother took a job at an East Coast college, where the opponent got her BA and MBA before returning to Smallville five years ago. Maily might also be sad to learn that the incumbent mayor grew up in Shelbyville, a rival town ten miles from Smallville. Not that it matters, really.

Day 15: The printer finishes preparing Maily for delivery to ten thousand homes. Each copy of Maily contains the name and address of a different voter (or household). The campaign manager had given a list of households to the printer using three criteria: this piece goes only to those voters who participated in at least two of the past three local elections, have been registered in the county for fifteen or more years, and are at least fifty years of age.

Day 25: Maily's excitement at being printed wore off while Maily languished in the downtown post office's bulk mail room for a week. Just five days before the election, though, Maily is sorted and placed into each mail carrier's truck for delivery the next day. Maily is happy to have good company in another five pieces of direct mail, which each mail carrier has bundled together inside a grocery store's weekly coupon advertisement. The grocery ad appears on a low-grade newsprint that makes Maily itch.

Day 26: The big day arrives, and Maily leaps into one mailbox after another, drops down into mail slots, and is jammed into walls of small apartment boxes. The first household to see Maily is a small bungalow where Maybelle Anders lives alone. Maybelle greets the mail carrier and sorts through her mail on the way from her birdhouse-shaped mailbox to the front door. She catches Maily's eye and sees the big headline and colorful photo for 2.5 seconds before she drops all her political mail into the recycling receptacle on her front porch. The grocery store circular makes it into the house, along with a bill and a card from her grandson.

Maily is sad, lying in a pile of moldering mail, plastic newspaper bags, and paper scraps from a craft project. Smallville's recycling program keeps Maily in the circle of life, but, more important, Maybelle's brief glance was enough to make Maybelle wonder why an out-of-towner would be so audacious as to run against the incumbent. A few more mailings—followed by a couple phone calls and some television ads—will secure Maybelle's vote to reelect the mayor.

Direct mail is just one of the tools candidates use to get their message to voters, but the story of Maily illustrates key features of contemporary elections—large expenditures on campaign advertisements, the construction of simple (often deceptive or misleading) strategic messages, and a no-holds-barred struggle to win the votes of those most likely to cast a ballot on election day. The deliberative perspective on campaigns tries to calculate the sum of these sorts of campaign communications and interactions. Can there be such a thing as deliberative elections, and, if so, how common are they?

The Golden Days of Elections

When some modern critics speak of how dirty and petty modern campaigns have become, it can be useful to step back and ask whether the golden days of years past were really so golden. It is true enough that the United States electoral system was designed to promote a deliberative electoral process. In the 68th *Federalist*, Alexander Hamilton explained that the proposed system of electors would be appropriate for choosing a president because these men— and, yes, they were all men—would "be most likely to possess the information and discernment requisite to such complicated investigations."[2] Though today the electoral college is a curious anachronism for most, at the nation's founding it was a real process for selecting judicious electors who would deliberate on the merits of rival candidates in a process as rigorous and serious as any.

As Kathleen Hall Jamieson writes in her history of presidential campaigns, "The ideal unraveled rapidly." When George Washington stepped down from the presidency at the end of his second term in 1797, it "precipitated the nation's first contested election," which included communications and public events "that venerated and vilified the leading candidates." As Jamieson recounts, "Republican handbills praised [Thomas] Jefferson as an atheist and pilloried [John] Adams as a monarchist."[3] The charges and countercharges were printed on fliers and posted on doors, posts, and wherever else they could hang. Riders distributed bags of these ancestors of modern direct mailings.

Even if the media system of Jefferson's day sounds antiquated, the message itself should sound familiar. The atheist charge should be reminiscent of the claim that only George W. Bush understood the visceral experience of Christianity by being born again. The monarchist label parallels the argument often heard in 2000 that electing Bush would promote a dynastic family, as Bush Jr. would be following his father's presidency by just eight years.

Even the sordid details of President Bill Clinton's extramarital affairs with Monica Lewinsky and Gennifer Flowers are no match for campaigns from years past. When Grover Cleveland ran for president as the Democratic nominee in 1884, his opponents attacked his fitness for the office by claiming that Cleveland, a bachelor candidate, was the father of a child born out of wedlock (called at the time an illegitimate child). In public, Cleveland neither affirmed nor denied the charge, but he did acknowledge that he paid child support to the child's mother. The campaign against Cleveland developed the chant, "Ma, Ma, where's my Pa?" When Cleveland won the election, the Democrats answered the slogan with "Gone to the White House! Ha ha ha!" High-brow stuff, that.

Though attack politics have existed since the founding of the United States, one might still wonder whether the golden age had something we still lack today—real debates on real issues. The most famous debate from our political history was the famed Lincoln-Douglas debates, in which Abraham Lincoln debated Stephen Douglas on slavery seven times during their 1858 Illinois

Senate campaigns. These debates, communication scholar Michael Schudson pointed out, are "frequently upheld, to this day, as a high point of American deliberative politics. Here was a time," he wrote, "when people would stand outside for hours listening to detailed, erudite, complex arguments on the nation's most pressing political controversy."[4] But were these debates really such a great example of a deliberative election?

Schudson investigated this question and found answers that may be surprising. First, "no one who attended the debates for three hours on hot summer afternoons in small Illinois towns ever actually voted for Lincoln or for Douglas."[5] This was before the Seventeenth Amendment, which provided for the direct election of U.S. senators. The only people voting in the 1858 Illinois Senate election were members of the state's legislature, which chose to reelect Douglas as senator.

These were not election events so much as they were popular entertainment. The debates took place in a time before the National Football League, the multiplex, or even the evening radio broadcast. Schudson argued that "this was the best show in town." People assembled in festival-sized crowds, with children in tow, to "cheer their champions to victory." Rather than furrowing their brows and nodding their heads, audiences shouted, "Hit him again!" or "He can't dodge you!"[6]

As for the debaters, Schudson concluded that "Lincoln and Douglas were neither as high-minded nor as reasonable in their addresses as myth supposes." The debates were often as personal as they were substantive: "Lincoln, for instance, in the opening debate at Ottawa, advanced the groundless argument that Douglas had conspired with former President Franklin Pierce, current President James Buchanan, and Chief Justice Roger Taney to expand slavery throughout the nation. Evidence? Lincoln did not require any." Instead, he was happy to draw together an assemblage of circumstantial evidence and move on.[7]

And so it went, back and forth, through not only reasoned arguments and counterarguments but also ad hominem attacks and other instances of what would today be called negative campaigning. The point is not that the debates were without merit, for they were useful not only as political theater but also as a venue for airing serious arguments about the future of the nation. Rather, the point is that the history of campaigns and elections is not so different from their modern practice. The media have changed, as discussed in Chapter 2, and the election laws and electorate have changed, but the ideal of deliberative elections—and the limitations of actual elections—are more constant than most might guess.

A Deliberative Electoral Process and the Deliberative Voter

There are many varieties of elections, but in defining deliberation here, we focus on one variety—the election of public officials in a representative democracy. In a large representative system like that in the United States, or in any major city for that matter, the bulk of the decision making is done by a handful of individuals selected by the mass public during periodic elections.

In theory, representative elections ensure accountability through lively competition between incumbents and their challengers and the careful voting decisions of the public, who act as the sober-minded electors.[8] In the ideal election, voters begin with a relatively well-developed sense of their own self-interests and some conception of the public good. Though those views may shift slightly over the course of an election, voters remain steadfast in their values and never lose sight of their primary concerns. Meanwhile, a list of qualified and diverse candidates appears for every public office, and voters have a wide range of choices to consider. Voters examine the candidates by meeting them face-to-face, attending public forums, listening to speeches, watching debates, and sampling the offerings of a wide variety of relevant printed and electronic media. If there is an incumbent seeking reelection, or if both candidates have experience as elected representatives, voters consider how each candidate has performed in office. The candidate voters judge most suitable is then charged with pursuing the public's interest as its representative, either as an executive,

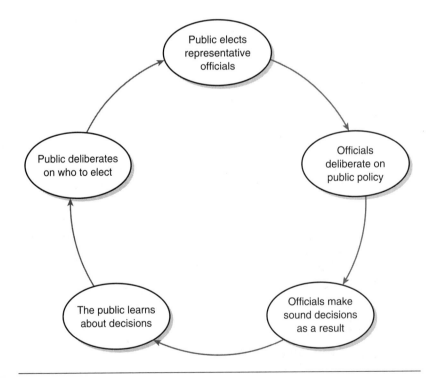

Figure 4.1   An Idealized Relationship Between Deliberative Elections and the Deliberation of Elected Representatives

an administrator, a judge, or a member of a legislative body. Figure 4.1 provides a visual summary of this virtuous cycle, which is, once again, an ideal, not an empirical model of how elections actually work.

The basic idea is that a modest amount of public deliberation during elections ensures the selection of a set of public officials who then undertake more detailed deliberation before making decisions on the full range of public issues that demand their attention. Put another way, voters deliberate leading up to Election Day so that they don't have to deliberate again until the next election.

When looked at more closely, there are really two questions. Chapter 3 considered deliberation from the perspective of media producers and users, and in this chapter we look at deliberation from the perspective of both an entire electoral system and individual voters. The system-level perspective is even more helpful in the electoral context because the information provided and views expressed during an election come from an even wider range of sources, from political parties and candidates to private and public organizations and vocal activists. But just as mediated deliberation involves news providers and users, so too do elections involve the larger electoral system and the individual voter.

Figure 4.2 shows how deliberation applies to elections. The left-hand column shows the now familiar analytic and social process criteria used in Chapters 1 through 3, with the middle column extending these to the electoral system and the right-hand column restating them from the perspective of a voter. Beginning with the system, the "problem" that electoral deliberation must analyze is whom to elect to public office. (In an initiative election, the question is whether to vote for or against a piece of legislation, but it is easier to focus on just candidates for the time being.)

A deliberative electoral system provides all necessary information to voters about a broad range of candidates. The system highlights the most relevant features of each rival candidate and contrasts each office-seeker in those terms, thereby revealing the pros and cons of supporting one candidate or another. The system also ensures that the analytic process ends with each voter's choice being counted and incorporated into the final decision.[9]

The social process criteria for an election ensure that every candidate's campaign, as well as the campaigns of other interested parties, has the opportunity to present its own views of candidate strengths and weaknesses. Allowances must be made for the views of independent and minor-party voices, though a system can understandably emphasize those candidates who make a serious effort to campaign. In addition, the messages produced by all the various communicators in an election should be comprehensible and free of both deceptive devices and disrespectful invective that show a pointless lack of civility. This is not to say that candidates cannot clash and make impassioned arguments; rather, these requirements merely stipulate that a deliberative process involves straightforward, honest, and relevant exchanges, many of which involve legitimate criticisms and sharp disagreements.

	Electoral System	Individual Voter
Analytic Process		
Create a solid information base.	Make vital information on candidates and ballot measures easily available to the electorate.	Learn what there is to know about the candidates' backgrounds and positions.
Prioritize the key values at stake.	Facilitate the exploration of relevant values and other criteria for selecting candidates. Clarify what is at stake in the election.	Identify the values and criteria most important to you as a voter.
Identify a broad range of solutions.	Ensure a pool of diverse and viable candidates in primaries and general elections.	Study each viable candidate and party, not just the ones getting the most attention.
Weigh the pros, cons, and trade-offs among solutions.	Provide clear contrasts between candidates with different experiences, values, and objectives.	Consider how parties and candidates embody or subvert your values and assess how well they will do their job.
Make the best decision possible.	Ensure that every voter's final decision is counted.	Take personal responsibility for your final voting choice in each election.
Social Process		
Adequately distribute speaking opportunities.	Ensure that all campaigns have an effective public forum in which to discuss and debate candidates' backgrounds and positions.	Make time to listen to people supporting other parties or candidates and add your own voice when appropriate.
Ensure mutual comprehension.	Make campaign messages clear and understandable, free of deceptive or manipulative prose.	When a party or candidate's record or positions are unclear, seek to learn more.
Consider other ideas and experiences.	Make room in the electoral process for minor parties and independent candidates.	Reflect on the experiences and values that shape party and candidate platforms different from your own.
Respect other participants.	When debating or criticizing an opponent, a party or candidate should still show respect for his or her opposition.	Even when arguing with fellow voters, remain respectful and avoid being antagonistic.

Figure 4.2   Key Features of Deliberative Elections

Within such a deliberative electoral environment, voters have responsibilities similar to those they have when seeking out and processing media. Voters should reflect on their own values, then consider the full range of candidates by weighing the benefits and disadvantages of electing one over another. In the end, each voter should make a decision according to his or her best assessment of the rival office-seekers. Though voting may seem like the solitary act of private individuals standing in voting booths with the curtain drawn, deliberative voters recognize that during campaigns they are part of a social process. Voters should take the time to talk with people who back other parties or candidates. They should speak plainly and respectfully to one another and try to reflect on the experiences and values that inform the platforms advocated by the political parties and candidates a voter does not presently endorse.

Once again, the purpose in spelling out such an ideal is to imagine a reality that does not, in fact, exist. The question is, how much do the electoral system and voting behaviors described in Figure 4.2 differ from actual electoral practices? To answer that question, we turn to the best available research on political communication and deliberation during elections.

The Modern Electoral System

Most Americans' experience of elections is far from ideal. The political observer Murray Edelman put it this way: "Everyone who grows up in our society is bound to become aware, at some level of consciousness, that an individual vote is more nearly a form of self-expression and of legitimation than of influence."[10] The experience of voting, though, is just the end of the story. Our tale begins with an electoral system that fails in many regards to promote a deliberative process. Each of these systemic features merits careful attention before considering the experiences of individual voters acting within the larger system.

SAFE INCUMBENTS IN UNCOMPETITIVE ELECTIONS

Deliberation requires the consideration of alternatives. In the case of elections, this means that two or more candidates must have a chance of winning the election, and these opponents must have different policy positions (or qualifications) from one another, along with sufficient competence to act effectively in elected office. Many elections for local, state, or federal office feature only one viable candidate and thereby fail to meet even this most basic criterion for deliberation.

Why is it often the case that there is no viable opposition to an incumbent? One reason that potential candidates often decline to oppose an elected official is that they dislike the personal criteria by which candidates often are judged.

For the highest offices, media coverage of campaigns devotes considerable attention to uncovering the character of candidates by scrutinizing their personal lives. Tempting targets, such as Gary Hart and Bill Clinton, have habituated the media to looking for personal weaknesses while covering the candidates in presidential primaries. Though the media pay scant attention to the personalities and family lives of lower-level candidates, there remains a widespread perception that campaigning for any political office exposes one to careful scrutiny of one's personal choices and circumstances.

For similar reasons, fierce negative campaigning also has turned away potential candidates. Citizens contemplating a career in public service cannot help but notice the harsh attack television ads and mailers exchanged by candidates in other races. Though a low-intensity campaign against an incumbent might never prompt such an attack on the challenger, prospective candidates must still weigh the odds that they will be unfairly attacked or that their past missteps will be broadcast for all to see. Whether running for federal, state, or local office, the fear of becoming the target of a negative campaign makes qualified citizens wary of seeking election.[11]

But even angelic candidates and thick-skinned sinners avoid running for office because of the long odds of defeating an incumbent. By virtue of their position, elected officials have numerous advantages over challengers. Members of Congress, for instance, can send mail to constituents without charge. They have travel and communication allowances, constant invitations to public events, regular media exposure, a district office, and paid staff.[12] During a campaign, the electorate is normally quite familiar with the incumbent's name but cannot recognize that of the challenger.[13]

The greatest advantage of incumbency, however, is fundraising ability. The rising price of seeking the presidency has received considerable attention, but costs are climbing for other offices, as well.[14] A tremendous amount of money has been spent on U.S. House and Senate races nationwide for decades, and the cost of election has continued to grow. To make matters worse, congressional scholar Gary Jacobson explained, "a vastly disproportionate share of the growing pot of campaign money has gone to incumbents and candidates for open seats."[15] Challengers for Congress each must now expect to raise at least one million dollars to begin to be viable, meaning that they have a real chance of competing with the incumbent. High-profile, competitive races involve much greater sums. When long-time incumbent Senator Jesse Helms fought off the challenge of Harvey Gantt in the 1996 North Carolina Senate election, Helms nearly outspent his opponent two to one, even though Gantt spent eight million dollars.[16]

If these factors were not enough, one more serious obstacle stands in the way of effective competition. Redistricting often further limits voting options in district races, as opposed to those where candidates seek a statewide, countywide, or citywide office. After each U.S. Census, many states ask the legislature to set the boundaries for state and federal districts, while county- or city-level councils draw local district lines. In many cases, those drawing new district lines deliberately pack like-minded voters together to make it impossible for one major party to lose an election in that district. This is called gerrymandering, a word created in reference to the American politician Elbridge Gerry, who drew his district to his political advantage in a shape resembling a salamander.

The worst cases are those states that make redistricting an explicitly political process, in which incumbents from both major parties agree to protect their own party's seats. Thus, after redistricting for the 2002 election, California had no unsafe U.S. congressional seats: incumbents had an eighteen percent or more margin of victory in their reelection campaigns. Compare this with Iowa, which uses a neutral redistricting commission to create balanced districts. The result of the commission's work has been to make as many as four of the state's five congressional seats competitive.[17]

Even when an incumbent retires in one of the "safe" districts drawn in states like California, the general election remains uncompetitive because a single party represents the overwhelming majority of registered voters. In these cases, one might hope for a competitive primary election within the dominant political party, but it is often the case that only one viable candidate appears when it is time for voters to cast their ballots. As mentioned before, many potential candidates shy away for fear of personal attacks and negative campaigning, but others cannot raise sufficient funds quickly enough, and still others simply lack the support of the party leaders, who often informally coronate a candidate before the election is held.

CANDIDATE DISCOURSE

Even if an election is competitive, with two or more candidates having a legitimate chance of winning, the question still remains as to the quality of the candidates' campaign discourse.[18] After all, the point of a competitive election is to present voters with clear choices among viable candidates, and this only occurs if the messages voters receive during the campaign help them understand the most relevant strengths, weaknesses, and commitments of the candidates. Such discourse, in turn, should help voters make informed, reflective choices.

Negative Advertising

Many critics of contemporary campaign discourse point to the prominent role of negative advertising. In the American political vernacular, a negative ad is any written or broadcasted campaign advertisement that criticizes an action or a quality of an opponent. A negative ad might remind voters that an incumbent voted for a tax increase, or an attack ad might focus on the criminal background of a candidate's family. The purpose of negative ads is to win elections by winning over undecided voters, persuading an opponent's supporters to switch allegiance, or causing undecided or opposing voters to not vote.[19] There has been some debate about the third of these effects, but both experimental and field studies of attack ads show that such advertising often results in a modest (five percent) drop in voting for a given election.[20]

From the deliberative standpoint, however, there is nothing wrong with a negative ad, per se. One needs to distinguish between substantive criticisms, such as a factual contrast between two candidates' stances on abortion, and illegitimate attacks. The former is an important—probably essential—kind of talk that occurs during a deliberative election, whereas the latter includes many different kinds of "illegitimate" discourse, whether negative or positive in tone.

Moreover, it is unnecessary to focus on campaign advertising, per se, to find manipulative discourse in politics. Nearly every elected official, as well as many of their administrative (and even judicial) appointees, engages in a kind of permanent campaign—an ongoing effort to secure their own reelection or the long-term fortunes of their political party. What an official says at a press conference is at least as interesting as what a candidate says (or has someone else say on his or her behalf) in a television commercial. Thus, to understand the nature of manipulation in political discourse, it is useful to look at both elections and "normal" politics, as practiced by government.

Powerful Words

One need not tell an outright lie to deceive, misdirect, confuse, or otherwise manipulate voters. One way in which both candidates and officials try to shape public debate without uttering outright fabrications is with the use of powerful words that are capable of framing reality in a way that obscures certain facts and promotes certain beliefs, whether or not they are founded in fact. In *Political Language* and other works, political scientist Murray Edelman documented many such words, and famous among them is the word *crisis*. To say that we are in the midst of a crisis—budget crisis, health care crisis, poverty crisis, terrorism crisis, global warming crisis—is to say that a rare event is occurring, one that requires immediate action that likely will require exceptional sacrifices. Surmounting a crisis also requires unity, and those who resist acknowledging or addressing the crisis are dangerously misguided or worse.

There surely are true crises, but Edelman pointed out that public officials routinely deploy the term *crisis* in a way that deliberately misleads: "While political rhetoric evokes a belief in a critical threat to a common 'national interest,' the impacts of each crisis inevitably reflect internal conflicts of interests and inequality of sacrifice."[21] Thus, a state government may be facing a real budget crisis, in the sense that it does not have the money to pay for its desired public programs, but the crisis language may be used to encourage the state's population to accept a general sales tax increase that places the burden of sacrifice disproportionately on the state's lower income residents. Second,

if the crisis label is successful, it often "relaxes resistance to governmental inter-
ferences with civil liberties and bolsters support for executive actions, including discouragement or suppression of criticism and governmental failure to
respond to it."[22]

The *national security crisis* phraseology deployed by the Bush administration after the Al-Qaeda attacks on September 11 had this effect by providing
linguistic justification for heightened federal powers (e.g., the passage of the
Patriot Act) and characterizing any opponent of President Bush's policies as
being blind to the crisis faced by a nation at war. Such language simultaneously
bolstered the Bush administration's political capital and remade the image of a
president who successfully pursued reelection in 2004.[23]

Manipulative political discourse, however, is as much about what one's
language hides as it is about what it highlights. Successful campaigns and governments deploy words that are vague and powerful in their ambiguity. Words
like *democracy, social justice, human rights, freedom,* and *terrorism* do not lend
themselves to simple definitions. Scholars and international treaties can give
precise definitions to these words, but the words themselves can never be teth-
ered by such treatises or declarations.

There are at least three simple advantages of using these words. First, using
such a word allows listeners to infer a multitude of meanings, causing them to
agree with the speaker for entirely different reasons. Second, ambiguity can
serve as camouflage: "By using very abstract, undefined or very vague terms,"
explained linguist Ruth Wodak, "unpleasant facts are less obvious, ignorance of
the speaker is easier to hide, and it is easier to deny a statement afterwards."[24]
Third, George Orwell argued that the repetition of meaningless and "dead"
words anesthetizes listeners' brains, making them less critical and more receptive.[25] In a sense, what Orwell described is the use of peripheral cues—symbols
that speakers provide to bolster their credibility and, potentially, distract listeners from the weakness of the core argument. Such cueing can be an effective
means of persuasion, especially in the short term.[26]

Twisted Syntax

More subtle uses of syntax can also have the effect of distracting or misleading the listener. A now famous example was President Bill Clinton's artful
dodging when asked about his sexual relationship with intern Monica
Lewinsky in 1998. Testifying before a grand jury, he insisted that he told the
truth when he said that "nothing *is* going on" between him and Lewinsky,
despite that they had been sexually involved. Clinton offered the following
explanation:

> It depends on what the meaning of the word "is" is. . . . If "is" means "is and
> never has been," . . . that is one thing. If it means "there is none" [at present],

that was a completely true statement. . . . Now, if someone had asked me on that day, "Are you having any kind of sexual relations with Ms. Lewinsky?"— that is, asked me a question in the present tense, I would have said, "No." And it would have been completely true.

Clinton's grammatical subtlety amuses because it resembles a teenager's equivocations in response to questioning by concerned parents. The matter is more serious when it involves covering up the loss of human life or other serious transgressions. Consider the controversy surrounding President Bush's (possibly illegal) authorization of domestic "wiretaps."[27] (Wiretapping is covertly listening in on electronically transmitted conversations.) The careful use of pronouns in such a situation can mask responsibility. When asked about this matter, President Bush could have uttered any of the following sentences:

1. I have found it necessary to use domestic wiretaps.

2. We have found it necessary to use domestic wiretaps.

3. The National Security Agency found it necessary to use domestic wiretaps.

4. A national security crisis made it necessary to use domestic wiretaps.

Which sentence one uses has a significant impact on where the listener places responsibility. The first sentence says that *I* (the president of the United States, in this case) am responsible for the wiretapping. The second moves to a more ambiguous *we*, such as *the administration*, but still includes oneself among those responsible. The third sentence redirects responsibility to a third-party agency, even though in this case the agency got its authorization from the president. The fourth sentence returns us to Edelman's *crisis*, remarkably placing the onus on the broad shoulders of our national crisis, which forced the action on helpless public officials and agencies.

Summary

Along with euphemisms, technical jargon, loaded words, myths, inapt metaphors, and other distracting or misleading language, imprecise words and misleading syntax often conflict with the need for explicit argumentation in a deliberative election.[28] If candidates and public officials are intentionally (or even unconsciously) concealing their messages, voters have a more difficult time understanding and comparing their voting choices. In effect, oratory becomes sophistry, and the exchange of perspective sans ideas becomes a competition among discursive manipulators. Language has inherent ambiguity, but political actors routinely exploit the mixed or hidden meanings in our lexicon and syntax in a way that undermines deliberative elections.

MEDIA COVERAGE OF ELECTIONS

Kathleen Hall Jamieson, whose insights on the history of elections were noted earlier in this chapter, lamented that candidates eschew the deliberative ideal. It is all too rare that candidate discourse is "fair, accurate, contextual, comparative, [and] engaged"; that candidates "take responsibility for the arguments they make"; and that they "defend or repudiate claims made by others on their behalf."[29] At the same time, though, Jamieson places some of the blame on the media for their coverage of elections. Why, she asks, can we not have "news coverage that engages the candidates on matters of public concern" and call them to account for "their past as well as their promises"?[30]

Media coverage of elections does, at times, include these elements. Occasionally, a media outlet goes so far as to counter the low-quality discourse of the campaigns. Candidate advertisements, for instance, sometimes contain outright falsehoods or blatantly misleading statements. Some broadcasters began to address this problem systematically in the 1990 election by reporting on the ads. This adwatch approach aimed to critique campaign ads and reveal to voters any false or exaggerated claims that candidates made. Unfortunately, studies of the adwatch approach suggest that it is not always effective: a study of a 1992 Pat Buchanan attack ad on President George Bush found that viewing an adwatch caused voters to discredit the ad somewhat; however, a study of an attack ad in the 1992 North Carolina gubernatorial campaign found that by rebroadcasting the negative ad, the adwatch format can enhance the intended effect of the ad.[31]

Such adwatch efforts, even if unsuccessful, represent the best impulses of broadcasters and publishers to promote thoughtful deliberation during elections. Unfortunately, the most prominent models of media coverage of elections suggest that these efforts are the exception, not the norm.

Elections as Ritual Dramas

Dan Nimmo and James Combs provided one bleak frame for election news: the ritual drama, in which "the elements of a drama repeatedly relate to one another in a ritualistic fashion." The U.S. presidential election, in particular, stages a dramatic confrontation between two sides, each of which fantasizes about "an ideal America either lost but to be regained, or one yet to be found." Thus, the election is "a recurring, emotionally compelling, seasonal ritual" that "possesses all the requirements of melodrama."[32]

Some of the dramatic fantasies that Nimmo and Combs see in the presidential election—and occasionally in others—are the longing for a "new face" that helps us forget our failed past, the ritualized parading of beauty pageant contestants in the party primaries, the self-congratulatory conceit of staging and witnessing a "great debate," and so on. Each of these fantasies is played out in the course of each presidential election, and the certainty of the recurring drama provides continuity from one election season to the next. Above all else, the "overarching fantasy formed through the mediation of campaign hype is one of hope. Presidential contestants differ with, criticize, bicker at, and attack one another" but, in the end, all candidates must "enunciate a rhetorical vision of hope."[33]

In this sense, election coverage is the antithesis of deliberation. Rather than stimulating careful reflection on different candidates and opposing ideals and contrasting means of achieving public goals, the ritualized drama of the election promotes universal adherence to the belief that all is well, that the electoral system works, and that whether your candidate wins or loses our nation will prosper. Amid the adversarial clashes characteristic of competitive elections, this ritualistic media coverage has value, in that it keeps the nation's partisan divisions from rending us apart. This particular ritual drama does not, however, provide a useful basis for public deliberation.

Horse Race Coverage

Another dramatic metaphor commonly used to describe media coverage of elections is the horse race. Recall from Chapter 3 that Cappella and Jamieson described how strategic frames shape coverage of issues, such that the content of a news story is more likely to discuss the motives, tactics, and fortunes of partisans fighting over a policy question than the substance of the debate itself. Horse race coverage focuses on who's in front, who's falling behind, and the larger spectacle of political sport. By at least one accounting, this variety of coverage accounts for nearly half of the coverage in major newspapers, network, and cable news.[34]

What has spurred this horse race style of coverage? One likely reason is the popularity of such reportage. News organizations have come to embrace more strongly than ever the singular purpose of maximizing market share, and the conventional wisdom in major media organizations is that even when it comes to elections, the public wants the excitement of live coverage of a sporting event, not the bookish tone of an academic lecture. This entertainment-driven news coverage blurs the line between hard news and popular culture in the name of giving viewers what media providers believe they want.[35]

Deeper reasons lie in the culture of the newsroom and the aspirations of reporters, editors, and columnists. Reporters seek to provide timely information about important events whose outcomes remain uncertain, and elections fit this mold, with the reporter's emphasis on trying to resolve the uncertainty by investigating the likely outcome. Moreover, reporters and columnists alike believe they are more likely to make a mark as prescient prognosticators than as reviewers of important campaign issues. Couple this with the production of polls by news organizations, and a culture of contest, sport, and prediction permeates the news media.[36]

Negativity and Sensationalism

Another common feature of media coverage of elections is a focus on the negative. Just as campaigns produce charges and countercharges, so do the media repeat—or even construct—negative attacks. This is not simply a matter of passively transmitting candidate messages to the public. For instance, a study by the Center for Media and Public Affairs found that during the 1996 presidential campaign, only twenty-six percent of candidate messages were "negative" attacks, but critical remarks made up fifty-two percent of the candidate quotes that appeared in the coverage of those same campaigns.[37]

From the deliberative standpoint, however, this is not a problem in and of itself. After all, when candidates are making warranted, relevant criticisms of their opponents, they are helping voters understand the choice that they must make in the election. The media actually help this process by playing up key points of contrast in their coverage.

There is a problem, however, when the media focus not on substantive criticisms and important contrasts but instead on nonissues and seemingly important dramas and pseudoscandals that say little about the merits of the candidates as potential public representatives. The word *scandal* evokes images of presidential candidates caught in extramarital affairs or questionable business dealings. When such events reveal a candidate's moral hypocrisy, personality flaws, doubtful judgment, or incompetence, such news has real value. Too often, however, the pursuit of emotional or sensational video obscures more substantive issues that—if well presented—could capture public interest. Local television, in particular, has come to rely on low-cost, high-drama video, and this causes an emphasis on simple dramas. As one summary assessment concluded, "any local political campaign that is not competitive or does not have a scandal associated with it gets almost no attention."[38]

Less Is Less

Given that most campaigns lack the drama of torrid affairs or fistfights, it is not surprising that beyond the presidential campaign and the handful of other high-profile races, most campaigns struggle to gain any media interest. In the popular imagination, our thinking about candidates, campaigns, and media is shaped by the high-energy coverage of the presidential election. Because of its importance and stature, the presidential election has attracted the most attention from voting scholars. The most influential works on elections have studied presidential contests, and this narrow focus may have caused past research to overgeneralize from one exceptional election to all others.[39]

For many elections, even a sensationalized horse race news story on their campaign would be like an oasis in a desert. For many elections, it is hard to get the attention of reporters and editors. This is true even in the case of races for U.S. Congress. Political scientist Girish Gulati and his colleagues offered the following explanation in their review of campaign news coverage:

> Most information about Congressional races is found in smaller papers. Reporters working the congressional beat tend to be young and new to the profession. Most have limited experience in analyzing politics and campaigns and do not regard their assignments as desirable. Congressional coverage is considered the "dog beat" of the newsrooms, because reporters are required to spend long grueling hours working during the election cycle and are left with few stories to write once the campaign is over.[40]

But there is a strata of elections even beneath the so-called low-information congressional races, and here lies the vast majority of elections for public office. Presidential and congressional elections correspond to just the federal government, which is but one of the more than 80,000 units of government within the United States. Most races for office in the fifty state governments are very low profile, as are the vast majority of elections to office in more than 3,000 counties, 19,000 municipalities, 16,000 townships, 14,000 school districts, and 33,000 other special districts across the United States.[41] Most voters will read, see, or hear almost nothing about these state and local elections in their area, with the exception of gubernatorial and many mayoral contests.

Even when candidates receive coverage, voters rarely get the chance to hear candidates lay out arguments in any detail. This phenomenon led to the neologism *sound bite*, referring to the brief period of time allotted for a candidate or other public figure to speak during a news broadcast before cutting to something else. A famous 1992 study found that the candidates in presidential elections spoke an average of forty-three seconds at a time in 1968, compared to just nine seconds in 1988.[42] We have come to accept brief statements as conventional. Nearly a minute of unbroken speech sounds quite long to the modern ear. Even if taken for granted, the status quo of sound bites is an important part of the electoral landscape, as it reflects the relative scarcity of in-depth, fully developed argument in day-to-day media coverage of elections.

The Deliberative Voter

The preceding survey of campaign discourse and media coverage might sound bleak because it implies that voters have relatively little high-quality information by which to judge candidates competing for public office delivered to their doorstep. If campaigns and media actually made such poor contributions to electoral deliberation, one would expect many voters to struggle to make careful, reflective judgments when filling out their ballots. Unfortunately, this appears to be the case. Research has found that voters routinely respond to such mundane cues as physical attractiveness, especially in an information-poor environment or one filled with ambiguity.[43] Moreover, through appeals to emotion with substance-free symbols, such as a waving flag or a smiling baby, voters can be induced into positive candidate evaluations. Voters have been found to misattribute the positive feelings generated by hearing music and see-ing symbols into positive appraisals of the candidates who happened to co-occur with these emotional triggers.[44]

From a deliberative perspective, this is worrisome, to say the least. There is more to voting, though, than impulsive responses to campaign symbols. To better understand the deliberative voter, we must first understand the values and aspirations (or interests) that voters have. We can then examine some of the shortcuts they use to arrive at voting choices when unaided by a more robust deliberative electoral process.

HOW VOTERS FORM ATTITUDES

A fundamental requirement for deliberative self-governance is that the vot-ing public must develop clearly defined interests that can be articulated during (and between) elections.[45] Does the typical American voter, in fact, know what policies are in his or her best interests? It is impossible to answer this question because there exists no independent ground from which to judge anyone's partic-ular conception of the public good. Some philosophers make compelling claims that freedom and equality are relatively neutral standards for making such a judg-ment,[46] but I wish to ask a more simple question: regardless of the substance of their views, do individual citizens have informed and coherent policy positions from which they can evaluate candidates, initiatives, or referenda in elections?[47]

An informed view is one that is based on a modest amount of relevant information—both facts about an issue and awareness of different perspectives on an issue. The more informed the average voter, the better the result. The public's policy judgments are coherent if they connect logically to one another and to underlying values. Different logic can lead from the same basic values to different policy choices, but the question is whether those connections have been drawn at all.[48]

Unsophisticated Voters

If Americans' policy views are well informed, then Americans should know a good deal about public issues and government. Michael Delli Carpini and Scott Keeter studied this question in depth in *What Americans Know about Politics and Why It Matters*. Using survey data from the National Election Studies, they found that "only 13% of the more than 2,000 political questions examined could be answered correctly by 75% or more of those asked, and only 41% could be answered correctly by more than half the public." The poor per-formance of respondents on these knowledge questions led the investigators to conclude that the American public's judgments are "hardly the stuff of informed consent, let alone of a working representative democracy."[49]

Evidence from both public surveys and psychological experiments shows that most Americans' political views are often not only poorly informed but also rather incoherent. One of the most comprehensive and well-supported theories of public opinion paints a humbling portrait of how we think about political issues. Political scientist John Zaller brought together previously unconnected findings on attitude instability, public opinion shifts, media discourse, reelection campaigns, and survey method effects to create the receive-accept-sample model of public opinion. According to this model, we routinely receive media messages on issues, and less politically sophisticated voters accept these messages uncritically. (Those more politically savvy simply filter out messages that conflict with their predispositions.) When asked to state our opinions (or cast a vote), we sample among the messages we have accepted, which have become "considerations" in our heads.[50]

For all but the most sophisticated voters, Zaller's receive-accept-sample model suggests that the main determinant of policy views is the balance of opinions expressed in the mainstream media. Voters without considerable political acumen simply average what they hear and read through radio, television, newspapers, magazines, the Internet, and other mass media and arrive at a kind of summary view that involves no judgment whatsoever. In this view, even if campaigns and media provided more substance in their discourse, the average voter would simply uncritically absorb it and engage in little critical analysis and weighing of rival claims.

Sophisticated Voters

And what of those voters who do have the political knowledge and skill to critically examine media and campaign messages? So long as these citizens have a clearly formed ideological or partisan bias, Zaller explained, they do not uniformly accept the messages they receive. These citizens can form what appear to be informed and coherent policy views by systematically accepting the messages that come from like-minded elites and filtering out those that come from messengers with rival viewpoints. Thus, so long as at least some of the mass-mediated voices that citizens hear represent their own orientation, ideological citizens can "learn" stable, consistent attitudes from those elites. In this way, Zaller argued, "Ideology can make a valuable contribution to democratic politics in a society in which people are expected not only to have opinions about a range of impossibly difficult issues, but to use those opinions as the basis for choosing leaders and holding them accountable."[51]

True ideology, though, is quite rare. Based on a careful examination of National Election Study data, it appears that roughly half of the American electorate is nonideological, in that their political attitudes show little consistency from one issue to the next. Moreover, only about twenty percent of the electorate shows unambiguous signs of ideologically organized policy views, such as along the lines of the liberal-conservative dichotomy that remains popular in American politics. Another third of the electorate demonstrates at least some higher-order structuring of their political beliefs but is hardly "ideological."[52]

But even for the one-fifth of the population who thinks ideologically, Zaller's characterization is far from flattering, at least in terms of deliberation. After all, citizens who are politically knowledgeable and ideological obtain large amounts of political information and simply filter out ideologically inconsistent views. The result is far from a well-reasoned set of attitudes. Instead, these citizens develop a crude copy of the views of elites who appear to share a similar ideological orientation.

Recent research conducted on a 2003 initiative election in the state of Washington suggests that these voters are not only more likely to adopt wholesale the views of their partisan elites, but they also are more prone to adopt uncritically false factual claims presented to them by those same elites. In this case, "sophisticated" conservative partisans, being subject to the messages passed on by conservative elites, were more likely to underestimate the number of people injured in the workplace and, consequently, oppose regulating workplace safety. Similarly, sophisticated liberals tended to overestimate the number of injuries and, therefore, support the regulation. These distorted beliefs about reality appeared to influence voting choices even after taking into account their partisan leanings and general attitudes toward business regulation.[53]

Further complicating matters, citizens' genuine interests do not always correspond to those of their favored ideological elites. In particular, elites and the lay public often diverge along class lines, such as when liberal and conservative elites underappreciate social and economic realities of average citizens.[54] More frequently, the unique circumstances of individual citizens result in a set of particular interests that diverge from generalized ideological positions. A liberal Kansas farmer, for instance, is likely to have many interests that differ from those represented by liberal elites. The most serious problem, however, is sorting out disagreements among ideologically similar elites. If one identifies oneself as a conservative, it is not enough to simply average the views of Pat Robertson and Steve Forbes. Within every ideological camp, there are deep divisions on important issues that make it difficult for citizens to learn and adopt consistent views.

More generally, elites model attitudes that dismiss alternative points of view, and they pass this extremism down to citizens who might otherwise prefer a more balanced policy position. This problem becomes acute when citizens seek to understand the larger public good. Ideological filtering of elite messages does not help a citizen develop a broad public perspective on current issues. Broadminded citizens listen to and incorporate diverse viewpoints and seek out common ground on which all parties can stand. Citizens cannot develop an inclusive public voice if they systematically dismiss ideologically divergent views.[55]

ELECTORAL CUEING FOR THE MASSES

Whatever the hazards of following elite cues to form beliefs on the issues of the day, at least sophisticated voters end up with relatively clear views and candidate preferences on which they can act. When it comes time to choose candidates or vote on ballot measures during elections, what does the rest of the electorate do? As it turns out, they, too, can resort to a variety of cues.

Retrospective Voting

The most widely studied race of them all—the presidential election—appears to trigger a special form of candidate evaluation. In presidential elections, citizens often engage in what Morris Fiorina called retrospective voting. Many Americans evaluate presidential incumbents based on the actual condition of the nation. In addition to taking into account candidates' stances on issues and promises for the future, voters take a hard look at what they have experienced under the president's administration before deciding whether to reelect.[56] To take an extreme example, events such as the Great Depression can doom a president's chances of reelection no matter how artful a dodger that politician may be. Though much modern presidential advertising threatens to mislead or even deceive unwary voters, it appears that the electorate selects presidents based on the economy and other "hard data." To paraphrase the famous sign posted in the Clinton campaign headquarters in 1992, "It is, indeed, the economy, stupid."

It turns out that such voting behavior is the exception and does not work very well outside of the presidential election.[57] Retrospective voting is usually an ineffective method of candidate evaluation. If a voter looks at the condition of the local or national economy and judges candidates on that basis, the voter is using an objective but not necessarily relevant piece of information. Moreover, voters often vote based on inaccurate perceptions of the economy's condition, which further distorts this process.[58] But even if voters' perceptions are accurate, forces beyond the control of public officials cause most economic shifts, and an incumbent may deserve neither credit nor blame for people's fortunes.

Few voters know much about the actual performance of most of their elected public officials. Some voters may judge presidents based on overall economic trends, but how many voters have solid indicators of the performance of state legislators, judges, school board members, and secretaries of state?[59] A study of the perceptions of city and county services in Kentucky found evidence of considerable error in citizen evaluations of the local government: citizens associated nongovernmental functions with public institutions, attributed functions to the wrong institution, and often failed to recognize some of the functions that local government performed.[60] In addition to these concerns, retrospective voting is also of little or no use when voting in an election with no incumbent to vote for or against.

Partisan Cueing

When voters are weighing alternative candidates, as opposed to ballot measures, there is a simpler cue they can often turn to, rather than trying to retrospectively assess incumbent performance. One simple piece of information—a candidate's party—can be enough to help a voter make a choice. This is commonly referred to by political communication scholars as the partisan cue because these voters take their cue for how to vote by comparing a candidate's party membership with their own allegiance.

Many voters put this partisan cue to use. Though only a fraction of the electorate has a strong ideological orientation, as many as three-quarters of the public identifies with either the Democratic or Republican Party. For example, in the 1998 House elections, seventy-three percent of voters described themselves as either Democrat or Republican. Eighty-nine percent of Democratic voters backed Democrats, and ninety-one percent of Republican voters backed Republicans. Nonaligned voters, by contrast, split their vote almost evenly between the two parties. Statistics for House elections from 1980–1996 show that seventy-seven percent to ninety-two percent of partisans voted for their party's candidate.[61] Numerous other studies found that political partisanship is the most powerful predictor of voting choices in a wide range of partisan general elections in the United States. For example, voter partisanship predicts roughly fifty percent of all voting in the presidential election.[62] Highly sophisticated partisans sometimes even use party-identification cues in nonpartisan elections by reading the voting guides or candidate slates printed for them by their state or local party organization.

Nonetheless, both the prevalence and value of partisan voting cues are overestimated. With regard to the exit poll itself, after choosing to vote Republican, for instance, it is more likely that voters will report identifying themselves as Republican. Also, some of the voters whose party identities and voting choices matched did so only incidentally; for some Democrats, as an example, voting Democratic in a particular race was a conscious choice based on the individual characteristics of the Democratic candidate. Even if voters chose at random between Democrats and Republicans, half of all partisans would support candidates of their own party anyway. In addition, the citizens who do not vote have weaker partisan loyalties.[63]

There is also considerable evidence that the power of the partisan cue is declining. After studying the past forty years of party politics in the United States, Martin Wattenberg concluded, "Once central and guiding forces in American electoral behavior, the parties are currently perceived with almost complete indifference by a large proportion of the population." Consistent with this view, surveys conducted in 1994, 1996, and 1997 found that between two-thirds and three-quarters of Americans report that they regularly vote for candidates from parties other than their own in at least one race per election.[64]

Not only is support for the two major parties declining, but partisanship is also most common among those voters who are the most knowledgeable and ideological. Strong Democrats are the most liberal voters, and strong Republicans are the most conservative; this relationship is even stronger for those voters with the most political knowledge.[65] For example, a national survey found that only thirty-two percent of partisans successfully distinguished the two major parties' positions on four out of four major policy issues. The thirty-seven percent of partisans who distinguished the parties on only one election, or none, gained less information from a candidate's party membership because they were not entirely sure what such membership implied.[66]

In addition, those less sophisticated voters who rely on partisan cues are more likely to have incidental party affiliations. For most Americans, political party membership is not a "fundamental belief . . . but rather an inherited trait."[67] When a person votes for Democrats because his or her parents voted for Democrats, that voting pattern represents the person's actual concerns only to the extent that child and parent share similar values, circumstances, and knowledge. Historical party realignments, such as the African American shift toward the Democratic Party during the civil rights era, show that people may change party membership in response to changing party platforms or shifts in voters' own attitudes. Nonetheless, party identity remains stable for most Americans regardless of changing personal and political circumstances.[68] Party membership influences other attitudes and candidate evaluations far more often than these beliefs influence membership.[69]

The ultimate failing of partisan cue reliance, however, is an inescapable feature of conventional American elections. Simply put, partisan cues are useless in nonpartisan elections and party primaries. When choosing among finalists in a nonpartisan general election (in which no candidate is identified by party on the ballot), less sophisticated voters usually remain unaware of the candidates' party loyalties; other times, the candidates may all happen to belong to the same party. Innumerable political observers have declared the party voting cue as the connection between public preferences and political representation, yet no such connection exists in numerous local and statewide nonpartisan races for judgeships, executive offices, councils, and boards. Though nonpartisan systems are often designed to make local government "less political" and avoid graft and corruption, the net result is the removal of the one cue that most voters rely on to distinguish among competing candidates. For this very reason, many political observers oppose the concept of nonpartisan elections, let alone changing some local elections from partisan to nonpartisan.[70]

Primary elections also offer no shortcut via the partisan cue. When two Democrats face off against one another for a chance to challenge a Republican incumbent in a general election, partisanship is of no use in judging the relative merits of the two Democratic candidates. A conventional winner-take-all general election still requires a prior choice among candidates of the same party in each party's respective primary. In districts and locales where the vast majority of residents belong to a single party, over-reliance on the partisan cue is particularly hazardous. The domination of one party in the general election means that the outcome of the election is actually determined in that party's primary election. For that crucial decision, voters must look past party membership for guidance. If voters have become accustomed to relying on partisan cues to choose candidates, they will lose their bearings in primaries and vote blindly or simply abstain.[71]

Cultural Cueing

Finally, there is a powerful cultural cue that many voters use when evaluating candidates. Partisanship and the liberal and conservative ideologies may even be an expression of this underlying cultural orientation. Research I conducted with colleagues Dan Kahan and Don Braman found strong evidence in support of a conception of culture first developed by anthropologist Mary Douglas and later refined by political scientist Aaron Wildavsky.[72] Douglas and Wildavsky believed that people could be arrayed on a two-dimensional cultural grid. One dimension distinguishes a more individualistic orientation from a more collectivist worldview, and the other dimension distinguishes egalitarians from those who believe in the importance of clear social, political, and economic hierarchies. Figure 4.3 shows this grid, with a solid black dot denoting a hypothetical individual who is strongly collectivist and modestly hierarchical. This person has a cultural orientation that believes in a well-ordered and tight-knit society that privileges the needs of the community over those of the individual and accepts inequalities that fit within what they view as the natural hierarchies of their society.

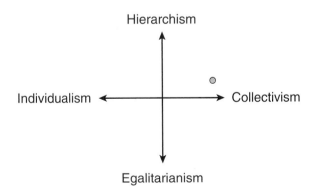

| Figure 4.3 | Placement of a Hypothetical Collectivist/Hierarchical Individual on a Two-Dimensional Cultural Grid |

The reason cultural orientation is so important to voters is that their culture comes not only with a worldview but also with a way of speaking and acting, a set of symbols, and rituals. Even if a voter is not politically sophisticated in the sense described by Zaller, he or she can easily notice whether a candidate wears a peace symbol button or an American flag pin, whether the candidate hunted as a child or lived in a kibbutz. Candidates also give off cultural signals by how they speak, including the words they choose and the way they say them. And, of course, the beliefs that candidates espouse can correspond more or less with one's own cultural worldview. Taking all these cues together, voters can use cultural signals to orient themselves toward candidates they perceive as being culturally like-minded.

The rationality of this cultural cueing is that a voter can presume that someone who shares their cultural outlook is most likely to pursue their core interests, principally their security and economic well-being. If their cultural values are also embodied in that candidate's actions as an elected official, all the better, but it is important to note that these cultural voters are oriented by culture—not necessarily motivated by it to pursue some culturally parochial agenda.

Summary

Whether following ideological, partisan, or cultural cues, or even taking part in the exercise of retrospective voting, voters are unlikely to participate in the sort of cognitive exercise described in Figure 4.2. Voters are not digging up information, reflecting on well-formed values, and carefully weighing the candidates' positions in relation to their own values, let alone the larger public good. What voters are doing is making decisions, often erratically and often, at best, by following faint cues like a bloodhound sniffing with a stuffed-up nose.

Deliberative Electoral Reforms

Some degree of cueing is inevitable with a busy and distracted mass public and a less-than-deliberative media and electoral environment, but there are ideas for how to make elections more deliberative, and we consider three of those in this section: campaign finance reform, a day devoted to deliberation, and deliberative citizen panels.

CHANGING VOTING RULES

One relatively technical change that might yield more deliberative elections is changing the rules by which votes are counted. Almost all elections in the United States are winner-take-all (or first-past-the-post) contests, where each

voter chooses one candidate, and the candidate who has the pluralit
wins. (A plurality is simply more votes than any other candidate rece
necessarily a majority of all votes, if there are more than two candid
only common exception is where a candidate must receive a majori.,
(50% + 1), and if no candidate earns a majority, a runoff election between the
top two vote-getters is held.

One reform that could change the dynamics of elections in the United
States is instant-runoff voting. In this system, voters rank candidates, rather
than vote for just one. A common argument for this proposal is that it allows
voters to state their true preferences, even if their preferred candidate is not one
of the two most popular candidates. Using the terminology popular under the
current system, voting for such a "minor" or "third-party" candidate amounts
to "throwing away your vote" because the candidate receiving the vote is not a
contender for winning. Under instant runoff, voters can rank their minor candidate as their first choice but rank other candidates, as well, by marking next
to each name a "2," a "3," and so on. During the ballot counting phase, if their
candidate receives the fewest first place votes, their ballot will be read for its
second choice, and so on. In this way, people express their true preferences
without fear of casting an irrelevant ballot.

Other variations go further, and a thorough consideration of alternative
voting systems would include consideration of fusion candidates (permitting
voters to support candidates nominated by more than one party), proportional
representation (where seats in a legislature are allocated according to a party's
percentage of the total vote, ensuring representation for sufficiently large
minor parties), and the single transferable vote method (combining the logic
of proportional and instant runoff voting).[73]

From a deliberative perspective, each of these alternatives facilitates the
serious consideration of multiple points of view—more than two parties or
candidates—for any given election. Even if a voting system reform doesn't
make more than two candidates viable, at least it encourages voters to express
their sincere preference; that, in turn, puts information into the electoral system of which future candidates might take note. More likely, though, these
reforms ultimately would broaden the public debate by making a wider range
of candidates and parties electable.

CAMPAIGN FINANCE REFORM

Earlier in this chapter, I remarked that elections have become increasingly
expensive. As Larry Makinson of the Center for Responsive Politics put it,
"Elections these days are big business."[74] Candidates without sufficient personal
funds or considerable backing by major donors rarely have any chance of victory and—unless extremely idealistic, self-promotional, or delusional—choose
not to run for office. Those serious candidates who run for office, with the

exception of some independently wealthy individuals, spend long hours trying to raise funds, and that fundraising takes time away from contacting voters.

To encourage more contact with voters and less fundraising, some political reformers have argued for full public financing of all major elections. The idea of taxpayer money replacing political action committee and individual contributions is not decidedly un-American: presidential campaigns are funded, in part, by citizens who voluntarily check a box on their federal income tax forms (and thereby send a few of their tax dollars to the presidential campaign fund). Advocates of public financing argue that virtually all other elections would benefit from full or partial government funding. Survey data suggest that, depending on the design of the system, the electorate might support such an idea. For instance, a 1996 Gallup poll of likely voters found that sixty-four percent favored a proposal for the federal government to provide "a fixed amount of money for the election campaigns of candidates for Congress, and that all private contributions be prohibited."[75] A 1997 Gallup poll found that support dropped to forty-three percent, however, if in conjunction with public financing "all contributions from individuals and private groups are banned."[76] After the 1998 election, Arizona and Massachusetts joined Maine and Vermont as states where voters have endorsed some form of voluntary public financing, though none of the laws has gone into effect.

Even if campaign finance reforms create more competitive races, however, that would not necessarily change the quality of the decisions that voters make. Just as the term-limits laws enacted in many states create a mandatory turnover in elected officials, more competitive elections might replace more incumbents. Nonetheless, the reforms do not necessarily improve the wisdom with which voters make those replacements.

DELIBERATION DAY

A far more ambitious reform directly aimed at improving electoral deliberation is a proposal that comes from legal scholar Bruce Ackerman and political communications professor James Fishkin. Ackerman and Fishkin propose that every two to four years we should have a national holiday devoted to face-to-face citizen deliberation on the parties and candidates in our national elections. This is not simply throwing a party to which everyone is invited but which nobody attends. Part of what makes this proposal original is that participants would be paid to deliberate. At the end of a daylong deliberation held two weeks before the election, each citizen participant would receive a $150 stipend. And though Ackerman and Fishkin acknowledged that "the food won't be great," their proposal allocates "enough money to make sure that it will be better than your memories of your standard high school meal." After all, they note, "Deliberation Day . . . *is* a holiday."[77]

The Deliberation Day holiday they propose is divided into three events. Citizens would gather together at a local deliberation site, where they would watch, via satellite, a real random sample of the nation's citizenry interact with the presidential candidates in a town hall format. Afterward, citizens would develop questions of their own in small discussion groups. Forming a local assembly of their own, citizens would then put those questions to local party officials and spokespersons who would be present with them. And back and forth it would go, as citizens refined questions, pressed for clear and satisfactory answers, and, ultimately, came away with a much better sense of where parties and candidates stand on issues that are most important to the citizens.

This idea of a national holiday for deliberation did not come out of the blue. Previous experiments in citizen deliberation, such as those described in Chapters 2 and 7, have laid the groundwork for such an event. These predecessors, such as Fishkin's deliberative poll (see Chapter 7), established that such events can produce serious talk, a modicum of give-and-take among citizens, and some novel questions that push candidates and parties to clarify their positions or extend their platforms to issues they had overlooked or tried to avoid.[78]

Though Deliberation Day comes with a price tag—roughly one or two millions dollars every four years[79]—it could be well worth the expense if it resulted in better representation. After all, as Figure 4.1 shows, one can expect more deliberative governance if the elections that put officials in place are themselves deliberative, and better deliberation in federal government would likely result in savings and increased efficiencies on the order of billions—if not hundreds of billions—of dollars each budget cycle. Spending small change on a deliberative investment could yield a return that would make any venture capitalist salivate, most likely profusely.

CITIZEN PANELS AND VOTING GUIDES

Another approach to deliberative reform takes as a given the public's reluctance to deliberate extensively, even for a single day. In a nutshell, this alternative proposal convenes random-sample citizen panels to deliberate for one week on the most important initiatives or referenda on a ballot, as well as on candidates seeking election. Each panel works separately, hearing testimony from and cross-examining advocates presenting contrasting points of view. In the end, each panel writes a summary description of the key differences among candidates or the pros and cons of supporting a ballot measure, along with the panel's final vote (for or against a measure or for preferred candidates).

In 2000, I presented this idea in *By Popular Demand*, but related proposals have appeared in Ned Crosby's *Healthy Democracy*, Ethan Leib's *Deliberative Democracy in America*, which makes citizen panels a new branch of government;

and John Burnheim's *Is Democracy Possible? The Alternative to Electoral Politics*, which supplants elections altogether with quasi-citizen panels.[80]

Imagine the simplest form of citizen panel—one that convenes to consider the merits of a single statewide initiative that will appear on the ballot. Figure 4.4 shows the three stages in such a panel. The secretary of state gathers the citizen panel using a representative random sample of all registered voters. This panel then interacts with witnesses selected by the initiative's chief proponents and opponents, followed by a period of deliberation that culminates in participants writing a one-page summary evaluation of the initiative. Alongside the full text of the initiative, the secretary of state publishes this evaluation in the voter guide mailed to all registered voters (also made available online, along with additional details from the citizen panel deliberations).

In a given election, there may be multiple initiatives and referenda appearing on the ballot. In the most elaborate version of the citizen panel proposal,

---

1. Preparation and Agenda Setting

   • The secretary of state pays a nonprofit polling organization to select a representative statewide random sample of twenty citizen panelists, each of whom are paid a stipend and have all their travel, lodging, and meal expenses covered.

   • The initiative's sponsors and its principal opponents select witnesses to provide testimony.

2. Deliberation

   • For two days, witnesses present testimony and cross-examine one another. Citizen panelists also address direct questions to the witnesses.

   • For the final three days, citizen panelists deliberate, receive feedback from witnesses, and then write a summary description of the initiative, along with rationales for and against it. Deliberation ends with a final up or down vote on the initiative.

3. Implications for Elections

   • The secretary of state provides voters with the citizen panelists' written summary, arguments, and recommendations through printed and online voter guides. The online guide includes links to witness testimony and the citizen panel's deliberation.

   • Voters refer to the guides and see the deliberative judgments of their peers on the ballot initiative.

Figure 4.4   Steps in Implementing a Panel on a Statewide Initiative

each of these is vetted by a separate panel. The same could be done at the county and city level for local measures, such that a voter has a complete set of citizen panel summary statements on each measure, along with recommendations in those cases where the panel came to general agreement for or against.

Would such a proposal actually influence voters? Independent studies of the official voting guides used in California and New Mexico both found that roughly a third of the registered voters referred to the guide before voting, but a recent survey in Washington found that closer to ninety percent of likely voters in that state used their voters' pamphlet when voting on initiatives.[81] For many voters in locales that have no such official guide, the League of Women Voters' guide is the only readily available source of information in low-intensity elections, such as those for state legislature or district judge. Poll workers often see voters walk into the voting booth clutching a printed guide, and those voters may read as they vote or refer back to selections they already marked on their guide.[82]

As Internet use increases among the general population and voters increasingly cast absentee ballots, the electorate is likely to rely even more on printed and online guides when filling out their ballots. The guides will also become increasingly popular as their design and content improve with the addition of citizen panel information. For example, the printed guides could provide voters with a one-page tear-out sheet summarizing citizen panel recommendations— something voters could easily carry with them to the polls or refer to quickly while filling out an absentee ballot. An ideal online voting guide would permit users to note candidate preferences and other votes as they navigated the site, then print out a marked sample ballot or a one-page summary of voting choices.

Conclusion

If any or all of campaign finance reforms, Deliberation Day, and citizen panels came to pass, they would go a long way toward making elections more deliberative. The pool of candidates would likely become more diverse and competitive as a result of reducing the financial advantages of incumbency, personal wealth, and the narrow range of viewpoints that effectively mobilize large donors. Deliberation Day would involve the larger public in a face-to-face conversation with local and federal party officials, forcing political elites to engage in a direct dialogue with the general public and sharpening citizens' own deliberative skills. Finally, the citizen panel reports would serve as an invitation to learn more about the panel's deliberations, and, more important, provide a deliberative voting cue to those voters who would not be able to (or not choose to) engage in substantial deliberation. Many voters will substitute the deliberative judgment of their peers for the directives of partisan or cultural elites, particularly when they feel weaker attachments to those same elites.[83]

One advantage of this approach is that it provides different kinds of information to different kinds of voters. When political scientist Keena Lipsitz investigated the kind of information that voters crave during campaigns, she found that the more politically engaged citizen wants a more interactive, deliberative campaign, whereas the less involved voter wants issues and choices laid out simply.[84] A citizen panel creates a process that invites the most interested voters to join in an intensive deliberative exploration of ballot issues, but the panel simultaneously creates a powerful voting cue for those who would rather follow the lead of their deliberative peers.

In this sense, the citizen panel approach asks relatively little of the average voter. In this sense, this constitutes a "weaker" or more modest strain of deliberative theory. This approach only asks citizens to spend a modest amount of time, by themselves and in conversation with others, engaging with the substance of issues in an election; failing that, citizens might attend to deliberative voting cues.[85]

An even more deliberative electoral system would result from the varieties of media reforms introduced in the previous chapter. In fact, those newspapers and other media outlets that practice public journalism have made efforts to improve how they cover elections, and research suggests that they can play an important role in covering deliberative public events[86] and even facilitating such deliberation.[87] In the meantime, however, it is fair to say that elections, as they are practiced in the United States, remain a relatively nondeliberative enterprise.

Notes

1. Barber (1984, p. 188).
2. Quoted in Jamieson (1996, p. 5).
3. Ibid.
4. Schudson (1998, p. 133).
5. Ibid., p. 135.
6. Ibid., p. 136.
7. Ibid., p. 137.
8. Portions of this section are adapted from Chapter 3 in Gastil (2000).
9. Figure 4.2 focuses on candidates. Ballot measures are similar but have differences, as described later in this chapter.
10. Edelman (1988, p. 97).
11. See Jamieson (1992) for a brief history of modern negative campaigning. Scher (1997) argued that name-calling and attack advertising (i.e., mudslinging) are old American traditions. The most comprehensive study to date of negative campaigning is likely Lau and Pomper (2004).
12. On the advantages of congressional incumbency, see Jacobson and Kernell (1981) and Alford and Brady (1993).
13. Jacobson (1997, pp. 89, 94). Cain, Ferejohn, and Fiorina (1987) discussed at length the power of the "personal vote" that incumbents develop through both mere

exposure and actual constituent service. They stress the value of "warm, humane interventions" by elected officials. But, they concluded, "Without constraints . . . such behavior can corrode the conduct of democratic government by undermining the ability of that government to act in ways that improve the lot of its citizens" (p. 229). Currying and maintaining the personal vote can make elected officials servants of particularistic interests rather than true public representatives.

14. For up-to-date information on fundraising activities and campaign finance law, visit George Washington University's Campaign Finance Institute at http://www.cfinst.org.

15. Quote is from Jacobson (1993, p. 119). Figures for 1981–1998 are official numbers compiled by the Federal Election Commission, available at http://www.fec.gov. Though past studies raised questions about the net added value of incumbent spending, methodologically refined studies have confirmed the electoral importance of this fundraising advantage in House races (Erikson and Palfrey 1998) and Senate elections (Gerber 1998).

16. On incumbent intimidation tactics, see Jacobson (1997). All spending data are provided by the Federal Election Commission. Aside from the daunting fundraising requirements of an effective challenge, congressional scholar Gary Jacobson noted that the personal financial cost of running has escalated: "The investment of time and energy . . . required to run an all-out campaign is daunting. A serious House candidacy is a full-time job—with plenty of overtime. Most non-incumbents have to finance the campaign's start-up costs while forgoing income from their regular work for many months" Jacobson (1993, p. 131).

17. Forgette and Platt (2005).

18. Portions of this section are adapted from Gastil (1992).

19. Budesheim, Houston, and DePaola (1996) found that issue-oriented attacks on an opponent work well with an audience in the advertiser's in-group, and character-based attacks work well within an advertiser's out-group. The in-group identifies with the advertiser's ideological similarity, whereas the out-group sees no such similarity and responds best to attacks with no issue relevance.

20. Ansolabehere, Iyengar, Simon, and Valentino (1997).

21. Edelman (1977, p. 45).

22. Ibid., p. 48.

23. Politics also often involve the creation of new words. Elites, resistance groups, and social movements have all invented neologisms. One of the more powerful examples from the late twentieth century was *nukespeak*. Nukespeak was intended to sound like the word "newspeak" used by George Orwell in his dystopian novel *1984*. It referred to the vocabulary created by those public and private organizations associated with the production and deployment of nuclear weapons. The political left brought the term into use in the United States and England in the early 1980s to provide researchers and political critics with a new way to describe the nuclear weapons culture. The creation of this term served to delegitimize the technocratic, euphemistic language of the nuclear establishment, including its own neologisms, such as *collateral damage* (the civilian lives unintentionally—but unavoidably lost—in a preemptive nuclear strike). See the collection of essays on the subject in Chilton (1985).

24. Wodak (1989, p. 144).

25. Orwell (1956, pp. 359–60).

26. Petty and Cacioppo (1981).

27. CNN.com reported this story under the headline "Bush says he signed NSA wiretap order," available at http://www.cnn.com/2005/POLITICS/12/17/bush.nsa/index.html.
28. More examples and analyses of such language are provided in Gastil (1992).
29. Jamieson (1992, p. 11).
30. Ibid.
31. On the Buchanan ad, see Cappella and Jamieson (1997), and, on the gubernatorial race, see Pfau and Louden (1994). For a review, see Kaid (2004, pp. 186–87).
32. Nimmo and Combs (1990, pp. 54–55).
33. Ibid., p. 68. See a summary on pp. 225–28.
34. Buchanan (2001, p. 370).
35. Underwood (2001, pp. 108–9).
36. Gulati, Just, and Crigler (2004, p. 240). Baker (2001, p. 356) argued that a caveat is in order here, however. It is certainly the case, Baker maintained, that the media address the needs of different constituencies, and among those is a group of people who have already made a reflective choice on their preferred candidate and now only need to know how "their side" is faring in the election. Providing horse race coverage for this constituency is certainly useful, but it is doubtful that partisan political sophisticates constitute a majority share of any major media outlet's audience, and even then the question remains as to whether this subgroup's appetite for forecasting outweighs the larger public's interest in grasping the considerations in upcoming elections.
37. Study cited in Buchanan (2001, p. 369).
38. Gulati et al. (2004, p. 245).
39. Election research routinely grounds itself in the observations of presidential election studies, such as *The American Voter* (Campbell et al., 1960) and *The New American Voter* (Miller and Shanks 1996). Perhaps tiring of presidential studies, election scholarship is turning increased attention to House, Senate and even gubernatorial races, but other state and local races still receive little attention.
40. Gulati et al. (2004, p. 247).
41. Figures come from Burns et al. (1996, p. 171). These low-intensity races fall below the radar of almost all political science research on campaigns and elections. If the conventional wisdom is that a typical House race is a "low-information" race, then these elections are close to "zero-information" races. One of the few studies looking at near-zero information elections is Dubois (1984).
42. Hallin (1992).
43. Ottati and Deiger (2002).
44. Isbell and Ottati (2002).
45. See Dahl's (1989, p. 98) "strong principle of equality."
46. This idea is advanced famously by Rawls (1971), and I return to the idea at the beginning of Chapter 10.
47. Another useful perspective on evaluating public opinion is Daniel Yankelovich's (1991) view that we should judge public opinion to be of the highest quality only "when the public accepts responsibility for the consequences of its views" (p. 24). I don't pursue that view further because there is not yet a sufficient corpus of evidence regarding the "responsibility" aspect of a public's opinion on issues. Regardless, Yankelovich is not optimistic that the public reaches this level of sophistication very often, though it does happen. He gives the example of the death penalty, whose proponents generally accept that a death penalty invariably results

in at least some innocent people being put to death—a grim "trade-off" that proponents are nonetheless willing to accept (p. 27).

48. As Delli Carpini and Keeter (1996, p. 56) wrote, "The more one knows about politics, the more effective—the more instrumentally rational—one's voice is likely to be." On how values and decision logics can go together for individuals and groups, see Macoubrie (2003).

49. Delli Carpini and Keeter (1996, pp. 101–2, 133). As for state and local elections, Burns et al. (1996, p. 11) observed, "Citizens generally take less interest in . . . and are less informed about their local governments than they are about their national government."

50. Zaller (1992, p. 308). In another widely celebrated review of public opinion research, Page and Shapiro (1992) presented a similar conception of public opinion. In their view, measurement errors and fluctuations in individuals' opinions cancel each other out and uninformed citizens simply follow elite cues: the result is a "rational public" with stable opinions that change only in response to changing objective conditions (as interpreted by elites).

51. Zaller (1992, p. 327). Some scholars have begun to lose their optimism about the fidelity of public reception of elite cues. Kuklinski and Hurley (1996), for instance, argued that citizens routinely misinterpret elite messages.

52. Figures are derived from Jacoby's (1991, 1995) analyses of 1984 and 1988 data. Using 1984 national survey data, Sniderman, Brody, and Tetlock (1991) also found twenty percent of the population to have "intense" ideological feelings. Respondents rated liberalism and conservatism on a hundred-point "feeling thermometer," and intense ideologues were defined as persons reporting a difference of twenty-five points or higher in their two thermometer ratings (e.g., giving liberalism a rating of fifty and conservatism a rating of seventy-five or more). Only seven percent of respondents could be categorized as intense liberals and thirteen percent as intense conservatives. The most influential writing on ideology and the American public was an essay by Philip Converse (1964), which found that only a tiny fraction of the public engaged in ideological thinking but that, again, roughly one-fifth of the public has "real" attitudes. These estimates are important because they suggest what percentage of the public uncritically filters political messages.

53. Wells et al. (2006).

54. Page (1996) shares Zaller's belief in the value of learning from elites, but he raised this concern about elite versus mass interests. In Chapter 6, I examine Page's view in detail.

55. Mathews (1994) promoted the use of the terms *public perspective* and *public voice* to remind us of the difference between aggregated self-interest and a broader public will.

56. Fiorina (1981).

57. Ibid., p. 208.

58. Svoboda (1995).

59. Sniderman et al. (1991) argued along these lines. Though the high-information voter engages in elaborate, issue- and party-based candidate evaluation, "the less well informed voter may have the information he needs provided he treats the choice before him as a choice for or against the incumbent; for poorly informed or not, he is in a position to judge if the incumbent's performance is satisfactory" (p. 178). I believe that evaluation of actual incumbent performance is more difficult than

other evaluations, and if low-information voters are making their choices that way, they are likely to make haphazard candidate choices in low- and medium-intensity campaigns.

60. See Lyons, Lowery, and DeHoog (1993, Chapter 6).

61. Statistics are from "A Look at Voting Patterns of 115 Demographic Groups in House Races," *New York Times*, November 9, 1998, p. A20. Voter News Service collected the data in this article through Election Day exit polling of more than 10,000 respondents in 1998. It is quite possible that these surveys overestimate party loyalty, but secret ballots permit no better measure of actual voting behavior. Also see Jacobson (1997), who found that roughly one quarter of voters cross party lines in congressional elections.

62. Miller and Shanks (1996). The greater predictive strength of partisanship in congressional elections is consistent with the fact that partisanship is a cognitive shortcut. When voters are exposed to tremendous amounts of information in the unique environment of a presidential election, many decide that a candidate from another party would better represent their interests. In other words, these crossover voters made a decision other than the one that the simplistic partisan cue would have suggested.

63. Ibid. Though some misidentification takes place during exit surveys, partisan identity predicts voting preferences even years later.

64. Quote is from Wattenberg (1994, p. ix). Wattenberg presented a detailed description of the decline of political parties in America. An April 4–7 survey by Princeton Survey Associates found that seventy-five percent of respondents said they voted for different parties in response to this question: "When you vote in an election for national, state or local offices, do you always vote for candidates from one particular political party, or do you vote for candidates from different parties?" A January 19–February 10 Roper Center/Institute for Social Inquiry survey found that sixty-five percent reported voting for different parties in response to this question: "When voting in elections do you typically vote a straight ticket—that is for candidates of the same party, or do you typically split your ticket—that is vote for candidates from different parties?" See *The Public Perspective* (1998, 9:2, p. 49). Tarrance, De Vries, and Mosher (1998, p. 35) pointed out that, according to University of Michigan surveys, ticket splitting is far more common now than it used to be: twenty-nine percent reported splitting in 1952 compared with sixty-three percent in 1996.

65. Delli Carpini and Keeter (1996, pp. 252–54).

66. Abramowitz and Saunders (1998, pp. 643–44).

67. Arnold (1990, p. 53).

68. Miller and Shanks (1996). Abramowitz and Saunders (1998) provided compelling evidence that partisanship is more ideological than it used to be. In their view, ideological debates between the two major parties made their differences more apparent, and the newest generation of voters includes many Republicans who have severed their Democratic family roots for ideological reasons.

69. Evidence of the strength of partisanship on attitudes is provided by Campbell et al. (1960), Fiorina (1981), Green and Palmquist (1994), and Miller and Shanks (1996), among others.

70. On the history of nonpartisan reforms, see Lee (1960). For criticisms of nonpartisan elections, see Hawley (1973).

71. Given the relatively low turnout in primary elections, most voters do not choose to exercise their right to vote, which often makes primaries unrepresentative of the views of the average party member. Since the most active voters are more ideological, primaries often result in the election of extremist candidates who do not reflect the views of the nonvoting partisans. A related concern is the frustration true independents feel in general elections, in which they also lack a partisan cue (since, by definition, they lack a party). Not surprisingly, independents have lower turnout rates than partisans, and their voting rates also have declined more rapidly from the 1960s to the 1980s (Keith et al., 1992, p. 58).

72. On cultural theory, see Thompson, Ellis, and Wildavsky (1990), Wildavsky and Douglas (1982), and Wildavsky (1987). My more recent work on cultural theory with a group of colleagues appeared in a variety of articles, including Gastil, Kahan, and Braman (2005) and Kahan et al. (2006). The most recent work from this project is available online at http://research.yale.edu/culturalcognition.

73. For an overview of voting systems, see Farrell (2001).

74. Makinson and Goldstein (1996, p. 3).

75. The Gallup survey was conducted October 29–30, 1996, with 714 registered voters. This result and similar findings have been assembled by Public Campaign at www.publicampaign.org/pollsumm.html

76. Gallup poll from January 31–February 2, 1997, cited in *The Public Perspective* (1998, 9:2 p. 47).

77. Ackerman and Fishkin (2004, p. 34).

78. See McCombs and Reynolds (1999) and Fishkin and Farrar (2005).

79. Ackerman and Fishkin (2004, Appendix A).

80. Gastil (2000), Crosby (2003), Leib (2004), and Burnheim (1989).

81. After the election, thirty-one percent of all Bernalillo County, New Mexico, residents reported reading the guide, and thirty-four percent of those who reported voting said that they had read it. See the University of New Mexico Institute for Public Policy's *Quarterly Profile of New Mexico Citizens* (1997, 9:Winter, p. 3). The California data can be found in Magleby (1984), and the Washington data is in Gastil and Crosby (2006).

82. Surprisingly, the League of Women Voters' national office knew of no formal research on the use of the voter guides, as I learned in a November 9, 1999, telephone interview. They did, however, lead me to contact a league member in Maryland, who found that direct mail distribution of voter guides slightly increased voter turnout in traditionally low-turnout precincts (Watkins, 1998). For a comprehensive review on the impact of Get-Out-the-Vote efforts, see Green and Gerber (2004).

83. When venturing into this territory, one should be cognizant of the danger of paternalism. Deliberative democracy need not treat voters as incapable agents who need deliberative instruction, but there is a tendency to do so in deliberative theory (Rostboll, 2005). In the context of initiatives, it is noteworthy that rank-and-file voters recognize their need for more information and overwhelmingly endorse ideas like the panel described in Figure 4.4 (Gastil & Crosby, 2006).

84. Lipsitz, Trost, and Grossmann (2005). This finding contradicts the more dire alarm sounded by Hibbing and Theiss-Morse (2002), who argued that the public generally eschews a deliberative campaign environment and would prefer that leaders quietly go about the business of governing without demanding much of the public. When

surveyed, it is not surprising to hear frustration with conventional political conflict; in practice, however, citizens relish genuine opportunities for meaningful public deliberation and have willingly participated in a variety of labor-intensive processes, such as those described in Gastil and Levine (2005).

85. Weithman (2005) contrasted weak and stronger versions of deliberative theory. The weaker version asks citizens only "to contribute to well-conducted public deliberation by offering a range of reasons, stories and narratives, and artistic contributions, all without a settled readiness to supplement any of these contributions with public reasons" (p. 283).

86. Reynolds (1999).

87. Charles, Sokoloff, and Satullo (2005).

SOURCE: George Bush Presidential Library and Museum. Used by permission.

5

How Government Deliberates

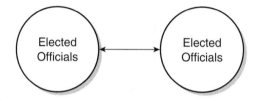

Elected Officials ⟷ Elected Officials

The mild voice of reason, pleading the cause of an enlarged and permanent interest, is but too often drowned, before public bodies as well as individuals, by the clamors of an impatient avidity for immediate and immoderate gain.

—James Madison[1]

On September 6, 2005, Representative Jean Schmidt (R-Ohio) spoke her first words on the floor of the U.S. House of Representatives, just minutes after being sworn in. Schmidt had become the newest member of the 109th Congress a month earlier in a special election, replacing fellow Republican Rob Portman, who had resigned his seat earlier that same year. As recorded in the *Congressional Record*, Representative Schmidt introduced herself with these humble but profound words:

> Mr. Speaker, I stand here today in the same shoes, though with a slightly higher heel, as thousands of members who have taken the same oath before me. I am mindful of what is expected of me both by this hallowed institution and the hundreds of thousands of Americans I am blessed to represent. I am the lowest-ranking member of this body, the very bottom rung of the ladder, and I am privileged to hold that title.

Photo 5.2 Representative
Jean Schmidt (R-OH)

This House has much work to do. On that we can all agree. We will not always agree on the details of that work. Honorable people can certainly agree to disagree. However, here today I accept a second oath. I pledge to walk in the shoes of my colleagues and refrain from name-calling or the questioning of character. It is easy to quickly sink to the lowest form of political debate. Harsh words often lead to headlines, but walking this path is not a victimless crime. This great House pays the price.

So at this moment, I begin my tenure in this Chamber, uncertain of what history will say of my tenure here. I come here green with only a desire to make our great country even greater. We have much work to do. In that spirit, I pledge to each of you that any disagreements we may have are just that and no more. Walking in each other's shoes takes effort and pause; however, it is my sincere hope that I never lose the patience to view each of you as human beings first, God's creatures, and foremost. I deeply appreciate this opportunity to serve with each of you. I very much look forward to getting to know you better, and I humbly thank you, Mr. Speaker, for allowing me to address this . . . body.

Representative Schmidt's words went largely unheard, as is typical for such formal addresses, but the words appear here for two reasons. First, they clearly articulate the idea that deliberation is more than a cognitive, analytic process of weighing information and facts. Instead, deliberation is also a social process, one that works best when participants express and hold respect for one another as people and for the value of open, principled disagreement and the open exchange of ideas.

But, sadly, we come here today on this solemn occasion—the opening stanza of Chapter 5—not to praise Representative Schmidt but to bury her. Nary a month later, on November 18, 2005, Representative Schmidt took to the floor and, in the words of her inaugural speech, likely determined "what history will say" of her "tenure here":

House Speaker Pro Tempore:	The gentlelady from Ohio is recognized for one minute.
Rep. Schmidt:	Thank you. Yesterday I stood at Arlington National Cemetery attending the funeral of a young Marine in my district. He believed in what we were doing is the right thing and had the courage to lay his life on the line to do it. A few minutes ago I received a call from Colonel Danny Bubp,

Ohio representative from the 88th district in the House of Representatives. He asked me to send Congress a message: Stay the course. He also asked me to send Congressman Murtha a message, that cowards cut and run, Marines never do. [Some members of Congress can be heard to murmur, then some shout protests, amidst a banging gavel. The volume of Schmidt's voice begins to rise, until she is shouting over the din.] Danny and the rest of America and the world want the assurance from this body that we will see this through.

Speaker: The House will be in order. The House will be in order. The House will be in order. The House will be in order. The House will be in order. The gentlelady will suspend, and the clerk will report her words. [Pause, as murmuring dies down.] All members will suspend. The gentleman from Arkansas has demanded that the gentlelady's words be taken down. [This invokes a House rule designed to censure a member of Congress for inappropriate speech on the House floor.] The clerk will report the gentlelady's words. [Long pause.]

Speaker: The House will be in order. [Shouted repeatedly.] The gentleman from Tennessee will take a seat. All members take seats. [Repeated, with occasional gavel pounding.] The gentleman from Massachusetts will cease and take his seat. All members will take their seats. [Repeated.] The House will be in order. Members please take seats. The gentlelady from Ohio.

Rep. Schmidt: Mr. Speaker, my remarks were not directed at any member of the House and I did not intend to suggest that they applied to any member. Most especially the distinguished gentleman from Pennsylvania [Representative Murtha]. I therefore ask for unanimous consent that my words be withdrawn. . . .

Rep. Snyder: I appreciate the gentlelady's words and I accept her . . . offer to have her words withdrawn. But I encourage all of here tonight to recognize the seriousness of what we're about and to choose our words carefully. Our side [the Democrats] is greatly offended by this process, and I suspect you [the Republicans] have a number of members who are not satisfied with it either. My suggestion would be that the resolution be withdrawn and we come back and discuss another

day. However [pause amidst clapping], I have no objection
Mr. Speaker.

Speaker: Without objection, the gentlelady's words will be withdrawn.[2]

Where to begin? The participants in this sophomoric bit of name-calling
were elected in contests that routinely cost, as discussed in the last chapter,
upwards of one million dollars. The salary for rank-and-file members is
$165,000. Their job is a sacred trust, as the representatives of a self-governing
people who have relied on Congress for thoughtful legislative deliberation for
more than two centuries. With all that history, significance, and responsibility,
it might seem remarkable that a representative could transition from a poetic
inaugural speech on the virtue of dialogue and mutual respect to a petty
schoolyard taunt, delivered in the third person by way of a state legislator. But
such is a day in the life of Congress.

In this chapter, we look at how deliberation takes place in government,
focusing on legislative bodies like the U.S. Congress. The emphasis on legislatures reflects the presumption that these are the more deliberative bodies of
government, but before concluding this chapter, we also look very briefly at
how deliberation takes place—or fails to occur—within the executive branch
of government and the Supreme Court. Little has been written about deliberation in the latter bodies, but much needs to be said about the importance of
deliberation within these other critical governmental institutions.

A Foundational Moment in Deliberative History

For many Americans, there is no clearer historical example of the deliberative
ideal than the Constitutional Convention of 1787. Stretching from May to
September, the marathon convention wore out the seats of many pairs of
pants. Likely of more importance, the convention managed to bring together
representatives of such divergent views that none could foresee accurately the
ultimate shape the Constitution would take. Fortunately, the participants in
the convention did foresee the future significance of their meetings, and they
kept journals, notes, and letters that have made it into the hands of historians.
Historian Jack Rakove brought together those documents to produce *Original
Meanings: Politics and Ideas in the Making of the Constitution,* a Pulitzer
Prize–winning account of the convention.

Rakove argued that the convention was simultaneously an exercise in
political philosophy and a pragmatic negotiation among the states, whose representatives all sought to improve the unwieldy Articles of Confederation that

held them together as a weak union—less than a whole nation. "At the most abstract level," Rakove wrote, the convention debates "were indeed concerned with such fundamental questions as the nature of representation and executive power, federalism, the separation of powers, and the protection of individual and minority rights." Quite rightly, the delegates "believed that what they did would have lasting implications not only for their constituents but for a larger world." Both James Madison and Alexander Hamilton asserted that the convention's decisions would "decide for ever [sic] the fate of Republican Government."[3]

But the convention's task was one of practical deliberation as well. "Here the real challenge did not involve solving theoretical dilemmas posed by Hobbes or Locke or Montesquieu," Rakove explained. Instead, it required the following tasks:

> efforts to accommodate the conflicting interests of different states and regions on such matters as the apportionment of representation and taxes, the regulation of commerce, and the extension of the slave trade. Rather than view the Convention as an advanced seminar in constitutional theory, historians and many political scientists have preferred to describe it as a cumulative process of bargaining and compromise in which a rigid adherence to principle yielded to the pragmatic tests of reaching agreement and building coalitions.[4]

This pragmatic purpose could have overwhelmed the convention and narrowed the delegates' vision were it not for the fact that the delegates had no final authority. As Delegate Edmund Randolph explained to those who insisted on conforming to the articles, "Our business consists in recommending a system of government, not to make it." Whatever the convention ultimately proposed would only become law if ratified by the various states. Thus, Delegate James Wilson offered that he felt himself "at liberty to *propose any thing* [sic]" precisely because he had the power "to *conclude* nothing." As Rakove wrote, "The fact that the Convention could not simply promulgate a constitution on its own authority thus had an immensely liberating effect on its deliberations."[5]

Balancing principle and practicality, the convention waded through the full range of issues facing the nascent nation. The mythic accounts and celebrated portraiture of the convention present the delegates as sober, thoughtful, and public-spirited throughout, but Rakove's more vivid account suggested otherwise. One of the most famous disagreements among delegates concerned the composition of the federal legislature. The delegates from larger states favored allocating all seats in proportion to each state's population, whereas the representatives of smaller states, such as Delaware, insisted on one of the bodies in a bicameral legislature having an equal number of members from each state.

The key vote on this issue occurred on Monday, July 16, with the small-state coalition winning sufficient support to have its view prevail. Rakove recounted that, after the vote, "There followed an interlude that revealed how the tensions of the past weeks still festered. For a few minutes parliamentary decorum prevailed, as the framers moved on to the next item on their agenda." Soon thereafter, Virginia Delegate (and sitting governor) Edmund Randolph insisted that the vote to reject proportional allocation of seats in the Senate had undermined the logic of the proposed constitution. He then suggested, as a warning, "that the large States might consider the steps proper to be taken in the present solemn crisis of the business, and that the small States might also deliberate on the means of conciliation."[6]

New Jersey Delegate William Paterson called Randolph's bluff. He suggested that "it was high time for the Convention to adjourn . . . and that our Constituents should be consulted." If Randolph was serious in his intent to propose adjournment, Paterson offered to "second it with all his heart."[7]

Randolph immediately backed down, protesting shock that his words "had been so readily and strangely misinterpreted." He offered that he only meant to adjourn for the night, and when Paterson seconded this less dramatic motion, the New Jersey delegate could not help advising the "larger states to deliberate further on conciliatory expedients." Happily, as Rakove recounted, the next day's proceedings quickly moved on to other issues and became "a full and rich day of discussion that marked significant progress on several major questions, and which thus helped dissipate lingering ill feelings while pointing the delegates toward the work ahead."[8]

Though the convention had its moments of levity and pique, it was largely a serious affair and accomplished a remarkable feat—creating a draft constitution that a wary confederation of states ultimately ratified. Had the ratification campaign failed, few would have hailed the deliberation that preceded it. But, in the end, the "grand compromise" constitution succeeded, and it is doubtful that it would have come into existence without the convention's thorough deliberation.

What Would a Deliberative Legislature Look Like?

The Constitutional Convention serves as an abstract symbol and illustration of deliberation, but it is necessary to develop a more precise model of deliberative governance. The emphasis here remains on legislative deliberation. Thus, Figure 5.1

	Agenda Setting	Issue Consideration
	Analytic Process	
Create a solid information base.	Maintain a reliable and broad research base that can identify emerging social, economic, and environmental problems.	In committee, carefully study the issue being considered, getting information from reliable sources.
Prioritize the key values at stake.	Identify the public's core values and interests, not merely those that are expressed most often.	Acknowledge the full range of values and considerations relevant to an issue, not just the most obvious ones.
Identify a broad range of solutions.	Consider the full range of problems that need to be addressed, not just the ones that receive the most attention.	Avoid latching on to a single solution. Instead, develop a range of alternative pieces of legislation.
Weigh the pros, cons, and trade-offs among solutions.	Consider the relative human and ecological costs of setting one issue aside to address another.	Honestly assess the long-term impact of proposed legislation and its alternatives.
Make the best decision possible.	Prioritize issues on the agenda based on which ones most need to be addressed.	Make the decision that is in the public's best interest, whatever the political cost.
	Social Process	
Adequately distribute speaking opportunities.	Ensure that every point of view gets expressed clearly during committee hearings and floor debate, including some opportunity for voices outside the legislature.	
Ensure mutual comprehension.	Avoid speaking in coded language or unnecessary abstraction. Make sure all voting members understand one another.	
Consider other ideas and experiences.	Reflect on the experiences and values of legislators who are undecided or who do not vote the same as you do.	
Respect other participants.	Committee sessions and floor debate should maintain a professional decorum. Criticism should be substantive, not personal.	

Figure 5.1   Key Features of Legislative Deliberation

identifies the key features of deliberation as it should be practiced by an ideal legislative body. In addition to the social aspect of deliberation, this figure makes an analytic distinction between issue consideration and agenda setting. The conceptions of deliberation in Chapters 2 to 4 took for granted that certain questions were already on the public's agenda, but in reality there can be as much deliberation on which issues merit discussion as there might be on the issues themselves.

AGENDAS VERSUS ISSUES

Within a legislative body, a considerable portion of the deliberation concerns this problem of agenda setting—deciding which issues are of the highest priority. Even local school boards and county commissions routinely have more issues to address than their meeting time permits, and this is always the case for state and federal legislative bodies. Thus, when looking at the analytic process in a legislature, it is equally important to judge its deliberation about what to consider as it is to evaluate how it considers the issues that become top priorities.

For example, consider the "weigh pros and cons" aspect of deliberative analysis. In the agenda-setting phase, the charge for a deliberative legislative body is to "consider the relative human and ecological costs of setting one issue aside to address another." If it chooses to debate a trivial, symbolic issue and simultaneously dodges a politically contentious issue, such as immigration law, in spite of the latter issue's importance to human health, the economy, and foreign policy, the assembly has failed to deliberate adequately on its agenda. Once a given issue is on the legislature's agenda, then this criterion instead requires the legislature to "honestly assess the long-term impact of proposed legislation and its alternatives." At this junction, the alternatives constitute different solutions to the problem under discussion—not alternative issues vying for a slot on the agenda.

This distinction between agenda setting and issue deliberation could equally well apply to many other deliberative situations, such as which issue a discussion group chooses to address, which issues the media cover, or which referenda or initiatives make it onto the ballot in an upcoming election. The idea of agenda setting, however, applies best in the context of governmental deliberation, and we return to it when we look at the role the executive branch of government plays in deliberative governance.

DELIBERATING AS REPRESENTATIVES

Another important difference between Figure 5.1 and previous definitions of deliberation concerns the unique role of public representatives, be they legislators, executives, or judges. In the kinds of informal discussions described in Chapter 2, participants might try to look beyond their own private perspectives, but doing so is merely an exercise in open-mindedness. For public representatives, doing so is their job. This is true in two senses: representatives have a specific constituency on whose behalf they speak, but those same constituents often expect them to think and act in terms of the larger public good—beyond even the boundaries of a representative's particular district or political base.

For example, consider an elected U.S. senator from Georgia. She has obligations to the people of Georgia, to the particular people who put her in office with their votes (and support), and to the nation as a whole. It may be the senator wants one approach to U.S. foreign policy, the people of Georgia want a different one, the partisans who supported her want yet another, and the senator recognizes that a fourth alternative likely best serves the nation's larger interests, beyond, say, Georgia's particular concerns about the textile industry. Thus, the charge in Figure 5.1 to "make the decision that is in the public's best interest, whatever the political cost" could ask too much of a senator in the midst of a hard-fought reelection campaign. Serving the interests of the nation may or may not be politically expedient.

In such a situation, which public must she answer to? From a deliberative perspective, the ultimate task of the larger legislative body is to serve the greater public's interest (in this case, that of the nation), but individual legislators are sometimes torn between representing their state constituents and the nation as a whole.

In the same way, prioritizing key values in Figure 5.1 refers to the broader public—not just one's personal values or those of one's constituents. In practice, the legislature is doing its job if individual members bring different and complementary voices into its deliberation. The point, however, is not simply to aggregate distinct perspectives: doing so results in "prioritizing" simply by counting (e.g., "since sixty percent of us privilege national security concerns over privacy issues, we'll presume that security is the more important value"). Rather, the point is to bring to bear the full range of values and concerns and arrive at a deliberative judgment as to how to weigh those in the course of studying an issue under consideration by the legislature. Doing this conscientiously is one of the best ways legislators can represent the interests of their varied (and shared) constituencies.

A more subtle consequence of serving as representatives is the special role legislators, executives, and judges play as role models for deliberation. Voters choose their representatives not only to speak clearly and forcefully but also respectfully. Even those public officials who are hoped to promote a particular political agenda aggressively can do so in a way that reflects well or poorly on those who elected them. U.S. Senator Bob Dole's vice presidential (1976) and presidential (1996) candidacies were damaged by his reputation as a "hatchet man" likely to attack the integrity or values of an opponent. In the October 15, 1976, vice-presidential debate (the first such debate ever held), Dole cemented forever this reputation when he observed, in a clumsy digression, that the wars in Vietnam and Korea, along with World Wars I and II, were "all Democratic wars, all in this century." He famously added, "I figured up the other day. If we added up the killed and wounded in the Democrat wars in this century, it would be about 1.6 million Americans, enough to fill the city of Detroit. If we want to go back and rake that over and over again, we can do that."[9]

Assigning political blame for what were largely bipartisan war efforts amounts to foolishness for any speaker, but as a representative of his state of Kansas, and the national Republican party, which had named him as their vice-presidential candidate, his gaffe reflected poorly on those who had elevated him to such public stature. He failed not as a private speaker in a closed-door discussion but as a designated representative in a public debate.

In a related sense, public representatives have special deliberative responsibilities as role models. Modeling is one of the most powerful educational processes,[10] and to the extent that public representatives model deliberation in how they analyze problems and interact with their fellow officials, they serve the larger cause of deliberation by setting a high standard for political or judicial discourse. If they treat each other poorly, ignore one another's values, and refuse to consider important facts, their constituents learn to do the same in their own interactions with fellow citizens.[11]

RULES OF ORDER

Probably as a result of its profound consequences on public life, legislative deliberation differs from day-to-day discussion in the degree to which its process becomes codified in rules and procedures. Formal rules and well-established norms shape both the analytic and social aspects of deliberation in representative bodies that have endured through many generations of members.

Underlying the practice of formal legislative bodies, from the U.S. Congress to smaller school boards or community foundations, is a "common law of parliamentary procedures." As explained in Alice Sturgis's *Standard Code of Parliamentary Procedure*, this common law "is the body of principles, rules, and usages that has developed from court decisions on parliamentary questions, and is based on reason and long observance."[12] After centuries of practice, beginning in England and spreading across the globe, there is now a foundation of parliamentary conventions in most quasi-democratic countries.

Those procedures are often formalized through the adoption of a set of procedural statutes unique to a legislative body (such as the U.S. Congress), or simply by noting in an organization's bylaws that all of its proceedings are subject to the rules of an established parliamentary reference guide. The most famous among these in the United States is *Robert's Rules of Order*. General Henry M. Robert wrote this rulebook to permit citizens to work with familiar rules within the many civic and public associations they might happen to join. Robert viewed his book as a way of codifying his conception of democracy, which was ultimately majoritarian but respectful of minority views in a way consistent with deliberative visions of democracy:

> The great lesson for democracies to learn is for the majority to give the minority a full, free opportunity to present their side of the case, and then for the minority, having failed to win a majority to their views, gracefully to submit and to recognize the action as that of the entire organization, and cheerfully to assist in carrying it out, until they can secure its repeal.[13]

Robert's Rules provides procedures for both agenda setting (establishing a main motion) and issue consideration (debate on the main motion). In fact, the rules have procedures—or at least principles—that correspond to every aspect of the deliberative process. Figure 5.2 shows each of these connections. Adopting the rules does not make a group deliberative, but it doesn't necessarily impede deliberation, either. A group following the rules need not get lost in formalism by fetishizing the minutiae of parliamentary procedure, quibbling over arcane rules, or appointing a parliamentarian who must repeatedly rule on points of parliamentary law. Rather, the rules can serve as the backdrop General Robert envisioned, respecting the place in debate of both dissenting minority views and emergent majority opinions.

SUMMARY

In sum, legislative deliberation, as well as executive and judicial deliberation, is a special context because it involves public officials working on behalf of a larger people. These officials have a sacred trust to look beyond their particular perspectives and to consider the larger public good while comporting themselves as models of professional, respectful debate and discussion. How well do they fare in this respect?

Unfortunately, the literature on deliberation in government is relatively thin, compared to that which has been written about informal discussion, mediated deliberation, and elections. The reason for this is that deliberative democratic theory has the public as its central emphasis, and the public is not (directly) present in a discussion of how public officials deliberate. Nonetheless, these officials serve as public representatives, particularly in the case of a legislative body, so it is necessary to glean what we can from the available research on how these bodies do (or don't) deliberate. Thus, we now examine deliberation within government, beginning with our principal focus—the quality of deliberation in legislatures.

Analytic Process	
Create a solid information base.	Refer questions to committees to draft investigative reports. During debate, permit points of information to obtain necessary facts before proceeding.
Prioritize the key values at stake.	No specific procedures, per se, but encouragement of balanced debate, vocal minority, and persuasive appeals encourage raising value questions.
Identify a broad range of solutions.	Permit tabling main motion without rejecting it so that other motions may be considered in course.
Weigh the pros, cons, and trade-offs among solutions.	The chair generally balances speakers for and against the main motion. Require two-thirds majority to close debate when "calling the question."
Make the best decision possible.	Permit amendments to main motion to add desirable elements to the proposal and to excise undesirable features.
Social Process	
Adequately distribute speaking opportunities.	None may speak a second time when others yet to speak wish to do so. Interrupting speakers who "have the floor" allowed only for special reasons.
Ensure mutual comprehension.	Give precedence to points of information (seeking clarification on facts) and parliamentary inquiries (seeking procedural clarification).
Consider other ideas and experiences.	In large assemblies, permit informal consideration of issues in "break-out groups" (e.g., ten to twelve persons each) to generate more in-depth dialogue.
Respect other participants.	Decorum is stressed. The chair can reprimand rude members, "call a member to order" (issue warning), or "name an offender" (e.g., remove the member).

Figure 5.2   Deliberation as Facilitated by Adoption of *Robert's Rules of Order*

SOURCE: Procedural details taken from Robert (1990).

Legislative Deliberation

The sparse literature on legislative deliberation makes it necessary to be selective in topics, addressing those subjects that have already received the attention of at least some scholars. Moreover, the overwhelming majority of research to date has focused on the U.S. Congress, rather than state or local legislatures. In this review, therefore, we focus on the setting of Congress, and we look at decorum and civility among congressional representatives, the substance of floor speeches and committee work, and the role of lobbying in legislative deliberation.

CIVILITY IN CONGRESS

America has a long-standing tradition of debate and conflict, and its democratic political philosophy and institutions are primarily adversarial in nature.[14] Nonetheless, even within the larger genre of adversarial public discussion, we can distinguish between spirited, thoughtful debate and petty, childish argument. The case of Representative Schmidt, which opened this chapter, showed that even a newly minted member of Congress understands this distinction yet is susceptible to the temptations of public squabbling.

Government scholar Eric Uslaner provided one of the most useful analyses of civility in the U.S. House of Representative and Senate. The latter body is often hailed as the more mature and deliberative body, and this reputation stems back to the debate at the Constitutional Convention reviewed earlier in this chapter. Originally, the state legislatures elected Senate's members, shielding it from direct public elections. The idea was not only to give the states control over their representatives but also to create, in James Madison's words, "a necessary fence" against the "fickleness and passion" of the larger public and its House of Representatives.[15]

In Uslaner's view, however, "it is a fundamental mistake to talk about a House of Representatives out of control and a Senate that keeps the republic on an even keel."[16] Not only are these bodies more alike than distinct in this regard, but also the source of their waxing and waning civility is the same. These bodies, Uslaner argued, as much reflect public partisanship and incivility as they produce it. He tracked the decline of legislative civility that began in the 1970s by noting that they "saw an outbreak of incivility in both Congress and in public life." People at that time became more pessimistic about the future: "In such a world, it makes less sense to trust other people and to be willing to make the compromises that underlie reciprocity."[17]

Those serving in office could see the change as it unfolded. Senator Joe Biden (D-Delaware) remarked in 1982, "There's much less civility than when I came here ten years ago. There aren't as many nice people as there were before. . . . Ten years ago, you didn't have people calling each other sons of bitches and vowing to get at each other."[18]

But this generalized legislative incivility "became increasingly partisan in the 1980s," with Democrats and Republicans regularly sparring with one another. In 1985, Representative Bob Dornan (R-California) burnished his macho credentials by grabbing Representative Thomas Downey (D-New York) by his tie and "accusing him and other Democrats of being weak on defense." A decade later, Representative James Moran (D-Virginia) returned the favor by shoving Dornan's good friend Randy Cunningham (R-California) in a squabble over patriotic credentials.[19] The tradition continues to the present day, minus wrinkling ties and shoving matches, with the antics of Representative Schmidt and uncivil colleagues in both parties.

Even if one views such breakdowns in decorum as inconsequential, Uslaner convincingly argued that incivility has real significance for policy making by making compromise difficult. Uslaner illustrated this by tracking the steady increase in ideological extremism from the mid-1960s to the present. During these years, members of both political parties in both the House and the Senate became more rigid in their voting patterns.[20]

Far from an innocent bystander, the public spurs congressional incivility. Uslaner's research found that as the public shifts toward liberalism, for instance, the Democrats become emboldened and drift toward ever-increasing ideological rigidity in their voting patterns by rejecting more opportunities for compromise or crossover voting. During these same periods of rising liberalism, by contrast, the Republicans "circle the wagons and become increasingly conservative," making their response "countermajoritarian."[21]

In the end, rising or falling liberalism and conservativism in the public is unlikely to restore civility in Congress. Instead, Uslaner's theory asks us to put our hope in public trust: only if the public can regain its sense of security, mutual trust, and optimism for the future can we expect our political parties to restore the norms of public-spirited compromise and good-faith bargaining.

SPEECHES OF SUBSTANCE

Moving from the tone or tenor of Congress to the substance of its speeches, political communication researcher Stephanie Burkhalter looked at the talk that occurs during floor debate to see what purposes it serves. In a deliberative ideal, such speeches serve as the most publicly visible stage in congressional debate on current issues.[22] The floor speeches that occur in the House and Senate could be where the most stirring rhetoric occurs, crystallizing arguments and marshaling passions, evidence, and logic to persuade not only fellow members of Congress but also the larger public.

What Burkhalter unearthed was not so inspiring. Her initial foray into the subject focused on the case of debate on welfare reform. What she found was a stubborn symbolic crusade by the Republican Party and conservative Democrats to promote an increasingly narrow stereotype of welfare recipients as either "welfare queens"—those exploiting the system to become wealthy while posing as poor—or lazy, undeserving "deadbeats," who are capable of work but refuse to do so as long as the government provides sufficient housing and handouts. The message being conveyed through a barrage of speeches was simply that "the poor are not like the rest of us." The net effect was to shift the discourse of both parties toward a narrow range of policy alternatives for addressing poverty. The complex reality of welfare was reduced to a simplistic metaphor for the purpose of narrowing the range of policy alternatives under consideration.[23]

This initial foray into congressional speech led Burkhalter to conduct a larger, more systematic study of floor speeches, which became her doctoral dissertation, *Talking Points: Message Strategies and Deliberation in the U.S. Congress*.[24] This study looks at message discipline within the Democratic and Republican parties across a range of issues debated in the U.S. Senate and House. Burkhalter created a method for assessing the degree to which messages in a debate are organized and orchestrated—in a word, *disciplined*. Both pro and con sides of any given proposal put before Congress have many arguments that can be marshaled, which include points of fact, value emphases, and other important considerations. A disciplined party brings out a parade of speakers, each of whom says almost nothing original and largely ignores whatever words have been said in opposition to their own. In both the Senate and the House, and in both parties, Burkhalter found that the general rule was high message discipline, with both parties repeating the same arguments repeatedly and in sync with the talking points each party had set in advance.

Burkhalter's research provided a concreteness to the lingering sense among both scholars and elected representatives that deliberation is waning in Congress. In a more informal first-person survey of floor speeches in state legislatures, from Nebraska to New Mexico, I came to the same conclusion. Though there are periods of spirited debate now and again, anyone entering a state legislature should take a seat in the viewing gallery expecting to see a session of "legislative karaoke." Like its more musical namesake, legislative karaoke consists of one speaker after another giving an amateur performance of a prewritten script, occasionally glancing up from their notes in an effort to make brief eye contact. The speaker and the listener both know the script, and the reading is merely a performance. While one speaker "sings" his or her talking points, the other legislators can be as rude as even the seediest bar crowd, noisily unwrapping and eating food on their desks, reading mail, talking to one another, and even answering phone calls. Meanwhile, the person next in the queue goes over his or her notes and gets ready to take the microphone when signaled to do so by the DJ (aka the presiding officer of the chamber).

Even members of Congress recognize that floor speeches have become little more than recitations of strategic messages with close to zero persuasive value for fellow legislators. Consider the restrictions that congressional leaders have placed on C-SPAN, the cable television network that covers all of the floor debates. At its inception in 1979, Democratic leaders placed tight restrictions on what it could show: the cameras had to remain on the speaker and could not show reaction shots or pan the chamber to show that there was no audience for a speech (something a C-SPAN camera operator once did to the outrage of congressional members). When Newt Gingrich and the Republican Party took control of the House after the 1994 elections, C-SPAN chairman Brian Lamb was optimistic about the prospects for loosening these rules. Before leading the "Republican revolution," Gingrich had been among the first to welcome cameras onto the floor and had used them to his advantage. *Congressional Quarterly* editor Ronald Elving offered the following recollection:

> For a time, Lamb was seeing nothing but green lights—cameras at Gingrich's daily briefing for reporters, a camera just off the floor, cameras allowed to pan the chamber and show reaction shots (but still controlled by House employees). With members warned in advance, the loosened rules were tried in late March during a racially charged debate over welfare reform. Then things started to fall apart. Members in both parties suddenly had reservations. Thirty-one Republicans signed a letter asking Gingrich to go back to showing whoever was speaking, period. Democrats were also leery, raising questions like these: What if the roving camera eye found a group of members smiling and joking in some part of the sprawling House chamber during a speech on a deadly serious subject? Or Democrats and Republicans quietly working together off to one side? Or members smoking cigarettes somewhere else?[25]

In the end, C-SPAN was defanged once more, and the floor speeches were able to continue as a succession of poorly sung hits from each party's songbook. It is no irony that the same debate that caught Burkhalter's interest was the one that revoked the freedoms briefly exercised by C-SPAN's camera operators.

If one looks for an exception to this bleak portrait, one might find it in the unconstrained floor time in the House of Representatives. Political scientists Forrest Maltzman and Lee Sigelman studied these brief speeches, which air live on C-SPAN to an audience of millions. They found that "rather than simply providing electorally insecure members a free forum for reaching their constituents," these speeches were used principally by party leaders and the most ideologically extreme (and electorally secure) members of the House, particularly those in the minority party. Matlzman and Sigelman concluded that these speakers, unconstrained by the normal rules of floor debate, appear to be "driven by policy and political considerations beyond their own reelection."[26] It is surely the case that some of these speeches advance the public debate on the issues they address, and that alone is heartening. If nothing else, they show that elected representatives in Congress certainly have the capacity to speak to the issues of the day, if not so often in a deliberative mode of discourse.

THE SECRET LIFE OF COMMITTEES

If there is deliberation in Congress, or other legislatures generally, it is likely to occur in the quieter chambers of the committee rooms. Recall that *Robert's Rules of Order* encourages forming committees and breaking into smaller study groups to permit more thorough examination of issues and facilitate open dialogue among members. Particularly in large assemblies, the only place where in-depth exchanges of ideas, information, and aspirations occurs is in committee rooms, offices, and other smaller—sometimes even private—settings.

In this web of committees, conferences, and meetings, there is evidence of deliberation in both the House and Senate. Government scholar Joseph Bessette's *The Mild Voice of Reason* documented many instances of deliberative practice in Congress, including case studies of three famous legislators and the committees on which they worked:

- Wilbur Mills (D-Arkansas) serves as an example of how working hard on the creation of good public policy can earn a representative considerable prestige. Mills served as the chair of the powerful Ways and Means Committee and his influence came, in the words of one Republican peer, from "his knowledge, the fact that he does his homework." The model of what is now called a policy wonk, Mills was said to be so "single minded" that he "never goes out" and has "no social life or cocktail parties."[27]

- In the U.S. Senate, Edmund Muskie (D-Maine) illustrated how credibility earned within one's committees could translate into political power. Muskie successfully chaired a range of committees during his career, but his most famous actions may have been defending the spending targets developed by the Budget Committee, even against popular programs like the school lunch program that he (and his constituents) supported. In the end, Muskie achieved many of his political goals, in part due to respecting the integrity of compromises struck in his committees.[28]

- Pete Domenici (R-New Mexico) demonstrated how a U.S. senator could develop a national profile as a tough-minded legislator in a way that strengthened one's prospects for reelection. Domenici took on issues that were politically risky in his politically divided home state, which included a strong and vocal Democratic constituency. Domenici took stands that went against the material interests of some of his key supporters, such as when he supported the elimination of oil and gas price controls (opposing New Mexican energy industrialists) and encouraged cutbacks in Social Security (opposing New Mexican retirees). In the end, stances like these earned him national praise, which was then echoed by the New Mexican press corps in a way that made voters proud to have elected (and reelected) him.[29]

Bessette used these particular representatives, along with other cases and examples, to make a more general point about legislatures. The three most obvious goals motivating representatives are making good public policy (virtue), securing influence within government (power), and ensuring their reelection (security). Popular accounts emphasize the latter two goals—power and security, with personal greed often thrown in as a reason for exercising power. Bessette, however, shows time and again that many elected officials aspire to shape laws in pursuit of their particular political philosophy or a less well-defined sense of the common good. What is most valuable about Bessette's analysis is that it shows how pursuing the public good can ensure greater power and security. In other words, even if officials are often motivated by power and are determined to win reelection, they might seek to make good laws precisely to augment their power and security.

LOBBYING AND THE PUBLIC'S VOICE

Examining committees, though, also takes us in another direction. In both Bessette's study of legislators and Burkhalter's analysis of floor speeches, a powerful influence is often working behind the scenes to shape deliberation. Bessette found both professional and amateur lobbyists seeking legislators' ears at every turn, and Burkhalter found she could sometimes trace the talking points recited on the floor directly back to the briefings and policy papers previously written by think tanks and special interest organizations.

Effective lobbying can change votes on upcoming legislation, and it can influence which bills officials introduce or which causes they champion.[30] The term *lobbyists* refers to the full universe of influential interest groups, which includes policy institutes and think tanks (e.g., American Enterprise Institute, Brookings Institution, Heritage Foundation) and, more commonly, special and public interest groups (e.g., American Medical Association, American Association of Retired Persons, National Right to Life Committee, Mothers Against Drunk Driving, People for the American Way, Conservative Caucus, National Federation of Industrial Businesses League, Sierra Club, and so on). Often, the actual individuals and firms representing these interests are professional lobbyists and public relations mercenaries (e.g., Hill & Knowlton), and it is increasingly common for lobbyists and their firms to represent multiple interests.[31]

Though the research and arguments developed by lobbyists can contribute positively to a larger deliberative process, the conventional practice of lobbying is far from the deliberative ideal.[32] Lobbyists and advocacy groups generally present narrow or partisan viewpoints, thus earning them the label *special interest*. Lobbyists who visit the offices of legislators focus on specific policies of concern to their sponsors. When defeating a single amendment or obtaining a particular ruling means outright victory for a lobbyist, he or she will speak unambiguously on that specific point. As one example among thousands, Boeing's $5.2 million lobbying campaign in 1996 focused on tax "mitigation" and "avoidance." Though costly, the campaign succeeded in winning the company deductions and credits resulting in a $33 million rebate—the equivalent of a negative nine percent tax rate.[33]

More generally, lobbying is an unrepresentative form of public voice because its influence depends largely on the wealth that funds it.[34] "One dollar, one vote" is a closer approximation to lobbying's ethic of representation. The most influential individual donor-lobbyists come largely from a single social strata: a recent study of federal campaign contributions of $200 or more cross-referenced donor zip codes with census data and found that donations disproportionately came from predominantly wealthy, white neighborhoods.[35]

Standing behind many lobbyists are political action committees (PACs), which can contribute thousands of dollars to candidates each election. Moreover, many congressional candidates receive the maximum legal contribution from multiple members of a family whose commercial or ideological interests are represented by a single lobbyist or lobbying organization. Even more indirectly, PACs and individuals can contribute indirectly to national parties, who then send the money to candidates or spend it on their behalf. Contributions can also go to nonprofit organizations that run their own, quasi-independent advocacy campaigns. By making campaign contributions conditional on incumbent responsiveness, lobbyists can buy a measure of influence, especially from candidates concerned about reelection.

Other lobbying organizations have both money and members. Behind them stand not only a well-funded and media-savvy public relations arsenal but also a large membership and a skilled organizing staff. One of the most striking examples of this lobbying tool is the membership of the American Association of Retired Persons (AARP). Through a system of incentives, the AARP has built a membership exceeding 30 million, and the organization has become skilled at mobilizing its members to contact specific officials who might otherwise fail to respond to the AARP's voice. As political communication scholar Lance Bennett explained, "Those millions of letters, postcards, and phone calls that arrive on Capitol Hill and at the White House promise revenge at the next election" if officials do not protect Social Security or other policies backed by the AARP.[36] Elected officials recognize the importance of these letters because they represent more than diffuse constituent concerns; rather, they are a clear reminder of AARP's ability to influence thousands of votes in any single district.

Though it is certainly influential in the legislative process, lobbying generally represents an exclusive, nondeliberative form of discourse. The most public-spirited interest groups sometimes promote public dialogue on an issue by convening public meetings or engaging in televised debates, but the purpose behind such activities is to increase the amount of public support for a preset policy position. Persuasion through argument is an important part of the deliberative process, but orchestrated public discussions often become manipulative. For example, Murray Edelman argued that policy advocates attach themselves strategically and psychologically to a particular plan of action and then cast about for problems that justify their prefabricated solutions. Thus, an organization might promote public meetings to discuss a problem only to lead the public to support a particular solution.[37]

Most interest groups lack even internal deliberation. As Jane Mansbridge observed, "Few interest associations in the United States or Europe institutionalize any formal deliberative processes among their membership, let alone deliberative processes designed to promote identification with the public good." Mansbridge's own research on the movement for an Equal Rights Amendment found that "even in this democratic and public-spirited movement, the elites never learned what the grass-roots activists would have formulated as good public policy if both elites and activists had taken part in a more extensive process of deliberation."[38]

Deliberation and the Executive Branch

If it causes one dismay to see such a bleak portrait of deliberation in the legislative branch, the good news is that there are more places one can look. Though legislatures are the most obvious place to look for governmental deliberation, one can also hope to find deliberative moments and practices within the executive branch of government. One may think of the executive as simply a solitary decision maker, but this portrait is not accurate for mayors and governors, let alone a president who hopes to make decisions on behalf of an entire nation.

We consider two particular aspects of the executive deliberation: the importance of information gathering and the perils of decision making with tight-knit groups of advisors. Both of these reveal a new facet of deliberation that applies more generally to government as a whole but has special significance for the executive.

GATHERING INFORMATION

One of the most mundane ways in which the executive branch facilitates deliberation is through the collection of information. Gathering data may not sound glamorous, but recall from Figure 5.1 that one basic task in deliberation is to "create a solid information base." As Joseph Bessette explained, "Both Congress and the executive branch have invested heavily in the collection, analysis, and dissemination of substantive, policy relevant information."[39] Congress set up the Congressional Research Service, the General Accounting Office, the Congressional Budget Office, and the Office of Technology Assessment, and it has innumerable committees, subcommittees, ad hoc committees, and personal staff conducting research. The executive branch disperses its research functions "among the two-million-member bureaucracy," but it also concentrates the research function "within specific agencies whose main business is the production of statistical data for policymakers." Prominent agencies include the "bureaus," who conduct the U.S. Census and collect statistics on labor, health, justice, and the environment. More indirectly, the federal government sponsors basic and applied research through institutions such as the National Institute of Mental Health, the Centers for Disease Control and Prevention, and the National Science Foundation, which has even funded some of the research reported in this volume.

Without such extensive information gathering, both the executive and Congress would be even more reliant on the lobbying groups described earlier. High-quality government information can provide a counterpoint to what are often biased data collected by groups advocating particular interests or points of view. A lobbyist will rarely provide a government official with information that runs counter to their objectives, but government agencies routinely deliver news to executives (and to the wider public) that they would rather not have heard. When we hear in the news that unemployment is rising, that a war costs ten times the original estimate, and that the trade gap is widening, we are hearing information that the government has collected on our behalf. Recalling Murray Edelman's observation that governments sometimes seek to create the perception of a crisis when none exists, official statistics can also be unwelcome when they deliver good news—our rivers are cleaner, our violent crime rates are dropping—that undermines a crisis frame designed to justify a corresponding environmental or criminal policy agenda.

The constructive purposes of such information are relatively straightforward. Bessette offered the following explanation:

> [Federal government information] may serve a variety of distinct purposes in a deliberative process. First, it may educate policy advocates themselves as they fashion specific administrative or legislative proposals. Second, policy advocates (or opponents) may use information to try to persuade other decision-makers of the merits (or shortcomings) of proposed policies. Finally, the contestants in the policy process may gather, distill, and disseminate information in order to mobilize support for, or opposition to, a policy initiative outside of the governing institutions themselves, among, for example, the media, state and local officials, interest groups, or the broader public.[40]

If the function of gathering data and commissioning research seems mundane, one had best remember that it is only neutral or objective by degree. There has always been the temptation to "cook the books"—to redefine how unemployment, for example, is calculated so that the statistic appears to go down, and so on. Though all executives have engaged in such practices, the Bush administration appears to have gone further than those that came before it. A popular account of this trend appears in Chris Mooney's *The Republican War on Science*.[41] Mooney documented numerous ways in which the Bush administration has violated long-standing norms of routine scientific data collection:

- Has "stacked" advisory committees with industry representatives and Christian conservatives lacking the training necessary to collect or evaluate policy-relevant data.

- Required the National Cancer Institute to assert in its publications that abortion can cause breast cancer, despite the preponderance of evidence collected by the institute and others refuting this claim.

- Forced the Centers for Disease Control and Prevention to remove from its Web site information regarding the benefits of condom use.

The exact motivations underlying such actions are harder to glean, though they certainly include the promotion of a partisan agenda and a general skepticism toward the benefits of science in making policy decisions. The point here is not to vilify the Bush administration but rather to recognize the value of establishing and maintaining quasi-independent agencies within the executive (and legislative) branch whose job is to collect data and promote research without regard to the particular biases or aims of the current administration.

EXECUTIVE AUTHORITY AND GROUPTHINK

A distinguishing feature of the executive branch of government is precisely that—the executive authority given to the mayor, county commissioner, governor, or president. All other deliberative groupings and bodies considered herein—even a court consisting of judges—require a measure of agreement among members to be able to reach a decision, or even glean a sense of the group's direction. The executive, by contrast, independently makes decisions and the decisions are the executive's responsibility alone.

Under this circumstance, is deliberation possible in any meaningful sense? Yes, it is, in that the executive can set aside his or her authority for the duration of a group discussion and let the group draw on the wisdom and insight of all of those present, yielding a group recommendation, albeit not a final decision. This is precisely what a president has the opportunity to do when calling together a cabinet, a committee, or an advisory council. In many cases, the judgments of such groups are tremendously helpful to the executive, yet at other times those bodies fail to engage in a thorough analysis of a problem and fall into a trap that has come to be known as groupthink.

Irving Janis cemented the popular understanding of that term in his book *Groupthink: Psychological Studies of Policy Decisions and Fiascoes.*[42] Janis found that under the wrong circumstances, groups of well-intentioned and highly capable experts, policy advisors, and executives could devolve into a kind of discussion that invariably leads to flawed decisions. The symptoms of groupthink include:

- An illusion of invulnerability, wherein a group comes to doubt that it can fail (a member might proclaim, "Failure is impossible" or "Failure is not an option," etc.)

- An unquestioned belief in the group's inherent morality ("We are on the side of God" or "You're either with us, or you're with the evildoers")

- A collective rationalization of warnings that one's plan may be mistaken ("Their information is not as good as ours" or "We have taken that into account already")

- A stereotyped view of an opposing group's motivations ("They are all evil/ stupid/cowardly")

- Careful self-censorship of deviations from the emerging group consensus (members might write doubts in their journal but fail to speak up during meetings)

- An illusion of unanimity (members perceive complete agreement, but it is not present)

- Application of direct pressure on dissenters ("You shouldn't question his authority" or "We really need you on board with us")

- The emergence of self-appointed "mindguards" (members who keep unpleasant information or dissenters away from the leader)

The bad news is that Janis found these symptoms to be present in the historical record for many important executive meetings of the executive branch. Groupthink appears to have been partly to blame for such fiascoes as the Bay of Pigs invasion in Cuba, strategic errors committed during the Korean and Vietnam wars, and the failure to anticipate the attack on Pearl Harbor during World War II. Since Janis wrote *Groupthink*, other scholars have pointed to groupthink as a potential explanation for other policy disasters.[43] One can speculate that more recent miscalculations, such as the lack of preparation by the Bush administration for postwar Iraq, may have also involved groupthink.

The good news is that groupthink is far from inevitable. As shown in Figure 5.3, Janis believes that a cluster of group features is necessary for groupthink to occur. A group must be highly cohesive, structurally flawed, and in a provocative situational context. Of particular significance from a deliberative standpoint, groupthink is more likely when a group lacks an impartial leader and methodical procedures for conducting its discussions. In other words, the more autocratic and arbitrary the leadership, the less deliberative the group's discussion.

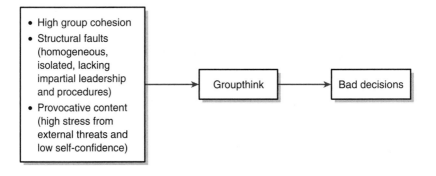

Figure 5.3   Basic Elements of Groupthink Theory

When one looks at Janis's suggested remedies, each is consistent with the kind of open-ended, deliberative discussion described in Figure 2.1. Janis suggested critically evaluating ideas—even by having a member play the role of devil's advocate (effectively weighing pros and cons), inviting in outside experts (strengthening information base, etc.), forming subgroups to generate competing proposals (broadening the range of solutions to consider), meeting without the leader (promoting more balanced participation), and so on. Such procedural steps can turn even a dysfunctional group into a highly competent one, as in the case of Kennedy's advisory groups, which went from the Bay of Pigs fiasco to the successful negotiation of the Cuban missile crisis through making precisely these sorts of changes.[44]

Judicial Deliberation

Finally, what of the judicial branch? This is not an easy governmental body to study, as justices do not generally discuss cases with one another—even when they sit on the same court—and when they do, they do not generally share their discussion with the public. Nonetheless, it is useful to at least reflect on the unique character of deliberation that occurs on courts, and in the United States the only one that has received sufficient attention to merit mention is the Supreme Court.

Political philosopher John Rawls argued that the highest Court is "the branch of government that serves as the exemplar of public reason."[45] The Court safeguards a "democratic constitution," which is "a principled expression in higher law of the political ideal of a people to govern itself. . . ." The "public reasoning" of the Court serves to "articulate this ideal" by clarifying, for instance, how the principle of freedom of speech applies to changing social circumstances.[46]

Does the Court meet this ideal standard in its deliberations? The clearest window into the court's functioning is *The Brethren: Inside the Supreme Court*, a unique piece of investigative journalism by Bob Woodward and Scott Armstrong in 1979. The authors described the workings of the court from 1969 to 1975, relying on "at least one, usually two, and often three or four reliable sources in the chambers of each Justice" for the duration of their study.[47] Such access was rare indeed, and since the book's publication, the Court has allowed no other observer a similar vantage point from which to write.

One distinguishing feature of judicial deliberation is that it is private deliberation. No other interested parties are permitted to speak with the justices through any channel other than formally submitted legal briefs. Such norms are most clear when they are violated, and Woodward and Armstrong related one such incident. A private-practice lawyer, Thomas "Tommy the Cork" Corcoran, sought to influence the Court regarding a recent issue involving the El Paso Natural Gas Company, and he made an appointment to see Justice William J. Brennan:

> Brennan had no idea why Corcoran, whom he did not know well, had requested an appointment. He greeted Corcoran warmly [at his office]. The two Irishmen sat and exchanged a few pleasantries. Corcoran quickly got to the point. Why was the Court determined to ruin El Paso [Natural Gas Company]? . . . Brennan stood. He said that he, of course, could not and would not ever discuss a pending case, and showed Corcoran the door. He immediately went to tell his clerks. Something awful just happened, he said. His shock was evident on his face as he described Corcoran's visit. . . . It was outrageous, a lawyer coming to lobby a Justice.[48]

Formal argument does, occur, of course through normal court proceedings, as the Court hears from those appealing prior rulings, along with those asking that appeals be dismissed or prior decisions upheld. In each phase, the justices also hear from each other, directly and indirectly. During the agenda-setting phase of court decision making, the justices meet in a secret cert conference and choose to hear a small subset of the thousands of cases appealed to the Court each year. In a nod to minority rights, only four of the nine justices must vote to hear a case for it to make it onto the Court's docket.

Once the Court agrees to hear a case, it then evaluates written arguments in the form of legal briefs, followed by brief oral arguments in open court. The briefs come not only from the formal representatives on either side of a case but also from interested parties who are filing an ever-increasing number of amici curiae briefs to advance their own views of a case.[49] The oral argument period consists of attorneys for each side stating their core arguments and the Justices repeatedly interrupting them, with questions both helpful and unhelpful to an attorney's cause. The questions Justices ask are meant as much to communicate openly with one another as to engage the attorneys.

Shortly thereafter, the Justices engage in the closest thing to a face-to-face deliberation in the Court—a closed-door case conference. This ends with an initial vote, after which a Justice is assigned to write the majority opinion. (If the chief justice is in the majority, she or he makes this assignment; otherwise, the senior justice in the majority assigns this responsibility.) During the next several months, justices engage in deliberation-by-text as they begin writing the majority opinion, concurrences (agreements with the majority that make additional points), and dissents (minority views). Before the final opinions are published, justices can "join" others' opinions, reducing the total number of different opinions written into the decision. The majority opinion becomes legal precedent, but any concurrences or dissents also influence the interpretations of law, as they provide legal rationales for different directions the Court could head in the future.

We cannot know what level of discussion is typical at the Court during case conference meetings and the written deliberation that takes place thereafter, but *The Brethren* reminds us that justices are human. The Court can reach high-minded judgments that pull together diverse points of view, but it can also become less than deliberative. In this regard, Woodward and Armstrong recounted that the summer of 1975 was a low point for the Court, with all but one justice underperforming. "At conferences," Woodward and Armstrong wrote, "the Chief read verbatim from clerks' memos" instead of engaging in discussion with his fellow justices. Most of the others fared no better:

> Brennan's bitterness at the direction of the Court's decisions made him a voice crying in the wilderness. It was sad . . . [He] gave knee-jerk liberal reactions. Stewart was hard-working but distracted. Marshall appointed Brennan. Blackmun was tormented and indecisive, searching for a way to duck issues or narrow the final opinion as much as possible. Rehnquist was clearly very intelligent and hard-working but too right wing. His willingness to bend previous decisions to purposes for which they were never intended was surprising . . . Powell seemed the most thoughtful, the best prepared, the least doctrinaire. White was the most willing to discuss an issue informally before it was resolved, but he could become unnervingly harsh.[50]

The net result of this constellation of justices was a string of decidedly nondeliberative cert and case conference meetings:

> The absence of intellectual content or meaningful discussion at conference was the most depressing fact of Court life. Stevens thought that the nation's highest Court picked its way carelessly through the cases it selected. There was too little time for careful reflection. The lack of interest, of imagination and of open-mindedness was disquieting. By the end of the term, Stevens was accustomed to watching his colleagues . . . shading the facts, twisting the law . . . [and] warping logic. . . . What Stevens could not accept, however, was the absence of real deliberation.[51]

Once again, this is not to say that the Court routinely fails to meet a high standard of deliberation. This excerpt does illustrate, however, the susceptibility of the Court to the same distortions, distractions, and failures that other deliberative bodies experience. Without a record of the Court's deliberation, one can only judge its deliberation by the legal quality of its judgments, but that, alas, is a task beyond the scope of this book.

Conclusion

How can a government become more deliberative? There are surely countless ways, but little has been written in the deliberation literature about how to raise the internal workings of government to a higher standard. Nonetheless, I wish to consider one controversial reform regarding governmental deliberation, then foreshadow the next two chapters by considering how bringing the public into government decision making can help to produce more deliberative governance.

Looking at the Supreme Court as a model of deliberation may be surprising because its most important deliberations are held in secret. But, as law professor John Kang argued, "The Supreme Court would seem to stand as a cultural exemplum of everything conducive to critical interaction—a collection of highly learned, highly intellectual, and apparently dispassionate individuals who publicly present themselves not as representatives for special interests, nor even as representatives for the people as a whole, but as fellow travelers in the search for truth."[52] In particular, Kang emphasized the following point about the Court's regular conference meetings:

> The strictly confidential nature of the meetings affords the justices ample opportunity to assume the sort of devil's advocate extolled by Mill to speculate and to experiment in a way unavailable in the public glare of reporters and visitors who would mark the justices' every word and demeanor. At the conference, the justices are confronted with having to persuade their opponents

and to defend their positions, and there may even be opportunity for the justices to learn something from those who diametrically oppose their views. These Court meetings would seem to represent, then, the sort of vibrant and potentially extraordinary deliberation idealized by some advocates of deliberative democracy.[53]

Is what's good for the Supreme Court good for other branches of government? The Bush administration made precisely this argument for permitting the executive branch to hold closed-door meetings with regular advisors, occasional guests, and task forces. As recounted by the watchdog group Public Citizen, "President Bush and Vice President Cheney have asserted that the advice they received . . . both from executive branch employees and from outside lobbyists, is protected from disclosure to the public by executive privilege." The Federal Advisory Committee Act, however, requires that "committees formed to advise the government on policy matters that include persons who are not government employees" are required to have "balanced membership and open meetings."[54]

Regardless of how the courts ultimately resolve this and similar legal challenges, the question remains as to whether secrecy can be a valuable and appropriate part of executive deliberation. The experience of the Supreme Court suggests that secrecy can create space for honest exchanges that might not occur otherwise, but the research on groupthink warns that insulating a group from outside criticism risks reaching increasingly unrealistic decisions.

This question also applies, though somewhat differently, to the legislative branch of government. After culling the recent historical record for examples of deliberation, Joseph Bessette concluded that if we "take seriously the deliberative responsibilities of national legislators," then we "may come to view the issue of secrecy and accountability somewhat differently." A cynical distrust of members of Congress leads us to demand open meetings, but if we, instead, recognize that public officials generally pursue some vision of the public's will, "then the question becomes whether the glare of public scrutiny and formal accountability for every vote in committee and most votes on the floor contributes to or hinders deliberation in service of the public good."[55] In Bessette's view, open meetings result in more partisan posturing, make it easier for lobbyists to hold legislators accountable, and force legislators to act on behalf of narrow constituent interests more often than in the larger national interest.

In the end, there remains a balance between the need for public scrutiny and "transparent" public institutions and the move to secure space for more private deliberation.[56] The aim here is not to elevate secret meetings, which clearly have the potential to undermine democratic control of government, so much as to raise the question as to when it might be appropriate for elected public officials to confer in closed-door sessions. We take for granted the need for private deliberation, and we need to remain open to the periodic need for such meetings in other branches of government.

In any case, the principal means of augmenting deliberation in government is to give the larger public a more meaningful, direct, and substantive role in discussions leading up to governmental decisions. The jury system plays this role in the judicial branch of government, and we look more closely at how the jury functions as a means of public deliberation in the following chapter. In the legislative and executive branches of government, there have been many successful experiments in public deliberation, and we consider those in Chapter 7.

By way of a preview, consider two different strategies for increasing public involvement in governmental decision making. Peter Levine, Archon Fung, and I distinguished between inside strategies, which entail "creating relationships with policymakers or enacting administrative or legal requirements that compel them to incorporate public deliberations into their decisions." This ranges from simple public comment periods to the establishment of citizen authority via neighborhood councils or zoning boards. Outside strategies, by contrast, "rely on generating political and social pressures that compel officials to respect the results of public deliberation" that occurred outside the confines of government.[57]

There are many other issues to consider when tightening the connection between citizen deliberation and government decision making, but this preview gives a glimpse of the kinds of reforms that are considered in detail in Chapter 7. Before turning to these alternative practices, however, we turn our attention to the American jury—an established form of deliberation so obvious and taken for granted that it often goes unnoticed. The next chapter helps us understand this practice of face-to-face citizen deliberation and how it fits into the larger judicial branch of government.

Notes

1. Quoted in *The Federalist*, No. 42. Available online at http://usinfo.state.gov/usa/infousa/facts/funddocs/fed/federa42.htm.
2. This transcript was written by the author, based on the video provided by C-SPAN.
3. Rakove (1996, p. 14).
4. Ibid., p. 15.
5. Ibid., p. 102.
6. Ibid., p. 80.
7. Ibid., p. 80.
8. Ibid., p. 81.
9. Transcripts of portions of the debate appear at http://www.pbs.org/newshour/debatingourdestiny/dod/1976-broadcast.html.
10. Modeling is the principal concept in the behavioral approach to psychology. For a judicious explanation of this theory, see Bandura (1986).

11. No direct study has demonstrated this observational learning effect, but Mutz and Reeves (2005) showed that watching particular vicious televised debates undermines trust in government, and the connection to behavior is not a large leap, especially considering the strength of the behavioral modeling paradigm in social psychology and education (Bandura, 1986).
12. Ibid., pp. 2–3.
13. Robert (1990, p. xliii).
14. On the philosophy of adversary democracy in America and its alternative, see Mansbridge (1983).
15. This quote remains of such significance that it appears on the official history of the U.S. Senate available at http://www.senate.gov/artandhistory/history/minute/Senate_Created.htm. For the deliberative (and antideliberative) strains in Madison's political theories, see Wilson (1990).
16. Uslaner (2000, p. 34).
17. Ibid., pp. 36–37.
18. Quoted in ibid., p. 39.
19. Ibid., pp. 37–38.
20. Ibid., pp. 45–47. There was a momentary exception for Senate Republicans in the mid-1970s, but the trends are generally consistent across both chambers and parties.
21. Ibid., p. 49.
22. Weithman's (1995) philosophical defense of the deliberative perspective emphasized the importance of legislative deliberation as a model form—not necessarily in practice but in theory. The legitimacy of the social contract—our commitment to work within a binding political system—hinges on the deliberative quality of the process through which legislation takes shape.
23. Burkhalter (1997).
24. Burkhalter (2006). For an insider's view confirming these concerns, see Gore (2007).
25. Elving (1995).
26. Maltzman and Sigelman (1996, p. 828).
27. Bessette (1994, pp. 110–15).
28. Ibid., pp. 115–20.
29. Ibid., pp. 121–8.
30. Portions of this discussion of lobbying are adapted from Chapter 5 in Gastil (2000).
31. Salisbury (1986) reported the results of a survey of lobbyists in the early 1980s that show how lobbyists develop a professional expertise that transcends particular issue domains.
32. John Stauber and Sheldon Rampton's *Toxic Sludge Is Good for You* (1995) provided a very readable critique of public relations, which often supports lobbying campaigns.
33. Lewis's (1998) book, *The Buying of Congress*, is replete with such examples of successful lobbying, particularly by corporate interests.
34. For a critical analysis of lobbying as a means of preserving the interests of the economic elite, see Parenti (1995, Chapter 12). Parenti acknowledged the role of unions as a lobbying group but argued that their influence is weak relative to business interests. Dahl (1998) summarized the problem succinctly: "Because market capitalism inevitably creates inequalities, it limits the democratic potential of polyarchal democracy by generating inequalities in the distribution of political resource" (p. 177).

35. Fletcher (1998). Rosenstone and Hansen (1993) also found a clear relationship between income and campaign contributions based on Roper Surveys conducted in the 1970s and 1980s.
36. Bennett (1994, p. 297).
37. Edelman (1988, pp. 21–23).
38. Mansbridge (1992, pp. 501–2).
39. Bessette (1994, p. 50).
40. Ibid., p. 51.
41. Mooney (2005). An edited commentary on Mooney's book is available at http://www.parlorpress.com/pdf/lookingforafight.pdf. Al Gore has also described this phenomenon in his recent book *The Assault on Reason* (2007).
42. Janis (1982). This second edition was a substantially expanded revision of his 1972 book, *Victims of Groupthink*.
43. For a review and suggested revisions to the original theory, see Street (1997) and Park (1990).
44. Janis (1982, pp. 14–47, 132–59).
45. Rawls (1995, p. 231).
46. Ibid., p. 232.
47. Woodward and Armstrong (1979, p. 4).
48. Ibid., p. 80.
49. Samuels (2004, p. 7).
50. Woodward and Armstrong (1979, p. 442).
51. Ibid., pp. 442–43.
52. Kang (2004, p. 324).
53. Ibid.
54. The most famous contemporary example of this issue is the administration's insistence on protecting the Cheney Energy Task Force from public scrutiny. See "The Cheney Energy Task Force" at http://www.bushsecrecy.org/page.cfm?PagesID= 27&ParentID=1&CategoryID=1.
55. Bessette (1994, p. 223).
56. For a more detailed analysis of this problem, see Chambers (2004).
57. Levine, Fung, and Gastil (2005, p. 277).

SOURCE: iStockphoto. Used by permission.

6

Deliberation in the Jury Room

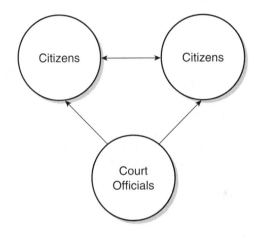

A jury consists of twelve persons chosen to decide who has the better lawyer.

—attributed to Robert Frost[1]

M any Americans, sooner or later, will receive a summons from a city, county, or federal courthouse requesting that they appear for jury duty. Many of us dread such a summons and view jury duty as a burden. One study even suggested that compiling the summons list from the list of registered voters causes people to cancel their registration just to avoid the specter of jury duty.[2]

Serving on a jury, however, is one of the few—if not the only—opportunity most citizens ever have to practice deliberation as a representative of the government (or, as political scientists call it, the state). After all, the normal role of a citizen consists of electing representatives who act as agents of the state—passing laws, and so on. As a juror, a citizen not only sees the state up close—through the workings of its judicial branch—but actually becomes an arm of the state, by virtue of the jury's authority to render verdicts and judgments in criminal and civil cases, respectively.

Consider the experience of one private citizen, D. Graham Burnett, who happened to receive a summons to appear for jury duty in New York City. He ultimately served on a jury for a murder trial, and he recounted his experiences in the riveting work *A Trial by Jury*. After hearing ten days of testimony and evidence regarding a gruesome Manhattan murder, the jurors retired for what would become four days of jury deliberation. The twelve jurors were as diverse in their backgrounds as they were in their opinions of the case. As the jury plowed through the evidence, a consensus began to emerge—with the jurors concluding that the accused may have, indeed, committed the murder but that the evidence was not strong enough to convict. Jurors worried that they might be holding the prosecution to too high of a standard. Were they taking too literally the requirement that guilt must be proven beyond a reasonable doubt?

As he prepared for the final day of deliberation, Burnett had the following insight:

> For the last three days, we had struggled to come to terms with the burden of proof that the prosecution had to meet: it seemed unreasonable, exaggerated, impossible. But here was a way to understand it: the burden of proof was so high exactly because the state was so powerful. . . . All of us probably would have agreed in the abstract, before the trial even started, that the state was powerful. But after four days of sequestration, we had developed a new and immediate appreciation of just what this power meant: the state could take control of your person, it could refuse to let you go home, it could send men with guns to watch you take a piss, it could deny you access to a lawyer, it could embarrass you in public and force you to reply meekly, it could, ultimately, send you to jail . . . without even accusing you of a crime. . . . For (mostly) law-abiding citizens with no experience of the criminal-justice system, with no experience of what it feels like to be made wholly impotent by the force of legal strictures and the threat of legal violence, this discovery had been shocking. . . . If we as a jury wanted to understand why the burden of proof fell on the prosecution, and fell with such gravity, we needed only to reflect on what we had discovered directly about the real power of the state and its agents.[3]

Burnett shared this view with the jury and swayed the last reluctant juror to agree to a not guilty verdict. What Burnett did not recognize, or at least acknowledge to fellow jurors, was that at the moment of rendering a verdict, they were the state. In essence, they were holding themselves to a high burden of proof. Once he left the courtroom, Burnett once again became subject to the powerful state apparatus. He and his fellow jurors had held up a democratic principle that requires proof of guilt beyond a reasonable doubt because one would want that same standard applied to oneself if the state ever chose to send "men with guns" to one's home.

A more familiar—and powerfully controversial—example of the jury's check on state power is the 1995 criminal murder trial of O. J. Simpson. Whatever one thinks of the jury's verdict, one member of the Simpson defense team pointed out that it had the effect of "setting a more demanding standard of performance" for the Los Angeles County coroner's office, crime laboratory, and police officers.[4] Regardless of the other evidence at hand, the misconduct of individual officers and the clerical and procedural lapses of crime lab staff were sufficient to sway the jury. In fact, two of the most renowned jury researchers reviewed the evidence presented at the trial and concluded that "the possibility of some evidence contamination seemed convincing" and that "some of the most incriminating bloodstains were questionable."[5] Since the Simpson trial, the higher bar that both officers and staff must now clear to win conviction increases the pressure on the state to conduct itself with the highest integrity and care when attempting to prosecute its citizens.

Neither the Simpson jury nor the one on which Burnett served tell the whole story. And it is vital that the experience of the American jury be told because it is the only institutionalized deliberative experience most U.S. citizens are likely to ever have. I begin the story by recounting the unique history of the jury system; then I define more precisely what it means for a jury to deliberate effectively. A review of the modern research record on juries then answers a series of questions: Do juries render good verdicts? How often are juries really deliberating? And how are juries woven into the larger fabric of civic life? This chapter concludes by considering how reforming the jury—and the larger legal system—might make juries an even more effective deliberative institution.

Legitimacy and the Origins of the Jury System

Before considering the contemporary practice of juries, it is important to understand the jury's historical origins. To understand the jury's history requires first understanding the relationship between deliberation and legitimacy. The idea of legitimacy is central to many modern theories of deliberation, and it merits a brief discussion in its own right.

LEGITIMACY AND DEMOCRACY

A decision is said to be legitimate in a democracy if the public consents to it as a legal policy arrived at by an appropriate decision-making body or executive.[6] The revolutionary cry of "no taxation without representation" is in this spirit; it challenges a tax policy's legitimacy on the grounds that it was established in a way that was illegal, inappropriate, and generally unworthy of the public's trust.

Recalling the definition of democracy introduced in Chapter 1, what distinguishes a democracy from noncoercive political systems, such as a pure anarchist collective, is a democracy's readiness to enforce its decisions on its members. In a benign anarchy, decisions are not binding on members—they are strictly provisional agreements reached by a provisional consensus. In a democracy, even those who nobly resist the law through acts of civil disobedience still must accept that their actions earn them time in jail.[7] Thus, in a democracy, it is critical that decisions have legitimacy, lest a restive public refuse to follow its laws.

In the context of deliberative democracy, political theorist John Dryzek argued that "outcomes are legitimate to the extent they receive reflective assent through participation in authentic deliberation by all those subject to the decision in question."[8] In practice, this can be a challenge. As we have seen thus far, it is a challenge to find compelling examples of authentic deliberation. The greater difficulty, however, is to somehow ensure "participation . . . by all those subject to the decision." In a nation, or even a large city, that is not practical. Thus, the conventional solution is to elect representatives, such as those discussed in the previous chapter. So long as the public elects them through a deliberative process and the representatives, in turn, demonstrate deliberative judgment, the public may come to view the decisions of these executives, legislators, and judges as legitimate.

There is another solution, however, and the jury illustrates this alternative. Rather than electing or appointing representatives, authority and deliberative responsibility can be placed in the hands of the public itself, as represented by a randomly selected microcosm. This approach solves the government's legitimacy problem by passing the problem on to the larger public. How the jury came to play such a role is the question to which we now turn.

THE CREATION OF THE JURY

Happily, there exists a voluminous historical record on the jury and its origins. One of the most entertaining and insightful syntheses of this historical record was written by William Dwyer, a federal judge who served many years in the Western District of Washington State. Dwyer viewed the jury as a "civilized fight"—an institution designed to civilize the resolution of conflicts through a ritualistic, formalized procedure culminating in the judgment of one's peers. "The first task of law," wrote Dwyer, is "to deal with raging quarrels—to stop anger from turning to murder."[9]

Prior to the jury system, Dwyer explained, the preferred method of resolving conflicts was "trial by ordeal," which had a "long and surprisingly successful run" across the globe. In England, where the jury was to first emerge, "there was no clear distinction between church and state," and there was no centralized state in the modern sense. The local priest was held to be the best judge of God's will, and when an accused remained steadfast in his or her professed innocence, the local priest would use trial by ordeal to divine the truth. One method was to severely burn the palm of the defendant's hand, bandage the wound, then check after an adequate stretch of time to see how the hand was faring. Spreading infection meant guilt, whereas a clean but scarred palm meant innocence—and only modest disfigurement. But there were alternatives, such as this:

> [T]he accused was bound, hands beneath knees, and lowered at the end of a rope into a pond sanctified for the purpose. If he floated he was guilty; the water had rejected him, and execution or mutilation would follow. If he sank he was innocent, as shown by the pond's acceptance of his body. The innocent, if lucky enough, would be fished out in time to avoid drowning.[10]

The shift from these and other methods of divine revelation to trial by verdict "took about two hundred years," from the arrival of the Norman conquerors in 1066 to approximately 1275, when "a statute directed that accused persons who refused to submit to jury trial be jailed under harsh conditions until they gave in."[11] What led to this shift? Among the causes was the inescapable fallibility of the ordeal and similar methods of judgment:

> Even the most devout began to feel skeptical when divine signs clashed with firsthand knowledge. A recognition grew that the outcomes could be wrong—the innocent hanged, or the guilty freed, as the cases were seen by human reason. The sense of injustice, a sometimes dormant part of our mental equipment, was awakening.[12]

Meanwhile, the Normans reached out to local noblemen to try to seize control over the scattered towns and principalities dotting the English countryside. These "sworn informants" served as a quasi-jury by reporting, under oath, on the size and productivity of local estates, such that the Normans could tax them all in proportion to their value. By 1166, this institution had spun off into the grand jury, whereby the local sheriff or royal judge periodically assembled a group of respected citizens and asked them to write up "a list of notorious criminals" in their locality.[13]

Behind the growing authority of these juries was "friction between church and crown." While King Henry II held the throne from 1154–1189, he systematically undercut the authority of the church, including such traditional practices as the ordeal. Simultaneously, the head of the church in Rome denounced the practice. The convergence of these changes, Dwyer wrote, "left a gaping void in English law. The ordeals were gone, but nothing was at hand to take their place." One might assume that into this legal vacuum would leap eager and power-hungry civil authorities, but local magistrates and judges, Dwyer explained, "were loath to seize for themselves the case-deciding power and the risks of blame and downfall that would come with it. . . . So they turned to a solution at hand—to the jury, which already existed for other purposes."[14]

In effect, the jury solved the local officials' legitimacy problem. The divine authority of the ordeal had vanished, and the authority of the existing royal officers in England did not always extend into the world of legal judgment. What the jury provided was a body that would weigh evidence and present a judgment seemingly independent from the local authority. That judgment would have the same mystical finality of a trial by ordeal, but poor judgments could now only raise doubts about the wisdom of one's fellow subjects—not judges or priests.

It would not be until 1671, however, that English law would establish that the jury could render a verdict independent of the opinion of the judge.[15] Jury deliberation emerged not as a check on state power but, essentially, as a means of shoring up the state's legitimacy. Over time, the jury would claim increasing independence and become a body with which the state had to reckon. The jury would come to challenge the state's prosecutorial ambitions, as in the cases introduced at the outset of this chapter, and juries would be the vehicle through which persons could successfully sue the state when its officials violated their own laws.

Defining High-Quality Jury Deliberation

Given its political origins, it is remarkable that most modern political communication scholars do not think of the jury as a political institution worthy of careful attention. Texts on politics and political communication generally omit the jury. Deliberation scholars have sometimes drawn the connection between juries and other deliberative practices, but this is often done to ask, skeptically, whether the average jury actually deliberates. Thus, political scientist Lynn Sanders argued that "when Americans assemble in juries, they do not leave behind the status, power, and privileges that they hold in the outside world."[16] In this view, juries do not deliberate in the fullest sense of the word.

The linguistic problem here is that, in the vernacular, all juries *deliberate*. When a judge sends a jury out of the courtroom to deliberate, the jury retires to the *deliberation room* and begins their *deliberations* on the case. In this text, though, we work with a more demanding meaning of the word *deliberation*. It might help to put it this way: In the case of juries, we can still ask whether their deliberation was of the highest quality. Thus, Figure 6.1 presents

Analytic Process	
Create a solid information base.	Consider all of the facts and testimony provided during the trial. Avoid adding personal experiences and biases.
Prioritize the key values at stake.	The paramount values are ensuring justice and the rule of law.
Identify a broad range of solutions.	The judge specifies a range of verdicts or sentences (judgment) the jury can give. No others are available.
Weigh the pros, cons, and trade-offs among solutions.	Consider whether each possible verdict or sentence upholds the relevant laws identified by the judge and serves the larger cause of justice.
Make the best decision possible.	Follow standards for reasonable doubt and other guidelines to render the appropriate verdict or judgment.
Social Process	
Adequately distribute speaking opportunities.	The foreperson and others should ensure a balanced discussion by drawing out quiet jurors and welcoming dissenting jurors to speak up.
Ensure mutual comprehension.	Speak plainly to each other and ask for clarification when confused. Ensure understanding of technical evidence or finer points of law.
Consider other ideas and experiences.	Listen carefully to what others say, especially when you disagree with their view of the case. Try to understand their unique perspective on the case.
Respect other participants.	Presume that each juror is honest and well intentioned. Remember that cases go to trial most often because the parties involved see the facts of the case differently.

Figure 6.1   Key Features of High-Quality Jury Deliberation

a definition of *high-quality jury deliberation.* I refer to *deliberation* as a short-hand for the longer *high-quality* phrasing, but the basic question is, what kind of talk does a jury engage in when it is in the midst of a high-quality discussion of a case?

LEGAL CONSTRAINTS ON DELIBERATION

The left-hand column in Figure 6.1 should look quite familiar by this point, as it includes each of the components of deliberation presented in the preceding chapters of this book. The right-hand side is quite distinctive, though, because juries have a special kind of task unlike any of the others we have seen thus far. What makes the jury special is that so much is preset by the court before the jurors even assemble in the courthouse, let alone deliberate.

Starting at the top of Figure 6.1, jurors receive their information base through the arguments, evidence, and testimony that attorneys and witnesses present to them. In fact, judges admonish jurors to only consider the evidence presented during the trial. In the 1957 movie *12 Angry Men*, the lead character stabs into the jury's meeting table a knife he bought at a store near the murder site.[17] He uses the knife to show that the murder weapon shown at trial was not unique—that the defendant's knife need not have been the same one used to commit the murder. In actual practice, such behavior constitutes grounds for a mistrial, with a juror expanding the information base set by the judge during the trial. As written in Figure 6.1, the deliberating jury is only to "consider all of the facts and testimony provided during the trial" and must "avoid adding personal experiences and biases" into their discussion.

High-quality jury deliberation also does not venture beyond the values of justice and the rule of law when weighing the case. One might think that values do not come into play at all in the best deliberation, with the jury merely applying the facts to the case and taking the law as given. As one justice typically instructed his jurors, they must apply to the facts of the case "the law as the court will give it to you. You must follow that law whether you agree with it or not."[18]

In fact, American juries have the right to "nullify" existing law when they believe that following the law is an unforgivable miscarriage of justice. Until 1894, this fact was well known to juries, who knew they were free to exercise their independent judgment, though asked to remain mindful of the law. In that year, the U.S. Supreme Court declared that the jury no longer had "the right to determine questions of law," yet it affirmed that juries still had the final say on cases.[19] In other words, juries retained their right to independence but lost the right to be informed of that authority. This paradoxical state of affairs has resulted in the occasional jury defying what they consider unjust applications of the law. Unaware of this power, and likely reluctant to disregard the law in any case, the practice is exceedingly rare.[20] Nonetheless, it is because of the authority of nullification that Figure 6.1 stipulates that juries are to consider the law itself and ensuring justice as the key values in judging a case.

As for the range of solutions a jury can consider, there are none but those provided by the court—often nothing more than a choice between guilty and not guilty or finding for the plaintiff or defendant. The evidence either supports or refutes these alternative verdicts or findings, and the jury ultimately must reach a decision that best upholds the law and justice in relation to the facts of the case.

Whereas the jury's discussion procedures and rules are highly structured, the social aspect of jury deliberation more closely resembles the general discussion process described in Chapter 2. In a high-quality deliberative process, jurors take turns speaking, address each other in terms they can understand, and consider carefully what each other has to say about the case. Like the Gricean maxims in Figure 2.2, the jurors presume one another's honesty and good intentions, even when honestly disagreeing about the facts of a case or the interpretation or application of the relevant legal statutes. Though within the narrow parameters of a legal proceeding, these are essentially the relational qualities of any deliberative discussion.

DELIBERATING BEFORE ENTERING THE DELIBERATION ROOM

One other feature of jury deliberation makes it special. Paradoxically, jury "deliberation" begins before the jurors even get to speak to one another face to face. Imagine yourself sitting on a civil trial in which you hear evidence for and against the contention that the defendant committed malpractice, causing the plaintiff to suffer avoidable complications after receiving cosmetic plastic surgery. During the course of the trial, you hear from experts who explain what can be reasonably expected from such surgeries, what routine risks they involve, and how often serious complications occur. You also see documents—legal contracts between doctor and patient, perhaps an e-mail exchange from after the surgery. Both parties testify, along with other character and ancillary witnesses, and the attorneys point you to relevant laws and precedents that support their arguments. How could you possibly absorb all that information without processing it? Could you somehow hold all these facts, claims, and arguments at once, without turning a single one over in your mind before formally deliberating as a jury?

The evidence suggests that jurors process information as it comes up during trial. Communication researcher Ann Pettus interviewed jurors who had recently completed trials and made the following conclusion for the average juror:

> The decision making process begins early in the trial. Points in the trial when the jurors make their decisions include: when they see the defendant for the first time, when the information is read, during opening statements, and during

the presentation of prosecution witnesses. While some jurors might form their opinions at specific points during the trial, others begin the process with the "sense" or intuition that the defendant is guilty or not guilty. As the trial proceeds, that decision becomes more certain. Thus, although jurors are instructed to wait to form an opinion until after all the evidence has been presented, this study indicates that they do not wait.[21]

Larger samples of juries have confirmed that jurors routinely make up their mind about a case before leaving the courtroom to deliberate. Jurors are ready to vote by the first straw poll (a nonbinding vote by ballot or raised hands to see where the balance of opinion lies), and in nine out of ten cases, the initial vote a jury takes predicts the ultimate outcome.[22]

Even if jurors could suspend their processing abilities until face-to-face deliberation began, it is not so clear that it would be advisable. Recall the discussion in Chapter 3 of Australian philosopher Robert Goodin's insight regarding the deliberation that occurs within us as we read fiction or watch a documentary. What he calls deliberation within is precisely what juries do while watching a trial. The only difference between them and someone sitting at home watching CourtTV is that the jurors are physically present in the courtroom. Except in those courts that permit jurors to ask questions (which I discuss later), jurors remain silent witnesses to the trial.

In Goodin's view, this is likely just as well because the independent judgments of individual jurors may add up to a more sound judgment than the verdict that would be reached through discussion. Here, Goodin deploys the Condorcet jury theorem. The gist of the theorem is that the probability of a group majority being correct rapidly increases as the group's size increases, so long as the members are assumed to have a better-than-chance likelihood of reaching the right decision.[23]

In the context of the modern American jury, this means that we should have a good deal of confidence in the initial majority that forms through jurors' independent weighing of the evidence in the case prior to meeting as a group. With regard to the definition of high-quality jury deliberation, this suggests that it is preferable that jurors begin their deliberations within—processing and reflecting on information as it comes up during the course of the trial. This should not lead them to reach fixed judgments, such that they are unwilling to yield their initial judgment as a result of deliberation. It does, however, mean that much of the important deliberation that occurs during civil and criminal trials takes place before the judge sends the jury to the deliberation room.

Jury Deliberation and Decisions

One of the reasons we pay so much attention to how and when jurors deliberate is that it can be difficult to judge the quality based on the result of the deliberation.

If we know that a jury overlooked key facts, misunderstood the relevant laws, or acted on impulse without reflection, we can say that the jury's deliberation was not of the highest quality and, on that basis, judge it as having failed to do its job. But is it also possible to judge the jury's final decision on its own merits? Before considering how well juries deliberate, we can attempt to judge the quality of jury verdicts.

JUDGING THE QUALITY OF JURY VERDICTS

The challenge with judging the output of any deliberative process is establishing an independent basis for making the judgment. After all, as Judge Dwyer's historical account of the jury explained, the point of the jury is to provide a means for rendering binding decisions in situations where there is at least some degree of uncertainty about the proper resolution of a civil dispute or criminal allegation.

One means of judging juries is to compare their verdicts to the opinions of the judges who presided over them. In the 1950s, Harry Kalven and Hans Zeisel of the University of Chicago Law School launched a project that undertook precisely this task. This single study, published in *The American Jury*, remains a benchmark in jury research, cited to this day despite being half a century old. It has been difficult to collect comparable data in the years since, so it remains necessary to lean on its findings.

As part of this project, five hundred judges completed questionnaires after 3,576 separate criminal trials, and in each case they reported how they would have ruled on the case had each been a bench trial (i.e., one in which the defendant relied on the ruling of the judge, rather than the verdict of the jury). In seventy-eight percent of the cases, the judge and jury would have reached the same verdict. For nineteen percent of the cases, the judge would have ruled guilty but the jury returned a not guilty verdict, and in the remaining three percent, it was the reverse. In a comparable number of civil trials, the judges and jury again agreed on seventy-eight percent of trials, with the judge alone ruling for the plaintiff in ten percent of cases and the jury alone finding for the plaintiff in the remaining twelve percent of cases.[24]

Kalven and Zeisel examined the cases of juror disagreement with judges and found that the juries were particularly lenient when defendants had no prior criminal record or the defendant came across in the trial as a sympathetic character. What did not cause the jury-judge disagreement was the complexity of the evidence in the trial, and this weighed against the interpretation that jurors were simply ignorant, careless, or confused.[25]

In the end, it is difficult to know in any absolute sense whether the jury was "right" or "wrong" in those twenty-two percent of cases where they disagreed with judges. Nevertheless, that they generally agreed should give us confidence that juries generally yield sensible verdicts. Moreover, to say that juries perform well in the United States is to say, frankly, that they perform well as a whole, since more than ninety percent of the world's trials occur in the United States.[26]

ARE JURIES REALLY DELIBERATING?

It could be, though, that juries are rendering sensible verdicts despite engaging in low-quality deliberation. In other words, even if juries are doing a good job of meting out verdicts, can we attribute their success to deliberation? The first answer is that we will, in an important sense, never know exactly what juries are up to in the deliberation room. Jury deliberation happens in private sessions, and only in a handful of rare exceptions has a judge allowed the recording of what happened in the jury room. Recall from the previous chapter that closed-door sessions can be conducive to more honest, deliberative legislative discussions, and for that same reason judges believe it is best that jurors not have their deliberation open for public scrutiny.

When judges allow researchers into the courthouse, they occasionally permit them to ask jurors a few questions about themselves and their experiences in the jury room. Researchers who want more in-depth data can stage their own mock juries—groups of people who come together as a simulated jury and discuss real or hypothetical cases. In these studies, mock jurors answer extensive questions about themselves and their jury experience, and researchers often videotape and transcribe the deliberation.

One finding that has proved consistent across studies of both real and mock juries is that about ninety percent of the time a jury ends up with a verdict that a majority of jurors favored before entering the deliberation room.[27] In the famous movie *12 Angry Men*, the lone dissenting juror sways his fellow jurors and turns the tide in favor of a not guilty verdict, but in reality such changes are uncommon. However, there is nothing that says that bona fide deliberation must produce dramatic swings in opinion. I already reviewed research showing that much deliberation within a juror's mind occurs before juries enter the jury room, and it is reasonable to expect the majority is more likely than not to have reached a reasonable preliminary verdict. As one review of past research concluded, it is remarkable that ten percent of trials result in a verdict shift: "Thus, the issue of whether or not deliberation matters essentially amounts to a choice between viewing the deliberation glass as 90% empty or 10% full."[28]

Regardless of whether the initial majority's view prevails, we can examine the process juries go through and compare it to the definition presented in Figure 6.1. One set of studies found that juries often proceed in one of two ways—either using a verdict-driven or evidence-driven style of decision making.[29] Verdict-driven juries typically begin with an initial straw-poll vote, in which jurors informally say (or write on secret ballots) which verdict they would support if it were an actual final vote. The discussion then proceeds through an analysis of the verdict options and the arguments for each. Remember that in many trials a jury has more than two choices. In criminal trials, guilty versus innocent is the basic choice, but often the defendant faces multiple separate charges, yielding multiple choices, or the jury must answer additional questions, such as when considering the aggravating or mitigating circumstances of a murder in a potential capital punishment case. In civil trials, juries often have to answer a series of questions and then choose from among a broad range of potential judgments or name an exact amount for an award. All told, there is often much for a verdict-driven jury to discuss without requiring it to sort through the evidence per se.

By contrast, an evidence-driven jury goes through a structured discussion of the testimony, physical evidence, judge's instructions, and arguments presented about each piece of information. Because it encourages a more thorough analysis of the law and evidence in the trial and allows more space for considering minority arguments about these subjects, an evidence-driven style better approximates the deliberative ideal in Figure 6.1. The happy news is that juries tend to be more evidence driven.[30]

The evidence-driven jury, however, is far from a fact-sifting machine. The most compelling account of jury deliberation to date suggests that juries instead sort through evidence looking for the most compelling story. Social psychologists Reid Hastie, Steven Penrod, and Nancy Pennington developed this narrative view of the jury in their landmark study *Inside the Jury*. Looking at how mock juries deliberated in the evidence-driven style, these investigators saw that jurors review evidence "without reference to the verdict categories, in an effort to agree upon *the single most credible story* that summarizes the events at the time of the alleged crime. And the early parts of deliberation are focused on the *story construction* and the review of evidence."[31]

A jury following this story model of deliberation proceeds through three overlapping but distinguishable stages, as described by Hastie, Penrod, and Pennington:

1. The jury begins by attempting to comprehend and organize the evidence "into one or more plausible accounts describing 'what happened' at the time of events testified to during the trial." In doing so, jurors draw on abstract understandings of how human behaviors typically sequence themselves; they try to fit the specific evidence and accounts into these more general "schema" to construct detailed but broadly comprehensible stories explaining the unfolding of events, as seen from the opposing sides in the trial.

2. Next, the jury tries to describe each "verdict category" (e.g., guilty or innocent) in terms of its "defining features and a decision rule specifying their

appropriate combination." For instance, a jury might ask itself, what does a not guilty verdict mean in terms of our understanding of the events described during the trial?

3. Finally, a jury seeks "the best match between story features and the verdict category features." Simply put, the jury asks which verdict category best fits the most plausible narrative account of events. In a criminal trial, did the prosecution or defense end up creating the most compelling story, as supported by the evidence presented at trial, and how well do their respective stories fit the verdict categories available? Once a jury finds the most plausible story that fits a verdict category, it is ready to return to the courtroom and report its verdict to the judge.[32]

One reason a jury might closely follow this deliberative sequence is that a foreperson guides jury members through each stage. Research has found that forepersons can have tremendous influence over the jury deliberation process and the outcome.[33] Though the foreperson is sometimes randomly appointed by the court, the jury often selects their foreperson, and juries tend to disproportionately appoint men and other high-status individuals.[34] This combination of factors should raise concerns about the adequacy of nonforeperson speaking opportunities, particularly if jury members hold a view (and a social status) different from that of an influential foreperson. Could the story model of deliberation lead the group to effectively exclude a juror who wanted to tell an alternative version of events? Even on criminal juries where the court requires a unanimous verdict, the pressure to conform to the majority view could silence dissent.

One of the most forceful critiques of deliberation came along these very lines. In her 1997 article "Against Deliberation," Lynn Sanders argued that "when Americans assemble in juries, they do not leave behind the status, power, and privileges that they hold in the outside world."[35] Sanders acknowledged that evidence-driven juries are likely to be inclusive of diverse views, but she insisted that "to meet the concern of equal participation," those advocating democratic deliberation should, at the very least, "explicitly attend to issues of group dynamics and try to develop ways to undercut the dominance of higher-status individuals."[36] Failure to do so might lead to privileging high-status views on matters of public (and sometimes explicitly political) controversy. Sanders saw a danger in high-status jurors being more likely to convict the accused (presumably to protect their property and the stable society they rely on for their status privileges), but the fact that individuals with more formal education lean toward political liberalism might counter than tendency,[37] given that educational attainment is likely one of the strongest status cues at work in the jury room.

It helps shed light on this controversy to ask jurors about their experience. Renowned jury researcher and legal scholar Valerie Hans found that both mock jurors and actual jurors tend to rate their deliberative experience very positively. In Hans's mock civil juries, for instance, the average juror rated the deliberative experience as a 7.3, close to the top of a ten-point satisfaction scale. By contrast, only 3.8% of all jurors gave a rating below the scale midpoint.[38]

This finding is consistent with a study of fifty-six juries that colleagues and I conducted in the Seattle Municipal Court. Our data permit a more careful look at jurors' perceptions of deliberation, and Table 6.1 summarizes the main results.[39]

The five survey items shown in the table correspond to different aspects of jury deliberation, as defined in Figure 6.1. In each case, jurors described their experience as tremendously positive. For example, on the five-point response

Table 6.1   Average Scores on Deliberation Measures in Fifty-Six Municipal Criminal Juries

Survey Item	Response Scale	Average	Percentage of Juries With Minimum Response Level		
			High (4–5)	Neutral (3)	Low (1–2)
Jurors thoroughly discussed the relevant facts of the case.	1 = Strongly disagree 5 = Strongly agree	4.52	89	9	2
The jury thoroughly discussed the instructions the judge provided.	Same as above	4.35	67	27	5
All of the jurors listened respectfully to each other during deliberation.	Same as above	4.41	89	7	4
The other jurors gave me enough of a chance to express my opinions about the case.	Same as above	4.50	95	4	2
How were you treated by fellow jurors?	1 = Less than satisfactory 5 = Excellent	4.40	71	24	7

scales given for each item, the average response was close to 4.5, and roughly ninety-five percent of the juries—about fifty-four out of fifty-six—had not a single juror deliberation rating below the scale midpoint. In other words, the overwhelming majority of jurors agreed that "the other jurors gave me enough of a chance to express my opinions about the case," "the jurors listened respectfully to each other during deliberation," and the juries thoroughly discussed both "the relevant facts of the case" and "the instructions the judge provided." Overall, seventy-one percent of jurors felt the treatment they received from fellow jurors was "excellent" or "very good."

This study also looked at juror participation in deliberation and found that eighty-nine percent of the jurors tried to "explain evidence or facts" to fellow jurors at least once. Ninety-five percent expressed their "own views" of the case at least once, with sixty-eight percent of jurors doing so "three or more times." These findings suggest a broad degree of at least minimal active participation in the discussion when it came to weighing evidence and stating points of view. By way of contrast, consider that forty-two percent of jurors did not "speak about" their "own experiences," with only fifteen percent doing so more than once or twice. In other words, jurors in this Seattle courthouse engaged in focused deliberation on the merits of the case through consideration of relevant evidence and law, rather than relying on their own personal frames of reference.

Again, because one cannot see into the jury room, the evidence of jury deliberation is always indirect. What we have seen thus far is that juries generally make high-quality decisions; that mock juries more often than not follow rigorous, evidence-driven discussion styles; and that jurors recall their experiences as being deliberative. Taken together, that constitutes sufficient circumstantial evidence to find the jury not guilty on all charges of incompetence, recklessness, and sloth.

Connecting Jury Service and Civic Life

There is another angle from which one can see the real power of jury deliberation. In 1995, law professor Vikram David Amar wrote an article in the *Cornell Law Review* that shed new light on the political significance of jury service. In that essay, Amar argued that jury service is closely related to other forms of political participation, particularly voting. The surface resemblance is obvious, in that the government calls on jurors to give their say in a very well-structured process, just as it calls on citizens to participate in regular elections. Moreover, "Jurors *vote* to decide the winners and losers in cases—that is what they do."[40] The connections run deeper, though; Amar pointed out that "the link between jury service and other rights of political participation such as voting is an important part of our overall constitutional structure, spanning three centuries and eight amendments." When we talk about participation rights, discrimination, and equal protection, we could be just as easily talking about jury service as voting, and the courts have ruled similarly on both forms of participation.[41]

The framers of the United States Constitution certainly viewed jury service as a critically important feature of self-governance and enshrined the right to serve on juries in the Seventh Amendment. Not long ago, the U.S. Supreme Court reaffirmed this view by noting that "with the exception of voting, for most citizens the honor and privilege of jury duty is their most significant opportunity to participate in the democratic process."[42]

However, from the time of the drafting of the Constitution to today, many defenders of the jury system have argued that it is more than a good way of resolving legal disputes: it is also a means of civic education.[43] The jury system has the ability to elevate ordinary citizens into self-governors. In the aforementioned U.S. Supreme Court ruling, the justices cited the French political observer Alexis de Tocqueville, the author of the popular 1835 monograph *Democracy in America*. In that classic work, de Tocqueville made the following point:

> The institution of the jury raises the people itself, or at least a class of citizens, to the bench of judicial authority [and] invests the people, or that class of citizens, with the direction of society. . . . The jury invests each citizen with a kind of magistracy; it makes them all feel the duties which they are bound to discharge towards society; and the part which they take in the Government. . . . I do not know whether the jury is useful to those who are in litigation; but I am certain it is highly beneficial to those who decide the litigation; and I look upon it as one of the most efficacious means for the education of the people which society can employ.[44]

The confidence that citizens take their responsibility to serve on juries seriously places jury service in a special role of ensuring popular oversight of the judicial process.[45] In theory, elections play a similar role in ensuring that the larger public holds sway over the legislative and executive branches of government. (Chapter 4, however, showed that voting in elections is not on par with jury service, at least in terms of the depth and quality of citizen deliberation.)

But do juries really lift the civic spirits of those who serve on them? In a series of studies, colleagues and I addressed this question by studying how jury service is linked to voting and other forms of political engagement in the United States. Our initial study looked at a single locale—Thurston County, Washington—home to the state capitol of Olympia.[46] We collected court and voting records for a period of years and merged them by matching jurors' full names with unique matching records in the voter database. This first study found that after controlling for other trial features and past voting frequency, citizens who served on a criminal jury that reached a verdict were more likely to vote in subsequent elections than were those jurors who deadlocked, were dismissed during trial, or served as alternates. The effect was augmented by the number of charges against the defendant, with trials including more charges yielding greater increases in jurors' voting rates.

A grant from the National Science Foundation made possible an extensive follow-up to the Thurston County study, and this study yielded three interrelated findings.[47] First, in-depth interviews with a small sample of jurors revealed that citizens typically recognize jury service as a basic civic duty, and two-thirds, without further prompting, compared it to voting. In other words, jurors drew a cognitive connection between jury service and voting.

Second, a data set gathered from Colorado, Louisiana, Nebraska, North Carolina, Ohio, and Washington found the same pattern of increasing voting rates, except that this larger data set revealed that the critical distinction was between those who deliberated (including hung juries) and those who did not. Once again, the number of charges against the defendant had an additional, significant effect on postservice voting rates. This study was also large enough to permit breaking down participants into two subgroups, and this analysis found that the increased voting effects were apparent only for previously infrequent voters (voting less than half of the time) who served on criminal trials. Frequent voters and all of those who served on civil juries did not have a significant increase in voting after jury service.

A third study looked in-depth at jurors in King County, Washington. By combining survey data with court and voting records, we found that subjective experience was also a critical variable in predicting changes after jury service. Specifically, results showed that for both empanelled jurors and those reporting for service but not empanelled, the degree to which the jury service experience exceeded their expectations was positively associated with increased postservice voting rates. In other words, those who found jury service to be better than they expected were more likely to vote in the future relative to those whose expectations were barely met (or worse). A follow-up study found that those with similarly rewarding jury experiences were also likely to have subsequent conversations about local and national affairs, stay informed about current issues, and engage in direct political action.[48]

Summarizing across these studies, meaningful participation in jury service can have a significant impact on people's broader civic participation. Whether it has such an effect depends on the person and the jury experience—with the clearest effect being for those persons who come into jury service with lower levels of civic engagement, have an engaging experience deliberating on a jury, and come away with a positive view of their time spent in the courtroom.[49] Others might restate these findings to say that when citizens get a tangible sense of procedural justice, playing meaningful roles in a public process in concert with responsible, respectful public officials, they come away with a renewed respect for larger democratic procedures and principles.[50]

This is, in the end, a kind of indirect evidence that juries are engaging in meaningful deliberation. We will likely never know if a neutral outside observer would view the jurors' thoughts and discussions about the trial as fully deliberative, but we now know that jurors not only rate their deliberations favorably but also change their behaviors in a way that shows a lasting impact of this experience.

Making Juries More Deliberative

To think about how juries can deliberate more effectively, we return to the desk of Judge Dwyer, who earlier gave us a history lesson in the origins of the jury. Judge Dwyer presided over numerous jury trials during his career, and by his account those juries demonstrated considerable wisdom. He reflected that "in the rare instances where I have thought the jury went astray, no celestial sign reveals that I was right and the jury was wrong."[51]

Nonetheless, after reflecting on his own courtroom experiences and after reviewing the literature on juries, Judge Dwyer concluded that there are "six deadly sins" commonly practiced in the courtroom—or in the larger legal system—that interfere with the jury's important work. The jury system would be even more remarkable if the court system confessed these sins and repented through reform. On the following pages, Figure 6.2 shows the sins and the path to absolution for each, and it may be surprising to learn that Dwyer, himself a judge, found that much of the blame lies with his fellow judges. Dwyer insisted that most of the reforms outlined here "can be accomplished, with no amendment of the rules, simply by judges using their existing powers to make trials better."[52] Some require changing state laws, but even then the remedy does not call for radical change in the essential nature of the system. The most far-reaching reform (equity) might require considerably more investment in the system of public defenders, but that is simply making good on a promise already written into law.

Conclusion

The civic benefits of jury deliberation cannot be taken for granted because the jury system is perpetually under attack. Many other countries have scaled back or eliminated juries over the past century,[53] and in the name of procedural efficiency, many U.S. courts have reduced the size and frequency of jury trials.[54] The plea-bargaining process has further reduced the deployment of criminal juries, and many critics suggest drastically reducing the use of civil juries or dispensing with them altogether.[55] Even without the most radical reforms, there is already a trend toward decreased reliance on jury trials. Plea bargaining, alternative methods of dispute resolution, and other changes in the legal

The Sin	The Absolution
Overcontentiousness. The adversarial trial system is designed to present both sides of a dispute clearly, and it is adversarial to its core as a contest among rival viewpoints. However, there is no need to let courtrooms become overly contentious, with attorneys throwing up smoke, demonizing the opposing view, and spending more time on nonspecific assault and caricature than on evidence.	*Decorum.* Just as deliberation among jurors requires respect, so might judges require both sides in a trial to refrain from theatrics. Lawyers need to tell stories to explain their evidence, but they need not transform the courtroom into a playhouse to do so. Respectful disagreement helps the jury avoid polarizing and failing to review the evidence because it is caught up in the conflict.
Expense. Many potential defendants and litigants have strong cases but cannot afford to marshal all the necessary evidence. This leads criminal defendants to plea bargain prematurely and leads some civil plaintiffs to forgo trial altogether. When these cases go forward, the courtroom often has one side outmatched by the other simply because of the differential in resources.	*Equity.* The courts must take seriously the responsibilities of the public defender and make sure that a poor defendant has no disadvantage in the trial. Judges can also limit the glitz of a high-priced legal effort by requiring modesty in the style and manner of courtroom presentations. The reward is that more persons get their day in court, and the juries get a more balanced trial from which to draw their verdicts.
Delay. The stereotype of a slow trial is not always apt, as many trials last only one to three days. Some trials, though, drag on for weeks, and even the brief ones often include unnecessary delays. The jury experiences many of these delays, but even more occur before the case finally comes to trial. As the saying goes, "justice delayed is justice denied," so all of these slowdowns have a real price. When they occur during trials, they can make juries restless and confused. Word also gets out, and jurors avoid service for fear of being caught in the tedium of a slow trial. Those jurors who can least afford to take time off from responsibilities at work or home become, effectively, excluded from jury service.	*All due haste.* Judges have considerable control over the pace of a trial. Opposing counsel may want more time when they believe it will benefit their side (or steal momentum from the opposition), but judges should keep a trial moving forward. If judges ask both sides to limit their repetitiveness, everyone in the courtroom benefits. In the end, jurors will have a more focused trial and will be able to deliberate more effectively. Moreover, juries will better represent the wider community, as trials will ask for less of their time.
Aimlessness. A close cousin of delay, this is when a trial digresses into an unfocused, purposeless exercise. A lax judge can let opposing counsel review documents and witnesses at a level of detail irrelevant to the core issues in the trial. Summary arguments can become orations that stray far beyond the point. The sum of all this is a trial that even CourtTV fans would declare unwatchable, and this can lead jurors to become bored and distracted.	*Focus.* Once the jury arrives in the courtroom, both sides should know their tasks and carry them out efficiently, not digressing or unnecessarily drawing out testimony. A well-organized and fast-paced trial should not move so quickly that a jury cannot keep up, but it can move at a steady pace that keeps the jurors interested and alert. The reward is a jury that has less clutter to sift through and can recall the key facts of the case when deliberating toward a final verdict.

The Sin	The Absolution
Hypertechnicality. Some measure of technical detail is often necessary in a trial, as when a criminal investigation involves DNA evidence or a civil case requires reviewing a company's finances. Hypertechnicality, however, is when a trial digresses into a level of detail not germane to the trial and even leads to technical debates between dueling expert witnesses that have no bearing on the case at hand. There is a real danger that in these cases, jurors become confused.[a]	Plain talk. The only beneficiary of hypertechnicality is to the side in a trial with a weak case that must rely on a smokescreen of meaningless detail to sway the jury, or at least make them feel unable to reach a verdict due to hopeless confusion. Judges can ensure that testimony and evidence not digress beyond what is pertinent and comprehensible. More radically, judges can bring in court-appointed experts to offer a neutral view of complex evidence and investigative methods. In some cases, jurors have even received simple notebooks summarizing—at an appropriate reading level—the nature of complex evidence. Juries in such courtrooms will be able to grasp even complicated cases and reach reasoned verdicts.
Overload. Nearly all of the aforementioned sins contribute to what may be the most grievous problem in the court system—the overcrowded court docket. When cases soak up unnecessary hours and pretrial shenanigans waste a judge's time, less time is available to even get to, let alone try, the new cases that arrive each week. On top of this, many cases of limited significance—particularly the more petty, nonviolent, drug-related offenses—crowd out other cases that come before the court. The consequences are legion, including distracted judges, pressure for plea bargaining, and the herding of jurors like cattle.	Sensible law, adequate resources. A two-pronged approach is necessary to overcome this challenge. We must always consider the consequences of our actions when writing new laws. Every statute forbidding an action—along with every new police cruiser crawling down the street—promises to heap more cases on an already overloaded system. Thus, we must show restraint when criminalizing and policing, but we must also ensure that the courts have sufficient resources to try the cases we bring before them. With enough judges and staff, and with first-rate courthouses, we can make the juror feel like a respected magistrate, rather than a hurried member of the herd. Better treatment, in this case, ultimately leads to better behavior, with jurors feeling they have been given the time and resources necessary to do their job.

Figure 6.2   The "Sins" of the Court System and How to Seek Absolution for Them

SOURCE: Adapted from Dwyer (2002, chapter 7).

a. See also Hans (2000, pp. 222–25).

system have reduced the rate at which cases come to a full jury trial. In federal courts, the percent of criminal charges that end in jury verdicts dropped from 10.4% in 1988 to 4.3% in 2000, and the percent of civil cases resolved by juries declined from 5.4% in 1962 to 1.5% in 2000.[56]

Numerous scholars share the general public's concern about stagnant voter turnout, low levels of social capital, and limited civic voluntarism in American society.[57] The jury could prove a bulwark against further civic erosion. Others who question the extent of America's civic decline could still recognize that the jury, like other public institutions, plays a valuable role in sustaining a healthy civic culture.[58] Regardless, once the jury is recognized as perhaps the most explicitly deliberative public institution in American government, it is likely to be understood as more than merely a means of administering justice in the courts. Though the jury is not often a political body in the cheap sense of staging partisan political conflicts, the deliberative perspective highlights its vital role in a democratic society. The jury serves as a classroom where citizens learn how to deliberate in the wider array of public meetings held in one's community. It is to these meetings that we now turn our attention.

Notes

1. Frost quotation from www.quotationspage.com.
2. Oliver and Wolfinger (1999).
3. Burnett (2001, pp. 160–61).
4. Uleman (1996).
5. Hastie and Pennington (1996).
6. Parkinson (2003, pp. 182–84).
7. For an extended discussion of this issue, see Dahl (1989, Chapter 3).
8. Dryzek (2001, p. 651). Habermas (1975) was an early, influential writing on the relationship between system legitimacy and public discourse.
9. Dwyer (2002, p. 11).
10. Ibid., pp. 29–30.
11. Ibid., pp. 31, 35.
12. Ibid., pp. 32–33.
13. Ibid., p. 33.
14. Ibid., pp. 34–35.
15. Ibid., p. 58.
16. Sanders (1997, p. 364).
17. Henry Fonda won an Oscar for his portrayal of this character (Juror #8, aka "Mr. Davis").
18. This is how Judge Dwyer instructed his juries in federal court. See Dwyer (2002, p. 61).
19. Ibid., pp. 72–73.
20. Jonakait (2003, p. 258).
21. Pettus (1990, p. 94).

22. The figure comes from Kalven and Zeisel (1966, pp. 488–89). For a review of previous research, see Leigh (1984).
23. Goodin (2003, pp. 95–96).
24. Kalven and Zeisel (1966).
25. Ibid.
26. Casper and Zeisel (1972, pp. 135–36).
27. Field studies of actual juries include Kalven and Zeisel (1966) and Sandys and Dillehay (1995). An example of a mock jury study with this finding is MacCoun and Kerr (1988).
28. Devine et al. (2001, p. 701).
29. See Hastie, Penrod, and Pennington (1983, pp. 163–65); Hastie, Schkade, and Payne (1998).
30. Hastie et al. (1983) and Sandys and Dillehay (1995).
31. Hastie et al. (1983, p. 163, emphasis added). The idea of a story model of jury deliberation originated in Pennington's doctoral dissertation, as reported in Hastie et al. (1983, p. 22).
32. Hastie et al. (1983, p. 22).
33. On process, see Manzo (1996), Simon (1967), and Strodtbeck and Lipinski (1985); on the outcome, see Boster, Hunter, and Hale (1991) and Eakin (1975).
34. Boster, Hunter, and Hale (1991); Beckham and Aronson (1978). See generally Hans and Vidmar (1986).
35. Sanders (1997, p. 364).
36. Ibid., p. 367.
37. See Phelan et al. (1995), who give a more precise analysis of the liberal spirit imbued by education.
38. Hans (2000, pp. 226, 260).
39. Adapted from Gastil, Burkhalter, and Black (2007).
40. Amar (1995, p. 205).
41. Ibid., p. 206.
42. *Powers v. Ohio* (1991, p. 407).
43. See the 1997 uncredited research note "Development in the Law, the Value of the Civil Jury," *Harvard Law Review* 110: 1421–41.
44. de Tocqueville (1835/1961, pp. 334–37).
45. See Gastil and Weiser (2006).
46. Gastil, Deess, and Weiser (2002).
47. Gastil, Deess, Weiser, and Larner (forthcoming).
48. Gastil and Weiser (2006). This and other studies on the civic impact of jury service are available at the Jury and Democracy Project Web site at www.jurydemocracy.org.
49. Studies have also demonstrated that voting and participating in campaigns can have similar reinforcement effects on participants (Finkel, 1985; Green and Shachar, 2000). What makes the jury findings more remarkable is that they have connected very distant cousins (jury service and voting) among the behaviors that make up public engagement.
50. Besley and McComas (2005, p. 427). Segall (2005) extended this view to procedures like citizen juries, discussed in Chapter 7; in this view, the key to juries' civic impact is that they entrust citizens with real responsibilities, rather than asking them to "just talk." On the effects of deliberation on citizen efficacy, see Fishkin and Luskin (1999) and Morrell (2005).

51. Dwyer (2002, p. 136).
52. Ibid., p. 178.
53. Vidmar (2000).
54. See Dees (2001), Hans (2002), and Hans and Vidmar (1986).
55. Adler (1994).
56. Glaberson (2001).
57. Putnam (2000).
58. For a critique of civic decline, see Bennett (1998). On institutions, see Skocpol and Fiorina (1999).

SOURCE: iStockphoto. Used by permission.

7

Citizens and Officials in Public Meetings

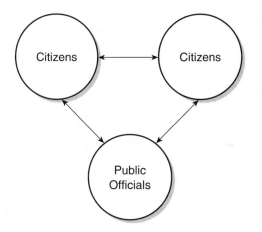

One of my fellow council members would occasionally start a public hearing by announcing that he already knew what position each witness would take. And he was usually correct. I figure I spent nearly 2,000 hours in formal public hearings over the last eight years. It was not time well spent.

—A former county council member in Maryland[1]

L et's be clear about something at the outset of this chapter: Holding a series of public meetings can be a complete waste of time. By comparison with the juries discussed in the previous chapter, participants in a public meeting may never reach a verdict or have any direct or indirect influence on policy, themselves, or anything else. Like the hearings recounted by the Maryland council member quoted in the opening of this chapter, public meetings can be a formal process that accomplishes precious little. More often than not, such meetings are far from deliberative.

That said, there have been many deliberative public meetings both large and small that have changed our social and political landscape. Many of these meetings succeed by breaking out of the mold of conventional public hearings and the like, bringing together citizens and policy makers in novel settings and for special purposes.

The recent experience of British Columbia, Canada, provides a good illustration of this new kind of public meeting. But first, a little history. As in the United States, British Columbia's provincial elections (akin to U.S. state legislative contests) occur in geographically separate districts, with the top vote-getter in each district (called a riding in Canada) being elected to the provincial assembly. By winning with narrow margins in key districts, a party can capture a majority of district elections with less than a majority of the overall vote. In 1996, the New Democratic Party (NDP) won thirty-nine percent of the votes across the province yet managed to retain a majority in the house (thirty-nine out of seventy-five seats). The party winning the second-most seats, the BC Liberals, won a greater proportion of the total votes yet earned fewer seats. This prompted the Liberals' leader, Gordon Campbell, to promise that if the Liberals won a majority in the house, they would create a special citizen body to reform the system by which votes are counted in the provincial elections.

In 2001, the BC Liberals won fifty-seven percent of the vote provincewide, and the same distortion occurred, this time in their favor: the Liberals took a remarkable seventy-seven of the seventy-nine seats in the province. In spite of winning nearly every seat under the existing electoral system, Premier Campbell pushed forward the proposed idea of having average citizens develop campaign reforms, and this came to fruition in the 2004 British Columbia Citizens' Assembly.

The assembly consisted of 160 randomly selected citizens, one man and one woman from each riding, plus two at-large aboriginal members. Over the course of the year, the assembly met face to face several times to study different electoral systems and consider how they could be adapted to British Columbia. The assembly also held public hearings across the province, giving the general public the chance to comment and offer suggestions as the assembly weighed different alternatives to the current electoral system. In October 2004, the assembly voted 146 to 147 in favor of replacing British Columbia's electoral system with a single transferable vote model, which lets voters rank candidates within multimember districts.[2]

Photo 7.2   Citizen Assembly Members Meet Face to Face at the Morris J. Wosk
Centre for Dialogue in Vancouver, British Columbia

SOURCE: BC Citizens Assembly. Used by permission.

Part of what made the assembly's meetings unique was the power they
wielded. From the outset, it was understood that the assembly's recommendation would be put before the people of British Columbia for ratification.
Indeed, the assembly's proposal was submitted to the electorate as a referendum
in the May 17, 2005, provincial election. A majority of voters in seventy-seven
of British Columbia's seventy-nine ridings approved the assembly's proposal,
with fifty-seven percent of all votes cast in favor of the proposal. Unfortunately,
British Columbia's legislature had set the bar for passage at sixty percent of the
popular vote. Because of the large majority supporting the proposal—and
because of the short duration of the campaign—British Columbia's government chose to let the voters consider the proposal one more time in 2009.

The British Columbia Citizens' Assembly was a bold step forward. In 2006,
the province of Ontario convened an assembly of its own, with 103 of its citizens deliberating on the same question of electoral reform, followed by a referendum vote in 2007. The assembly concept has spread beyond Canada, with
advocates for the process appearing in California, Australia, the Netherlands,
and elsewhere. A serious proposal based on the British Columbia model is
under consideration in California.[3] Other innovative public meeting designs
have appeared across the globe in recent years. We look at many of those in this

chapter, but before doing so, it is useful to step back and look at some of the historical meeting designs that have shaped the practice of public meetings.

Archetypal Public Meetings

An archetype is something that inspires numerous derivations, copies, or imitations. In popular culture, the character of Superman provided the archetype of the superhuman with a secret identity and hidden weakness (kryptonite, in Superman's case), and the man in tights spawned countless subsequent heroes, nearly all of whom wore tight clothing, had a set of special powers, maintained a secret identity, and could be thwarted (albeit only temporarily) once their arch-enemy figured out their weakness.

Similarly, in the world of deliberative public meetings, some archetypes continue to stimulate (and sometimes constrain) the public's imagination to this day. The most prominent of these is the Athenian assembly of ancient Greece. By 400 BCE, Athens had solidified a model of citizen deliberation that certainly had terrible flaws by modern standards—principally the exclusion of all but a subset of Athenian males. Nonetheless, Athens was an exceptionally democratic government for its time.

Princeton classics professor Josiah Ober wrote a series of books on this period of Greek history. As he explains in *Mass and Elite in Democratic Athens: Rhetoric, Ideology, and the Power of the People*, citizens governed through an interlocking set of institutions:

> The primary decision-making bodies were the citizen Assembly, the legislative bodies of Lawmakers. . . , and the popular courts. All of these bodies met openly; the Assembly and courts met frequently. Assembly meetings were open to all citizens; boards of Lawmakers and juries were selected randomly and by lot from the citizen body. The Agenda of the Assembly was determined by the Council, whose members were selected annually, by lot, from the entire citizen population; discussion in the Assembly was open, and every citizen had the right to take part in it, although normally members of the elite took the most active part. The decisions of the Assembly were subject to review only by the people's courts. The decisions of the courts were final. . . . Virtually all important legal judgments were by popular juries who decided legal disputes on the basis of Athenian law and their own ideological predilections.[4]

Despite their differences, it is easy to trace connections from the bodies of lawmakers to the modern legislatures described in Chapter 5 and from the popular courts to the modern jury described in Chapter 6. The Athenian assembly, in turn, is the model for many modern forms of deliberative public meetings, many of which also bring a random sample of laycitizens together for face-to-face deliberation. The British Columbia Citizens' Assembly has each of these features, including the *assembly* label.

Nevertheless, the Greek archetype has a feature often overlooked by its modern imitators, and it is important to keep it in mind when critiquing modern practices. Recall that Ober noted that although all Athenians could speak before the assembly, "normally members of the elite took the most active part." This was due, in part, to the logistics of conducting decisive assembly meetings in a reasonable period of time with eight thousand citizens in attendance. The limited time of deliberation in relation to such a large assemblage of citizens required a procedure that could filter out the most important speeches that could influence the assembly's weighty decisions.[5]

The informal solution to this problem was the emergence of professional rhetors, whom we might today call politicians, pundits, or, perhaps, public intellectuals. The rhetors were those the citizenry had "recognized as active political experts" and who "addressed the Assembly frequently and who competed in political trials with other rhetors."[6]

Just as the contemporary term *politician* has at least as many negative as positive connotations, saying a speaker was "able or clever at public address" could have negative implications. The word *demagogue* comes from a Greek word (*demogogos*) that could be used for praise or scorn, and the word *rhetoric* carries mixed meanings even today.[7] In sum, when the Athenians brought the general public together to meet and conduct business, they still presumed that there were special roles within those participatory processes for the most educated, articulate members of the community. Even in this archetypal democracy-by-lot meeting, in other words, there was role specialization among participants.

A second archetype for the modern public meeting, at least in the United States, is the New England town meeting. Political scientist Jane Mansbridge looked to these meetings in her 1983 book *Beyond Adversary Democracy*, one of the forerunners of modern deliberative democratic theory. She chose to focus on town meetings in the state of Vermont because of that state's unique political history. "In all the other New England states," she explained, "settlement took place under the auspices of a larger, central government." The lands within the modern state of Vermont, by contrast, were "subject to no superior authority" because New York and New Hampshire were fighting over them. Only when the independent towns in the area saw an advantage in joining the Union in 1777 did they come together to draw up a state constitution.[8]

These towns were the essential political unit in Vermont, governing themselves through regular meetings of the full electorate. In practice, only twenty to sixty percent of those eligible actually attended, though as many as three-quarters might attend during times of sharp conflict. (As in ancient Greece, many people did not qualify as full citizens: nonwhites, women, and landless males were excluded from the meetings.)

What makes the town meetings of Vermont such a powerful archetype was that everyone who chose to attend the meetings had a vote and could, in theory, have a say during the deliberation. Though townsfolk typically elected boards and clerks to handle the day-to-day business of their community, they also conducted business at the town meetings. Thus, the meetings were a kind of direct democracy in which the educated political experts, charismatic leaders, and rank-and-file citizens came together to debate and settle the issues of the day.

Did such meetings attain an exceptional level of public-spirited deliberation? After reviewing the records of these historic meetings, Mansbridge concluded that "although communities were more highly integrated than they are today, descriptions of the meetings suggest that feelings of duty and concern for the public weal were mixed with the call of private interest." In Mansbridge's view, there never was "a golden era" when Vermont towns "could act as pure unitary democracies." Instead, consensus on local policy came only after suppressing "the interests of the least powerful" and asking the larger public to "put their trust in the kinds of men who had always held power in the town."[9]

It is not too far a stretch to say that this process of elite leadership within the context of an otherwise egalitarian, participatory town meeting bears much resemblance to the emergence of gifted rhetors in Athens. In both cases, the general public retained direct authority but let itself be steered by influential local elites. In both cases, it is likely that minority views did not get the hearing they probably deserved. As Mansbridge observed in the case of a contemporary series of meetings in one Vermont town, "The deference accorded the expert, in particular, or even majority opinion often leads to premature closure" of debate.[10]

Whatever their merits, the town meeting remains a vital piece of local government throughout New England. Table 7.1 shows that these meetings govern over eight percent of the towns in five states, along with sixty-five percent of the towns in Rhode Island. Regardless of the limitations of the actual meetings, like the Greek assembly, the New England town meeting archetype continues to inspire modern conceptions of deliberation. Often the idea is simply to adapt the historic town meeting with modern communication technology to create an "electronic town meeting" or a "town meeting for the 21st century."[11] More subtly, the norms emergent in town meetings, such as disciplining oneself to speak to the issue, become broader, taken-for-granted cultural norms.[12]

Other times, the influence of the town meeting model is more profound. In their 1989 manifesto, *The Vermont Papers*, political reformers Frank Bryan

Table 7.1   Proportion of New England Towns Governed by Town Meeting

	Maine	New Hampshire	Vermont	Massachusetts	Connecticut	Rhode Island
Number of towns	497	221	246	312	169	31
Number of town meetings	475	197	230	262	160	20
Percentage of towns governed by town meeting	96	89	93	84	95	65

SOURCE: Williamson and Fung (2004, p. 7).

and John McClaughry took the Vermont example further than have any others. They argued that smaller is better in almost all aspects of policy making. They suggested handing over state, county, and even some town power to newly formed political units they called shires. A Vermont shire would usually draw together two or three towns, although the one or two cities in the state would have more than one shire. A constitutional convention would establish the shires, the boundaries of which would then evolve as citizens suggest joining or leaving their original shires. The authors claimed that these shires would benefit society by connecting people more directly with policy making. At the heart of each shire's government would be, of course, participatory town meetings, which, the authors argued, still serve to empower citizens and help them form a strong sense of local identity.[13]

Fortunately, one need not return to ancient Athens or break apart one's state or province into shires to get a taste of the Greek assembly or the Vermont town meeting. Instead, it is easy to see how the best features of these historic bodies live on in contemporary deliberative meetings. Before looking more closely at the contemporary practices these archetypes have influenced, however, it is useful to begin by describing an ideal public meeting from the deliberative perspective.

Convening a Deliberative Public Meeting

What would a modern public meeting look like if it were fully deliberative? The answer is a recipe that combines the ideals of conversation and discussion described in Chapter 2 with the deliberative legislative and jury models detailed in Chapters 5 and 6. Changing the proportion of each set of ingredients yields a different public meeting. Put in more conversation and you get a public meeting of assorted participants engaging in dialogue and sifting through the public's different views. Put in more legislative formality, and you get an agenda-setting and decision-making body with special roles for experts and elected representatives. Fashion it more like a criminal jury and you get a citizen panel that hears testimony and then deliberates on its own.

The hypothetical public meeting described in Figure 7.1 is a relatively even mix of these ingredients. The figure presumes that the meeting already has an agenda in place, but there is no reason the same process could not be used to decide what to put on the agenda at a future meeting. Regardless, the public meeting's analytic process relies both on professional research and personal experiences to establish its information base. This language stresses that there is a role in this process for both the content expert and the laycitizen. For example, imagine a public meeting discussing where to build a new transitional home for persons leaving the state prison. The meeting's deliberation would benefit from hearing statistics on the number of persons released into the community each year, recidivism (the rate at which former inmates become repeat offenders), and so forth, but it would also be valuable to hear the personal, emotional experiences of both former inmates and community members who have had ex-convicts as their neighbors, for better or worse.

LINKING EXPERTS AND LAYCITIZENS

This balance between the role of expert and laycitizen is not unlike the difficult balancing between the local elites and the general public in ancient Athens and colonial Vermont. Moreover, the balancing act becomes even trickier when moving beyond building an information base. Prioritizing the public's central concerns and aspirations requires integrating the public's articulation of its core values with technical and legal expressions and social, economic, and environmental costs and benefits.

For instance, when a member of the general public makes a value statement in a public meeting, it may sound like this: "I fear for the safety of my kids if we willingly invite into my neighborhood known violent criminals, even if the state tells me they've been 'reformed.'" It is easy enough to hear the value (public safety, particularly for the most vulnerable residents), and one can even ferret out a value trade-off (public safety of the community prioritized over the personal liberty of the ex-con). But often it is necessary to calculate a more precise weighing of those values. How much liberty can be sacrificed in the name of how much public safety? And sometimes neutral experts with no personal

Analytic Process	
Create a solid information base.	Combine expertise and professional research with personal experiences to better understand the problem's nature and its impact on people's lives.
Prioritize the key values at stake.	Integrate the public's articulation of its core values with technical and legal expressions and social, economic, and environmental costs and benefits.
Identify a broad range of solutions.	Identify both conventional and innovative solutions, including governmental and nongovernmental means of addressing the problem.
Weigh the pros, cons, and trade-offs among solutions.	Systematically apply the public's priorities to the alternative solutions, emphasizing the most significant trade-offs among alternatives.
Make the best decision possible.	Identify the solution that best addresses the problem, potentially drawing on multiple approaches when they are mutually reinforcing.
Social Process	
Adequately distribute speaking opportunities.	Mix unstructured, informal discussion in smaller groups with more structured discussion in larger groups. Create special opportunities for the reticent.
Ensure mutual comprehension.	Ensure that public participants can articulate general technical points and ensure that experts and officials are hearing the public's voice.
Consider other ideas and experiences.	Listen with equal care to both officials and the general public. Encourage the public to speak in their authentic, unfiltered voice.
Respect other participants.	Presume that the general public is qualified to be present, by virtue of their citizenship. Presume officials will act in the public's best interest.

Figure 7.1   Key Features of Deliberative Public Meetings

stake in the issue can introduce the real policy trade-offs overlooked by passionate community members: If the released prisoners will not live in a transitional halfway house, where will they live? If not in your community, then in whose? A successful public meeting facilitates a back-and-forth discussion between citizen and expert that can move both the public and policy makers in attendance to a level of values clarification never before reached. In the same way, this interplay can lead to a rigorous, thorough assessment of pros and cons that yields a well-informed and reflective decision.

BRIDGING THE OFFICIAL WITH THE UNOFFICIAL

The final decision reached in a public meeting often differs from that of a legislative body because a public meeting is not limited to legislative choices. When public meetings are held within a smaller geographic area, such as a neighborhood, town, or small county, the meeting participants and their extended social networks can represent a critical mass of local residents. As such, they possess the capability of implementing communitywide solutions that rely on social influence and local norms more than legislative rules and formal enforcement mechanisms. Thus, Figure 7.1 notes that public meetings often need to "identify both conventional and innovative solutions, including governmental and non-governmental means of addressing the problem." In the example of the halfway house, one part of the solution might be raising the level of community awareness about the new facility—something that is often better accomplished by resolving to keep each other informed through informal conversation than by legislating an official communication channel. Because of the value of these extragovernmental approaches, the best solution may, in the end, draw on multiple approaches that are mutually reinforcing.

A decision that incorporates both official policy and informal social commitments presumes a healthy working relationship between public officials and the larger community. The social process of a deliberative public meeting should strengthen that relationship. In this sense, mutual comprehension and considering other ideas and experiences refer to communication between citizens and public officials. All participants should "listen with equal care to both officials and the general public," but there is greater stress on ensuring that public officials and "experts and officials are hearing the public's voice." This emphasis reflects the fact that the gathered public has been attuned to hearing the voices of elites and experts since the earliest meetings of the Athenian assembly.

Even if the experts and officials need to be reminded to listen to the voices of the laycitizens, both elites and citizens often need a reminder to show respect. Not too long ago, a national survey of U.S. citizens found that the general public held an exceedingly negative view of their elected officials.

Eighty-eight percent agreed that "government leaders tell us what they think will get them elected, not what they are really thinking." Seventy-three percent reported believing that "politicians work for themselves and their own careers, not the people they represent."[14] These views are certainly true for some public officials, but there is little evidence that these constitute apt descriptions of most elected officials, particularly at the local level. The job of school board member, city councilor, or even state legislator is often a thankless, underpaid job sought more by idealists and reformers than it is by self-interested manipulators.

Thus, to ensure sufficient respect for public officials, citizen participants in an ideal deliberative public meeting are asked to presume officials will act in the public's best interest. This does not forbid skepticism, nor does it prevent a citizen from recognizing when an official does, in fact, go back on what he or she promised at a public meeting simply for personal or political gain. What it does require, though, is the willingness to work with public officials in a constructive partnership based on a provisional—but real—mutual trust.

In turn, of course, public officials must "presume that the general public is qualified to be present, by virtue of their citizenship." If citizens suspect selfish, political motives on the part of public officials, the officials (and nonpolitical experts present at the meeting) tend to doubt the wisdom and goodwill of the citizens present. Even to the extent that citizens are obtuse, officials and experts must work with the public they have. After all, in a democracy, the public has the final say on how it governs itself. This does not mean officials and experts should facilitate mob rule. On the contrary, constitutional and other legal protections of minority rights supersede the whims of the majority. Nonetheless, until the public transforms into a violent or tyrannical mob, officials and experts must accept that citizenship alone entitles the public to make its voice heard.

PROCESS DESIGN

The description of an ideal public meeting in Figure 7.1 leaves unanswered an important question: How does one design a deliberative public meeting? The conversations and discussions in Chapter 2 tend to be loosely structured, whereas legislative and jury deliberation in Chapters 5 and 6 tend to be rigidly structured in particular ways. Mediated and electoral deliberation, described in Chapters 3 and 4, are system-level processes that cannot be structured in the same way as face-to-face processes. Public meetings, however, can come in a wide variety of designs, and how one designs the meeting has great significance for which kind of talk takes place.

Throughout this chapter, it will be important to notice how meetings are orchestrated—who is invited, how the agenda is set, how the meeting's task is framed, and how the discussion is organized. Different configurations of participants and varied discussion procedures constitute different solutions to the problems posed by public meetings, particularly the challenge of balancing public values and experience with expert insight and the perspectives of public officials.

One example of such a design concern is in the recommendation for ensuring speaking opportunities, outlined in Figure 7.1: "Mix unstructured, informal discussion in smaller groups with more structured discussion in larger groups. Create special opportunities for the reticent." The idea of using different discussion formats within the context of a single public meeting reflects the fact that every design has its advantages. In this case, relatively informal small-group discussions are used to ensure that the quietest participants get their chance to speak. More specific procedures within these groups might involve the use of something as simple as a round-robin format, wherein the discussion proceeds in a circle from one person to the next. This removes the need to seize the floor through a quick interjection or interruption. You don't even need to even raise your hand. When it's your turn, it's your turn.

More complex design issues come up in every public meeting of consequence. What are the roles of public officials? When do experts get the chance to speak, and how will the laycitizens get the chance to query experts and use them as a resource? How much time in a meeting should be devoted to absorbing information versus engaging in open-ended discussion? As we discuss different kinds of public meetings and their varied outcomes, consider the consequences of the different designs being deployed in each case.

The Default Process: A Public Hearing

Perhaps because of the mundane nature of public meetings, there has been relatively little research to date on their conventional practice.[15] When public agencies or officials seek to interact with the public in formal meetings, the gatherings that take place are often unremarkable in their design and consequences. One of the basic purposes of public meetings is to give the public the chance to be heard in the context of an ongoing legislative deliberation,[16] and the most common form of such meetings is the public hearing.

The term *public hearing* has been used at times to refer to any kind of public meeting, but here we consider a more specific form of meeting. As defined by government scholars Abigail Williamson and Archon Fung, a public hearing is "an open gathering of officials and citizens, in which citizens are permitted to offer comments, but officials are not obliged to act on them or, typically, even to respond publicly." By these researchers' estimates, thousands of state and federal public hearings occur each year, many of them fulfilling public meeting requirements written into law.[17]

At its best, the hearing brings together—or at least juxtaposes—opposing views on current issues of importance, such as a proposed piece of legislation or a crumbling bridge that needs to be repaired or replaced. A public hearing can bring the public's many voices on the matter into a single room and record their interplay.

When this exchange of ideas and perspectives is inclusive of different perspectives, and involves attentive listening and clear articulation, it can amount to a kind of public deliberation. A sincere meeting between a school board and a group of concerned parents, for instance, can change the way both parties view an issue, as well as how they see one another. Careful discussion and debate can cause people to critically examine the problem they face, their own perspectives, and the views of their opponents. This leads citizens toward a more enlightened understanding of their interests and a more accurate understanding of the policy problem under discussion. This, in turn, can lead to an articulate presentation of the public's shared and divergent interests.[18]

In practice, public hearings routinely fail to resemble even a crude form of deliberation. Often conducted as a straightforward way of meeting federal, state, or local public meeting requirements, a typical hearing has citizens take turns speaking before a panel of government agency employees and elected officials. Public policy scholars Thomas Webler and Ortwin Renn witnessed hundreds of hearings in the United States and abroad, and their experience suggests that neither citizens nor policy makers value the public hearing process:

> To a citizen, the thought of attending a public hearing immediately conjures up negative images. Citizens often picture the public hearing process as disempowering. Typically, attendance is slight. To regulatory officials, experts, and project sponsors, the public hearing hall is a battle zone. Legal obligations must be met, hopefully without raising the hackles of the local populace. A well-attended meeting is bad news.[19]

Webler and Renn suggested that public hearings usually fail to produce deliberative and influential public deliberation both because of their timing within the policy-making process and the "structure of discourse within the public hearing process."[20] When public officials schedule hearings late in the process after they have reached a preliminary (or final) decision, the hearing only permits citizens to complain or implore a change in plan. Under those circumstances, the process becomes adversarial because citizens perceive that those "hearing" their input have already chosen to ignore it.

The structure of discourse at public hearings is a more subtle problem. Even when an elected official convenes a hearing before making a decision, the typical public hearing encourages a nondeliberative process by constraining public expression to a series of statements and limiting official response to periodic counterpoints. Hearings also tend to frame issues in an unduly technical manner, making it difficult for well-meaning citizens to address officials in their own terms.[21] Daniel Fiorino, the director of the Waste and Chemical Policy Division at the U.S. Environmental Protection Agency, acknowledged that when agency hearings are held, they "usually do not allow interested parties much of a chance to engage in full discussions with the agency and other parties or to influence the outcome" on issues before the agency.[22]

One increasingly common variation on the public hearing invokes the New England tradition with the name *town hall* or *town meeting*. On these occasions, officials invite the general public to discuss a particular issue with them. Depending on the topic, timing, and advance publicity, the meeting rooms typically become either empty meditation chambers or rousing political theater houses. When attendance is light, there can be a pleasant informality at such affairs, but there is little discussion. The attendees at a given meeting might include a few party activists, one or two residents who saw a note in the paper, and possibly a fretful lobbyist who has had trouble getting a one-on-one meeting with an official. The poor attendance can give representatives the impression that the public does not care about an issue or that it endorses whatever position the official might have.

Other town halls draw large crowds and may result in bedlam. In the view of some observers, the tendency toward acrimony and name-calling at public meetings is on the rise.[23] Daily newspapers routinely provide accounts of hostile adversaries sparring with one another at these public events, with the proceedings making little progress. The fear of such a result often leads forum organizers to design a highly formalized meeting process, rather than let opposing sides both air and debate their views.

When the House Republicans set out to orchestrate a public discussion on immigration reform in 2006, they chose to hold public hearings of this variety. Ruben Navarrette, a member of the editorial board at the *San Diego Union-Tribune*, witnessed the first of these and found the event "cynical and cowardly." Since the hearings concerned legislation on which Congress had already voted, he asked, "Why hold public hearings on bills that have already passed? . . . Besides, these aren't really public hearings per se; committee members don't hear from the public, as much as from invited guests—many of whom simply tell committee members what they want to hear." Moreover, Navarrette found that the House members hosting the hearings usually "spend more time talking than listening," and this event was no exception.[24]

One common alternative to this sort of meeting is to hold an online town hall, perhaps with the hope that in this format, cooler heads would prevail. A reporter for the *Boston Globe* recently found that such sites have proliferated but may now be falling out of favor:

> Randy Perry, vice president of Virtual Town Hall LLC, which helps create and run official Web sites for 57 municipalities in Massachusetts, said many cities

and towns ask if they should host official message boards, and his company advises them not to because of the pervasive lack of civility. At the request of two municipalities, in Connecticut and New York, the company closed two message boards because of the unbridled attacks.[25]

Few of these sorts of public meetings prove both deliberative and influential, and almost none are representative of the larger population. The most comprehensive study of participation in public meetings found that in the United States in 2003, twenty-five percent of citizens reported attending one or more such meeting in the past year. The overwhelming majority (eighty-five percent) of those who had not attended any meetings said that they had never been invited to one. Those who attended were somewhat more educated and affluent than nonattenders, but it is striking to compare meeting goers with those who participated in neither meetings nor other forms of political talk (conversations, Internet chats). Sixty-nine percent of meeting attendees had at least some college experience, compared with only thirty percent of those outside of the ongoing public discourse. Only twenty-one percent of meeting attendees made less than $30,000 in household income during the previous year, but a majority (fifty-one percent) of noncommunicators had a comparable income.[26]

Most public representatives recognize that meeting attendees are not a representative cross-section of the population and sometimes dismiss contrary sentiments expressed at public meetings on those grounds. As an anonymous county commissioner remarked to an investigator, "I think frequently you get your vocal minority" at public hearings "instead of a balance of opinion."[27]

Finally, there is the problem of integrating the perspectives of technical experts with those of laycitizens and activists. Sociologist Nina Eliasoph described the difficulty that environmental health activists had in trying to participate meaningfully in public meetings regarding the construction of a toxic incinerator. From the perspective of the officials running the meetings, the role of citizens is to request and receive information, but as Eliasoph explained, "Not all questions of citizenship can be addressed with information alone." In theory, she explained, "activists have no reason to object to technical and bureaucratic language." After all, "scientific language discovers physical, chemical truths" and "bureaucratic language discovers rules for democratic accountability, by tracing decisions through the agencies that control decisions." Over time, however, the activists began to object to the officials' approach, "because officials used bureaucratic and scientific languages to crowd other ways of talking and reasoning out of the conversation. Publicly minded reasoning and moral reasoning were 'out of place' in public."[28]

Once again, this is not to say that a conventional public hearing is always fraught with these problems. But the considerable expenditure devoted to run-of-the-mill public meetings often yields poor attendance, perfunctory public interaction with officials, and few tangible outcomes. Given that many public agencies are required to hold public meetings, it is important to understand how one can design more deliberative, productive meetings.

Deliberative Meetings With Elected Officials

In response to the problems with conventional meeting designs, public-spirited government officials and civic reformers have invented and implemented a wide range of innovative meeting designs. What these all have in common is a format and purpose aimed to promote deliberative talk among participants. Talk in these public meetings sometimes veers toward the kind of heated debate seen in well-attended public hearings, and it sometimes digresses into the kind of idle conversation one might see at a poorly attended hearing. More often than not, though, each of these designs generates considerable deliberation.

Figure 7.2 compares the design of three of the many different kinds of modern public meeting formats in terms of the deliberative criteria introduced earlier. Each of these meeting designs brings public officials together with the general public and the stakeholders.

A stakeholder is just that—a person who holds a stake in a given decision. As used in the public participation and management literatures, the term has come to refer more specifically to persons who represent organizations, communities, or alliances that have a particular stake in a decision. The less-flattering term *special interest representative* is often an apt label, but a stakeholder might speak on behalf of interests or groups that are more general than special, such as public health.

TWENTY-FIRST CENTURY TOWN MEETING

It is best to start with the meeting format that inherits the already-familiar town meeting tradition. In 1995, Carolyn Lukensmeyer founded America*Speaks* to find a way to better expose public officials to the values and common sense of the general public. Years of experimentation with different meeting design elements led Lukensmeyer and her colleagues to develop the ambitiously named 21st Century Town Meeting (hereafter, Town Meeting). America*Speaks* has held more than forty such Town Meetings spread over more than half of the states in the nation.

This format is powerful because it can bring together hundreds—or even thousands—of people to develop and record their collective judgment about a specific issue in the course of a single day.[29] Lukensmeyer offered the following description of the format:

	Twenty-First Century Meeting	Sequenced Forums	Municipal Council
Analytic Process			
Create a solid information base.	Participants read briefing materials and interact with experts.	Experts central to planning process.	Well-informed stakeholders are central players.
Prioritize the key values at stake.	Values emerging in separate groups are integrated in plenary.	Citizen forums flesh out underlying values.	Stakeholders represent distinct interests and values.
Identify a broad range of solutions.	Briefing materials introduce range of solutions; more arise in discussions.	Citizens and experts both contribute design ideas.	Stakeholders advocate and debate competing solutions.
Weigh the pros, cons, and trade-offs among solutions.	Discussion structured to force consideration of trade-offs.	Experts apply criteria systematically to various designs.	Stakeholders and officials present key pros and cons.
Make the best decision possible.	Participants privately express their views, which are integrated in the plenary.	Officials select design based on citizen input and expert analysis.	Council reaches a final decision by consensus or vote.
Social Process			
Adequately distribute speaking opportunities.	Emphasis on small groups promotes broad participation.	Mix of venues creates different opportunities for citizens and experts.	Regular meetings provide ample time for all participants.
Ensure mutual comprehension.	Small groups let participants move at their own pace.	Weak links among events could cause misunderstanding.	Ongoing interaction lets participants develop knowledge.
Consider other ideas and experiences.	Mixing participants in small groups promotes discovery.	Citizens learn from experts and vice versa.	Professional stakeholder roles promote advocacy over dialogue.
Respect other participants.	Direct interaction and cooperation in groups promote mutual admiration.	Honoring distinct expert and citizen roles may foster mutual appreciation.	Equality of influence on council essential for maintaining mutual respect.

Figure 7.2   Comparison of Three Public Meeting Designs Integrating Citizens, Stakeholders, and Public Officials

The day begins with brief opening comments from key political leaders, to set the context for the issues under discussion. Participants begin by answering a series of demographic questions using polling keypads, both to get oriented to the technology and to find out who is in the room. Before any deliberation on key content, there is a vision- or values-based discussion to allow participants to learn what is important to them regarding the issues at hand. The critical vision or values identified by participants lay the foundation for the next four to five hours of discussion on key issues and policy options. . . . In each segment of the agenda, discussion begins at individual tables, is themed in real time, and is then presented back to the whole for clarification and modification, and, finally, for voting.[30]

To get a sense of this meeting, imagine yourself participating in one of the better known America*Speaks* Town Meetings, the "Listening to the City" forum held in New York City on July 20, 2002.[31] Had you attended, you would have found yourself among more than four thousand fellow New Yorkers, along with city planners, public officials, and various advocates and activists. Most of the day you would have remained seated at a round table along with a facilitator and people hailing from different parts of the community. What brought you all together was a concern about what to build at the site of the former World Trade Center.

Periodically, the insights of your small-table discussions are integrated with those from other tables through the use of computer technology and a theme team: Each table submits a list of values, concerns, or ideas, and a team of trained facilitators integrates those into a manageable number of core themes, which then appear on a giant screen that everyone in the room can see. Back and forth it goes, with each stage of the agenda building on those before it. After identifying the most important values connected to rebuilding lower Manhattan, groups then move on to considering various proposals for the site,

Photo 7.3   Thousands Gather at a New Orleans 21st Century Town Meeting in 2006

SOURCE: © Lenny Lind/CoVision 2006. Used by permission.

using those values as a basis for evaluation. Or at least, that's what you would have done had you been there.

The impact of this particular town meeting was considerable. The headline in the *New York Daily News* said it all: "Plans for WTC Ripped: So, Back to the Drawing Board." Though the Town Meeting also yielded new ideas and concrete suggestions, the bottom line was that the development process had misjudged—or failed to take into account—the public's real priorities for rebuilding the World Trade Center site. The redevelopment plans that emerged in October of that year reduced the amount of office space and included many specific ideas from the Town Meeting, such as the construction of at least one tall building to connect with the larger New York City skyline.[32]

SEQUENCED FORUMS

A limitation of the Town Meeting format is that it sometimes happens in something of a vacuum—a one-day event that may make a splash but is soon forgotten. As it happens, the Listening to the City forum fed into an ongoing design process, but an alternative meeting design explicitly intersperses large public gatherings with more focused meetings that work out the details of public policies.

I have dubbed this second meeting type *sequenced forums,* a name that is unlikely to stick but that describes the key feature of this process—a sequence of well-integrated forums.[33] One concrete example comes from Pennsylvania, where a team of scholars, city planners, and concerned citizens joined forces to create the Penn's Landing Forums. The forums aimed to inject into city waterfront planning a more clear and influential public voice.[34]

One of the cocreators of the forums was Harris Sokoloff, a University of Pennsylvania professor who works in both the Graduate School of Education and the School of Design. Sokoloff and his colleagues organized a series of events that sharply defined the roles played by policy makers, technical experts, the public, and the media. The sequence of the Penn's Landing Forums let each party step to the forefront at each of the six stages:[35]

1. The first event was a panel presentation that integrated insights from realtors, waterfront designers, architects, developers, and historians. The information base created by the panel was echoed through articles in the *Philadelphia Inquirer* and a project Web site.

2. The next event brought together Philadelphia residents to set the criteria for evaluating waterfront development. Recruitment through the *Inquirer* brought a large but not entirely representative set of citizens to the meeting. The event began with an overview of the background information on Penn's Landing, then citizens broke into small groups to discuss their experiences and ideas, ultimately arriving at seven principles that future development at the landing

must follow. Principles included keeping it a publicly accessible space, making it a distinctive signature site for the city, and making the Delaware River a prominent feature in any design.

3. Organizers then used these principles to create three design scenarios. This was a closed process involving the forum staff, who drafted three loose scenarios that incorporated core principles and also highlighted conflicting ones. The choices presented were a public park, a new neighborhood, or a tourist attraction.

4. Next, the forums team convened a design charrette, which is an intense and focused work session aimed at solving a design problem. This one was not open to the public, but rather included "well-known local architects, planners, landscape architects, engineers, economists, artists, students, and faculty members." The charrette participants created a design for each scenario, and these appeared in the *Inquirer* and project Web site.

5. The *Inquirer* invited city residents to a final public meeting held at a museum on Penn's Landing. After providing summaries of each design scenario and a reminder of the previously established design principles, organizers randomly assigned the 350-plus participants to small groups. In a process incorporating elements of a 21st Century Town Meeting, participants discussed the scenarios at length and then provided summary ratings of each one, with the results presented at the end of the meeting for everyone to see the public's preferences.

6. The capstone event was a summary of the process by the organizers themselves. Sokoloff and other organizers wrote an *Inquirer* commentary on the final meeting and delivered a final report to the mayor, who also heard a detailed presentation on the process and its recommendations. In this final stage, the emphasis was on communicating effectively with public officials, and the message appeared to get through. The mayor has continued to use the principles and, consequently, has redirected development at Penn's Landing.[36]

There are many distinctive features to the Penn's Landing Forums, but the most important feature of the more general sequenced forum approach is to assign special roles to experts, citizens, and policy makers. In this case, the meeting process experts served to frame questions and distill recommendations, whereas the content experts provided background and fleshed out alternative choices. Citizens established principles and made recommendations, whereas policy makers—the mayor, in particular—ultimately considered and acted on those principles and suggestions.

MUNICIPAL COUNCIL MODEL

A third approach, the municipal council model, suggests a way to convene regularly scheduled public meetings to address ongoing policy problems, rather than special issues, such as rebuilding at the World Trade Center site or reinvigorating a waterfront. In this third model, the general public not only regularly participates in meetings with government officials, but the public also maintains a degree of direct control over policy. Whereas the 21st Century Town Meeting or the sequenced forums aim to inform and influence duly elected public officials, this third model gives citizens and stakeholders positions of power within government.

This idea of participatory government can be challenging for those accustomed to the representative model of government. Even one of the most famous advocates of direct democracy, the eighteenth century French philosopher Jean-Jacques Rousseau, lamented, "It is impossible to imagine that the people should remain in perpetual assembly to attend to public affairs." He believed in the power of local governance, whereby the public might be divided into small electorates that maintain an intimate relationship with their representatives, but even he did not hope for anything more.[37]

Two centuries later, and across the Atlantic Ocean, the seemingly impossible notion of perpetual assembly has taken root in South America. In 1988, Brazil adopted its seventh constitution after a long period of autocratic military rule. This modern constitution created a framework for governance that emphasized the role of direct public participation in governance. The most widespread participatory institutions emanating from this constitutional arrangement are the municipal councils, which oversee specific policy areas.

One glimpse of this system is provided by Vera Schattan P. Coelho, a researcher at the Brazilian Center of Analysis and Planning, and her colleagues. They analyzed the design and outcomes of Municipal Health Councils, which have responsibility for developing and implementing local health care delivery plans. There are well over 5,000 local health councils in Brazil, and they have directly involved more than 100,000 citizens in setting health policy across the country.[38]

The first defining feature of the municipal council model is how it balances membership among different stakeholder groups. Half of the thirty-two seats on a council go to members of civil society—the network of voluntary civic and social organizations prevalent in democratic societies. These sixteen seats include social movement organizations promoting public health, associations representing the needs of people with disabilities or particular ailments, as well as general labor unions. Another ten seats go to organizations representing professional health care providers (e.g., doctors and nurses, clinic staff) and producers (e.g., pharmaceutical companies). Finally, six seats go to governmental institutions, principally the municipal health secretariat, which is the official administrative branch of the council. Thus, government employees hold fewer than one-fifth of the council seats, and experts occupy roughly a third of the seats, with the remaining seats going to diverse stakeholder groups representing the general public and those with special health care needs.[39]

The second key feature of the council is its explicit authority. As Schattan P. Coelho and her colleagues explained, "The strength of these councils largely lies in the law that grants them veto power over the plans and accounts of the health secretariat. If the council rejects the plan and budget" drafted by the secretariat, the federal "Health Ministry does not transfer funds" to the municipal secretariat.[40] The council can exercise this veto power when it gathers its full membership in the Deliberative Assembly, a body that meets at the secretariat's headquarters each month, as well as any time the health secretary (acting as the council's president) or a majority of its members declares the need for a special meeting. The participants at assembly meetings make all decisions and remain open to public observation.

How deliberative are the actual meetings? Unfortunately, there exists no systematic accounting of actual proceedings on the council. Though Coelho is optimistic about the long run, she has expressed concerns about the distribution of information among council members. Limited "access to and dissemination of relevant information," she explained, "makes it more difficult to establish the cooperation essential for the exercise of *controle social*," a Portuguese term that roughly translates as government accountability to the larger society.[41] The authors stressed that "all the participants in deliberative processes of this kind have all the relevant information needed for deliberation." Unfortunately, "in the model of democracy prevalent in most countries, the bureaucracy has the majority (if not the totality) of the information necessary for the decision-making process" and this thwarts "effective participation."[42]

In spite of problems such as this, what makes Coelho hopeful is the structure of the council. After all, the government has a fraction of the council's seats, and if a majority of council members have difficulty accessing information or comprehending the proceedings due to government obfuscation, they can simply veto the secretariat's budget or plan. A prolonged deadlock can be painful for all health care stakeholders, but the local secretariat, if it wishes to maintain its federal funding through the federal Health Ministry, ultimately must work as a partner with the other council members.

The other representatives on the council come to the council meetings having already developed considerable expertise in their particular niche of the health care system or larger society. Trade unionists know a great deal about labor relations, nurses know about patient needs and their own working conditions, and so on. Elected for no more than two consecutive two-year terms, these stakeholders also gain considerable council-specific expertise in the course of their service.

STAKEHOLDERS AND THE GENERAL WILL

Each of these three processes relies to varying degrees on stakeholders as key participants, with the Brazilian municipal health councils relying entirely on stakeholder representatives. From the standpoint of deliberative theory, this approach raises a particular concern. If rogue gene-sequencers found a way to reanimate Jean-Jacques Rousseau, á la *Jurassic Park*, the French philosopher would delight in the municipal council model but would surely worry whether an assemblage of special interests could truly discover the "general will." Groggy from having his body reassembled, Rousseau might decline an impromptu speech and simply read the following passage from his 1762 treatise, *The Social Contract*:

> There is often a great deal of difference between the will of all and the general will; the latter considers only the common interest, while the former takes private interest into account, and is no more than a sum of particular wills. . . . If, when the people, being furnished with adequate information, held its deliberations, the citizens had no communication one with another, the grand total of the small differences would always give the general will, and the decision would always be good. But when factions arise, and partial associations are formed at the expense of the great association, the will of each of these associations becomes general in relation to its members, while it remains particular in relation to the State. . . . If the general will is to be able to express itself . . . , there should be no partial society within the State, and . . . each citizen should think only his [or her] own thoughts.[43]

Rousseau's assembly would bring together all of the citizens in a municipality (or nation) to speak only for themselves, not for any special interest. But quoting from the very same chapter, Rousseau might hesitate and rediscover his more practical side. He reasoned that when factions arise, as they inevitably do in large societies, "It may then be said that there are no longer as many votes as there are men [and women], but only as many as there are associations." Put another way, the factionalized society becomes one association, one vote. Moreover, Rousseau added, "If there are partial societies, it is best to have as many as possible and to prevent them from being unequal. . . . These precautions are the only ones that can guarantee that the general will shall be always enlightened, and that the people shall in no way deceive itself."[44] In the end, Rousseau's suggested framework sounds a good deal like the seat allocation in the municipal council model, with interests spread across a wide range of factions and balancing the voluntary sector against the professional and governmental factions.

Citizen-Centered Public Meetings

Nonetheless, Rousseau's dream of the general will continues to disturb the sleep of those seeking to create more deliberative public meetings. Many models of citizen deliberation have emerged that limit experts and stakeholders to the role of advisors, making the rank-and-file citizenry the centerpiece of the public meeting process. More specifically, these citizen-centered models have all stressed the importance of bringing together a representative microcosm of the public to simulate the assembly-of-all imagined by Rousseau.

The purpose in bringing people together is not simply to marvel at seeing society sitting in a single room, something that often captures the imagination of an onlooker who sees a deliberative event for the first time. Rather, the point is to have the public brush up against itself—to have citizens present with others whose views differ from their own. Contemporary political philosophers, civic reformers, and even economists have argued that something transformative happens in these settings. The public discovers itself, and individuals can come to think and speak in terms of something like Rousseau's general will. Even if citizens persist in disagreeing with one another, deliberating together can enlarge citizens' perspectives in a way that yields different decisions than had they simply studied the issue privately and then had their views aggregated.[45]

The problem is that even well-intentioned efforts, such as the Penn's Landing project or Listening to the City, inevitably draw out particular sectors of the population more so than they do others, and the citizen-centered approach puts a premium on addressing this problem.[46] How, then, can one efficiently and reliably bring together a microcosm of the general public?

RANDOM SAMPLES

The solution is to draw a random sample. We have already seen how one can create a representative microcosm through modern random-sampling methods. Chapter 3 showed how random-sample public opinion polls changed how the media gathered public opinion, and the proposals for Deliberation Day and citizen panels in Chapter 4 demonstrated how random samples could be incorporated into elections. Even the jury process, described in Chapter 6, takes a stab at gathering a random sample. Finally, this chapter began with the British Columbia Citizens' Assembly and its distant forerunner, the Athenian Assembly, both of which also drew participants by lot.

The definitive work on the use of sampling in democracy is *Random Selection in Politics*, by Australian researchers Lyn Carson and Brian Martin. Combining expertise on science, technology, government, and public participation, Carson and Martin reviewed both ancient and modern arguments for random sampling, along with the various means through which the samples are employed. The examples range from paying randomly selected citizens to ride a public bus and report on their experience to sponsoring intensive "planning cells" and "consensus conferences" that have randomly selected citizens work through public problems.[47] It is important to note that in many cases, participants were not simply invited but were also paid for their labors, receiving at least compensation for travel and often an honorarium or substantial hourly wage.

Their careful review of the historical record led Carson and Martin to conclude that random selection "is a significant tool to transform politics. On its own it can increase fairness in decision making," but, when "integrated with deliberation and consensus building, it can become a powerful means to achieve social justice and genuine democracy."[48] Though not always popular among those already in positions of power—whether as elected officials or influential stakeholders—the random sample approach makes it possible to bring together Rousseau's citizens who "'think only their own thoughts.'"

Carson, Martin, and other like-minded Australians have applied this principle in a wide range of contexts. They have used the other two methods to be introduced in this chapter—deliberative polls and citizen juries—to address local, regional, and national issues in Australia. Even when combining procedures, they always foreground the random sample of citizens to ensure that the general public has a strong voice in the process.[49]

THE DELIBERATIVE POLL

The most famous of all random-sample procedures may be the deliberative poll, which blends conventional large-sample surveys with group discussion. A deliberative poll begins with a predeliberation poll, followed by the distribution of a discussion guide. After participants meet and deliberate face to face (or online[50]), in small groups and in large assemblies with experts and officials, they complete a postdeliberation questionnaire. The main "finding" of any deliberative poll is the change in public opinion that occurs over the course of the deliberative event.[51]

The poll's originator and champion is James Fishkin, the same political communication professor whose Deliberation Day proposal was introduced in Chapter 4. Fishkin devised the deliberative poll to find a way for the general citizenry to reason through morally complex public problems together. Fishkin argued that a deliberative opinion poll can create "a direct face-to-face society for its participants and a representative institution for the nation state." The results of a deliberative poll are "something that begins to approximate what the public *would think*, given a better opportunity to consider the questions at hand."[52]

When Fishkin originally proposed the deliberative poll in 1988, other experiments in modern random sample democracy had already taken place, such as the televote, planning cells, consensus conferences, and the citizens jury (discussed later).[53] A television network had already invented the Granada 500, which brought five hundred English voters together to discuss contemporary political issues with candidates.[54]

Since its inception, more than fifty deliberative polls have taken place across the globe. One of the most carefully studied deliberative polls was the 1996 National Issues Convention (NIC), held in Austin, Texas, on January 18, 1996. More than 450 randomly selected strangers from across the United States spent three days in small-group discussions on U.S. foreign policy, the economy, and the family. Participants ventured off to classrooms to talk in groups of ten to twenty persons each, then periodically came together as a full assembly to ask questions of policy experts and presidential candidates.

By some accounts, the NIC managed to achieve something of Rousseau's ideal, in that participants gravitated toward a sense of the general will in their discourse. Particularly on foreign policy, participants came to view each other as parts of a common nation, rather than as partisans or members of factions.[55] In more concrete terms, there was also some convergence in public opinion, with, for example, the public developing even stronger support for long-term investment in public education and investment.[56]

As for being a representative microcosm of the nation, the convention fared relatively well. The poll began with a traditional door-to-door survey of a random national sample of households, and seventy-two percent of those initially contacted by interviewers took part in the pre-NIC survey. Of those six hundred respondents, only fifty percent made the trip to Austin. That resulted in a thirty-six percent response rate, which falls well below the standards of professional polling organizations in the United States. The National Opinion Research Center, which administered the survey, made a concerted effort to convince a higher percentage of respondents to come to Austin, but the free round-trip ticket, a $325 honorarium, and regular contacts by paid liaisons were not enough for many respondents, some of whom remained skeptical about the NIC's purposes. Nonetheless, demographic and attitudinal data suggested that the NIC attendees were similar to the national population in most respects.[57]

One striking finding in the convention's pre- and postdeliberation polling was the increase in knowledge that participants made over time. On average, participants became more accurate in their beliefs about the percentage of Americans on Aid to Families with Dependent Children (AFDC), the main U.S. trading partner, the unemployment rate, and the ideological orientations of the major political parties in the United States.[58] Fishkin and his colleagues found similar "information gains" in other deliberative polls, and they have even demonstrated that these gains in information can explain much of participants' attitude changes.[59] In other words, participants appeared to change their policy preferences as a result of becoming more informed.

Even more striking is the finding that participants in deliberative polls may be tending to move the public's views in a particular direction, even across issues and across nations. Chiara Bacci, Michael Dollinger, and I worked with a team of undergraduates to "code" each of the deliberative poll survey questions that elicited a change in the public's opinions. For example, our coders labeled each survey item as promoting or opposing cosmopolitanism," which we defined as the recognition of interdependence among nations and people in general. Across a wide range of issues, people tended to express more cosmopolitanism views after deliberating. This finding would likely warm the heart of Rousseau, who would view this as evidence of private individuals, through deliberation, coming to place greater value on their coexistence as members of an interconnected general public.[60]

Aside from changing their minds on particular policy questions, participation in the NIC made attendees feel more positively about themselves and the government—not unlike the changes shown for jurors in Chapter 6. For instance, the proportion of those who believed that "public officials care a lot about what people like me think" rose from forty-one percent to sixty percent. After studying the survey of convention participants' experiences, observer Tom Smith made the following conclusion:

> For almost all of the delegates, [the Convention was] a positive, moving experience. For some it was an epiphany that they felt would transform their lives, making them better citizens, changing them into more complete Americans. . . . Overwhelmingly, it was empowering, making them believe that they could and should make a difference.[61]

In the end, the convention proved to be a great demonstration project— showing what a deliberating public might look like in practice. It did not, however, have the intended effect of promoting a more focused, deliberative primary election.[62] Many of the deliberative polls held since have had clearer impacts on public policy. One of the most striking examples is the deliberative poll held in Wenling City, in the Zhejiang province near Shanghai. A write-up in the *China Economic Review* recounted the event. Fishkin and He Baogang, an associate professor in the University of Tasmania's School of Government, "convinced Wenling officials to give the system a try." Fishkin explained in a brief:

> The participants weighed the merits of 30 proposed projects. . . . They were given carefully balanced briefing documents, participated in small group discussions with trained moderators, and brought questions developed in the small groups to two large group sessions with a panel of 12 different experts. . . . The sample started with 275, 11% of them illiterate, and over 250 completed the process. Decisions leaned towards the practical—yes to sewage treatment, no to building an image park (or new square) but yes to a recreational park, yes for a new road linking the township's two main centers and no to other road projects.
>
> Fishkin says the cadres following the progress of the poll came away impressed not only by the transparency of the exercise but by the depth of dis-

cussion and the fresh ideas that came out of it. But the most amazing feature of this experiment in democracy . . . was that the resulting wish-list of
12 projects was taken away and passed en bloc by the local people's congress—
making it the first time deliberative polling results had actually been passed
into law.[63]

It may be ironic that China became the first country to directly implement
the findings of a deliberative poll, but doing so provided local officials the
opportunity to make large-scale investments without suffering charges of corruption or resistance to the public will. Moreover, though the Chinese government uses an authoritarian form of one-party rule, its official ideology is
entirely consistent with the direct expression of the public's will. Thus, procedures like the deliberative poll might facilitate the slow transition to democratic governance in China, beginning as an expedient way to hold on to power
but gradually becoming a way of doing politics that Chinese citizens come to
take for granted as a basic right of public expression.

CITIZEN JURIES

The final deliberative public meeting design discussed in this chapter has
an even longer history of practice, emerging from the 1971 doctoral dissertation of Ned Crosby, who was earning his graduate degree in political science at
the University of Minnesota. Before thirty years had passed, Crosby had over-
seen more than thirty citizen juries, and many more had sprung up spontaneously in other countries, particularly Australia.

Like the deliberative poll, Crosby's aim was to "create a process that would
enhance reason and empathy among citizens as they discussed a public policy
matter."[64] The process that evolved followed a set of design principles, many of
which parallel those of the deliberative poll (i.e., gathering a microcosm of the
community, providing high-quality information, minimizing staff bias, and
producing a fair agenda), with the most superficial difference being the size
and duration. Whereas a deliberative poll always involves hundreds of participants, gathered for two or three days, the typical citizen jury assembles roughly
two dozen citizens for four to five days.

These differences are superficial in that it isn't the number of people or days
that is important.[65] These numerical contrasts simply reflect a deeper difference
in purpose and philosophy. Whereas the deliberative poll seeks to track how a set
of individual opinion statements change when survey respondents are hit by a
wave of information, the citizen jury seeks to learn whether a mix of information
and in-depth deliberation can bring diverse individuals to a broad consensus on
a more narrow set of questions. Given the demands of the jury's task, it is necessary to reduce its size and extend the duration of its deliberation.

Consider these examples of jury tasks, which are typically called the charge a jury must meet: Should we pass a levy to improve our local schools? How should we manage the impact agriculture has on water quality in our state? Shall we restructure our state property tax system? Should we support the president's health care plan? How should we reconfigure the federal budget? How should we understand and address global climate change?[66] For each of these issues, reaching agreement on a set of detailed recommendations requires intensive learning and deliberation. In every instance, the citizen jurors ended up feeling tremendously satisfied with their discussion process and their resulting judgments, and jurors rarely thought they could have accomplished their task with less deliberation.[67]

The finer details of a citizen jury have varied considerably from one jury to the next. The jury analogy is most vivid when the jurors hear testimony from advocates and their opponents, judging the quality of one side's viewpoint versus the other's. Also in the tradition of a jury, this procedural approach can involve cross-examination of one side by the other. Unlike the typical jury, the citizen jurors also get the chance to directly question both sides' witnesses. This "hearing" phase of the citizen jury turns the tables on the conventional public hearing process because the citizens become the ones listening and asking questions, with the experts and officials pleading their case before the citizen deliberators.

When colleagues and I adapted the citizen jury process to attain public input on New Mexico highway department appropriations, we made this reversal starkly apparent by placing the citizens at a long table at the head of the room, with the experts sitting in the front row of the audience, facing the citizen table. Those testifying had the chance to make a brief opening statement, then they took questions from citizens, who were persistent in asking follow-up questions and taking the conversation wherever they felt it needed to go. The bottom line was that everyone in the room—the experts, the audience, and the citizens charged with deliberating—knew that the randomly selected body of citizens was in charge of the proceedings.[68]

In full-fledged citizen juries, the jurors have even more control over the proceedings: They can call back witnesses if they wish to hear more from them, alter the agenda to provide more time for background information, schedule more time for small-group deliberation, and even dismiss their facilitator or do nearly anything else they need to finish their task to their satisfaction. The only rule Crosby has enforced is that jurors not have "so much control that they can overturn the fair balance of witnesses worked out in advance of the hearings."[69]

CITIZENS' ASSEMBLY REVISITED

The comparison of citizen-centered public meeting formats ends where this chapter began, with the British Columbia Citizens' Assembly. Figure 7.3 contrasts the assembly process with the citizen jury and deliberative poll in terms of deliberative criteria. The main differences come from the sheer amount of time the assembly allows for discussion. The British Columbia Citizens' Assembly lasted several months, with citizen deliberators meeting repeatedly over a series of weekends. Instead of a brief question-and-answer period with experts, the assembly members had access to a regular staff of experts, plus various people flown in from across the globe to address specific questions. The assembly even had a middle-stage during which citizens held public hearings across the province to gather input from any British Columbians who wished to speak.

In this sense, the assembly more closely paralleled an earnest legislative committee, which has a professional staff at its disposal, studies an issue, hears testimony, and holds public hearings before reaching a decision. The analogy is even more apt, in that the Assembly had a power that is normally held only by a legislature—the authority to put a referendum before the people of the province. By contrast, Fishkin was surprised and delighted when the Chinese deliberative poll became the first to have its recommendations immediately implemented, and Crosby has bemoaned the lack of influence that citizen jury recommendations often have had on local, state, and federal officials.[70]

Conclusion

All six of the deliberative public meeting processes detailed in this chapter have clear advantages over traditional public meetings, but the question remains whether public officials or agencies will want to incorporate more of these processes into their regular activities.[71] Why would elected or appointed public servants cede the power and control vested in them to some mix of stakeholders, citizens, and experts? After all, isn't it their job to deliberate on the public's behalf?

One answer to these questions is that it depends on one's conception of democracy. In its grandest sense, the deliberative perspective challenges conventional modes of democracy that give relatively limited roles to citizens and rely on representative institutions to get the hard work done.[72] In the spirit of the Brazilian constitution, the deliberative perspective sees public officials as stewards of the public's best interests, with one of their main responsibilities being to help stimulate and channel the energy invested in broader public participation and deliberation.

Even if a public official rejects this view, there are reasons for traditional representatives to turn to more participatory, deliberative public processes when conducting meetings. For instance, public policy professor Kathleen Halvorsen has demonstrated that "beliefs about [government] agency responsiveness can be significantly transformed with one public meeting." In particular, "exposure

	Deliberative Poll	Citizens Jury	Citizens Assembly
Analytic Process			
Create a solid information base.	Citizens read briefing materials and have question-and-answer period with expert panel.	Citizens get to cross-examine pro and con witnesses.	Citizens have ongoing interaction with experts and resource staff.
Prioritize the key values at stake.	Values come up in small-group discussions.	Values revealed through structured discussion of evaluation criteria.	Values emerge through ongoing debates among alternatives.
Identify a broad range of solutions.	Potential solutions are referenced in briefing materials and questionnaires.	Initial solutions are preset, but alternatives may emerge in discussion.	Expert testimony, discussion, and hearings reveal diverse alternatives.
Weigh the pros, cons, and trade-offs among solutions.	Trade-offs and disagreements among citizens may or may not surface.	Pros and cons emerge as jury hears testimony and weighs alternatives.	Pros and cons emerge as assembly hears testimony and weighs alternatives.
Make the best decision possible.	Participants privately express their views in a survey but make no group decision.	Jury votes for a final set of recommendations, sometimes with a written dissent.	Assembly adopts recommendations that the largest majority can support.
Social Process			
Adequately distribute speaking opportunities.	Mixes informal group discussion with more plenary question-and-answer period.	Mixes formal question-and-answer period with extensive small-group deliberation.	Mixes small-group interaction with full-assembly discussion.
Ensure mutual comprehension.	Group discussion processes new information in question-and-answer period.	Extensive back-and-forth during question-and-answer period, plus deliberation.	Education materials printed for citizens; expert staff available.
Consider other ideas and experiences.	Goal of self-education promotes listening, learning.	Citizens have ample time to explore different viewpoints.	Public hearings provide additional opportunity to listen.
Respect other participants.	Briefing materials and facilitators emphasize importance of mutual respect. Important and distinct responsibilities given to citizens, experts, and officials help participants respect one another's roles.		

Figure 7.3   Comparison of Three Citizen-Centered Public Meeting Designs

to meaningful discussion" can boost perceived responsiveness. This, in turn, "helps to build public support for that agency." As a result, the public is more likely to trust an agency's judgment and accept its decisions.[73] Halvorsen produced these findings in the context of a forest service project in the midwestern United States, but her findings also square with the research cited earlier on other deliberative processes and the jury system.

This returns us to a theme raised in Chapter 6—the potential of deliberative processes to maintain, or even restore, the legitimacy of public institutions. In the modern era, many people have come to expect the kind of role in governance that Brazilians can gain through municipal councils. A study in Australia, for example, found that citizens viewed decisions on health policy as legitimate only to the extent that public officials' decisions were directly informed by the general public and representative stakeholders. Study participants placed particular emphasis on the public's role in setting principles and priorities, not unlike those generated in the design meetings held in New York and Philadelphia.[74] There is no compelling reason to believe Americans are any different. The historical record is clear, with Americans repeatedly demanding access to government and never relinquishing new powers given them, be it the direct election of senators, the ballot initiative, or any other participatory process.

Without public support, it is difficult for a government to govern. If deliberative processes are one of the wellsprings of legitimacy for both elected officials and public agencies, at the end of the day "giving power away" through more deliberative and influential public processes may ultimately provide public officials with greater power to act. Those actions will have to fit within the parameters given by the public, be they principles, prioritizations, or even more specific policy guidelines. But so long as those deliberative decisions follow the best available technical knowledge and incorporate the diversity of values and concerns held by the broader public, officials will find that the public has given them the freedom to act decisively, precisely along the lines that will best serve the public interest.

In spite of these advantages, public officials are likely to reconfigure their meetings in this way only when the larger society becomes more clearly committed to—and practiced in—deliberative politics. It is that possibility that focuses the discussion in the next chapter.

Notes

1. Adams (1995, p. 20).
2. See Ratner (2004a, 2004b) and Warren and Pearse (forthcoming) for details on the assembly.
3. For up-to-date information on Citizen Assemblies, see the blog of New America Foundation senior research fellow J. H. Snider, http://snider.blogs.com/citizensassembly.

4. Ober (1989, pp. 4–5).
5. Ibid., p. 325.
6. Ibid., p. 105.
7. Ibid., p. 106.
8. Mansbridge (1983, p. 127).
9. Mansbridge (1983, pp. 134–35). For contemporary accounts of the town meeting, see Bryan (2004) and Zimmerman (1989).
10. Mansbridge (1983, p. 121).
11. See, for example, Kirp (1992) and Lukensmeyer, Goldman, and Brigham (2005).
12. Townsend (2006).
13. Bryan and McClaughry (1989).
14. Kay (1998, p. 2).
15. Recent work theorizing the nature of public meetings suggests that this will change. Important advances in theories of public meetings include Kelshaw (2003) and Tracy and Muller (2001). The gist of all three works is that public meetings represent a complex exchange of ideas, problem frames, and respect/legitimacy between public officials and citizens. Interestingly, each of these scholars has at least as much interest in the experience and perspective of public officials as in citizens; this suggests that the literature on public meetings has begun to recognize public officials as active (and often confused, unsure) partners in conducting these meetings, rather than purely rational strategic actors.
16. Weithman (1995) stressed that the legitimacy of deliberative legislative processes hinges on the viability of the public's opportunity to be included in such deliberation, even in a system that elects its representatives. One inclined to coin such phrases might even go so far as to call this the deliberative paradox, that we elect people to deliberate on our behalf yet then insist that we be included in the deliberation itself. The resolution is simply that the public provisionally delegates authority but does not yield its undelegated right to participate in ongoing deliberation on public policy.
17. Williamson and Fung (2004, p. 8).
18. Again, the term *enlightened understanding* is used by Dahl (1989) as a criterion for the democratic process.
19. Webler and Renn (1995, p. 24). As one county commissioner put it, "At a public hearing you are more or less on trial" (Kettering Foundation, 1989, p. 11).
20. Webler and Renn (1995, p. 24).
21. Checkoway (1981).
22. Fiorino (1990, p. 226).
23. Mahtesian (1997).
24. Navarrette (2006).
25. Abelson (2004).
26. Cook, Delli Carpini, and Jacobs (2003, pp. 11, 29–30).
27. Kettering Foundation (1989, p. 11).
28. Eliasoph (1998, p. 190).
29. Lukensmeyer et al. (2005, p. 160).
30. Ibid., p. 159.
31. For a record of the event, visit http://www.listeningtothecity.org.
32. Lukensmeyer et al. (2005, p. 161).
33. There is no one way to sequence forums. Other examples can be found in Carson and Hartz-Karp (2005).

34. Waterfront development is experiencing a renaissance in many cities, and it presents a special opportunity for public involvement in urban planning. See Raymond Gastil (2002).
35. Charles, Sokoloff, and Satullo (2005).
36. Ibid.
37. This observation appears in Rousseau's discussion of democracy in Book 3, Chapter 4 of *The Social Contract*; see Rousseau (1762/1950). This text is also available online at http://www.constitution.org/jjr/socon.htm. For a clear example of Rousseau's influence on deliberative theory, see Mansbridge (1983).
38. Schattan P. Coelho, Pozzoni, and Cifuentes Montoya (2005, p. 176).
39. The election of the members is a complex matter, as yet understudied. See Schattan P. Coelho et al. (2005, pp. 177–80).
40. Coelho et al. (2005, p. 176).
41. Coelho, de Andrade, and Cifuentes Montoya (2002, p. 70).
42. Ibid.
43. Quoted from Book 2, Chapter 3 of *The Social Contract*; see Rousseau (1762/1950). Italics have been added for emphasis. The insertion of "[her]" is meant to translate into the present context, but Rousseau deliberately excluded women from the assembly, relegating them to a support role for the male deliberators. For a feminist critique (and appreciation) of Rousseau, see the edited volume by Lange (2002).
44. Rousseau (1762/1950). For a clear example of Rousseau's influence on deliberative theory, see Mansbridge (1983). Former Clinton cabinet member Robert Reich (1985) demonstrated the enduring power of Rousseau's idea, when he argued that "public deliberation allows people to discover latent public values that they have in common with others, and in the process to create new public values" (p. 1635).
45. For a philosophical account of this, see Warren (1992), who argued that deliberation can transform participants' self-interest, as well as instill a stronger orientation to the public good. From an economic perspective, Howarth and Wilson (2006) suggested that group-based deliberation has a special advantage over conventional "contingent-valuation" survey approaches because it requires individuals to take into account not only their own but also others' valuations of alternative policy outcomes. Mathews (1994) and Yankelovich (1991) are among the many who argued that deliberation fundamentally transforms the judgments people reach on issues.
46. For more discussion of the problem of how to invite participants, see Ryfe (2005).
47. Carson and Martin (1999). On the latter two procedures, also refer to Hendriks (2005).
48. Carson and Martin (1999, p. 4).
49. On how to integrate diverse deliberative procedures, see Carson and Hartz-Karp (2005).
50. On the online deliberative polls, see http://www.stanford.edu/dept/news/pr/03/onlinepoll129.html.
51. On the mechanics of deliberative polling, see Fishkin and Farrar (2005).
52. Quotes are from Fishkin (1991, p. 93), and Fishkin (1995, p. 43). Deliberative polling is a trademark used by the Center for Deliberative Democracy (http://cdd.stanford.edu).
53. The deliberative poll idea appeared in Fishkin (1988). On other processes, see Becker and Slaton (2000), Renn et al. (1993), and Crosby and Nethercutt (2005).

54. Denver, Hands, and Jones (1995).
55. Hart and Jarvis (1999).
56. Fishkin and Luskin (1999).
57. Merkle's (1996) tables show only modest demographic differences between attendees and the population, except that the attendees were somewhat more politically active and involved than the general population. For an extended discussion of the representativeness of the NIC, see Fishkin and Luskin (1999).
58. See Fishkin and Luskin (1999).
59. See Luskin, Fishkin, and Jowell (2002). Other researchers looking beyond this particular issue have found limited impacts from participating in deliberative polls (Denver et al., 1995; Sturgis, Roberts, and Allum, 2005).
60. Given the deliberative poll's emphasis on information, it is not surprising that this (and other attitude shifts) were more common on questionnaire statements that were more factual in nature, rather than policy evaluative. See Bacci, Dollinger, and Gastil (2006).
61. Smith (1999).
62. This outcome is likely one of the many reasons that Fishkin ultimately chose to propose the more engrossing Deliberation Day design for electoral reform.
63. The full text of the *China Economic Review* article is available at http://cdd.stanford.edu/press/2005/cer-power.pdf.
64. Crosby and Nethercutt (2005, p. 112).
65. There are limits to this. Schkade, Sunstein, and Hastie (2006) reported on the findings of discussions that lasted just fifteen minutes, without facilitation, and the results were strong polarizing and questionable deliberation. One can design deliberative events that last only a few hours or a couple days, but there are real differences in what one can expect from processes that are brief versus those that last a full week—or longer.
66. These examples are taken from Crosby (1995) and Crosby and Nethercutt (2005).
67. Crosby (1995, p. 164).
68. Gastil (2000).
69. Crosby and Nethercutt (2005, p. 114).
70. On citizen juries, see Crosby and Nethercutt (2005, p. 115). On the Chinese deliberative poll, see the previously cited *China Economic Review* article at http://cdd.stanford.edu/press/2005/cer-power.pdf.
71. For a compendium of deliberative processes public officials might use, see Gastil and Levine (2005). For recent international examples, see the last 2007 edition (Volume 46, Issue 4) of the *European Journal of Political Research*.
72. Barber (1984) forcefully argued against this older notion of democracy, contrasting it with a more participatory vision he called strong democracy.
73. Halvorsen (2003, p. 541). See also Reich (1985).
74. Wiseman, Mooney, Berry, and Tang (2003).

SOURCE: FIMA.

8

Deliberative Communities and Societies

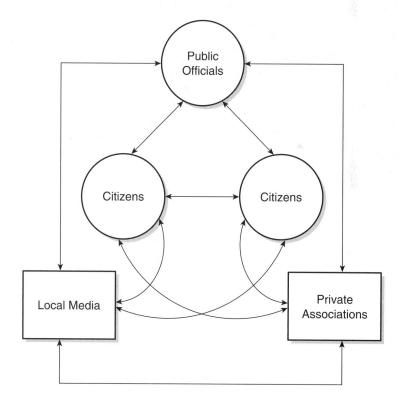

[We] envision a future in which all people—regardless of income, position, background or education—are able to engage regularly in lively, thoughtful, and challenging conversations about what really matters to them, in ways that have a positive impact on their lives and their world. We envision a society in which systems and structures support and advance inclusive, constructive dialogue and deliberation.

—Mission statement of the National
Coalition for Dialogue and Deliberation[1]

C ivic reformers often speak of democracy as every reasonable person's preferred form of government. From the vantage point of the average person, though, democracy can be exhausting, especially if we think of its deliberative strain. One could spend a fair portion of each week reading, listening, talking, thinking, debating, and strategizing on the issues of the day, yet still not do everything deliberative democracy could ask of a fully engaged citizen. Consequently, deliberative democracy may be hard to build in a country, state, or city that is underprepared for its demands.

To get a better sense for what this means, a side trip to Italy is in order. In 1993, public policy and government scholars Robert Putnam, Robert Leonardi, and Raffaella Nanetti presented the world with the results of their twenty-plus years of collaborative research on Italian government. Their landmark book, *Making Democracy Work: Civic Traditions in Modern Italy,* was an academic Helen of Troy, a book that launched a thousand peer-reviewed articles.[2]

The research by Putnam and his colleagues took advantage of an accidental, nationwide experiment of sorts. In the early 1970s, the Italian federal government implemented a plan to establish powerful regional governments across the country. Putnam wondered if the success or failure of these new regional governments—the newly built democratic institutions—would ultimately depend on the varied characteristics of the diverse local communities in Italy. "The practical performance of institutions," reasoned Putnam, "is shaped by the social context within which they operate."[3] In particular, the research team found that "some regions of Italy . . . are blessed with vibrant social networks and norms of civic engagement, while others are cursed with vertically structured politics, a social life of fragmentation and isolation, and a culture of distrust."[4]

These cultural differences—between the egalitarian, sociable regions and the more hierarchical, isolated ones—were long-standing dissimilarities that traced from the modern era back to the mid-1800s, more than a century before the Italian federal government implemented its experiment in local governance. More important, these differences proved powerful predictors of the performance of the newly created regional institutions, as measured by these governments' ability to develop stable and efficient local services and infrastructure.[5]

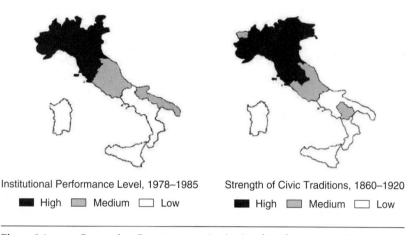

Institutional Performance Level, 1978–1985   Strength of Civic Traditions, 1860–1920

■ High ▨ Medium □ Low   ■ High ▨ Medium □ Low

Figure 8.1   Comparing Contemporary Institutional Performance and Historical Civic Traditions in Italy

SOURCE: Adapted from Putnam (1993, pp. 84, 150).

Figure 8.1 provides a visual summary of just how strong the correlation was between the performance of the new governments and the older civic traditions in each of fifteen regions.[6] Though the same regional governmental structures were built into each region, only the northern regions enjoyed high performance from their new regional governments. The same northern regions were roughly the ones that had highly participatory, sociable civic traditions dating back more than a century. By contrast, the southern and island regions had both weak traditions of civic engagement and low performance from their new institutions. Finally, the regions with moderately strong civic traditions had mixed success with their new regional governments, with most—fittingly—showing only modest levels of performance. As Putnam wrote, "The pattern is stark: One could have predicted the success or failure of regional government in Italy in the 1980s with extraordinary accuracy from patterns of civic engagement nearly a century earlier."[7]

The experience of Italy holds meaning for other countries hoping to transition to more participatory, democratic systems of government. Putnam also discovered that this same research had tremendous significance for his own home country, the United States. The core concept Putnam adapted from the Italy project was social capital, which he defined broadly as the "features of social life . . . that enable participants to act together more effectively to pursue shared objectives." This includes, principally, "trust, norms, and networks," the social glue that made Italy's northern regions so fertile for democratic innovation.[8]

In 1995, Putnam sounded the alarm with "Bowling Alone: America's Declining Social Capital," an article published in the *Journal of Democracy* and later adapted into a book of the same name.[9] The titular metaphor pointed out that bowling remains modestly popular in the United States, but people are increasingly more inclined to bowl alone (or with close friends and family) than in bowling leagues or as part of other civic outings. Putnam marshaled considerable evidence, demonstrating that this was no fluke but rather an instance of a wider trend in dwindling social capital.

Critiques of Putnam's diagnosis have stressed that many aspects of civic life remain healthy in the United States.[10] Though the public's trust in the media, politicians, and nearly every public entity is in decline, various observers have argued that citizens have simply shifted their attention from formal and group-based politics to more private civic engagement.[11]

The lesson for understanding deliberation and democracy is that patterns of public trust and communication merit careful study if we are to understand the health of a political system. The development of deliberative democratic practices in a society will involve altering more fundamental social practices, norms, and institutions. Looking at formal institutions, such as media systems, elections, legislatures, juries, and public meetings, is not enough. The conversational patterns described in Chapter 2 form part of this deeper societal layer, but there is much more that merits our attention.

The bottom line is that a deliberative democratic society is just that—a society, not merely a system of political and legal institutions. To illustrate this link more precisely, this chapter begins by showing how a society becomes more deliberative through democratic social movements, which constitute a particularly powerful means of systemwide transformation. After describing what a modern deliberative community might look like, we explore the underpinnings of a deliberative society. Finally, we consider two examples of contemporary efforts to make local communities more deliberative in their attitudes, habits, and norms.

Old-School Deliberation in Historic Social Movements

If Putnam and his colleagues found that a participatory civic culture helps democracy to thrive, one might then wonder how a culture becomes participatory in the first place. Recall that in the Italian case, the civic traditions in the different regions had remained relatively stable for nearly two centuries. In a dynamic society, what can cause such cultural habits to change?

One possibility is a social movement. These are collective actions typically loosely organized by a series of groups and organizations whose principal aim is either changing people's habitual practices and beliefs or changing larger legal, political, and economic systems—or the movement might aim to change both practices and systems. Among the most famous and influential movements of the past century are the American civil rights movement, the women's movement, the pro-life movement, and the Ghandian nonviolent movement for Indian independence.[12]

A vigorous social movement, by definition, has the power to transform how a society thinks and acts in everyday life. Among the many effects such movements might have is strengthening the public's democratic skills, dispositions, and commitments. Historian Sara Evans and civic scholar Harry Boyte studied precisely these changes in their review of twentieth century democratic social movements in the United States. Evans and Boyte found that the key to democratic social change in each of their historical case studies were free spaces:

> [Free spaces are] public places in the community . . . in which people are able to learn a new self-respect, a deeper and more assertive group identity, public skills, and values of cooperation and civic virtue. . . . Free spaces are settings between private lives and large-scale institutions where ordinary citizens can act with dignity, independence, and vision. These are, in the main, voluntary forms of association with a relatively open and participatory character . . . grounded in the fabric of community life.[13]

In reality, free spaces are never so "pure." Evans and Boyte explained that free spaces, along with the social movements that produce them, are "partial in their freedom and democratic participation."[14] They also do not generally bring together the larger public but rather particular communities of interest. Free spaces "exist on the borders, connecting as well as differentiating community and public arena." They help connect smaller communities to the larger public, however, because they always "look outward toward the larger world" to address the issues that spawned the social movement in the first place. In essence, those who dwell in free spaces often come hoping to meet their personal needs but end up becoming highly skilled democratic citizens interested in addressing larger, public concerns.

Consider the example of the civil rights movement in the United States. The main stretch of the civil rights era started with the unanimous 1954 *Brown v. Board of Education* Supreme Court ruling, which rejected the "separate but equal" principle of school segregation, and ended with the 1969 formation of the Congressional Black Congress by thirteen black members of the U.S. House of Representatives.[15]

This movement, along with many of its most famous leaders, such as Martin Luther King, Jr., grew out of a network of churches in the black community. These churches provided free spaces in ways that are both straightforward and surprising. Generally, Evans and Boyte explained that "the autonomy of the church," which remained relatively intact after emancipation, "proved a bedrock for community cohesion and autonomy, and its religious resources furnished . . . the main wellsprings of cultural renewal."[16]

Not every minister of every church was eager to mix worship with political struggle, but "even where ministers proved hesitant . . . the churches became drawn into the struggle through the activities of church members, and the language of black religion furnished the central themes of the movement."[17] Historian William Chafe, in *Civilities and Civil Rights*, explained that "the churches provided a training ground for political leaders and a meeting place where the aspirations of the black community could find collective expression."[18]

One of the early leaders of the movement, Ella Barker, saw in the churches the potential to develop not just strong leaders but strong citizens, capable of taking coordinated and sustained action. In her view, the movement could "develop individuals who were bound together by a concept that provided an opportunity for them to grow into being responsible," becoming active players in the movement rather than blind followers of a small cadre of leaders.[19]

One of the most important means of achieving this goal was the creation of citizenship schools, local free spaces devoted to adult civic education. Evans and Boyte explained that these schools "connected diverse communities and taught ordinary people new skills of public life." These schools, along with the larger movement, taught practical skills about how to vote, present grievances to government, and organize to promote social change. Perhaps more important, the lessons taught in the schools, as well as the churches, helped transform personal struggles with racism and segregation into a political struggle to make real the democratic promise of equality for all. It was that powerful democratic message that gave the civil rights movement, in Evans and Boyte's words, "a moral power that resonated the world over."[20]

Before closing this case, it is important to notice the more subtle kinds of free spaces provided by black churches a century before the civil rights movement had taken its first steps. A free space can engender participatory, empowering social relations without being explicitly political. In the case of the black church, one example is the practice of gospel music. Gospel music served as an opportunity to learn improvisation and a type of participatory collective action. As the gospel pioneer Thomas A. Dorsey once explained, "A white chorus of one hundred voices will buy one hundred copies" of a gospel song, but a black chorus will buy just two, "one for the director and one for the pianist." The chorus itself freely adapted the music as it learned it. In this subtle way, members of the choir learned the same set of skills that are necessary to participate effectively in a democratic social movement, which requires even more self-confident improvisation and public-spirited coordination among its members.[21]

Evans and Boyte found the same mix of subtle and explicit civic education in other democratic social movements, such as those for women's and workers' rights. For our purposes, the most important lesson is that a vibrant, deliberative community requires an abundance of free spaces in which people learn how to take responsibility for themselves, work effectively with fellow citizens, and develop the self-confidence and basic communication skills necessary for active participation in public deliberation.

Visiting a Deliberative Community

If a society had a proliferation of free spaces and social capital, and it used those to sustain a deliberative public culture, what might it look like? Figure 8.2 provides an answer at the level of a community (a county, city, or town), rather than a nation, so that we can glimpse how the various social and political pieces fit together in a unit of manageable size.

INFRASTRUCTURE AND LEADERSHIP

Consider how such a community maintains its information base and keeps in touch with its core values. The first requirement in Figure 8.2 is that the community "maintain a rigorous self-awareness through formal community assessment and informal feedback channels." In more concrete terms, that means that the community maintains two forms of ongoing self-assessment. It should have semiformal associations or organizations that periodically assess the community's demographics, infrastructure, and social, economic, environmental, and political challenges. In addition, the community should have rich, informal social networks that convey similar information on a continuous basis.

With regard to values clarification, the community should also "ensure an infrastructure of persons, practices, and institutions that articulates a community's values, whether broadly shared or diverse." This includes a mix of different events, processes, and people. A community can honor and reaffirm its core values (freedom, justice, compassion, responsibility, etc.) through civic holidays (e.g., Fourth of July, Martin Luther King Jr. Day), theater and art that convey moral arguments (e.g., a historic monument, a classic play, or a challenging performance art piece), and its schools (e.g., efforts to teach character and virtue in elementary school or promotion of civic responsibility in colleges and universities).

A deliberative community's values are also sustained by a wealth of democratic leaders. These are people who not only serve as articulate spokespersons for the community but also are capable of empowering their fellow community members to discover and contribute their own voices.[22] The social movements discussed earlier created many such leaders through formal training processes and through the ad hoc crucible of movement activities. For example, the Highlander Folk School in Tennessee (now called simply the Highlander Center) served as a leadership training institute, training "rural and industrial leaders for a new social order."[23] The Rotary Club and other less well-known civic organizations have also conducted leadership training for years in many communities. The point is simply that without such training grounds, there is the risk that a single leader, or near-oligarchy of leaders, may emerge to rigidly define a community's values. With a broader and more

Analytic Process	
Create a solid information base.	Maintain a rigorous self-awareness through formal community assessment and informal feedback channels.
Prioritize the key values at stake.	Ensure an infrastructure of persons, practices, and institutions that articulates a community's values, whether broadly shared or diverse.
Identify a broad range of solutions.	Look to people with different expertise and perspectives to introduce new ideas for how to address a problem.
Weight the pros, cons, and trade-offs among solutions.	Consider how each potential solution would affect different community members, as well as the world outside the community's borders.
Make the best decision possible.	Make an informed decision that best reflects the community's core values
Social Process	
Adequately distribute speaking opportunities.	Maintain open public and quasi-public space in which people can congregate, but also ensure private spaces in which like-minded people can caucus.
Ensure mutual comprehension.	Cultivate a minimum level of shared language and symbols. Educate members to help them understand complex information and ideas.
Consider other ideas and experiences.	Promote the creative expression of different perspectives and experiences to help community members see the world through others' eyes.
Respect other participants.	Encourage a strong sense of community so that members see each other as having some shared identity, even when expressing different views.

Figure 8.2   Key Features of a Deliberative Community

diverse leadership cadre, a community can sustain a rich, ongoing conversation about its core needs, desires, and aspirations.

With a solid information base and a lively discussion of values, a community can then work through its common problems. The process of generating solutions and weighing alternatives is comparable to those described in earlier chapters, with the community drawing on diverse expertise and perspectives and considering impacts on different members of the community, as well as people outside the community who might feel the effect of its decisions.

Once again, the community relies on an infrastructure of deliberative norms and institutions. There must be a strong tradition of innovation and creativity to spur new approaches to long-standing problems and to reward, rather than punish, those who challenge conventions. Even if the community rejects new ideas, the point is to encourage the consideration of alternatives. Without these, the community does not have the ability to make choices. The community must also have ways of bringing together public officials, experts, and laycitizens through processes such as the public meetings discussed in Chapter 7. Unless a community can sustain such public meetings, community deliberation will remain disorganized even at the point of decision making. This can leave citizens and stakeholders feeling shut out, experts perceiving their knowledge as useless, and public officials viewing themselves as making decisions in isolation.

PUBLIC SPACES AND THIRD PLACES

The social process of community deliberation also emphasizes community infrastructure, and it is worth discussing briefly the concepts of public space and private space introduced in Figure 8.2. To ensure an adequate distribution of speaking opportunities, a community should "maintain open public and quasi-public space in which people can congregate, but also ensure private spaces in which like-minded people can caucus." In plain English, a private space is one in which you set your own rules and are free to associate and talk as you please, free from public control. Pure examples include private conversations in one's home and private associations meeting in privately owned buildings. Public space is a more contested subject, but for present purposes it simply refers to spaces publicly owned and regulated and open to everyone. Between these two extremes lies a third place: the quasi-public spaces, such as coffee shops, bookstores, and bars where the general public meets.[24]

The physical qualities of public and quasi-public space merit further discussion, however, because they are often taken for granted and poorly understood. Communication scholars Susan Drucker and Gary Gumpert provided a good illustration of the importance of such spaces: "Communication," they explained, "does not occur in a vacuum, but in an environment. Relationships are delineated by the circumstances of place or the conditions of time." Thus, it matters whether we are meeting and talking in particular "rooms, buildings, streets, squares, parks, etc." Architecture and urban planning shape how we talk as a public.[25]

To illustrate how regulatory and building choices shape a community's spaces, Drucker and Gumpert provided the example of Great Neck, New York, a suburban community near New York City. First, consider how land use regulations affect the marketplace. Great Neck, like many communities, has experienced a battle between large-scale superstores and smaller-scale neighborhood business districts. When a whole community converges on Wal-Mart, it brings the wider public together in one place, but only (or at least, principally) to shop. Neighborhood businesses, by contrast, invite more pedestrian traffic, which is more conducive to sidewalk conversations among neighbors. Such districts also often come with parks, benches, and other public spaces and facilities that promote public interaction. The bottom line is that where businesses are allowed to build—and on what scale—can shape patterns of public interaction.

A more subtle example is how we eat and drink in third places. When a new restaurant opens, it does so with various legal permits that govern its operation. The liquor license is perhaps the most familiar permit. But legal discussions of new dining establishments can also delve into more arcane issues, such as dwell time, which is the average duration of a patron's stay at a business. The faster the turnover, the more revenue a limited number of tables in a restaurant can generate; however, the more quickly patrons dine, the less space there is for conversation.

Drucker and Gumpert found that in Great Neck, issues such as these come up routinely, and they entail hidden assumptions about public venues and how they should use their space:

> Permit applications inquire into . . . the menu of a proposed food establishment and negotiate issues regarding take-out service and the type of containers and wrappers to be used in the name of keeping streets and sidewalks clean. This creates spaces devoid of pedestrians who stroll, saunter, and stop while consuming their purchases. The type of window openings and access to the street is considered by village decision makers. Fear and disdain accompany the image of those who congregate on the street corners consuming everything from pizza to frozen yogurt or ice cream.[26]

One does not need to travel to Great Neck to experience the impact of zoning debates such as these. College and university towns vary tremendously in the liveliness of their immediate surroundings. Some have vibrant shopping and eating districts just a short walk from student dorms and classrooms, with businesses encouraging informal strolling among both students and long-time locals who enjoy living in a university neighborhood. Others have a pristine shopping mall with limited hours, strictly regulated shopping and dining, and less lively spaces for interaction. Others have no such district. In the end, how we build our public and quasi-public spaces affects the number and quality of opportunities for public talk.

Societal Analysis

Thinking about a deliberative community clearly requires reflecting on a different level than is required when we talk about public meetings, forums, juries, and legislatures, all of which involve discrete sets of individuals meeting at specific times and places. The earlier chapters about the media and elections operated on this larger scale, but they had the luxury of focusing on a particular institution. To understand how a deliberative community can come into existence, one must look more broadly than at a particular institution or practice and conduct a societal analysis. At this level, one asks how the different practices and institutions in a society fit together. It is easy to get vertigo at this high level of abstraction, and to help us keep our bearings it is useful to hold on to something—in this case a particular theoretical approach to understanding society.

STRUCTURATION THEORY

British sociologist Anthony Giddens developed structuration theory to synthesize conflicting sociological theories regarding how people create their social worlds. His attempt at a "grand theory" of society was successful in that his model is so abstract that it can encompass any more refined model of social cognition and behavior.[27]

Giddens distinguished between entire social systems and structures, which are rules and resources that make up a larger system. In structurational terms, a system is the "reproduced relations between actors or collectivities, organized as regular social practices."[28] In other words, a system is a fully developed, large-scale, enduring social system, such as a society. Within a larger system, however, there are many smaller coherent systems that some might call subsystems. An example of a small subsystem is a corporation or government agency, which is made up of a network of people following a set of behavioral norms within a specific context and working toward specific goals. A small town is a more complex and larger subsystem, but still just a small part of a larger system.

Structures, on the other hand, are the "rules and resources . . . organized as properties of social systems."[29] Structures are the building blocks of systems; they are the rules, norms, resources, and everyday understandings that guide human action and enable complex social practices. In Giddens's terminology, the three types of structures are meanings, power relations, and norms. Thus, some structures predominantly have to do with what actions or things mean to the people involved, whereas others are primarily about social power, and still others create and reproduce interaction norms. Structuration is simply the creation, maintenance, and reproduction of social systems via these structures.

Seen from the vantage point of a single person, structures are typically microlevel guides to interactions (such as greeting rituals or norms about appropriate terms of address in the workplace), but the actions of large numbers of individuals over time have implications for the larger social system. Returning to the concept of social capital introduced at the beginning of this chapter, the Italian who joins a local club does so, typically, for personal reasons, such as a desire to see neighbors regularly and to meet new people. If such civic "joining" becomes the norm, however, it changes the character of the entire community—not only directly, by making it seem abnormal to isolate oneself from one's community, but also indirectly, by providing the social network infrastructure necessary for effective local governance. Thus, small individual actions have ramifications for the whole, and structures pertaining to one facet of a society can end up influencing other social practices and institutions.

What Giddens's structurational theory gives us is a more precise way of talking about how the actions of community members, from their everyday talk to the institutions they build, can add up to form a deliberative, or nondeliberative, society. There are many topics to discuss from this point of departure, but I begin by looking at civic culture and discourse, both of which have received considerable attention in the literature on democracy and deliberation. Afterward, I analyze a variety of theories about institutional infrastructure.

CIVIC CULTURE AND CONVERSATIONAL NORMS

One simple application of structuration theory is to think in terms of the norms that support political discussion within a community. Perhaps the most basic form of talk is conversation, and it is surely the most common form of everyday political interaction among citizens. The frequency—or even the possibility—of deliberative conversation, however, should not be taken for granted. In the extreme case of a totalitarian society, open, honest political conversations can be dangerous, as one risks saying the wrong thing to the wrong person. In such a circumstance, an existing set of structures of meanings for particular words (calling for *revolution,* decrying *tyranny*) may violate prevailing normative structures (e.g., "don't criticize the government"), and this norm violation could trigger the mobilization of existing power structures (e.g., the secret police visiting one's home). These interlocking structures together create a powerful social norm against speaking freely about politics. Competent social actors quickly learn this norm and abide by it, without the government ever directly forbidding such criticism.

Even in societies that fall well short of totalitarianism, a norm of caution may develop. Consider the case of Zimbabwe: Robert Mugabe has ruled the country as prime minister or president since 1980, when the nation won its independence. Mugabe and his political party, the Zimbabwe African National Union, have presided over many dubious elections and, despite some significant accomplishments, have a well-deserved reputation of rampant corruption. In the midst of this political-cultural climate, a 1999 survey found that nearly sixty percent of Zimbabwe citizens believed that "in this country, you must be very careful of what you say and do with regard to politics." Despite such caution, a quarter said that they managed to have political discussions "frequently," with another thirty-nine percent doing so "occasionally."[30] In other words, the prevailing norms in Zimbabwe permitted political talk but advised against speaking too freely, particularly when speaking with anyone but close friends and family.

One of the most famous works in political society included similar measures in its surveys of the United States, the United Kingdom (UK), Germany, Italy, and Mexico in the 1950s. Gabriel Almond and Sidney Verba's *The Civic Culture* drew controversy on its particulars, but there was no denying its core findings—that the attitudes and habits in a society can support or undermine democratic institutions.

A half century ago, Almond and Verba found dramatic differences among the five nations they studied. With regard to conversational norms, thirty-seven percent of Americans said that they did not "feel free to discuss politics" with many people—if anyone. Fewer residents of the United Kingdom felt the same way, with only thirty-two percent feeling constrained in their political conversations. Less freedom was felt in Mexico, with forty-three percent reluctant to talk politics, but the highest incidences of reluctance were in Italy (fifty-one percent) and Germany (fifty-five percent). Perhaps even more telling was the percentage of residents unwilling to tell a native interviewer which party they voted for in the last national election. After receiving reassurances of the confidentiality of their responses, only one to two percent of U.S., UK, and Mexican residents refused to say which party they supported, compared with sixteen percent in Germany and thirty-two percent in Italy.[31] In the 1950s, the prevailing norm was to state one's partisan allegiance when asked, but in Germany—and especially Italy—doing so was clearly abnormal among a subset of the population.

It is my hope that looking at other countries and other times in history will whet the appetite for learning where we stand today. Sadly, the prevailing norm in the United States is that it's okay to discuss politics, but that one should avoid doing so with people holding views different from one's own. In a comprehensive review of modern political conversation in the United States, political communication scholar Diana Mutz pointed out that the majority of U.S. citizens do not have a regular conversation partner who reliably votes or thinks about politics differently from how they do. In fact, most of us can't even name four people with whom we regularly discuss politics, let alone disagree. To make matters worse, those who are politically active and have larger, denser networks are even less likely to experience disagreement in their political conversations than their more retiring counterparts.[32]

Mutz views this as partly a problem of *manners,* a term that refers to a particular variety of social norms. At one point, Mutz quoted Miss Manners herself, a nationally syndicated columnist who advises people on rules of etiquette. A reader had written to her in 2004 because this concerned citizen perceived a social "barrier to participation in the world's most famous democracy—that being Americans' reluctance to consider political discourse to be polite conversation." Sadly, Miss Manners had to concur and suggested that the reader avoid talking politics at dinner parties because people generally lack the skill to "express their opinions politely and listen to others' respectfully."[33]

It should be no surprise that a society that views political talk as unsavory, argumentative, and impolite ends up limiting most political conversation to agreements among like-minded peers. The cost, according to Mutz's research, is that too few people come to understand the reasons behind points of view different from their own.[34] From the structurational perspective, the daily repetition of these practices adds up to significant problems at the societal level. At the least, it provides the kindling for partisan wildfires, which can burn away any carefully tended middle ground, leaving no hope of a public consensus. At the worst, these day-to-day conversational practices can lead to intolerance, with the emergent majority not only ignoring but also refusing to permit the other side to speak its mind. Thus, one should never take comfort in being in a "free" society if its underlying cultural norms discourage open—let alone respectful—political talk across lines of difference.

STRETCHING THE LIMITS OF DISCOURSE

If conversational norms govern how often we talk and with whom, there are other structures that govern what we talk about and how we talk about it, not only in conversations but also in media and other communication modes. Recall from Figure 8.2 that a deliberative community aims to "promote the creative expression of different perspectives and experiences to help community members see the world through others' eyes." Thus, deliberation thrives when the larger society permits the free discussion of the full range of potential public issues.

To understand what that can mean, consider a quasi-experiment carried out by a large team of communication faculty in Wisconsin and Texas. Randomly selected residents viewed and discussed a documentary film about the cultural divisions in Jasper, Texas, after the murder of James Byrd, Jr., an African American man dragged to his death by three white men. Viewing the documentary increased viewers' willingness to talk about race and even take political action to address racism. Taking part in the forum discussion of the issue also had an additional impact on participants' awareness of and willingness to discuss racism.[35]

In structurational terms, this experimental intervention illustrates how small changes in people's experiences can change their expectations and intentions. Exposure to the documentary—an artistic expression of historical information—can yield this effect, as can participation in discussion itself. In both cases, people experience a kind of discourse—frank talk about race and racism—and then recalibrate their sense of whether that kind of discourse is normal, safe, and common. Just as growing up in a foul-mouthed household makes one more likely to use profanity when talking with others, so does repeated exposure to deliberative discourse—in media and forums—habituate one to deliberation in other settings.

Other limits on public discourse can be far more subtle, constraining not only the issues we discuss but also how we discuss them. Law professor Mary Ann Glendon identified one such constraint on political discourse in the United States. "Discourse about rights," she argued, "has become the principal language that we use in public settings to discuss weighty questions of right and wrong." The particular way people talk about rights in the United States stands out from discussions of rights in other countries "by its starkness and simplicity, its prodigality in bestowing the rights label, its legalistic character, its exaggerated absoluteness, its hyperindividualism, its insularity, and its silence with respect to personal, civic, and collective responsibilities."[36]

Glendon was clear that the problem is not claiming rights, per se. The women's rights movement, the civil rights movement, and other efforts to secure the equal rights of citizens have played important roles in advancing the cause of democracy. What concerns Glendon is how pitifully narrow the range of arguments available in public discourse has become. In particular, Glendon bemoaned the fact that responsibility has nearly suffocated under the blanket of rights: "A near-aphasia concerning responsibilities makes it seem legitimate to accept the benefits of living in a democratic social welfare republic without assuming the corresponding personal and civic obligations."[37]

Being a legal scholar, Glendon found the roots of this problem not so much in the words of everyday conversation but in the way judges and elected officials talk and act. In making this point, she quoted Martin Luther King, Jr., who argued that "the habits, if not the hearts, of people have been and are being altered every day by legislative acts, judicial decisions, and executive orders."[38]

One example among many that Glendon cited is the now-established legal principle in the United States "that one does not have a duty to rescue a stranger in distress."[39] Far from a hypothetical point of law, the dominance of individual rights over a sense of collective responsibility leads to a distorted society, wherein one finds it hard to be taken seriously when making arguments about our obligations to, say, children living in poverty. One can talk about the rights of poor children, but in cases like these, the rights language misses the mark and results in a less forceful argument than one might otherwise be able to construct.

Since Glendon's study, which she published in 1991, rights talk has continued to hold sway, but considerable effort has gone into promoting the idea of public responsibility. The communitarian movement that percolated in the 1980s gained momentum in the 1990s, with works such as Amatai Etzioni's 1993 book, *The Spirit of Community.* This led reformers to call for reinvigorated "community politics" and "civic renewal," both of which emphasized the importance of community ties and collective responsibility.[40]

One more whimsical but culturally salient moment in the turn toward community was the final episode of the sitcom *Seinfeld,* viewed by an estimated seventy-six million viewers on May 14, 1998. In the finale, the main characters cruelly mocked a man who was being robbed across the street, only to find themselves arrested for failing to intervene. At the ensuing trial, a montage of previous episodes revealed the characters' lack of responsibility in every conceivable social situation.[41] Though played for comic effect, the episode acknowledged that *Seinfeld* had developed a cadre of critics who had grown weary of the main characters.

Though watching this final episode was far from the powerful documentary on racism mentioned earlier, it reached a critical mass of the general public and probably, in its own small way, likely pushed the question of civic responsibility higher on the public's agenda. No definitive study has measured such an effect, but the point here is simply to see how public discourse—from conversations to popular television—shapes how we talk. Day-to-day interactions and mass-mediated events contribute to the larger pattern of social norms that promote—or thwart—open discussion of a full range of public issues.

Institutional Infrastructure

Though structuration theory emphasizes the often-underestimated importance of day-to-day social encounters, it also recognizes that societies are typically more than the sum of informal interaction. Over time, a large-scale society invariably develops an array of institutions. As Giddens explained, "The structuration of institutions can be understood in terms of how it comes about that social activities become 'stretched' across wide spans of time-space."[42] In other words, if a practice becomes sufficiently regularized—and often codified or ritualized—across a wide enough stretch of time and space, we can come to recognize it as an institution.

Happily, here much of the news is good for deliberative society. In fact, it is likely that the modern emergence of the idea of deliberative democracy stands largely on the strength of the institutional infrastructure that has emerged in many countries, from Brazil to Australia, from the United States to the European Union. Key features of this underlying infrastructure include such diverse institutions as schools, civil society, and newly emergent discursive designs. We consider each of these in turn.

PUBLIC EDUCATION IN DEMOCRACY

A solid education, be it private or public, has become the norm in the United States, thanks to laws making general education mandatory for all children and the construction of thousands of schools, both large and small. According to the census conducted by the National Center for Education Statistics, in 2001 more than 91,000 public schools provided instruction to 47.7 million middle school and high school students in the United States.[43]

We take for granted the present state of affairs, but the rise of educational institutions must be understood as a remarkable historic accomplishment. Since the United States started systematically recording educational data in 1940, the percentage of the adult population (twenty-five years and older) with at least a high school diploma has risen from twenty-five percent to eighty percent. In other words, in just over half a century, graduating from high school has gone from something that only a quarter of the population do to something that all but one-fifth accomplish.

Figure 8.3 shows that this change was even more dramatic for racial minorities in the United States, with high school graduation rates rising from 7.7% to 72.3%. That 27.7% of African Americans—and 16.4% of whites—do not obtain a high school diploma rightly remains a source of concern, but there is no denying that the experience of going to school has become, in Giddens's language, sufficiently "stretched across wide spans of time-space" that we recognize it as a basic institution for all communities within the United States.

Across the globe, rates of public education from preschool to college have also risen dramatically over the course of the last century. There are now only a handful of countries in sub-Saharan Africa, the Middle East, and South Asia in which a majority of the population remains illiterate. This reflects dramatic improvements in education for both men and women. According to data compiled by the United Nations, if one looks back to 1970, 28.5% of men in the world were illiterate, compared to just 13.3% in 2005. For women, the comparable figures for a drop in illiteracy are from 44.6% to 22.3%.[44] Thus, for both men and women, the growth of educational institutions has cut illiteracy rates in half in just 35 years.

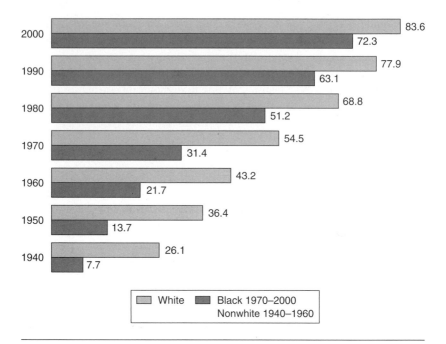

Figure 8.3   Percentage of the Population (Twenty-Five Years and Older) With a High School Diploma (or More), by Race

SOURCE: U.S. Census data from http://www.census.gov/population/socdemo/education/phct41/ US.pdf.

What is the significance of these institutions for democracy, political communication, and deliberation? In *Why Deliberative Democracy*, political theorists Amy Gutmann and Dennis Thompson explained the value of general education in this way:

> Democratic theorists have long recognized . . . [that] democracy cannot thrive without a well-educated citizenry. . . . Because the school system in a democracy appropriately aims to prepare children to become free and equal citizens, it constitutes one of the most important sites of rehearsals for deliberation. . . . Publicly supported and publicly accredited schools should teach future citizens the knowledge and skills needed for democratic deliberation. . . . If schools do not equip children to deliberate, other institutions are not likely to do so.[45]

The logic of this view is clear. A well-rounded education, particularly one that spans from kindergarten through college, can provide students with basic knowledge (history, economics, biology, etc.), critical thinking and learning skills, as well as personal value commitments that have withstood critical scrutiny by peers, educators, and oneself.[46] Surely a more knowledgeable, critical, and self-aware public is better prepared to deliberate or participate in any other form of political communication or engagement.

The uniformity with which democratic theorists adhered to this view of education prompted a team of researchers to investigate the matter more carefully. Norman Nie, Jane Junn, and Kenneth Stehlik-Barry pulled together a variety of cross-sectional and longitudinal survey data and found a far more complex pattern of results than might have been expected. Consistent with prior theory, they found that nearly every measure of political knowledge and engagement is highest among those with the greatest education, and the relationship is remarkably linear.[47]

Though the evidence of education's impact on political knowledge and engagement was clear, Nie and his colleagues probed further by investigating why education had these impacts. They found two distinct paths from education to political impact. First, the researchers reasoned that "an appropriate measure of the cognitive effects of education is one that captures the capabilities that are important to the words and language of politics." Taking a decidedly political communication perspective, Nie and his colleagues observed that "political struggles in democracy are waged in public arguments, amidst the rhetoric of public debate." In the world of politics, the ability to use language effectively is more important than, say, mathematical or spatial reasoning abilities, and education did, indeed, significantly boost people's "verbal cognitive proficiency."[48] This rising linguistic proficiency, in turn, had a direct impact on people's political knowledge of the principles of democracy and other current political facts, as well as on people's levels of tolerance for dissenting points of view.[49]

Contrary to the conventional view, however, education's impact on political engagement operated not so much through cognitive verbal learning, per se, but through education's impact on intermediary variables influenced by the political centrality of one's social network. Nie and his fellow researchers measured network centrality with a set of questions that asked respondents whether "they were personally acquainted with, or would be recognized by," particular public officials (e.g., a state legislator) or media professionals (e.g., a local reporter). Nearly half (forty-eight percent) of those surveyed had no such connections in their network, but network centrality varied by educational level. For instance, fewer than twenty percent of those with fewer than eight years in school knew at least two "political players," whereas sixty percent or more of those with at least eighteen years of education knew at least two.

Figure 8.4 greatly simplifies the results Nie and his colleagues found and makes it easier to see the crux of their findings. Whereas education shapes political knowledge through its effect on verbal proficiency, years spent in school promote political engagement through a complex set of indirect influences. As Nie

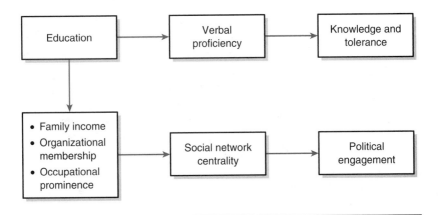

Figure 8.4   Indirect Effects of Education on Knowledge, Tolerance, and Political
Engagements

SOURCE: Adapted from Nie et al. (1996, pp. 85–88).

put it, time spent in educational institutions has a sorting effect by allocating
scarce income, membership, and occupational resources to those with the highest
educational attainments. Those resources, in turn, generate a political-social network closer to the centers of public status and influence, and that yields higher
levels of political engagement. After all, those closest to political power require the
least effort and gain the greatest rewards for their political engagement.[50]

Nie and colleagues were discouraged by their data. They have come to
view education as a competition for scarce social, economic, and (indirectly)
political resources. Though the rising rates of literacy and educational attainment have had a beneficial effect on society—and have mitigated some social
inequalities—the researchers concluded that "in the end, there is no compelling
evidence for either increasing or decreasing educationally based inequality in
political access." After all, "competition for scarce resources always produces
inequality, and there appears to be no simple recipe for altering the total amount
of inequality in political voice and access."[51]

Nie, Junn, and Stehlik-Barry provided a much-needed note of caution
about the power of educational institutions to transform the basic calculus of
political power, but when they moved away from the narrow question of equalizing formal political influence, they, too, recognized that widespread education can provide a more solid foundation for democracy:

> Increasing educational attainment clearly creates a more democratically
> enlightened citizenry. And a citizenry that is more committed to democratic
> values, as well as one that has a deeper and more sophisticated understanding
> of democratic processes, cannot help but provide greater protection for our
> democratic institutions and practices against whatever anti-democratic
> forces the future may hold.[52]

Once we begin looking for the broader purposes of education, it becomes apparent that schools can do even more to buttress a deliberative community. Education professor Walter Parker led the charge to make our educational institutions schools of deliberation. In his book *Teaching Democracy*, he explained that the opportunity for deliberative education could not be more obvious. Schools are, after all, "public places in which diverse populations of young people are congregated." Educators simply need to do three things: (1) "increase the variety and frequency of interaction among students who are different from one another," (2) "orchestrate these contacts to foster deliberation about the problems" that invariably arise in such settings, and (3) "strive to develop communicative competence, particularly the receptive practice of listening across social perspectives."[53]

One of Parker's suggestions is implementing a curriculum that looks a great deal like an extended dance remix of the National Issues Forums introduced in Chapter 2. In this curriculum, students analyze a problem, generate and consider alternatives solutions, and so on. That straightforward approach to deliberation is essential for learning how to deliberate on large-scale public policy problems.[54]

A more subtle example of in-school deliberation, however, comes from the work of elementary school teacher Vivian Paley. Parker explained that Paley chooses to "focus on the lived problems that her children experience in the classroom and on the playground." The most striking example is when Paley asked her kindergartners to deliberate on a rule she had imagined. The rule simply read, "You can't say 'you can't play.'" Initially, only the four young "outcasts" in Paley's class endorsed the idea. Paley continued the discussion by involving second and fourth graders at the school, and both classes were adamant that such a rule would only have done good had it been in place during their kindergarten years. When Paley took these views back to her own classroom's discussion circle, "her children listen, enthralled. . . . In the Socratic spirit, gently, she encourages them to support their views with reasons, and to listen carefully to and respond to the reasoning of other children."[55] In the end, the students agreed that the rule should be instituted as the law of the land starting the following year. The rule itself, of course, may have value, but for Parker, the greatest value was the deliberative process.

The point here is to underscore the missed opportunity for teaching deliberative skills and norms in school. This does not mean, however, that deliberation should be privileged above all other forms of public talk. Conventional debate programs certainly have their limitations, but they teach a mode of adversarial conflict that can play a valuable role in the political process. Moreover, teachers have come to recognize that students have different learning styles and appetites, and there is no need to starve aspiring debaters and gorge the natural deliberators. In sum, public education will best promote a deliberative society by teaching future citizens the virtues of a range of discursive styles, including those already most prevalent in society as well as those we might wish to make more prominent in the future.[56]

NONGOVERNMENTAL ORGANIZATIONS AND CIVIL SOCIETY

Though schools can help develop the political knowledge and communication skills essential for a healthy deliberative community, there is another set of institutions perhaps even more critical to sustaining public deliberation—the array of voluntary organizations between the private for-profit sector and the government. Earlier, we discussed civil society and voluntary associations, and it is useful to define these terms more carefully at this point. Political theorist Michael Walzer advanced one of the most popular definitions of civil society, describing it as the "space of uncoerced human association and also a set of relational networks—formed for the sake of faith, interest and ideology—that fill this space"[57] Civil society includes family life, sports clubs, religious associations, nonprofit organizations, neighborhood associations, political interest groups, and more. Voluntary associations simply constitute the bulk of the entities that make up civil society.

Scholars debate whether private businesses and political organizations also fall under civil society.[58] Herein, I exclude exclusively for-profit, market-oriented entities, which constitute much of "the market" or the business-oriented private sphere. These have a distinct market logic and purpose that play an important role in society but in a very different way. Other economic-minded associations, however, such as chambers of commerce, trade unions, and professional organizations, count as part of civil society because they address public issues and are largely voluntary.

One could also exclude from the discussion strictly political organizations, such as political parties. These could be set aside in a separate category sometimes called political society. I choose to count such voluntary groups as parts of civil society to the extent they are not simply instruments of the government, as in the case of governments based on one-party rule (e.g., the Institutional Revolutionary Party [PRI] in Mexico, which ruled from 1929 to the early 1990s). Nonetheless, to keep the discussion focused, I make reference not so much to their electoral activities as to their organizing role in society.

When thinking of civil society as the bedrock on which one can build a deliberative society, it is clear that civil society plays many important roles. As many previous examples have demonstrated, these associations can be training grounds for learning deliberative attitudes, habits, and skills. This is true of programs that explicitly promote discussion, such as the National Issues Forums outlined in Chapter 2, as it is also true of organizations that promote deliberative skills more incidentally, as in the case of social movements. In a sense, these voluntary institutions are vehicles of adult civic education, often picking up where the institutions of formal schooling left off. In this same way, civil society is also the pool from which emerge the civic reformers, discussion leaders, and activists who promote deliberation, per se, as well as the organizations that play formal roles in deliberative processes, such as the Brazilian municipal councils described in Chapter 7.

Aside from these obvious ways in which civil society draws private citizens into public life and equips them for political engagement, there are other interesting, complex connections between the civil sphere and deliberative citizenry. Consider the case of the Parent League documented by sociologist Nina Eliasoph. One evening, a new member named Charles "inadvertently violated the group's civic practice by implying that the group should talk more, to more people—that the group's quiet way of encouraging community involvement was misdirected."[59] In structurational terms, the league had drawn on conventional understandings of the limited role of parent organizations to limit its agenda to uncontroversial actions, such as fundraisers, and it had experienced modest success, further reinforcing this self-understanding. Eliasoph explained:

> Charles, an African-American parent, reported that some parents had phoned him about a teacher who said "racially disparaging things" to a student, "suggesting that blacks were not intelligent and such." Some kids in the teacher's class had tried complaining to the "appropriate authorities," but the authorities all claimed to be "too busy" to deal with it. The kids then told their parents and the parents told Charles, who was the local NAACP representative. . . . Since race riots had recently erupted in the school and at a nearby movie theater, and since the White Aryan Resistance was scheduled to hold a concert in town, Charles's testimony could have seemed especially noteworthy to the Parent League. . . .
>
> Instead, the group's response to Charles's speech was startlingly bland. None asked what the teacher actually had said. First Sheny minimized the problem of the lack of "proper channels," making the problem an interpersonal one, reminiscing about how hard it used to be for her own mother to talk to teachers.
>
> Mild-mannered Geoffrey cut in with a slightly cross edge to his voice: "And what do you want of this group. Do you want us to do something"—not as a question, but with a dropping tone at the end.
>
> Charles said, "I just thought more people would be at the meeting and it would just be something parents should know." He said parents should be more involved in general, not just to accomplish things, but to talk. Of course, members thought involvement was important, too—but Charles's urging the parents to get more people involved seemed simply an insult, since they assumed that they were doing all they could to invite involvement.
>
> In defense of the group, another parent, Ron, exclaimed, "Don't underestimate us—we make efficient use of small numbers of people! We get a lot done!"
>
> Charles slowly started restating the problem, but now Ron was impatient. He interrupted, "It's not up to us to do anything about the incident. That should go through the proper channels." Turning to Charles, as if it were

purely Charles's problem, he conceded, "It is unfortunate that the incident occurred—happened," using that special bureaucrat-ese that marked their discourse on "touchy" issues. "But it should go through the proper authorities."[60]

This incident, Eliasoph explained, "illustrates how people can create a sense of 'the public' that paradoxically shrinks their own meaning-making powers." This case "shows a paradoxical situation, in which committed, concerned citizens tried to do good precisely by hushing public-spirited conversation in public." She concluded:

> Thus, rejecting abstract, political, or principled talk was, paradoxically, volunteers' way of looking out for the common good. Volunteers assumed that if they want to show each other and their neighbors that regular citizens really can be effective, they should avoid issues that they considered "political." In their effort to be open and inclusive, to appeal to regular, unpretentious fellow citizens without discouraging them, they silenced public-spirited deliberation—which was just what someone like Charles thought the group needed to have in order to involve new members. This creation of "the public," this civic practice, itself dissipated the public spirit from public settings.[61]

The simplest lesson is that, if not careful, voluntary associations can actually suppress deliberation by too rigidly resisting the emergence of larger public or "political" concerns. By rigidly remaining separate from politics, an association can be not merely apolitical but actually antipolitical. To the extent that civil society serves as the wellspring of public life and vibrant political society, antipolitical actions can actually decrease the wider public's involvement in the work of self-government, including public deliberation.

Another sociologist, Theda Skocpol, took this concern even further in her historical study *Diminished Democracy: From Membership to Management in American Civil Life.* Skocpol noticed a tendency in the modern literature on civil life to celebrate local, apolitical associations in particular. Theorists, including the aforementioned communitarians, who have tried to resuscitate a sense of civic responsibility, portray civic life "as an aspect of local community, with national government at best irrelevant and at worst inimical" to civic virtue.[62] Conservatives speak in even stronger language, casting federal government institutions "as the chief enemies of 'natural' civic community, which they believe is rooted in autonomous families, neighborhoods, and local ethnic and voluntary groups able to solve social problems on their own, without involving extralocal government."[63]

After compiling an archive of more than one hundred fifty years of historical data on voluntary associations, Skocpol found that, at least in the U.S. experience, localism was hardly the hallmark of early civil society. "America," she wrote, "originally became a nation of organizers and joiners of membership-based voluntary associations *that operated in close symbiosis with representative government and democratic politics.*"[64]

One organization among many was the delightfully named Independent Order of Odd Fellows. With roots in England, this organization gradually established a network of lodges in the early 1800s, self-consciously modeling itself and its fraternal bylaws on the U.S. Constitution. From the outset, it aspired to be a "grand lodge of the United States," and, Skocpol recounted, other "immigrant-ethnic fraternals often established a full complement of state and national representative arrangements at a stage when they barely had enough members to fill a small number of local lodges scattered across several cities."[65] Far from being narrowly localist community groups, these early civic associations connected local membership identities with larger state and national association goals, including influencing government policy.

Today, there exists a far greater number of voluntary associations, and unlike the Parent League that troubled Eliasoph, most seek to maintain vital connections to state and national government. Nonetheless, Skocpol saw a diminished democracy because so many of these associations have lost their civic vitality. She wrote:

> [The United States] has the most pluralist polity in the world, yet associations claiming to speak for the people lack incentives and capacities to mobilize large numbers of ordinary people through direct personal contacts and ongoing involvement in interactive settings. Yawning gaps have opened between local voluntary efforts and the professional advocates and grant makers who seek national influence.[66]

BRIDGING DISCOURSE AND INSTITUTIONS

Having described the discursive practices and institutional architecture that can shape the prospects for deliberation, it is instructive to see how changing discourse can, in turn, lead to changing institutions. From the structurational perspective, this is a case where changing our language structures—the words we use and the frames of reference we apply to situations—can ultimately give rise to new institutions that change not only how we talk but also what physical and social resources are available to us for addressing public problems.

Political theorist John Dryzek provided the most powerful example of such a change through his theory of discursive democracy. Consistent with the central themes of this work and the larger field of political communication, Dryzek pointed out that democracy is not simply about mobilizing people to pursue their already-established interests; it is as much about talk—the way we frame and, consequently, understand ourselves, our common problems, and our malleable interests. Thus, a healthy democratic society needs not only participatory institutions, through which we lobby and vote, but also discursive institutions that embody "communicative ethics in rules of debate."[67]

The various deliberative forums described in earlier chapters provide examples of such discursive designs, but Dryzek highlighted other, more systemwide changes that have occurred in our discursive and institutional architecture:

> [The "incipient" deliberative designs] go by different names in different contexts, and none pays conscious tribute to communicative rationality [or deliberative ethics]. Examples include mediation of civil, labor, international, and environmental disputes . . . ; alternative dispute resolution procedures more generally . . . ; regulatory negotiation . . . ; and "problem-solving" workshops in international conflict resolution.[68]

Each of these processes has only become common practice in the course of the past three decades. Far from randomly evolving social practices, they all share these same features:

1. They address an ongoing problem of concern to all parties present.

2. The parties have conflicting views of what action should be taken to resolve the conflict.

3. A neutral third party, such as a "moderator" or "facilitator," orchestrates a discussion among the parties.

4. Discussion is given time to develop in face-to-face settings, following rules that adhere to the norms of honesty, openness, mutual respect, consensus decision making, or at least reasoned debate.

5. Discussion typically involves a reexamination of the parties' identities and relationships, often in a way that directly contributes to conflict resolution.

6. The final decision is by consensus of all parties.[69]

Having read this far in this volume, you will easily recognize the features of deliberation in these practices. The point is that these newly emergent discursive designs provide us with both a new way of talking about conflict and a set of semiprofessionalized and routinized practices we can draw on to address them. There now exists an abundance of mediation clinics, dispute resolution centers, and formal government procedures for negotiation. These institutions and the practices they preach become entrenched across time and space. Thus, it is fair to say that these designs have evolved into institutions, all of which indirectly support the practice of deliberation, which bears a close resemblance to these "normal" practices.[70]

Actively Creating Deliberative Society

The preceding discussion provides historical insight into the forces buttressing and undermining a deliberative society, and it also makes it easier to understand contemporary efforts to actively forge such a society. The most significant efforts to date have focused on local communities, but from the structurational perspective, it is undoubtedly the case that these local transformations could feed into even larger social changes.

INTRODUCING DELIBERATION TO A COMMUNITY

One straightforward strategy for developing a more deliberative community is to hold an ongoing series of deliberative forums, addressing a range of issues and reaching out to different corners of the community. One national civic association that promotes this approach is the Study Circles Resource Center (SCRC), founded in 1989. Since its inception, the center has shifted its focus from promoting self-guided, small-group discussions on current issues to helping communities transform the way they make decisions about public problems.

The best example of the SCRC's approach may be the case of Portsmouth, New Hampshire, a small community of just over 20,000 people in the southeast corner of the state. The SCRC began working with Portsmouth in 1999, when the Portsmouth Middle School asked them to design an event to address the perennial problem of bullying. With the help of local officials and community members, SCRC created "Days of Dialogue: Respectful Schools." In this process, two hundred sixth graders from the middle school discussed the issue with seventy-five parents and community members. The meetings took on an unexpected gravity due to a chilling coincidence: While Portsmouth students were describing their experiences of being bullied, two students at Columbine High School in Colorado shot and killed twelve students and a teacher, wounded two dozen others, and then took their own lives.

The timely forum on bullying helped educators and community members think through the issue at hand and take action to attempt to prevent such a tragedy as befell Columbine. The plans that emerged from these forums even included specific suggestions made by the student participants. Cameras on buses and more adult supervision at school events offered students more confidence that bullying would be noticed—and punished—wherever it happened in the context of the school. Another suggestion—the establishment of a peer mediation program—was important not only for its substantive effect on resolving student conflicts but also because it privileged student-to-student dialogue, creating one more way in which students can learn deliberative skills in school.

Like many other deliberative public meetings, this forum also held a mirror up to the community itself. As one Portsmouth resident involved in the forum commented, "Adults in the community . . . expressed surprise about how so many youth had meaningful things to say. They were also surprised to hear that, in certain areas of the school, the students wanted more, not less of an adult presence." The respect that emerged was mutual, by this participant's account, as the middle school students in attendance "were surprised that adults would even listen to what they had to say."[71]

Beyond the particular issue of bullying, this initial success demonstrated the potential efficacy of deliberative discursive designs in addressing difficult public problems. One of the attendees at the bullying forum was Nansi Craig, a member of the Portsmouth's school board. The following year, she commissioned the SCRC to design a series of study circles on redistricting schools, an issue that arouses public passion owing to its potential impact on school enrollments, budgets, and the plans parents have for where their children will learn.

Thinking back to the discussion of framing in Chapter 3, an event like this can become framed as either a public relations gimmick by an insincere government (buttressed by self-interested community leaders) or a genuine effort to involve the wider community in an honest deliberative process. The organizers of the redistricting study circles received the latter framing in local media coverage, as evidenced by an editorial that ran in the *Portsmouth Herald* in advance of the event. The portions that invoke a deliberative democratic frame have been italicized:

> For [redistricting] to be done successfully with the least amount of trauma, *public input is vital.* We strongly suggest *as many people as possible* take part, *add their ideas, express their concerns, and work toward solutions* to the problems which are bound to arise. . . . Portsmouth School Superintendent Lyonel Tracy has so far *fashioned a democratic approach* to solving challenges facing the school district: *creating a community solution to a community problem.*
>
> The School Board Redistricting Committee, the Greater Portsmouth Education Partnership Council, and the University of New Hampshire Public Conversations Project have combined to establish a process to *gather the information needed to make informed decisions.* They will use the Study Circle format similar to that used . . . at Portsmouth Middle School last year. . . . *This obviously requires some time commitment, but the argument that the future of our community must always be left to the dedicated few must be rejected. It would be nice to see some new faces involved.* . . . *Be part of the solution, not part of the problem.*[72]

This single editorial was just a few lines of print in the local paper, but it became one of many favorable characterizations of this study circle process and others that would follow. Table 8.1 shows how the SCRC helped spark an ongoing series of public forums in the Portsmouth community that moved beyond schools. Forums on race relations held in 2002 did not involve large numbers of citizens, but they did forge stronger network connections among key stakeholders in the community. For example, the deputy chief of the police department acknowledged that sitting down to discuss race with leaders from the African American community made him inclined to pick up the phone and call his newfound acquaintance at the local NAACP chapter if a racial issue arose in his department.[73]

Forums held from 2002 to 2004 involved the largest number of citizens and, ultimately, helped to shape the city's master planning process. Of all of the

Table 8.1   Study Circle Events Held in Portsmouth, 1999–2004

Date(s)	Sponsoring Organization	Discussion Topic	Total Participants
1999	Portsmouth Middle School	Bullying and school safety	275
2000	School board	Redistricting elementary schools	100
2002	Police department, NAACP, and the school district	Race relations	50
2002–2004	Portsmouth Listens, an association comprising city government, the Citywide Neighborhoods Committee, the Chamber of Commerce, and resident volunteers	The city's master plan (setting direction, in-depth exploration of specific plan elements, and review of the master plan in relation to study circles input)	440

SOURCE: Adapted from Scully and McCoy (2005, p. 201).

study circle processes, this one likely had the largest policy impact. As recounted in the *Portsmouth Herald*, the Planning Board began "acting on . . . the recommendations of the Portsmouth Listens study circles." During a pivotal board meeting, "time and again . . . city planners, in drawing their conclusions, cited suggestions made by community members." The most notable of the ideas that grew out of the forums was setting aside ten acres of green space alongside a local creek for the purpose of conservation.[74]

The net result of these processes on community development is hard to measure precisely. The study circles have demonstrated to a critical mass of public officials that dialogue and deliberation can play a productive role in helping community members listen to each other's concerns, make social connections, and create mutually acceptable solutions to some of their shared problems. But there has been no establishment of a specific institution or discursive design that can carry on this process in the future. The best candidate for this role is Portsmouth Listens, a voluntary association that spearheaded the master-planning forums and, unlike some other voluntary associations, has embraced its obvious connections to public officials and the larger political process.[75] Portsmouth Listens continues to hold study circles, including 2006 meetings on the city budget,[76] but it is unclear whether this association can sustain the movement toward deliberative community.

TOWARD DELIBERATIVE GOVERNANCE

By way of contrast, we can look at a relatively well-established deliberative community. If one travels five hundred miles south of Portsmouth, along the eastern coast of the United States, one finds Hampton, Virginia, a port city with a population of more than 150,000. Among the oldest American cities, Hampton has undergone a transformation in the past two decades—one that has changed its cultural practices and its institutions and made it into a remarkably deliberative community. Winner of a 2005 Innovations in American Government award bestowed by Harvard University's John F. Kennedy School of Government, a wide range of scholars and institutions have identified Hampton, Virginia, as an exceptional example of how government and volunteers can work together to build an engaged, deliberative community.

William Potapchuk, president and founder of Virginia's Community Building Institute, teamed up with two community leaders in Hampton to write a detailed account of Hampton's recent history. Summarizing the present state of affairs, these observers explained that in Hampton, "deliberation is not an 'event,' as it is in so many other places. Instead, deliberation is integral to deep reforms that have changed government and governance, reweaving and strengthening the community's civic infrastructure."[77]

When these authors referred to "government and governance," they were not being stubbornly redundant. The distinction between these words is important, and it helps us understand the case of Hampton. Briefly, *government* refers to official public institutions (e.g., courts, legislatures, executives, agencies), whereas *governance* refers to the process of making and implementing collective decisions—a process that can include not only government institutions but also the broader civil society, private sector, and general public.

It is no coincidence that Harry Boyte, who advanced the concept of free spaces presented earlier in this chapter, stresses this distinction. "Governance," he argued, "intimates a paradigm shift in civic agency and in democracy." If we think in terms of governance, rather than government, we shift from "seeing citizens as voters, volunteers, clients, or consumers to viewing citizens as problem solvers and co-creators of public goods." In the new governance paradigm, "government is a crucial instrument of the citizenry, providing leadership, resources, tools, and rules," but they are no longer "the center of the civic universe." If the larger civil society shares responsibility for governance, we then have the ability "to address complex public problems that cannot be solved *without* governments, but that governments *alone* can never solve."[78]

Returning to the specific case of Hampton, Potapchuk and his coauthors reported that before making a deliberative turn, "Hampton's city leaders found that many neighborhood trends were not healthy." In particular, leaders worried about the futures of the children growing up in the community and perceived that "the resources that the city could use to address these issues were shrinking. If the leaders wanted to address community problems proactively, they needed community partners" with whom they could collaborate.[79]

One important feature of Hampton's government was the long periods of service from its public officials. The city uses a city-manager model, whereby a part-time council with seven at-large members provides general guidance to a professional city manager, who oversees the various city agencies. It is not unusual for the manager to serve ten or more years, and the average department director is likely to serve twenty years. Coupled with routinely positive citizen evaluations of city services, this made it possible for Hampton city officials to advance civic reform without immediately hitting a wall of public skepticism.[80]

With the aim of shared governance, city officials teamed up with neighborhood leaders and undertook a series of interlocking initiatives, highlighted by the Neighborhood Initiative adopted by the city council in 1994. This initiative, and its offshoots, helped to make the community more deliberative, but rather than simply being a string of discrete deliberative forums, the Hampton approach involved the following programs:

1. *Youth Civic Engagement Initiative.* This initiative won Hampton the Innovations in American Government award. The design is simple: a deliberative voluntary association organized and populated by youth to discuss public issues, emphasizing the issues and concerns most pertinent to their own lives. Participants have learned skills in research, opinion research, deliberation, and collaboration, and youth representatives—even those not yet old enough to vote—have had a seat at the table for many significant city decisions. The net result is a cadre of motivated and skilled young people, many of whom will continue to use those skills as adults who have chosen to continue living in Hampton.

2. *Neighborhood College.* Whereas the Youth Initiative somewhat indirectly teaches civic skills to youths by involving them in issues of concern, the adult leadership college takes a more direct pedagogical approach, along the lines of the Highlander Folk School. Citizens attend six to twelve class sessions and complete homework assignments on subjects ranging from process skills (e.g., meeting facilitation, working with diversity) to policy making (e.g., budgeting, policing). By 2005, the college had "graduated" three hundred Hampton citizens, many of whom became community leaders, commissioners, or candidates for public office. In sum, this adult education program helped expand the pool of social capital that can promote deliberative governance in Hampton.

3. *Neighborhood Month.* Even in Hampton, most residents will not find themselves spontaneously drawn to join the aforementioned youth and adult education programs. To reach this larger public, the city created Neighborhood Month, a period during which local civic associations and the city schedule "house tours, celebrations, parties, and neighborhood clean-ups."[81] Just as the microjournalism efforts described in Chapter 3 help citizens connect with their immediate neighbors, these local parties and projects help citizens develop their ties with neighbors. Ultimately, these local ties may lead to becoming involved in citywide issues, but even when they don't, they build social networks

that reduce the number of Hampton residents who are truly disconnected from the larger social web that extends through the city.

4. *Neighborhood Commission.* This commission is one of the governance organizations that channels the energy generated by the preceding initiatives into real policy decisions and communitywide commitments for public action. The commission is a twenty-one-member body appointed by the Hampton City Council, and its membership includes members of city government, neighborhood representatives, civil society organizations, and youth. It not only makes recommendations to government, but it also has its own budget and undertakes its own initiatives, such as the creation of the Youth Initiative.

These and other efforts have made Hampton a community ever ready for deliberation, collaboration, and active public engagement on the issues that come before the city. Study circles, forums, and other processes have occurred with some regularity since the Neighborhood Initiative's adoption in 1994, but they are not the focus of the Hampton approach. Instead, the focus is on the kind of underlying community being cultivated. In this view, having a deliberative community in place is necessary to having ongoing forums that have real impact.

Conclusion

What Hampton, Portsmouth, and many other communities are working toward is a kind of ongoing deliberation that becomes stable and enduring. Government scholars Elena Fagotto and Archon Fung studied such efforts to investigate why deliberative habits sometimes fail to form in the communities where deliberative events take place. "It is quite possible," they wrote, "that specific instances of deliberation produce very short-lived impacts. That is, some community may adopt deliberation to resolve a conflict but then return to its more conventional, non-deliberative, business as usual practices."[82]

Fagotto and Fung undertook a series of case studies to investigate their hypothesis that "deliberative practices will yield more sustained effects when they are incorporated into—and thus when they transform—the communicative and decision-making routines of organizations, institutions, and the communities of which they are part." In their terminology, deliberation becomes "embedded" once it has taken hold in the most important local associations, institutions, and wider networks of community norms and attitudes.[83]

One can see a degree of embeddedness in both Portsmouth and Hampton, and Fagotto and Fung found signs of embeddedness in four other sites. Given these modest successes, it is far from utopian to hope that even stronger deliberative communities can emerge. After all, the modern reincarnation of the idea of deliberation in democracy has flourished for only two decades, at most.

Looking through the lens of structuration theory once more, one or two decades are but a blink in the longer stretch of time. Social practices, let alone institutions, take time to grow and establish themselves. Even longer periods of time are required when the desired social changes involve what Giddens called structural contradictions, such as that which exists between having a powerful autonomous government and having a lively, influential civil society.[84] Such structural contradictions may never resolve themselves, and the only hope for a deliberative community is to embed its new norms, understandings, and power relationships so strongly into the larger social system that it can resist its fundamental tension with strong, centralized government.

Finally, the gradual development of deliberative communities may or may not feed into a larger process of social change that extends beyond the borders of small towns or small states. It is at this level that advocates of deliberation begin to behave like members of a social movement. One aim of such movements is to cause members of a society to gain new insights into their existing ways of living, inspiring them to change their expectations, aspirations, and habits.[85] One can inspire fellow residents in one's town to become more deliberative for the immediate good of the local community, but if one asks for a more deliberative society, one is likely to carry a membership card in a social movement organization.

It is clear that many of those advocating more dialogue and deliberation in the United States have come to view themselves as part of such a movement. On the final day of the 2006 conference of the National Coalition on Dialogue and Deliberation, the hundreds of participants in attendance held small-group discussions that led to a final vote on the most important priorities for the coalition. One emerged as the clear winner: "Bring the perspectives and skills of dialogue and deliberation into the mainstream of society and its institutions."[86] That aspiration to reshape society is precisely the language of a social movement. This movement wants society to better incorporate the principles and practices of dialogue and deliberation.

Moving from the local community to a nation requires more than just a change in scale. It requires thinking somewhat differently about how civil society organizations might interlock, about how to teach deliberative skills to the public, and how to convene the public to deliberate. We return to these issues in the final chapter, but first we turn our attention to the largest scale of all—the aspiration for deliberation on the global stage.

Notes

1. Available at http://www.thataway.org/main/about/about.html.
2. Putnam (1993). To save the reader the trouble of checking this assertion, scholars have cited the book *Making Democracy Work* more than one thousand times, as

measured by the Web of Science citation index (www.isiknowledge.com). When checked in July of 2006, Putnam's name generated more than 300,000 hits on Google, and *social capital*—the key concept that he helped make famous—yielded more than 8 million hits.

3. Ibid., p. 8.
4. Ibid., p. 15.
5. Putnam (1993) provided the technical details on measurement of institutional performance and social capital in the book's appendices.
6. The correlation between the two was $r = .86$; see Putnam (1993, p. 151). The number of regions varied over the course of the past two centuries, as did the shape of Italy itself.
7. Ibid., p. 150. For a critique of Putnam's account, see Jackman and Miller (2004).
8. Quote from Putnam (1993, p. 167). See also Putnam (1995b).
9. Putnam (1995a, 2000). For a more general defense of the cultural approach to studying political communication, see Schudson (2001). Ryfe (2007) makes an even more pointed argument for thinking about deliberation, per se, as a sociocultural practice.
10. See, for example, Bennett (1998) and *The Public Perspective* 7:4 (1996).
11. Comparison of 1990 and 1994 surveys by Gallup and the Yankelovich Group shows declines in public trust in everything from the local media to religious organizations. For a summary, see League of Women Voters (1997). Also see Galston and Levine (1998, p. 36). Even with such disagreement, there exists a broad academic consensus that—however it may be measured—social capital matters.
12. Tilly (2004).
13. Evans and Boyte (1992, pp. 17–18). One way to conceptualize these spaces is that they are a particularly deliberative, democratic form of political microculture, a more generalized concept that Perrin (2005) used to distinguish among the different environments that promote (or retard) the growth of civic capacities. After all, Theiss-Morse and Hibbing (2005) have found evidence of civic associations that can actually undermine citizens' interest in public life. For more on social movement organizations, deliberation, and democracy, see Mansbridge (1983) and Polletta (2002).
14. Evans and Boyte (1992, p. 19).
15. See http://www.congressionalblackcaucus.net.
16. Evans and Boyte (1992, p. 49).
17. Quoted in ibid., p. 61.
18. Quoted in ibid., p. 61.
19. Quoted in ibid., p. 62.
20. Ibid., p. 68.
21. Ibid., pp. 49–50.
22. Gastil (1994) provided a definition of democratic leadership along these lines.
23. See http://www.highlandercenter.org.
24. Oldenburg (1997).
25. Drucker and Gumpert (1996, p. 280).
26. Ibid., p. 284.
27. The principal writing on structuration theory is Giddens (1984). For a useful review of structuration theory, see Craib (1992).
28. Giddens (1984, p. 25).
29. Ibid., p. 25.
30. Chikwanha-Dzenga, Masunungure, and Madingira (2001).

31. Almond and Verba (1989, pp. 80, 83).
32. Mutz (2006, especially pp. 17, 32).
33. Quoted in ibid., pp. 19–20.
34. Mutz (2006), pp. 63–83.
35. Rojas et al. (2005).
36. Glendon (1991, p. x).
37. Ibid., p. xi.
38. King quoted in ibid., p. 105.
39. Ibid., p. 89.
40. Filner (2002) provided an overview of key works in the community politics litera-
    ture. Briand (1999) and Sirianni and Friedland (2001) exemplified contemporary
    works influenced by it.
41. Ryan (1998).
42. Giddens (1984, p. xxi).
43. Figures available at http://nces.ed.gov/Pubs2003/Overview03/discussion/student
    membership.asp.
44. Data from UNESCO at http://www.uis.unesco.org/en/stats/statistics/literacy2000.htm.
45. Gutmann and Thompson (2004, pp. 35–36).
46. This is the argument made by many educators and social reformers over the years,
    including John Churchill (2006).
47. Nie, Junn, and Stehlik-Barry (1996, pp. 33–37). The clearest exception is voting
    rates, which are higher for those with only seven years of school than for any other
    educational group except those with eighteen years of education.
48. Ibid., pp. 40–41.
49. Ibid., Chapter 4.
50. Ibid., Chapter 4.
51. Ibid., p. 192.
52. Ibid., p. 194.
53. Parker (2003, p. xxi).
54. Ibid., Chapter 6.
55. Ibid., p. 84.
56. This important point comes from Jerome and Algarra (2005).
57. Walzer (1991, p. 293).
58. Foley and Edwards (1996) efficiently summarized these definitional issues.
59. Eliasoph (1996, p. 276).
60. Ibid., p. 276. Source: Cambridge University Press. Used by permission.
61. Ibid., p. 279.
62. Skocpol (2003, p. 9).
63. Ibid., p. 10.
64. Ibid., p. 18, emphasis added.
65. Ibid., p. 43.
66. Ibid., p. 231.
67. Dryzek (1990, p. 41).
68. Ibid., pp. 43–44.
69. Ibid., p. 44. Dryzek also noted that "such exercises are fluid and transient, lasting no
    longer than a particular problematic situation," but the professionalization of the
    dispute resolution field, coupled with the desire of some parties to have routinized
    vehicles for addressing conflicts, may no longer be the case.

70. In this spirit, reading Fisher and Ury's (1981) bestselling book *Getting to Yes* is as much an introduction to deliberation as it is to negotiation. The success of that book reflects the larger public's appetite for deliberation, but it also has helped to refine and articulate that aspiration. Nearly every veteran advocate of deliberation I meet has read that book, which was first published in 1981. Deliberation is not, however, the "normal"—or even preferred—mode of politics, even among activists who embrace its democratic character (Levine and Nierras, 2007).

71. Quoted in Mengual (2003).

72. "For Students' Sake, Join a Circle," *Portsmouth Herald* (September 26, 2000). Available at http://www.seacoastonline.com/2000news/9_26_e1.htm.

73. Adapted from Scully and McCoy (2005, p. 208). On the more traditional practice of study circles, see Oliver (1987). The SCRC is considering changing its name to reflect the fact that its programs have moved beyond reliance on the study circle method. For a broader account of community dialogues, see Walsh (2007).

74. DeConto (2003).

75. See, for example, the September 15, 2003, op-ed Portsmouth Listens published in the *Portsmouth Herald*: "Portsmouth Has Spoken, Now It's Time to Listen." This essay addressed both officials and candidates and warned them against ignoring the voices from the master planning forums: "If [our] opinions are ignored, if candidates who seek local office—for the first time, or through re-election—dismiss that energy, the community grows jaded and the subsequent disengagement will be impossible to overcome." Available at http://www.seacoastonline.com/2003 news/09152003/opinion/50271.htm.

76. See meeting announcement at http://www.seacoastonline.com/news/05302006/ business/105324.htm.

77. Potapchuk, Carlson, and Kennedy (2005, p. 255).

78. Boyte (2005, p. 537, emphasis added).

79. Potapchuk et al. (2005, p. 255–56).

80. Potapchuk et al. (2005) argued that when officials are all elected and falling in and out of their jobs with the ebb and flow of partisan politics, "citizens are constantly wary, never knowing whether a community process will be empowering, deliberative, and meaningful, or just a sham" (p. 256).

81. Potapchuk et al. (2005, p. 259).

82. Fagotto and Fung, (2006, p. 6).

83. Ibid.

84. Giddens (1984, p. 197).

85. Ibid., pp. 199–206.

86. Many details from the conference are archived at the Web site of the coalition at www.thataway.org.

SOURCE: NASA.

9

International Deliberation

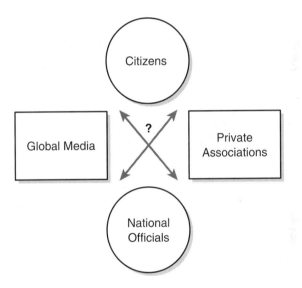

As substantial areas of human activity are progressively organized on a regional or global level, the fate of democracy . . . is fraught with difficulty.

—David Held[1]

M argaret Levi and David Olson, two political scientists at the University of Washington, stumbled into a significant moment in history when they chose to join a march led by the AFL-CIO in November of 1999. They became inadvertent witnesses to the "Battle in Seattle," which they summarized succinctly in *Politics & Society* a year later:

> Between 30 November and 3 December 1999, demonstrations against the World Trade Organization (WTO) precipitated a four-day closure of the retail core of Seattle. Militant, nonviolent protesters attempted to block the access of delegates to the meeting, while upward of 40,000 workers, students, environmental activists, and concerned citizens marched through the streets of downtown in a peaceful and legal march organized by the AFL-CIO. At the end of a long day, 30 bands of black-masked, black-clothed, self-proclaimed anarchists—linked by walkie-talkies and cell phones—began smashing windows while the peaceful and nonviolent protestors begged them to stop. The government's response to the anarchists turned Seattle into a police state, marked by battles in the streets of downtown and nearby neighborhoods. The Seattle police in full riot regalia, looking more like mockups of Darth Vader than Officer Friendly, used tear gas, pepper spray, rubber bullets, and percussion grenades to break up the growing crowds that turned out in defiance of city officials, the policy, and the WTO Ministerial.[2]

Another witness to the scene was Tico Almeida, a recent graduate of Duke University, whose first job out of college was as student-outreach organizer for the AFL-CIO. Reflecting on his experience on the first day of the protests, Almeida found the first half of the day "quite inspirational":

> It used to be that the politics of trade pitted American workers against foreign workers in an "us vs. them." But the 35,000 individuals who gathered at Memorial Stadium [in downtown Seattle] on that Tuesday heard something very different. We heard workers and unions from rich and poor countries alike stand together and say, "We want rules for workers' rights to be integrated into the global economy." There was a speech given by a worker from the U.S., a worker from Mexico and a worker from South Africa, together. There were also speeches from workers' advocates and union leaders from Malaysia, Africa, Brazil, the Caribbean, Central America, as well as from the U.S., Canada and Europe: all of them in solidarity with the same demand for the core labor standards to be added to the WTO rules and to be linked to all trade accords. . . .
>
> After the rally, the UW and SCCC students—with amazing street puppets and enormous signs in hand—all joined in and began the march towards the Ministerial Meeting together with the other protest groups. . . . For the first few miles of the march, we walked together in opposition to the status quo of trade policy. Eventually, the marchers split in two directions: tens of thousands heading towards the WTO meeting with the hopes of "shutting it down"; and other tens of thousands favoring a peaceful sit-down protest in the streets surrounding the hotel where many of the WTO delegates were stuck waiting while the events played out further downtown. This second action was particularly important because it created a safe protest option for families who had brought children, for senior citizens, and for those who hoped to reform, but not abolish the international trade system.

A few blocks away from this sit-down protest, members of the anarchist "Black Block" were beginning to smash windows and light fires. The Seattle Police Department was beginning its crackdown on both the violent and non-violent protestors. And I imagine that at that point, any journalists who had written news stories about the international union solidarity witnessed at Memorial Stadium just a few hours earlier were scrapping those stories in favor of accounts of the storming of Starbucks or NikeTown.[3]

In reflecting on the experience, Almeida believed what was most important about the Battle of Seattle was the series of "teach-ins and marches and peaceful protests," which had "slightly different messages" but "a common goal of democratizing the global economy." Almeida mused, "Those who focused only on broken glass, tear-gas and rubber bullets missed the story entirely."

Though the violent protests were not the only story, they were an important facet of the 1999 WTO protests in Seattle, as they have been for similar antiglobalization actions. When people begin to feel powerless against a powerful government they view as illegitimate, it is not uncommon for their discontent to lead to property destruction. The Boston Tea Party is now celebrated as a touchstone event during the American revolutionary era, but this 1773 event is remembered over other trade protests from that time because of the symbolic power of tossing hundreds of crates of tea into the Boston Harbor.

Just as the American colonists' protest presaged a coming revolution, so may the WTO protests in Seattle—and others like them in Prague, Quebec City, and

Photo 9.2   Old-School Trade Protests in Boston Harbor, 1773 (the Boston Tea Party)

SOURCE: http://upload.wikimedia.org/wikipedia/commons/2/27/Boston_tea_party.jpg.

elsewhere—signal a change in global governance. Joseph Nye, a preeminent U.S. foreign policy scholar, made this point in a 2001 issue of the sober policy journal *Foreign Affairs*. He summarized his argument thusly: "Civil society and the developing countries are growing more assertive. Meeting their concerns without jeopardizing multilateralism is the big test for policymakers. To fight this perception, global organizations need to increase transparency, improve accountability and think harder about norms for global governance." He continued:

> Trade ministers attend WTO meetings, finance ministers attend the meetings of the International Monetary Fund (IMF), and central bankers meet at the Bank for International Settlements in Basel. To outsiders, even within the same government, these institutions can look like closed and secretive clubs. Increasing the perceived legitimacy of international governance is therefore an important objective and requires three things: greater clarity about democracy, a richer understanding of accountability, and a willingness to experiment.[4]

This is precisely the point of the present chapter—to examine what it means to talk about deliberation and democracy on the global stage and to consider some of the experiments that have been conducted (or proposed) to improve the quality of bilateral, regional, and global governance.

We begin this journey by stepping backward. One useful starting point for understanding global governance is a brief review of the international bodies that have been designed to hold together a particular geographic region— Europe. This historical review is longer than those in previous chapters, because the concept of international governance simply requires more ink. The following three case summaries illustrate the variety of international bodies that have existed, as well as the progressive movement toward stronger international agreements and institutions.

From the League of Nations to the European Union

Europe has been the epicenter of a series of brutal wars, including many of the bloodiest in human history. To reduce the likelihood of future conflict, a variety of international institutions have been created over the years by Europeans and other interested parties. We consider a few of the twentieth century efforts to get a flavor of what international governance can look like, for better and for worse.

WEAK DIPLOMACY THROUGH THE LEAGUE OF NATIONS

In 1914, Europe fell into a four-year conflict that came to be known as the War to End All Wars, a name that subsequent events would require changing simply to World War I. The war took millions of lives and was further distinguished from prior conflicts by its gruesome trench warfare, with rival soldiers hunkered down in the mud, dying from artillery bombardments, close-range machine gun fire, and even poison gas.[5]

The war ended in a costly 1918 victory for the Allied powers, which included France, Russia, the United Kingdom, Italy, and the United States, with one result being the breakup of the vanquished empires of Austria-Hungary, Germany, and the Ottomans (Turks). After the signing of the Treaty of Versailles on June 28, 1919, many national governments sought a means of securing a lasting peace—one that could prevent the recurrence of such a costly and horrible conflict.

Months earlier, U.S. President Woodrow Wilson had presented to Congress a set of foreign policy principles he called the Fourteen Points for Peace.[6] The last of these read, "A general association of nations must be formed under specific covenants for the purpose of affording mutual guarantees of political independence and territorial integrity to great and small states alike." The aim was to create an association not for the purpose of international policy coordination but simply to make sure all parties remain true to their promise of respecting each other's sovereignty. If any future questions arose regarding two or more nations' "political independence and territorial integrity," this association would handle them rather than letting the disagreement lead the world back into war.

Along with many of his contemporaries in Europe, Wilson hoped to realize this fourteenth principle through a new body called the League of Nations.[7] In the year following the war, the League took shape, and it held its first general assembly of forty-one nations in its new headquarters in Geneva, Switzerland, on November 15, 1920. The League would last twenty-six years, and it managed to help resolve numerous minor territorial conflicts across the globe. Ultimately, however, the League was too weak to handle serious issues, as it had no military authority and relied on its individual members to muster influence, which they were reluctant to do. Despite Wilson's best efforts, the United States Congress never voted to join the League, nor did many other nations, and this damaged the League's credibility as a truly global institution.

As a deliberative body, the League was a failure. The League lacked the deliberative traditions, skills, and structures necessary to work as a cohesive body. Approval of any policy required consensus in the council (Britain, France, Italy, Japan, and rotating members), as well as a majority in the full assembly, and reaching that standard was difficult. The League was so indecisive that it could not even muster the collective will to agree on a flag or logo. When the world began to slide again toward a global war in the mid-1930s, the League's weakness was all too apparent, as it was unable to fulfill its most basic mission, namely, protecting the territorial integrity of the world's sovereign nations.

BARGAINING AT THE UNITED NATIONS

When the world took stock of itself after the Second World War, it was that much clearer that the prospects for peace were grim, indeed, without a stronger international body to govern relations among nations. All told, more than sixty-two million people died in this war, including six million or more European Jews and five million others in the Nazi Holocaust.[8] Moreover, with the United States' dropping of the atomic bomb on Hiroshima and Nagasaki, this war introduced the specter of nuclear annihilation, a potential fate that only grew in apparent likelihood and scope during the years afterward. It was clearer than ever in 1945, after six years of global warfare, that the world needed an international body far stronger than the all-but-defunct League of Nations.

It was in this context that the United Nations took shape. The international body's name was established on January 1, 1942, three years before the end of the war. On that day, twenty-six Allied governments signed the *Declaration by United Nations* to affirm their commitment to total victory against the Axis powers (principally Germany, Japan, and Italy). The United Nations (UN) became an official institution on October 24, 1945, after being ratified by the five members of the Security Council (China, France, the United Kingdom, the United States, and the Union of Soviet Socialist Republics) and a majority of the forty-six other member nations.[9]

From the outset, the Security Council has been the United Nations' greatest strength and its greatest limitation. The council has always included the five most powerful nations victorious in World War II, but it also includes rotating members, which increased from six to ten in 1965. To pass the council, a resolution must receive a majority of all votes, plus no "nay" votes from any of the five permanent members. Political theorist Jane Mansbridge calls this system "unanimity as self-protective veto."[10] In essence, the council does not seek to build consensus so much as avoid taking any action that a permanent member would view as a threat to its national self-interest.

This system has ensured that the UN does not make controversial decisions that force the angry departure of a permanent member, but it has also limited it from making bold decisions amid ongoing debate among the superpowers. During the course of the Cold War, which ran from roughly 1946 to 1991, this often resulted in a stalemate at the UN, with the Soviet Union (and often China) standing on one side of a question and the United States (with France and the United Kingdom) standing on the other. Since then, there has been more opportunity for international consensus on the Security Council, with the five permanent members often finding sufficient common ground to endorse UN intervention in other parts of the world.

The only UN body that includes a seat for every member nation is the General Assembly, which provides a global public forum for discussing international law and other issues of concern to the membership. With another nod toward seeking broad agreement, a two-thirds majority is required for passage on major votes, with only a simple majority required for lesser questions put before the assembly. The assembly's actions are often only symbolic, given that the council has the ultimate say and has often thwarted passage of controversial issues. Nonetheless, the assembly has provided an internationally recognized venue for the airing of grievances and the discussion of global issues.

Whatever its failings, the UN endured the Cold War. Though the UN has not always taken timely action to prevent genocide, famine, and other tragedies, it may well have helped to prevent a third world war, which could have resulted in a nuclear confrontation. Moreover, it has established widely respected programs, such as the Food and Agriculture Organization, which have provided invaluable expertise, services, and resources to developing countries. Moreover, the UN has always been a forum in which all member nations may speak before a global audience, and this minimal deliberative opportunity at least maintains an ongoing conversation within the larger world community.

ECONOMIC AND POLITICAL INTEGRATION THROUGH THE EUROPEAN UNION

The end of the Cold War created an opportunity for a new, more powerful and cohesive international body for the European continent. During the Cold War, the Eastern European nations had semi-integrated economies through the Council for Mutual Economic Assistance (aka COMECON), whereas many Western European countries worked out economic issues through the European Economic Community. After the breakup of the Soviet Union and the rapid, haphazard liberalization (and reconfigurations) of formerly Eastern Bloc countries, a large group of Western European nations met on February 7, 1992, at Maastricht in the Netherlands to sign the Treaty on European Union.[11]

In language confident of its historic significance, the treaty began, "By this Treaty, the High Contracting Parties establish among themselves a European Union, hereinafter called 'the Union.'" The first article of the treaty declared that it marked "a new stage in the process of creating an ever closer union among the peoples of Europe, in which decisions are taken as closely as possible to the citizen." Envisioning the reach of this union extending far beyond economic matters, the treaty declared the union's aim "to organize, in a manner demonstrating consistency and solidarity, relations between the Member States and between their peoples."[12]

Ratification in the signatory countries was not always easy, with opposition to the European Union (EU) quickly organizing in many countries. In the years since, however, all signatories have come to join the union, and its membership has steadily expanded to include most European countries, from Finland to Portugal and from Iceland to Italy.[13]

Far from a weak diplomatic meeting place or informal trade association, the EU has grown to become a powerful international body, tethering together the economies and governments of its members. Moreover, it has done so in a way that balances a desire for integration with the national character and interests of individual member states. Most visibly, the euro is now the sole currency used by a dozen member states (and likely more in the future), but more important, the EU has built a European common market by harmonizing commercial regulations, taxes, and trade policies across the union. The net effect has been to make the union, as a whole, the largest economy in the world.

As further evidence of its reach, the EU has enacted binding legislation regarding a wide range of policy areas. For example, the EU has made it possible for citizens of its member states to travel, live, or work in any part of the union, often without much fuss or paperwork at borders. The EU has established and enforced a clear-cut rule that "men and women must have equal pay for equal work," something that has not yet been achieved in other countries (such as the United States) without legal mandate. Myriad other rules, such as a ban on animal testing for making cosmetics, and coordinated actions, such as pooling resources to make the union the largest aid donor in the world, have further solidified the union's position as the most powerful actor in Europe.

The decision-making structure within the union differs considerably from that of the United Nations. The three main institutions within the union are the European Parliament, the European Commission, and the Council of the European Union. The parliament is directly elected by the people of Europe, making it an exceptionally representative international body, yet it has only limited authority, such as the right to amend or veto certain legislation. The commission is an executive branch, though it has the authority to introduce legislation. Each member nation nominates one commissioner; if approved by the full parliament, this person is then given responsibility for acting on behalf of Europe, rather than his or her nominating country. Finally, the most powerful body in the EU is the council, which includes representatives ("ministers") from each member government. The council has the power to make binding decisions, delegate responsibilities to the commission, and more. Analogous in some respects to the UN Security Council, the Council of the European Union always encourages consensus and sometimes requires unanimity among members. On some matters, it uses a qualified-majority voting system that requires a supermajority and gives more votes to the largest member nations.[14]

This voting system, along with more fundamental features of the union, is likely to evolve in coming years. The EU has its share of critics, but even skeptical observers and scholars are studying it carefully to assess its successes as a democratic body, as well as the potential for making it increasingly deliberative.[15] For example, its rampant use of committees, which often serve as powerful quasi-decision-making bodies, may be generating considerable small-group deliberation, or they may be creating unaccountable fiefdoms serving the interests of the individual member nations that steer them.[16] Beyond its formal decision-making bodies, the EU has certainly made a mark as a leader in sponsoring international deliberation among laycitizens, such as the Meeting of the Minds citizen panels convened to make recommendations on the future directions and implications of research on the human brain.[17] Whatever its limitations, the EU has certainly gone further than any previous body to bring the countries of Europe together. At the very least, the EU has helped make it seem less conceivable that its member states will face off against one another on the battlefield.

Conceptualizing International Deliberation

The League of Nations, the United Nations, and the European Union demonstrate that it is possible to build international institutions, but just as no nation is fully deliberative, none of these institutions could meet the highest standards of international deliberation. This then raises the question, what exactly would a fully deliberative process look like if it crossed national borders?

There is surely more than one answer, depending in part on the number and variety of nations involved and the issues they are willing to work through together. For instance, the EU has been careful to expand its membership only when candidate nations meet specified economic and political criteria, and this has made it easier for the union to reach consensus on major policy questions. The UN, by contrast, invites all established nations into its fold, and this makes for a maximally diverse—and at times contentious—body, with the permanent members of the Security Council unwilling to cede their control over the decision-making process to the full community of nations in the General Assembly. Even within the EU, there is reluctance to give the popularly elected European Parliament more influence in the union's affairs.

Given the varied circumstances of international cooperation, it may be a mistake to try to conceptualize a universal ideal model of deliberation at this level of analysis. An alternative approach is to imagine a deliberative process suited to a particular kind of relationship. One of the most promising and underused opportunities for deliberation beyond the nation-state sits with the smallest international unit—the bilateral relationship. Focusing on relations between two nations keeps the number of players conveniently limited, and it also conveniently highlights only a narrow range of issues. If the nations are neighbors, it also offers the practical advantage of facilitating regular face-to-face interaction, fact-finding in each other's territory, and other diplomatic and social exchanges. At the same time, this design is not necessarily easy, as bilateral issues can be among the most politically charged, especially among close neighbors, such as those between India and Pakistan and Taiwan and mainland China.

STRUCTURING A BILATERAL DELIBERATIVE PROCESS

Figure 9.1 sketches out what bilateral deliberation might look like if two neighboring national governments committed to the deliberative investigation of a problem that crossed their shared border. The figure provides an abstract ideal, but it is easier to discuss if we work with a concrete example.

One good candidate is the question of immigration between Mexico and the United States. According to 2002 figures from the nonpartisan Migration Policy Institute, more legal immigrants enter the United States from Mexico than from any other country, and roughly one-fifth of foreign-born legal U.S. residents are from there. In addition, roughly fifty-seven percent of the more than nine million undocumented immigrants in the United States hail from Mexico.[18] This tremendous outflow from Mexico to the United States has obvious significance for the shape of both countries' economies and societies, and it has more subtle effects on education, public health, and politics in both the United States and Mexico.[19] The aim here is not to grapple with the substance of immigration policy but, instead, to simply use this particular context for imagining the shape bilateral deliberation might take.

Referring to Figure 9.1, the analytic elements of bilateral immigration deliberation between the United States and Mexico would begin by setting up "an international body to study the issue systematically, drawing on people from both participating nations." Research institutes and think tanks, such as the Migration Policy Institute, already exist in both nations, and this first step might require nothing more than creating an umbrella organization that formalizes a partnership between these groups. Beyond the collection of hard numbers, however, an effort to truly understand this issue would turn to Mexican and U.S. civil society organizations. These groups could sponsor "open dialogues between people from both nations to share their relevant fears and aspirations," such as the prospects for economic development in Mexico, the impact of immigration on U.S. schools and the job market, and the maintenance of family ties across the border.

After digesting the fruit of these fact-finding efforts and open-ended discussions, the deliberation could then begin to generate a range of potential solutions. At this stage, it could be particularly helpful to reach out beyond the stakeholders in the two principal nations by bringing into the conversation "other members of the global community who have faced similar problems." Though the details of immigration between Mexico and the United States may be unique to those two countries, it is undoubtedly the case that other nations have helpful insights from their own experiences, particularly with regard to the variety of means available for addressing the issue. Hearing voices from other nations does not compromise the sovereignty of the United States and Mexico, no more than either country loses its autonomy by attending a UN conference on immigration.

Analytic Process	
Create a solid information base.	Support an international body to study the issue systematically, drawing on people from both participating nations.
Prioritize the key values at stake.	Cosponsor with civil society organizations open dialogues between people from both nations to share their relevant fears and aspirations.
Identify a broad range of solutions.	Generate solutions by bringing representatives of both nations together with other members of the global community who have faced similar problems.
Weigh the pros, cons, and trade-offs among solutions.	Convene a deliberative body consisting of official representatives and citizen-delegates from both nations to publicly examine the full range of solutions.
Make the best decision possible.	Elected officials and their representatives use formal legal procedures to finalize a decision that takes into account the findings of the preceding processes.
Social Process	
Adequately distribute speaking opportunities.	With incentives and outreach programs, draw voices from people of both nations into the bilateral deliberation, especially those who are often unheard.
Ensure mutual comprehension.	Go beyond mere language translation to promote cross-cultural exchanges, convene meetings in different regions within both countries, and so on.
Consider other ideas and experiences.	Ensure that participants in informal and formal meetings speak with people in the other country, particularly those in very different life circumstances.
Respect other participants.	Both nations must respect the political autonomy of the other, except in extreme circumstances of international aggression or wanton disregard for human rights.

Figure 9.1   Key Features of Government-Sponsored Bilateral Deliberation Between Nations

As the two nations move closer to reaching an accord, it would be beneficial to "convene a deliberative body consisting of official representatives and citizen-delegates from both nations to publicly examine the full range of solutions." More commonly, this stage involves public officials and their staff, with the occasional infusion of voices from civil society organizations and private business interests. It would be advantageous to keep at the forefront not only these conventional perspectives but also those of citizens without professional or political commitments. Different types of public meetings, along the lines of those described in Chapter 6, could involve citizens in a series of scattered forums, a special weeklong panel, or an ongoing process, all of which could eventually lead to concrete recommendations or assessments of proposals already under consideration. Whatever form they take, the requirement that all meetings be held openly is essential to make them transparent (clear and understandable) to all interested parties.[20]

Finally, at the decision-making stage, "elected officials and their representatives use formal legal procedures to finalize a decision that takes into account the findings of the preceding processes."[21] It is essential that representatives participating in this stage have a direct connection back to elected public officials. If the principal decision makers are individuals appointed by the president, for instance, it might be worth the effort to have their nomination approved by the national legislative branches of their respective countries. Alternatively, it might be best to have each legislature and executive send a handful of its members to form a bilateral committee that drafts a treaty that is then submitted to both nations' federal governments for ratification. Equally important is the visible incorporation of the earlier deliberative phases in this final decision. As foreign policy scholar Joseph Nye warned, if this process is to make a decision that appears legitimate to a public that expects open and deliberative self-governance, it is crucial to avoid the appearance of being a "closed and secretive club."[22]

GATHERING TOGETHER DIVERSE VOICES

As explained in all of the previous chapters in this book, the analytic side of deliberation has a social complement that stresses the relations among the participants over the content of their discussions. This aspect of deliberation is always important, but it takes on a special significance and added complexity in the international context. In any international process that involves two or more distinct languages, profound cultural differences, and disparities in resources and education, it is essential to provide the citizen deliberators with tremendous logistical support.

Figure 9.1 stipulates that to ensure equal consideration of the views of citizens in both countries, it is necessary to use "incentives and outreach programs" to draw in "voices from people of both nations, especially those who are often unheard."[23] In the case of the Mexico-U.S. dialogue on immigration, a starting point would be ensuring generous, equitable stipends for participants and a professional, bilingual staff to make necessary arrangements and provide for simultaneous translation. It would be helpful, however, to go much further. Identifying potential citizen participants would involve complex, culturally sophisticated interactions with those who reside at the margins of political power. Moreover, those most difficult to recruit may have a healthy skepticism of the prospects for influencing their own government, let alone a bilateral negotiation process. To obtain a representative sample, it would also likely be necessary to work with prospective citizen-delegates' extended families and local communities to provide the assistance they need to step out of their everyday lives and immerse themselves in a deliberative process of significant duration.

To ensure mutual comprehension and consideration of different perspectives, it would be necessary to "go beyond mere language translation to promote cross-cultural exchanges" and make certain that participants "speak with people from the other country, particularly those in very different life circumstances." In the U.S.-Mexico example, organizers could usher participants into a preliminary educational phase, in which the citizens learn about the life circumstances of people involved in different stages of immigration. This could involve visiting families in Mexican cities and rural communities, as well as in the U.S. cities and migrant farming communities where immigrants are often employed. Along the way, participants would also pick up some rudimentary skills in each other's language, making it more likely that informal exchanges and trust develop across the two nationalities. This process would also serve the interest of equalizing speaking opportunities, as the citizen participants in deliberative forums would then stand on a more equal footing with one another and with the officials and civil society representatives who would eventually address them, or even deliberate alongside them.

The last consideration interprets the principle of mutual respect in an international context, requiring that participants from both countries "respect the political autonomy" of the nations involved, making an exception for "extreme circumstances of international aggression or wanton disregard for human rights." This bedrock principle distinguishes international deliberation from deliberation, say, among cities within a state or states within a single nation. Cities are subject to the laws passed by the people of the state, and the states are subject to the federal constitution. Nations, by contrast, exist as independent entities, and participants in international deliberation must respect each nation's autonomy when working toward joint decisions.

The exception of "disregard for human rights," however, points to the limits of national boundaries in the twenty-first century. Some international scholars ask whether there now exists a kind of global constitution, or set of laws by which all nations must abide. Alternatively, perhaps there is a global public sphere in which nations must account for their actions to the world community. Has global civil society created sufficiently powerful discursive and political institutions that no nation can long remain independent of the influence of world public opinion? To address issues such as these, we turn to contemporary theories of international political communication and deliberation.

Is a Global Constitution Possible?

In simple terms, there exists no global constitution. There is no legally binding founding document that all nations have signed and sworn to uphold, under penalty of law. Nonetheless, argued German sociologist Hauke Brunkhorst, we can still talk meaningfully about the degree to which there exists something like an international constitution. For Brunkhorst, this is vitally important. Without a constitution granting legal/administrative authority, he argued, the global public is not strong, in the sense that its discussions are tightly coupled with consequential decisions. However, there can emerge a weak but real global public, possessing some sense of basic rights and possessing the ability to influence nations only through moral suasion. A weak global public can, for instance, shame and isolate some countries to the point that their regimes abandon unpopular policies or even crumble, as was likely the case in South Africa's apartheid regime, which collapsed in 1989. Surveying recent history, Brunkhorst came to the following conclusion:

> At least since the League of Nations . . . and especially since the foundation of the United Nations in 1945, a weak global public can be said to exist. The constitutional precondition of this weak public is realized in the existence of a core of binding legal rights and general principles of international law that are globally held. Its social precondition is enabled by the media of global communication and by a transnational network of associations.[24]

In his search for a global constitution, Brunkhorst begins by assuming that the constitution need not be coupled to a centralized international legal body. Brunkhorst asks us to "consider such international organizations as the UN, the World Trade Organization, or the European Union. The founding treaties of these institutions often have an effect on international or supranational law similar to that constitutions have on national law. Others still address the United Nations Charter as the 'constitution of the international community.'"[25]

When searching for signs of a strong constitution in bodies such as these, the most compelling evidence would be finding the will of powerful nations checked by the counterforce of legal, constitutional principle. The United Nations Charter, for instance, has a core principle of equal sovereignty, which holds that each state has an equal say in the international body. Within the charter itself, however, the veto authority of the permanent members of the Security Council violates this potentially powerful provision.[26]

IRAQ, THE UNITED STATES, AND THE LIMITS OF UN INFLUENCE

Consider the case of the United States' invasion of Iraq to overthrow the government of Saddam Hussein. On September 12, 2002, U.S. President George W. Bush addressed the UN General Assembly to ask the world community to prepare to take up arms against Hussein. Toward the end of his address, he explained his position thusly:

> My nation will work with the U.N. Security Council to meet our common challenge. If Iraq's regime defies us again, the world must move deliberately, decisively to hold Iraq to account. We will work with the U.N. Security Council for the necessary resolutions. But the purposes of the United States should not be doubted. The Security Council resolutions will be enforced— the just demands of peace and security will be met—or action will be unavoidable. And a regime that has lost its legitimacy will also lose its power.[27]

Reading this passage carefully, one can notice Bush acknowledging that the UN has authority with regard to authorizing military intervention (seeking "necessary resolutions" at the Security Council). Later, though, one sees Bush explain that the United States feels free to act without UN mandate, having its own "purposes" that may make action "unavoidable."

As he concluded the speech, Bush was more blunt: Only by joining the U.S. campaign against Hussein can the world "show that the promise of the United Nations can be fulfilled in our time." Otherwise, the United States "must stand up for security, and for the permanent rights and the hopes of mankind . . . by heritage and by choice."[28] Here, Bush simultaneously justifies the coming intervention on his reading of "the permanent rights" of humankind, without tethering his interpretation of those to an enforceable global constitution, let alone the UN itself. Instead, his actions are driven by the "heritage" of the United States, as well as by his own choice to act as the U.S. Commander in Chief.

In the months that followed, the United States successfully lobbied the UN to pass Resolution 1441 regarding Iraq, but the Security Council ultimately could not reach consensus on "enforcing" this resolution by authorizing the use of force against Hussein. Bush mixed frustration with the Council's resistance with a public optimism when he remarked shortly thereafter, "I believe when it's all said and done, free nations will not allow the United Nations to fade into history as an ineffective, irrelevant debating society. I'm optimistic that free nations will show backbone and courage in the face of true threats to peace and freedom."[29]

The United States, however, got no further support from the Council. France, Russia, and other nations required the United States to bring alleged

Iraqi violations before the Council. When it became clear that Bush would not win passage of more explicit language authorizing the use of force, he simply claimed that Resolution 1441 was, in and of itself, sufficient authorization to act. The United States, along with its "Coalition of the Willing," which included Britain and a ragtag mix of allies (not including France, Germany, and many other major allies), then invaded Iraq.

The UN charter, however, declares unequivocally in Articles 41 and 42 that the Security Council alone has the authority to marshal military force against any nation that defies its resolutions.[30] The UN had, in fact, authorized such action against Iraq in 1990, when the Council unambiguously authorized Kuwaiti allies "to use all necessary means" to expel Iraq from Kuwait if it did not do so by January 15, 1991. Thus, the U.S.-led expulsion of Iraq on January 17, 1991, occurred with the support of the UN,[31] whereas the most recent incursion did not.

At the end of the day, what power does the UN have to stop the United States from interpreting UN resolutions as it wishes? For that matter, how can it stop the United States from taking action in direct defiance of the UN charter or previously passed UN resolutions? In legal constitutional terms, the answer is none. Through its International Court of Justice (aka the "World Court"), the UN has tried to enforce its will against the United States in the past, such as in the 1980s, when it required the United States to comply with the Nuclear Nonproliferation Treaty and, on another occasion, to cease supporting attacks on the Nicaraguan government (and pay $2 billion in compensation). In these cases, and others, the United States has refused to recognize the court's authority.

Foreign policy scholar Stephen Zunes noted that "recent decades have seen increasing American hostility toward any legal constraints upon U.S. foreign policy," despite "America's strong legal tradition," its leadership role "in the development of international humanitarian law and related international legal constructs," and "the fact that the International Court of Justice has more often than not ruled in favor of the United States and its allies."[32] Thus, the ability of nations like the United States to defy the UN's councils and courts shows the weakness of any claim the UN might make to constitutional authority.

POWER AND EQUALITY IN THE WORLD TRADE ORGANIZATION

Questions of trade and economic policy are second only to security questions as subjects of international dispute. Consequently, questions of global constitutional authority are directly relevant to international economic institutions. Prominent among these institutions is the World Trade Organization (WTO).[33]

The WTO is the international body responsible for enforcing global trade rules, principally including the General Agreement on Tariffs and Trade (GATT). Since the WTO's establishment in 1995, all but a handful of countries in the world have joined the organization, and its members now account for well over ninety percent of the world's trade. The WTO Ministerial Conference meets at least once every two years, and any decisions it makes require at least a two-thirds majority vote, though normally a unanimous vote is achieved.[34]

The principle of consensus is consistent with the strongest ideal of deliberation, but do the WTO's members reach such a consensus as the result of genuine deliberation, with the member nations only arriving at agreement after careful scrutiny of the arguments advanced by all parties, with an eye toward the best interests of the global public? Moreover, do the member nations bind themselves by the core principles of the WTO, which might have some kind of legal/constitutional force?

Environmental studies professor Ilan Kapoor addressed these questions by directly assessing the degree to which the WTO fulfills the principles of deliberation and democracy. Holding the trade association up against the deliberative ideal advanced by Jurgen Habermas (which we discussed in Chapter 2), Kapoor found that in practice, the WTO functions as a medium through which powerful nations broker agreements among themselves, often at the expense of more numerous but less powerful nations. In meetings involving the full membership, the United States, the EU, and other powerful trading partners often threaten to reject a proposed set of rules unless their preferred provisions are included.[35]

Those provisions are worked out in so-called green room caucus discussions. Kapoor concluded that, above all else, "it is the repeated and systematic exclusion or neglect of many developing countries in key caucus meetings that is troubling." He added:

> [Within the WTO,] there are no clear and transparent (and dialogically generated) rules regulating such caucuses, ensuring for instance that all members are at least invited to them, or if not, spelling out the criteria for inclusion and exclusion. The absence of such rules means that the most powerful western members can continue their strong-arm tactics with impunity.[36]

Given their relatively low economic power, other members acquiesce to the rules drawn up by these private caucuses. Thus, consensus emerges owing not to persuasion through reasoned deliberation but simply because of the irrelevance of any decision that goes against the wishes of their most powerful trading partners. In the end, one might say that each country has a degree of power, but that power is proportionate to its raw economic power, unfiltered by any rules or norms that would equalize their status. In effect, the WTO has a de facto security council, with the "permanent members" simply meeting in private to decide which policies they will support in the Ministerial Conference.

In another parallel to the UN, the WTO also has something akin to the World Court. The WTO's Dispute Settlement Procedure allows a nation to bring before the organization any complaints it has about other nations causing it harm by violating international trade agreements. Paradoxically, this procedure gives member countries more flexibility by permitting them to violate trade rules without facing anything more than a fine equivalent to the damage done. Without such a procedure, a nation would be thwarting the entire trade regime any time it was seen to violate a rule, whereas this system labels a nation as a rogue state only when it repeatedly refuses to pay the required compensation for its past transgressions.[37]

At the present time, however, the Dispute Settlement Procedure continues to privilege more powerful nations, which are better equipped to use it effectively and more prepared to defy its judgments when they find it necessary to do so. Moreover, the WTO is not designed to uphold any principle but that of trade liberalization, and consequently disputes are routinely resolved without regard to the many other values and concerns held by the people living in the countries in question. Thus, dispute settlement rulings routinely deem nations' democratically established labor standards or environmental laws as violations of international trade agreements. Were those agreements the result of unfettered, democratic deliberation, this would be analogous to protecting the global constitution against national violations thereof. As it stands, however, the Dispute Settlement Procedure simply enforces the dictates of the more narrow economic and political interests of those nations that wield disproportionate power within the WTO.[38]

In light of this reality, Jeff Faux, president of the progressive Economic Policy Institute, argued that one of the greatest problems with "free trade" is the absence of a legitimate global constitutional framework. Economic development and trade within the United States, he noted, has always occurred "safely within the context of a democratic U.S. constitution." As a result, "over time, the power of corporate capital was balanced by protections for small business, labor, and the environment." By contrast, "the global economy has no such constitution," at least not yet.[39] Referring to the hundreds of pages of documents generated by his organization and others, the director general of the WTO once quipped, "We are no longer writing the rules of interaction among separate national economies. We are writing the constitution of a single global economy."[40] As Faux pointed out, "The question being raised in the streets" of Seattle and other protest sites was, "Where in this constitution are the rules that protect the rest of us?"[41]

DELIBERATION WITHOUT DEMOCRACY?

The prospects for creating a global constitution are not good, nor is it likely that the most economically powerful nations in the world will ever subject themselves wholly to the rulings of a supranational council or court, unless they indirectly wield de facto vetoes and disproportionate power within such bodies. So long as this remains true, international bodies cannot be categorized as democratic in any meaningful sense.

For this and other reasons, Robert Dahl, whose writings we discussed in Chapter 1, suggested that by its very nature "an international organization is not and probably cannot be a democracy."[42] Dahl pointed out that people in relatively democratic nations have a hard enough time influencing their own countries' foreign policy decisions; expecting them to effectively self-govern through international institutions is unrealistic.

Moreover, those nations that lack any degree of internal democracy cannot be said to be part of a democratic international process because their governmental representatives do not derive their authority directly from the people they govern. Whereas democratic principles require us to treat individuals as capable of representing their own interests (see Chapter 1), the same cannot be assumed of national governments that subjugate their own people.

As an alternative, Dahl suggested that we call the most functional international institutions "bureaucratic bargaining systems."[43] The institutions are responsive to their members only in the sense of an effective corporate manager, who knows how to work well with lower-level employees. Though not democratic, these institutions can play a valuable role in facilitating effective bargaining among competing interests, rather than letting the inevitable conflicts spiral out of control. Moreover, these international bodies can admit a degree of deliberation without being fully democratic. In this sense, the deliberation becomes more like the discussions described in Chapter 2, or those public meetings in Chapter 6 that were only advisory, rather than conclusive. Deliberation can thus facilitate a modest amount of responsiveness, even within a system that is, taken as a whole, undemocratic.

A Global Public Sphere and Discursive Designs

In light of these difficulties with formal international bodies and global constitutions, scholars and reformers seeking more democratic international communication systems choose to look beyond constitutionalism and formal decision-making bodies. The alternative, in this view, is the establishment of a powerful, global public sphere, including a vibrant, transnational civil society and prominent public spaces in which open and honest discussions can take place.

CONCEPTUALIZING THE GLOBAL PUBLIC SPHERE

The starting point for this discussion is understanding what it means to say that a public sphere exists. Political theorist John Keane offered the following definition of "public sphere":

> A public sphere is brought into existence whenever two or more individuals ... assemble to interrogate both their own interactions and the wider relations of social and political power within which they are always and already embedded. Through this autonomous association, members of public spheres consider

what they are doing, settle how they will live together, and determine . . . how they might collectively act.[44]

This way of defining public spheres ties back nicely to the structuration theory introduced in the previous chapter. In structuration theory, societies form and solidify through the establishment of routine behavioral patterns and shared understandings of the rules and power relations that govern society. When we make choices about how to behave, we are not always consciously aware of these patterns, rules, and relations, or even of our motivations, but we nonetheless manage to take competent actions in our own self-interest.[45] Following Keane's definition, when we enter into a public sphere we have the chance to "interrogate" our day-to-day interactions, as well as "the wider relations of social and political power" that operate in our society.

This is more than an exercise in self-awareness. Just as alcoholics make a positive step forward when they come to recognize their addictive behavior, so too can a public's self-awareness (and system awareness) be transformative. As Giddens explained, "Reflection on social practices," from off-hand insights to book-length social theories, "continually enter into, become disentangled with, and re-enter the universe of events that they describe." For this reason, social scientific research or less systematic deliberation in the public sphere can actually change the very practices they aim to describe. By contrast, "no such phenomenon exists in the world of inanimate nature, which is indifferent to whatever human beings might claim to know about it."[46]

With regard to the community of nations, are there such public spheres in which citizens from across the globe can interrogate one another's practices and self-understandings? Despite Brunkhorst's characterization of the global public as weak, he nonetheless sees potential for a stronger public—and more vigorous public sphere—in one domain of international relations: the establishment and defense of human rights. "If NGOs [nongovernmental organizations] and other global public agencies speak the language of human rights," he argued, "they speak a language which is still morally grounded, but already legally binding." Using moral language that invokes human rights can mobilize global "public interest and communicative pressure"; moreover, it is a legal language that "the political class and its administrative body of legal advisors, diplomats, etc. can understand and take into account for decision making."[47]

HUMAN RIGHTS DISCOURSE

The language of human rights is grounded in fundamental documents. Chief among these is the United Nations Universal Declaration of Human Rights, which was adopted by the UN General Assembly on December 10, 1948. Figure 9.2 highlights portions of the preamble and some of the articles in the declaration, which begins with the assumption that "all members of the human

Preamble: Whereas recognition of the inherent dignity and of the equal and inalienable rights of all members of the human family is the foundation of freedom, justice and peace in the world,

Whereas disregard and contempt for human rights have resulted in barbarous acts which have outraged the conscience of mankind, and the advent of a world in which human beings shall enjoy freedom of speech and belief and freedom from fear and want has been proclaimed as the highest aspiration of the common people,

Whereas it is essential, if man is not to be compelled to have recourse, as a last resort, to rebellion against tyranny and oppression, that human rights should be protected by the rule of law. . . .

Now, therefore, The General Assembly proclaims this Universal Declaration of Human Rights as a common standard of achievement for all peoples and all nations. . . .

Article 1: All human beings are born free and equal in dignity and rights. They are endowed with reason and conscience and should act towards one another in a spirit of brotherhood.

Article 2: Everyone is entitled to all the rights and freedoms set forth in this Declaration, without distinction of any kind, such as race, colour, sex, language, religion, political or other opinion, national or social origin, property, birth or other status.

Article 3: Everyone has the right to life, liberty and security of person.

Article 4: No one shall be held in slavery or servitude; slavery and the slave trade shall be prohibited in all their forms.

Article 5: No one shall be subjected to torture or to cruel, inhuman or degrading treatment or punishment.

Article 9: No one shall be subjected to arbitrary arrest, detention or exile.

Article 10: Everyone is entitled in full equality to a fair and public hearing by an independent and impartial tribunal, in the determination of his rights and obligations and of any criminal charge against him.

Article 13.1: Everyone has the right to freedom of movement and residence within the borders of each State.

Article 18: Everyone has the right to freedom of thought, conscience and religion.

Article 19: Everyone has the right to freedom of opinion and expression.

Article 20.1: Everyone has the right to freedom of peaceful assembly and association.

(Continued)

(Continued)

Article 21.1: Everyone has the right to take part in the government of his country, directly or through freely chosen representatives.

Article 21.3: The will of the people shall be the basis of the authority of government; this will shall be expressed in periodic and genuine elections which shall be by universal and equal suffrage and shall be held by secret vote or by equivalent free voting procedures.

Article 23.4: Everyone has the right to form and to join trade unions for the protection of his interests.

Article 25.1: Everyone has the right to a standard of living adequate for the health and well-being of himself and of his family, including food, clothing, housing and medical care and necessary social services, and the right to security in the event of unemployment, sickness, disability, widowhood, old age or other lack of livelihood in circumstances beyond his control.

Article 26.1: Everyone has the right to education. Education shall be free, at least in the elementary and fundamental stages.

Article 27.1: Everyone has the right freely to participate in the cultural life of the community, to enjoy the arts and to share in scientific advancement and its benefits.

Figure 9.2   Excerpts From the Universal Declaration of Human Rights

SOURCE: Full text of the declaration available in multiple languages at http://www.unhchr.ch/udhr.

family" have "equal and inalienable rights." These rights include such fundamentals as "life, liberty and security of person," but they go much further. They also include freedom from "torture" or "cruel" punishment, the right to "participation in the cultural life of the community," basic education, and "a standard of living adequate for the health and well-being" of oneself and one's family.

Human rights even encompasses basic principles of democracy and, more indirectly, deliberation. Articles 18 through 20 secure the freedom of "thought, conscience and religion," freedom of both "opinion and expression," and the right to "peaceful assembly and association." Article 21 further stipulates that "everyone has the right to take part in the government of his country, directly or through freely chosen representatives," with "the basis of the authority of government" being "the will of the people," as expressed through "periodic and genuine elections which shall be by universal and equal suffrage."

Numerous other documents, treaties, conventions, and national constitutions have since incorporated related language, thereby embedding the general principles of human rights throughout much of the international and national legal systems. The UN, the World Court, the EU, and numerous other regional and international associations have provided a forum in which people can discuss human rights and, more important, aggrieved individuals and associations can seek redress for what they perceive as violations of their basic human rights.

Sometimes this means making a formal appeal to a supranational body. For instance, in 1989, the Inter-American Court of Human Rights found in the case of *Velasquez Rodriguez v. Honduras* that the U.S. ally Honduras had failed to "implement its human rights obligations" in failing to protect the plaintiff from a politically motivated abduction and torture.[48] Other cases have been brought before the UN's World Court, the EU, and many other such associations, often resulting in at least partial redress of significant grievances.

At the same time, numerous organizations make direct appeals to the larger global community (sometimes while simultaneously working through the UN or other bodies). Among the most visible nonprofit associations promoting and protecting human rights is Amnesty International, which vows to be "concerned solely with the impartial protection of human rights." Explicitly tying itself to the UN's principles, the organization holds a "vision . . . of a world in which every person enjoys all of the human rights enshrined in the Universal Declaration of Human Rights and other international human rights standards." Nonetheless, it seeks to act as a nonpartisan civil society entity, "independent of any government, political ideology, economic interest or religion."[49]

Perhaps the most widely acclaimed of Amnesty International's activities is its Prisoner of Conscience campaigns designed to free political prisoners. Though critics have accused the organization of letting its biases determine which prisoners it spotlights, its overall mission may be vindicated by the fact that its critics cover the political spectrum, including the Congo, China, Israel, Sudan, the Taliban (Afghanistan), Vietnam, Russia, and the United States. In other words, the cases it has championed have challenged governments across the full breadth of the political spectrum. At least as important has been its diplomatic work within the UN, helping to strengthen the clarity and force of human rights language in international law.[50]

GLOBAL NETWORKS AND DISCURSIVE POWER

But again, Amnesty International is just one of thousands of associations, small and large, that combine with one another to form a powerful communication network—the global public sphere in which human rights claims can be contested. Though this global public sphere is enmeshed in established international bodies, it is important to appreciate the advantages it has as a freestanding entity. If human rights discourse was always subject to up-or-down votes in a body like the UN, it could be suppressed by self-protective member nations that themselves lack internal democratic processes.

Moreover, whereas the legal-institutional approach requires bringing together national governments, the spontaneous action of the global civil society can result in globalization from below (individual citizens and nongovernmental organizations working together across national boundaries). Though the focus here is on the issue of human rights, historian Jeremy Brecher identified numerous occasions in which concerned individuals and nongovernmental organizations worked across national boundaries and often outside of official international bodies to raise global consciousness. He offered the following example:

> Environmentalists identified globalization as a source of acid rain and global warming and saw global corporations and the World Bank sponsoring the destruction of local environments around the world. . . . Advocates for small farmers in both the First and Third Worlds identified new trade agreements as a means to destroy family farming in the interest of agribusiness. . . . College students became outraged that products bearing their schools' logos were being made by children and women forced to work sixty or more hours per week for less than a living wage.[51]

A scholarly consensus has emerged in the political communication literature that the rapid expansion of modern communication technology has enhanced the expressive power of rapidly forming global civil societies, whether their concern is human rights or any other number of issues. From the Internet to cell phones to handheld video cameras, inexpensive means of global communication have facilitated discourse across geographically dispersed networks. In addition, as political communication scholar W. Lance Bennett pointed out, "the introduction of open publishing and collective editing software . . . channeled through personal digital networks" have all facilitated media democracy, whereby consumers change into producers.[52]

At times, nongovernmental organizations have sufficient human and economic resources to not only produce their own discourse and media but also take decisive action on behalf of their issue. Thus, international aid organizations that see violations of the basic human right to "a standard of living adequate for the health and well-being" can coordinate their charitable and service activities to address immediate needs, so long as no state actor stands in their way. In this way, the public sphere can even become the "functional equivalent" of a state.[53]

A more subtle, and likely more powerful, influence of global public spheres on issues such as human rights is their creation of influential discourses. Political theorist John Dryzek, who stressed the importance of discursive designs, which were discussed in Chapter 8, defined a discourse as "a shared set of assumptions and capabilities embedded in language that enables its adherents to assemble bits of sensory information that come their way into coherent wholes." Moreover, "because discourses are social as well as personal," they also serve to coordinate "the behavior of the individuals who subscribe to them."[54]

In Dryzek's view, "the real power of transnational civil society" is its "communicative power"—its "capacity to affect the terms of discourse and change the balance of competing discourses."[55] The civil society organizations that have championed human rights have created one of the most powerful global discourses, which frames international foreign policy debates and can help or hurt domestic political organizations. An example of another powerful discourse is the traditional conceptualization of international affairs as anarchy, which places priority on ensuring national security in a chaotic global environment. Another discourse views the world as an open market, ascribing to the global economy the kind of equality and vitality characteristic of a more modest assemblage of vendors. Another popular discourse is that of sustainable development, which stresses the dangers of unplanned economic growth. When these discourses come into conflict, there are public debates about how we should understand the world, as in the case of whether one should view overseas corporations as natural resource "prospectors" or "pirates."[56]

The point, for Dryzek, is to obtain a sufficiently open and deliberative global public sphere to ensure that none of the prevailing discourses goes unchallenged. It is highly unlikely that we will see the emergence of a transnational democratic government giving order to our diffuse international system, but in the context of increasingly forceful, networked public spheres, we can certainly strive to build more democratic "discursive sources of order."[57]

DELIBERATIVE FORUMS "SOCIALIZING" THE GLOBAL SYSTEM

A loosely coupled network of civil society organizations can make up a relatively lively, discourse-rich public sphere, but the deliberative ideal is probably best served when this public sphere also spurs the creation of relatively organized forums—international gatherings analogous in many ways to the public meetings described in Chapter 6. Political theorist Jennifer Mitzen stressed the value of public forums within the global public sphere. She began by stressing that such forums need to be open, egalitarian, held in public view, and consistent with the minimal features of deliberative public meetings. She then assumed that the participants in these forums "care how they appear to others," at least in the sense that they hope to maintain a reputation that serves their interests.[58]

Though nations, and other stakeholders, typically enter such international forums seeking to maximize their self-interest, beneficial "forum effects" that none of the parties intended can result. First, Mitzen pointed out, "even selfish actors will want to appear impartial and fair," so they will frame their arguments "in terms acceptable to all." When participants do so, however, "they can find themselves subsequently compelled to follow through on commitments based on those rationales," an outcome philosopher John Elster called the civilizing force of hypocrisy. Even more powerfully, Mitzen argued, "With continued expectations that they will meet in forums, speakers get habituated to practices of reason giving and to relying on public criteria of acceptability." Over time, individual actors come to see themselves "less as 'selves' and more as 'members' of a group," such as the larger community of nations.[59]

International relations scholars Thomas Risse and Kathryn Sikkink put this idea in the context of human rights discourse and elaborated on Mitzen's argument by demonstrating how ongoing public discourse about human rights, in forums and other settings, can "socialize" nations to change their internal behavior, making them more likely to respect human rights, including the principles of democratic self-government. Advocacy networks (including organizations such as Amnesty International), nation-specific civil society associations, and sympathetic national governments can "link up with international regimes" to raise the public's consciousness about "norm-violating states." Pointing the finger at violators tends to remind the relatively democratic states "of their own identity as promoters of human rights." By protecting allied opposition groups within targeted countries, global human rights discourse also gives strength to the very people the human rights violators meant to repress. External pressure "from above" (supranational organizations) and "from below" (via domestic opposition) yields fewer opportunities for repression. In the end, the targeted country is often forced to enter into dialogue on its domestic human rights record, and once it begins arguing, bargaining, and compromising, it has already begun to habituate itself to a state of affairs in which it can no longer act without regard to global public opinion, or even its own domestic opposition.[60]

Conclusion

The preceding example leads to a final reflection on the potential power of global discourse on human rights and other issues to promote "democratization." Over the course of the past half-century, the number of nations in the world has steadily increased, but the number of quasi-democratic regimes has increased even more rapidly. There is no simple metric for measuring democracy, but by one straightforward measure, in the 1990s the number of at least quasi-democratic governments finally overtook the number of autocracies.[61]

An optimist cannot help but notice that the long-term forecast for democracy is positive. The preceding discussion of international regimes and global public spheres suggests that the promotion of deliberative institutions and discourses will contribute to that trend. Deliberative practices can have a procedural, socializing effect on nations, and the discourse of human rights, along with its accompanying legal infrastructure, can provide a substantive democratic influence. Moreover, these forces may combine to create the elusive "strong global public," an international civil society operating independently of, but in concert with, democratic regimes. With or without a constitution, this public might be sufficient to create a relatively powerful force to promote an increasingly deliberative international system.

At the same time, one should resist the temptation to simply "export" a particular conception of deliberation or democracy. One of the issues discussed in Chapter 8 was the importance of understanding the social infrastructure of a community when considering taking a deliberative approach to a problem. In an international context, this issue is all the more serious because of the widely varying cultural traditions across the globe. Consider the case of Japan, which held a series of consensus conferences on genetically modified foods. Public policy scholar Mariko Nishizawa studied this process and found that "the existing framework of public acceptance of GM crops, a technocratic policy style and the particular cultural norm of conformity prevented effective citizen deliberation from taking place" in these forums. "Without both an acknowledgement and a better understanding of the dynamics of the relationship between citizen deliberations and their social environments," he warned, "the [practical success] of deliberative approaches may be severely limited."[62]

This fact should not discourage so much as caution those who aim to promote the ideals of deliberation. One promising sign in the community of deliberation scholars and practitioners is the current research project led by the Kettering Foundation to better understand the diverse norms and practices related to deliberation in different countries. The foundation has assembled a team of researchers who are systematically doing what Nishizawa recommended—coming to terms with the social dynamics in different countries that might support or obstruct deliberation.[63] Going further, this study may help us develop a flexible understanding of deliberation that articulates itself differently in different nations. Just as this book aims to stretch the term across contexts, such a study may ultimately lead to a theory of democratic deliberation that carries shared meaning across a variety of cultures. Such work could go a long way toward laying the groundwork for meaningful, effective international deliberation.

Notes

1. Held (1998, p. 11).
2. Levi and Olsen (2000, p. 309).
3. This first-person narrative was archived at the WTO History Project, a joint effort of the University of Washington, the Harry Bridges Center for Labor Studies, and the Center for Communication and Civic Engagement. This transcript is available at http://depts.washington.edu/wtohist/testimonies.htm.
4. Nye (2001).
5. Tuchman (1994) provided a very readable account of the forces that triggered World War I. An equally readable account of the end of the war is MacMillan (2003).
6. The points are available online at http://www.yale.edu/lawweb/avalon/wilson14.htm. On the rhetorical career of Woodrow Wilson, including his speeches regarding the League of Nations, see Kraig (2004).

7. On the League and Wilson's efforts to make it a relevant global institution, see Thomas J. Knock (1995).

8. A comprehensive account of the war is provided by the *Oxford Companion to World War II* (New York: Oxford University Press, 2005). On the casualties in the Holocaust, see Hilberg (2003). The United States Holocaust Museum also has straightforward questions and answers on the subject online at http://www.ushmm .org/research/library/faq.

9. A useful description of the UN that looks beyond its peace-keeping role to its broader functions in the world is provided by Fasulo (2005). Former Secretary of State Madeline Albright (2003) published a vigorous defense of the UN's relevance and power as well.

10. Mansbridge (1983, pp. 260–61).

11. It was thoughtful of them to choose this author's birthday for the auspicious occasion.

12. Full text of this and other EU treaties are available at http://europa.eu/abc/treaties/ index_en.htm.

13. For a list of current EU members and candidate countries, see http://europa.eu/ abc/governments/index_en.htm.

14. For a lively discussion of this voting system and alternatives being considered, see http://news.bbc.co.uk/1/hi/world/europe/3562405.stm.

15. For an introduction to a range of theoretical perspectives of the EU, see Eriksen and Fossom (2000).

16. Pollack (2003).

17. For background on this project, see http://www.meetingmindseurope.org.

18. See Passel (2004).

19. On the history, demographics, and politics of U.S. immigration policy, see Hing (2004). On U.S. immigration policy, politics, and public health, see Fairchild (2004). On how Mexican migration to the United States influences politics in Mexico, see Smith (2003).

20. This parallels Nanz and Steffek's (2005) criterion of transparency, which they use for assessing the deliberation of international bodies.

21. This parallels Nanz and Steffek's (2005) evaluative criterion of transparency, which was discussed in more detail in Chapter 5.

22. Nye (2001).

23. This and subsequent criteria parallel Nanz and Steffek's (2005) access and inclusion criteria for evaluating international bodies.

24. Brunkhorst (2002, p. 680).

25. Ibid., p. 681.

26. Ibid., p. 687.

27. The text of this speech is available at http://www.whitehouse.gov/news/releases/ 2002/09/20020912-1.html.

28. Ibid.

29. Full remarks available at http://www.whitehouse.gov/news/releases/2003/02/ 20030213-4.html.

30. For a somewhat sympathetic account of the U.S. efforts to appeal to the Security Council, see Glendon (2003).

31. For a compilation of UN resolutions on Iraq, see http://www.state.gov/p/nea/rls/ 01fs/14906.htm.

32. Zunes (2004).

33. For a summary of the arguments lodged for and against the WTO, and free trade generally, see M. Lane Bruner (2002).
34. On the structure and history of the WTO and related trade institutions, see Barton et al. (2006).
35. Kapoor (2004, p. 528).
36. Ibid., p. 529.
37. These insights come from Rosendorff (2005), who concluded that the procedure makes disputes more common but, in the end, makes the entire system more resilient.
38. On the quasi-constitutional function of the Dispute Settlement Procedure, see Brunkhorst (2002, pp. 685–86).
39. Faux (2000).
40. For context on this famous quote, see the article "Investment Rules Not Dead, Yet," *South-North Development Monitor* (February 20, 1998) available at http://www.sunsonline.org/trade/process/followup/1998/02200198.htm.
41. Faux (2000).
42. Dahl (1999, p. 19).
43. Ibid., p. 33.
44. Keane (1984, pp. 2–3), quoted in Dryzek (1990, p. 37).
45. Giddens (1984, pp. 5–7).
46. Ibid., p. xxxiii.
47. Brunkhorst (2002, p. 690).
48. Case referenced in Gould (2004, p. 187).
49. This official Amnesty International self-description is available at http://web.amnesty.org/pages/aboutai-index-eng.
50. See Clark (2001).
51. Brecher (2000).
52. Bennett (2003, p. 144).
53. Rosenau (1998, p. 41).
54. Dryzek (2000, p. 121).
55. Ibid., p. 131.
56. Ibid., pp. 122–29.
57. See ibid., pp. 115–16, 138–39.
58. Mitzen (2005, p. 411).
59. Ibid., p. 411.
60. Risse and Sikkink (1999, p. 5).
61. These figures are based on the results of the Polity IV Project (http://www.cidcm.umd.edu/polity), for which the principal investigators are Monty G. Marshall (George Mason University), Keith Jaggers (Colorado State University), and Ted Robert Gurr (University of Maryland).
62. Nishizawa (2005, p. 486).
63. For updates on this project, refer to the Kettering Web site at http://www.kettering.org/programs/project.aspx?progID=29&workID=66.

SOURCE: Joe Goldman. Used by permission.

10

Toward a
Deliberative Democracy

Deliberative democrats must work not only to make the familiar institutions of democracy more friendly to deliberation but also to extend the scope of deliberation to institutions where it has not previously dared to go.

—Amy Gutmann and Dennis Thompson[1]

Imagine yourself a lonely, wispy soul, quietly floating through empty space, detached from any physical universe but soon to inhabit the body of a single person in one of many parallel earths. To prepare for your imminent embodiment, you have contracted with Corporeality Inc., a celestial matchmaking service. Each morning, a new promotional DVD arrives in your, um, mailbox, from an earth that wants you to choose to enter one of its soulless bodies. So far you have received four videos:

Alpha-Earth: Where the Strong Survive! Lonesome prairie images fly by with a gristly narrator speaking in a deep, gravelly voice. . . . "We invite the heartiest of souls to plop themselves down in the ruggedest little whistle-stop in the universe. There's a lot of elbow room on Alpha-Earth, and when you do bump into someone, the rules are simple—'might makes right.' As long as you're strong in body and strong in will, you'll thrive here. But if you can't make it on your own, remember: there's no wussy safety net, and no excuses."

Beta-Earth: The All-Inclusive Collective! A softly lit planet appears with many moons and a single tall tower rising above small villages. A soft-voiced narrator whispers to you. . . . "Everyone on Beta-Earth knows their place in this peaceful society, and it's the same place for everyone. Whether you are healthy or sick, smart or dull, everyone on Beta-Earth does what they can to promote the welfare of others, and each gets back what they need to live a decent life. Our laws are already well established, and there's no need for you to worry over them. We have a strong government that helps all souls find their way and has everyone's best interests at heart. And that's a promise you can take with you to the shamrock mines, the unicorn stables, or wherever you end up."

Gamma-Earth: Every Night Is Casino Night! The camera flies through a moon-lit sky, past smoky tin huts, and over a stand of glistening skyscrapers, revealing streets brightly lit in flashing neon. The narrator shouts, full of glee (and amphetamines, no doubt). . . . "Every city on our planet is a city of dreams! Each citizen has the chance of becoming a gazillionaire, and all you need to do is take a risk, apply yourself, and give the wheel a spin! Laws? We've got laws: Money is power, and if you want power, well go get some money! Our markets and our politics are all freely available to the highest bidders, so shake that hand and throw those dice! Who knows? Maybe you'll come out on top!"

And finally . . .

Delta-Earth: Make of It What You Will. You see a slideshow of a variety of neighborhoods and vistas, none too remarkable but none too shabby. An even-keeled narrator in a professorial drone begins speaking, slightly out of sequence with the images. . . . "Now, our fellow parallel planets will sell you this, and they'll sell you that, but we put it to you straight. The people of Delta-Earth make their laws together, abiding by a few constitutional principles—basic freedoms, rights, and procedures that we like to call 'deliberative democracy,' if you know what that means. When you come down to Delta-Earth, will we have universal health care? Could be. Will we have a regulated market economy? Maybe. Will we have gun control, capital punishment, or an Endangered Species Act? Couldn't tell you. It all depends on what comes out of the deliberative democratic process. Sorry I can't be clearer, but we believe that there are no fixed answers to these questions. If you don't think you can live with it, pick another planet, okay?"

If this book has gotten its job done, you would choose to send your soul down to Delta-Earth. If we were to ask moral philosopher John Rawls, he would turn over in his grave at this cheesy adaptation of his elegant treatise *A Theory of Justice.* Then he would argue that you would have no choice but to pick Delta-Earth, for a disembodied soul can't help but recognize that it's the best deal. You sacrifice your liberty, or worse, on the other planets. Rawls reasoned that if people did not know what lot they might draw in life, they would want a social system that protected the interests of the least well-off while granting all persons enough liberty to choose the course of their lives. The only guarantee about Delta-Earth is a deliberative version of democracy, but if those basic rules are well established and enforced, the planet will likely go a long way toward improving the fortunes of the least fortunate while preserving individual liberty.[2]

Putting the Pieces Together

One could read the preceding chapters of this book and still not be sure what, exactly, a deliberative democracy would look like when all its pieces are put together. This is somewhat by design, as this book is as much about integrating how we think about political communication as it is about deliberative democracy, per se. Nonetheless, if the principles of deliberation can serve as a powerful critical lens through which to study existing patterns of communication in public life, those same principles should also be capable of guiding us as we aim to establish and nurture future practices and institutions. Thus, in this final chapter, we consider what a full-fledged deliberative democracy might look like. In the end, I also suggest how we can help make such a democracy our reality.

Over the course of the past two decades, numerous political and communication theorists have sketched out visions of deliberative democracy.[3] Simone Chambers provided a concise summary of deliberative democratic theory's core tenets:

> Deliberative democratic theory . . . begins with a turning away from liberal individualist or economic understandings of democracy and toward a view anchored in conceptions of accountability and discussion. Talk-centric democratic theory replaces voting-centric democratic theory. Voting-centric views see democracy as the arena in which fixed preferences and interests compete via fair mechanisms of aggregation [e.g., elections]. In contrast, deliberative democracy focuses on the communicative processes of opinion and will-formation that precede voting. Accountability replaces consent as the conceptual core of legitimacy. . . . Accountability is primarily understood in terms of "giving an account" of something, that is, publicly articulating, explaining, and most importantly justifying public policy. Consent (and, of course, voting) does not disappear . . . [Deliberative democracy] is rather an expansion of representative democracy.[4]

That theoretical statement serves as a useful summary of the core idea of deliberative democracy as a means of self-government. Having read the preceding chapters, we can now flesh out a more concrete articulation of what that means in terms of social practices, institutions, power relationships, and so on. Figure 10.1 shows one such integration of the different concepts and models from Chapters 2–9.

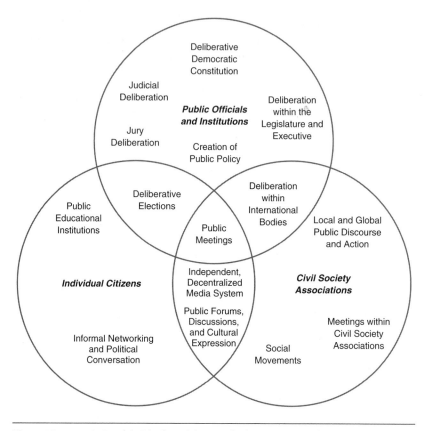

Figure 10.1   A Graphic Display of the Interlocking Features of Deliberative
Democracy

Figure 10.1 shows how individual citizens, civil society associations, and public officials and institutions all play important—and often overlapping—roles in a deliberative democracy. From informal conversations to formal public meetings, electoral competition to community dialogue, independent media to public education, jury service in municipal courthouses to contesting discourses in a global public sphere, and the establishment of a democratic constitution to the organization of a democratic social movement, each of these modes of communication and social interaction fits into a complex deliberative democratic system.

Another way to approach this summary of deliberative democracy is to refer back to the analytic and social aspects of deliberation and see how different institutions and activities ensure rigorous analysis and positive social relations among all participants. Figure 10.2 provides a checklist of some of the important ways a larger sociopolitical system might maintain its deliberative

Analytic Process	
Create a solid information base.	• Public journalism to help the public identify and understand its challenges • Public infrastructure for research • Strong institutional and public memory
Prioritize the key values at stake.	• Public dialogues with broad participation • Artistic community actively confronting contemporary issues
Identify a broad range of solutions.	• Innovative public policy think tanks • Multiple influential political associations representing a diversity of views
Weigh the pros, cons, and trade-offs among solutions.	• Deliberative electoral processes • Representative and influential citizen deliberation on policy • Rigorous governmental deliberation (legislative, executive, judicial, and jury)
Make the best decision possible.	• Elected officials confident in the political wisdom of enacting sound public policy • Public committed to implementation
Social Process	
Adequately distribute speaking opportunities.	• Constitutionally secure freedom of speech and association • Publicly sponsored issues forums • Numerous social ties facilitating conversation
Ensure mutual comprehension.	• Outstanding public education system teaching language and communication skills • Adult civic educational opportunities
Consider other ideas and experiences.	• Social and political connections across prominent socioeconomic differences • Appreciation of art, drama, and literature
Respect other participants.	• Celebration of cultural diversity • Strong trust in neighbors, fellow citizens • Respect for legitimate public institutions and their officials

Figure 10.2   Key Institutions and Practices in a Deliberative Democracy

character. For instance, at this institutional level of analysis, the creation of "a solid information base" is aided by promoting "public journalism to help the public identify and understand its challenges." Maintaining "public infrastructure for research" will provide a steady source of policy-relevant information, and "strong institutional and public memory" will ensure that the insights of journalists, researchers, citizens, and the wider civil society do not fade from the public's memory as it moves from one issue to the next.

Figures 10.1 and 10.2 are by no means comprehensive. There are surely other institutions and social practices that would aid deliberation but have not been addressed in this text. Moreover, there is always a deeper level of detail below the material provided herein. My aim here is simply to give enough detail and show enough links among related practices to help the reader organize the different ideas and lessons introduced in this book. Looking back over the previous chapters, I hope readers can now begin to see connections, such as those from public education to the development of an educated electorate, from an independent media to an accountable government, or from a vibrant civil society within democratic nations to the protection of human rights across the globe.

Taking Action

Whether one's own conception of democracy corresponds exactly to the one illustrated in the preceding figures is not as important as simply having a commitment to some vision of democracy. Like most other theories of democracy, explained political philosopher Simone Chambers, "deliberative democratic theory is a normative theory that suggests ways in which we can enhance democracy and criticize institutions that do not live up to the normative standard."[5] In other words, one can view deliberative democracy as an aspiration, a conception of a more fully realized democracy than our existing system. From that standpoint, one can readily develop precise critiques of one's existing system, then take action to reform that system to bring it closer to the ideal, even without ever entirely reaching it.

ASSESSING DELIBERATIVE DEMOCRACY IN THE UNITED STATES

The first form of action one can take to improve the quality of political communication in one's world, as well as the related institutions and practices, is to develop a systematic critique of "things as they are." Much of the research presented in this volume was the result of public scholarship—efforts by academics to conduct relevant research that can help us understand our world and, when necessary, the prospects for reforming it.[6]

But just as Lance Bennett argued for democratizing the media, so can one think of publicly relevant research as something that everyday citizens and voluntary associations can readily produce. Democracy advocate Jim Shultz stressed the importance of research and analysis in *The Democracy Owner's Manual: A Practical Guide to Changing the World.* "Ultimately," he explained, "advocacy is about pushing public change. Solid, reliable information helps us understand in which direction we ought to be pushing that change." As a side benefit, careful research "also strengthens our political credibility and clout along the way."[7]

One example of such advocacy research is the work of Fairness & Accuracy in Reporting (FAIR), a nonprofit association that conducts studies of mainstream media. One of its many ongoing investigations is into the use of think tanks as sources by newspaper, radio, and TV journalists. The aim of the study is to assess the degree to which media over-rely on these limited and unbalanced sources. In terms of deliberative democracy, this research assesses the extent to which professional voices dominate mediated discourse and whether the voices we hear fairly represent the range of views in a debate.

Figure 10.3 shows the results of the June 2006 FAIR report and focuses on the question of ideological bias in sourcing. The figure shows that a plurality of cited think tanks (forty-seven percent) can be categorized as politically centrist, but of those with an ideological bias, media cited three conservative sources for every one liberal think tank (forty percent versus thirteen percent). Data like these help FAIR make stronger claims about the extent of media bias and how to address it.

One can work with existing civil society associations or university faculty to take part in research like this, but it is also possible to conduct more modest research on one's own community. If you believe public libraries are an important part of adult public education, you might want to learn whether funding for your local library system has gone up or down in recent years. If you live in an ethnically or economically diverse community, does attendance at public meetings or forums reflect the diversity of the whole public? Answers to simple

Number of Media Citations, by Ideology	2005 (%)	2004 (%)
Conservative or center-right	10,937 (40)	11,921 (39)
Centrist	12,719 (47)	13,632 (45)
Progressive or center-left	3,573 (13)	4,666 (15)
Total	27,229 (100)	30,219 (100)

Figure 10.3   FAIR Report on Citations of Think Tanks in 2004–2005, by Political Orientation

questions such as these do not provide a comprehensive portrait of one's locality, let alone the forces that cause changes in figures such as these, but they can be a first step in developing a systematic empirical critique of existing practices.

INVENTING AND SUPPORTING REFORMS

At some point, you are likely to decide that the research base is sufficiently solid and that it is time to advance reform proposals. Even critics or dispassionate observers sometimes tire of being onlookers and feel compelled to act.

Sometimes there are road-tested reforms that you can propose or support. This text includes many such mechanisms. For instance, Chapter 2 showed that if you are concerned about the lack of high-quality discussion on important issues, you could start your own National Issues Forums in your community, school, or workplace. The materials for such forums can be obtained from the National Forums Institute, and you can even attend a regional or national training on how to organize and moderate a forum.[8]

Other prebuilt proposals may be of a grander scale and require you to join a cadre of reformers who have a vision of a new political institution or even a cultural shift along the lines of a deliberative social movement. Jim Fishkin and Bruce Ackerman's advocacy of Deliberation Day represents one such approach (Chapter 4), and there are many other proposals currently in play that are designed to change how people influence elections and policy making.[9]

You may also discover that you have ideas of your own for how to move society closer to the ideal of deliberative democracy. How can you change the way you live to provide an example for others? Can you influence the ways problems are discussed and the ways decisions are made within your own organizations and associations—your workplace, your school, or your political organization?

Democracy depends on the ingenuity and passion of its citizens, so it is no surprise that democratic reform relies on those same qualities. With a clear understanding of deliberative democratic theory, a solid critique of existing practices and institutions, and a commitment to practical and significant reforms, you may become not just an observer of political communication but a part of the ongoing struggle to make your own society more deliberative and democratic.

Notes

1. Gutmann and Thompson (2004, p. 56).
2. For the original formulation of his moral philosophy, see Rawls (1971). For relevant extensions, see Rawls (1995, 1999). On the application of Rawls to deliberative democratic theory, see Bohman (2003), Elkin (2004), and Freeman (2000).

3. There exists a wide range of writings on deliberative democratic theory. Some of the earlier, book-length treatments of the subject include Bohman (1996), Cohen (1989), Elster (1998), Fishkin (1991), Gastil (2000), Gutmann and Thompson (1996), Mathews (1994), and Nino (1996). In addition to Cohen's 1989 essay, the earliest modern works to foreground the idea of deliberation include Barber (1984), Habermas (1989), Mansbridge (1983), and, less often recognized, Reich (1985). For a sketch of the rise and fall of deliberative approaches to democracy in 20th Century America, see Gastil and Keith (2005).

4. Chambers (2003, p. 308).

5. Ibid.

6. On the role of intellectuals and scholars as critics, see Goldfarb (1998).

7. Shultz (2002, p. 83).

8. Visit www.nifi.org for more information.

9. Gastil (1993, 2000), Crosby (2003), Leib (2004), and Burnheim (1989). For updates on the activities of deliberative reformers, visit the online sites of the Deliberative Democracy Consortium (www.deliberative-democracy.net), the National Coalition on Dialogue and Deliberation (www.thataway.org), and the *Journal of Public Deliberation,* which includes sites designed for both scholars and practitioners (services.bepress.com/jpd).

References

Abelson, Jenn. 2004. Uncivil discourse blights online debates. *The Boston Globe,* January 5, 2004. http://www.boston.com/news/local/articles/2004/01/05/uncivil_discourse _blights_online_debates/ (acessed Accessed online October 21, 2006).

Abramowitz, Alan I., and Kyle L. Saunders. 1998. Ideological realignment in the U.S. electorate. *Journal of Politics* 60:634–52.

Ackerman, Bruce, and James S. Fishkin. 2004. *Deliberation day.* New Haven, CT: Yale University Press.

Adams, Bruce. 1995. Building a new political environment. *Kettering Review* (Fall):16–21.

Adler, Stephan J. 1994. *The jury: Trial and error in the American courtroom.* New York: New York Times Books.

Albright, Madeline. 2003. Think again: The United Nations. *Foreign Policy* (September/October). http://foreignpolicy.com/story/cms.php?story_id=34 (accessed October 24, 2006).

Alford, John R., & Brady, David W. 1993. Personal and partisan advantage in U.S. congressional elections, 1846–1990. In *Congress reconsidered,* ed. L. C. Dodd and B. I. Openheimer, 141–57. 5th ed. Washington, DC: Congressional Quarterly Press.

Almond, Gabriel, and Sidney Verba. 1989. *The civic culture.* 2nd ed. Newbury Park, CA: Sage.

Alterman, Eric. 2003. *What liberal media? The truth about bias and the news.* New York: HarperCollins.

Amar, Vikram David. 1995. Jury service as political participation akin to voting. *Cornell Law Review* 80:203–59.

Ansolabehere, Stephen, Shanto Iyengar, Adam F. Simon, and Nicholas Valentino. 1997. Does attack advertising demobilize the electorate? In *Do the media govern? Politicians, voters, and reporters in America,* ed. I. Shanto and R. Reeves, 195–204. Thousand Oaks, CA: Sage.

Aristotle. 1988. *Politics.* New York: Cambridge University Press. http://www.constitution .org/ari/polit_04.htm (accessed October 21, 2006).

Arnold, R. Douglas. 1990. *The logic of congressional action.* New Haven, CT: Yale University Press.

Bacci, Chiara, Michael Dollinger, and John Gastil. 2006. Does deliberation yield a consistent pattern of attitude change? Testing the underlying value dimensions of opinion shifts during Deliberative Polls. Paper presented at the annual conference of the National Communication Association, San Antonio, TX.

Baird, A. Craig. 1928. *Public discussion and debate.* Boston: Ginn and Co.

Baker, C. Edwin. 2001. Implications of rival visions of electoral campaigns. In *Mediated politics: communication in the future of democracy*, ed. W. L. Bennett and R. M. Entman, 342–61. New York: Cambridge University Press.

Bandura, Albert. 1986. *Social foundations of thought and action: a social cognitive theory.* New York: Prentice-Hall.

Barber, Benjamin R. 1984. *Strong democracy: Participatory politics for a new age.* Berkeley: University of California Press.

Barton, John H., Judith L. Goldstein, Timothy E. Josling, and Richard H. Steinberg. 2006. *The evolution of the trade regime: Politics, law, and economics of the GATT and the WTO.* Princeton, NJ: Princeton University Press.

Baym, Geoffrey. 2005. *The Daily Show:* Discursive integration and the reinvention of political journalism. *Political Communication* 22:259–76.

Becker, Ted, and Christa Daryl Slaton. 2000. *The future of teledemocracy.* New York: Praeger.

Beckham, B., and Aronson, H. 1978. Selection of jury foremen as a measure of the social status of women. *Psychological Reports* 43:475–78.

Bennett, W. Lance. 1994. *Inside the system: Culture, institutions, and power in American politics.* New York: Harcourt Brace.

Bennett, W. Lance. 1998. The uncivic culture: Communication, identity, and the rise of lifestyle politics. *PS: Political Science and Politics* 31:741–61.

Bennett, W. Lance. 2003. Communicating global activism. *Information, Communication and Society* 6:144.

Bennett, W. Lance, Regina G. Lawrence, and Steven Livingston. In press. *When the press fails: Political Power and the news media from Iraq to Katrina.* Chicago: University of Chicago Press.

Besley, John C., and Katherine A. McComas. 2005. Framing justice: Using the concept of procedural justice to advance political communication research. *Communication Theory* 15:414–36.

Bessette, Joseph M. 1994. *The mild voice of reason.* Chicago: University of Chicago Press.

Black, Laura. 2006. Deliberation, difference, and the story: How storytelling manages identity and conflict in deliberative groups. PhD diss., University of Washington.

Blanchard, Margaret A. ed. 1998. *History of the mass media in the United States: An encyclopedia.* Chicago: Fitzroy Dearborn.

Bohman, James. 2003. Deliberative toleration. *Political Theory* 31:757–79.

Bohman, James F. 1996. *Public deliberation: Pluralism, complexity, and democracy.* Cambridge, MA: MIT Press.

Bormann, Ernest G. 1996. Symbolic Convergence theory and communication in group decision making. In *Communication and group decision-making,* ed. R. Y. Hirokawa and M. S. Poole, 81–113. 2nd ed. Thousand Oaks, CA: Sage.

Boster, Franklin J., John E. Hunter, and Jerold L. Hale. 1991. An information-processing model of jury decision making. *Small Group Research* 18:524–47.

Boyte, Harry. 2005. Reframing democracy: Governance, civic agency, and politics. *Public Administration Review* 65:536–46.

Brecher, Jeremy. 2000. Globalization from below. *The Nation,* November 16, 2000. http://www.thenation.com/doc/20001204/brecher (accessed October 24, 2006).

Briand, Michael. 1999. *Practical politics: Five principles for a community that works.* Champaign: University of Illinois Press.

Bruner, M. Lane. 2002. Global constitutionalism and the arguments over free trade. *Communication Studies* 53:25–39.

Brunkhorst, Hauke. 2002. Globalising democracy without a state: Weak public, strong public, global constitutionalism. *Millennium: Journal of International Studies* 31:675–90.

Bryan, Frank. 2004. *Real democracy: The New England town meeting and how it works.* Chicago: University of Chicago Press.

Bryan, Frank, and John McClaughry. 1989. *The Vermont Papers: Recreating democracy on a human scale.* Port Mills, VT: Chelsea Green.

Buchanan, B. I. 2001. Mediated electoral democracy: Campaigns, incentives, and reform. In *Mediated politics: Communication in the future of democracy,* ed. W. L. Bennett and R. M. Entman, 362–79. New York: Cambridge University Press.

Budesheim, Thomas Lee, David A. Houston, and Stephen J. DePaola. 1996. Persuasiveness of in-group and out-group political messages: The case of negative political campaigning. *Journal of Personality and Social Psychology* 70:523–34.

Burkhalter, Stephanie. 1997. "The poor are not like the rest of us": The social construction of welfare mothers in congressional policy discourse. Paper presented at the annual meeting of the Western Political Science Association, Tucson, AZ.

Burkhalter, Stephanie. 2006. Talking points: Message strategies and deliberation in the U.S. Congress. PhD diss., University of Washington.

Burkhalter, Stephanie, John Gastil, and Todd Kelshaw. 2002. A conceptual definition and theoretical model of public deliberation in small face-to-face groups. *Communication Theory* 12:398–422.

Burnett, D. Graham. 2001. *A trial by jury.* New York: Vintage.

Burnheim, John. 1989. *Is democracy possible? The alternative to electoral politics.* Berkeley: University of California Press.

Burns, James M., J. W. Peltason, Thomas E. Cronin, and David B. Magleby. 1996. *State and local politics: Government by the people.* Upper Saddle River, NJ: Prentice Hall.

Button, Mark, and Kevin Mattson. 1999. Deliberative democracy in practice: Challenges and prospects for civic deliberation. *Polity,* 31:609–37.

Button, Mark, and David M. Ryfe. 2005. What can we learn from the practice of deliberative democracy? In *The deliberative democracy handbook,* ed. John Gastil and Peter Levine, 20–33. San Francisco: Jossey-Bass.

Cain, Bruce, John Ferejohn, and Morris Fiorina. 1987. *The personal vote: Constituency service and electoral independence.* Cambridge, MA: Harvard University Press.

Campbell, Angus, Philip E. Converse, Warren E. Miller, and Donald E. Stokes. 1960. *The American voter.* New York: John Wiley & Sons.

Cappella, Joseph N., and Kathleen Hall Jamieson. 1997. *Spiral of cynicism: The press and the public good.* New York: Oxford University Press.

Carson, Lyn, and Janette Hartz-Karp. 2005. Adapting and combining deliberative designs: Juries, polls, and forums. In *The deliberative democracy handbook,* ed. John Gastil and Peter Levine, 120–38. San Francisco: Jossey-Bass.

Carson, Lyn, and Brian Martin. 1999. *Random selection in politics.* Westport, CT: Praeger.

Casper, Gerald, and Hans Zeisel. 1972. Lay judges in the German criminal courts. *Journal of Legal Studies* 1:135–91.

Chambers, Simone. 2003. Deliberative democratic theory. *Annual Review of Political Science* 6:307–26.

Chambers, Simone. 2004. Behind closed doors: Publicity, secrecy, and the quality of deliberation. *Journal of Political Philosophy* 12:389–410.

Charles, Michelle, Harris Sokoloff, and Chris Satullo. 2005. Electoral deliberation and public journalism. In *The deliberative democracy handbook,* ed. John Gastil and Peter Levine, 59–67. San Francisco: Jossey-Bass.

Chasin, Richard, Margaret Herzig, Sallyann Roth, Laura Chasin, Carol Becker, and Robert Stains, Jr. 1996. From diatribe to dialogue on divisive public issues: Approaches drawn from family therapy. *Mediation Quarterly* 13:323–44.

Checkoway, Barry. 1981. The politics of public hearings. *Journal of Applied Behavioral Science* 17:567–82.

Chikwanha-Dzenga, Annie B., Eldred Masunungure, and Nyasha Madingira. 2001. Democracy and national governance in Zimbabwe: A country survey report. *Afrobarometer Paper No. 12.* www.afrobarometer.org/papers/AfropaperNo12.pdf (accessed August 22, 2006).

Chilton, Paul A. ed. 1985. *Language and the nuclear arms debate: Nukespeak today.* London: Frances Pinter.

Churchill, John. 2006. A liberating education. *Seattle Times,* August 20, 2006. http://seattletimes.nwsource.com/html/opinion/2003209223_sunchurchill20.html (accessed October 23, 2006).

Clark, Ann Marie. 2001. *Diplomacy of conscience: Amnesty International and changing human rights norms.* Princeton, NJ: Princeton University Press.

Coelho, Vera Schattan P., Ilza Araujo L. de Andrade, and Mariana Cifuentes Montoya. 2002. Deliberative fora and the democratisation of social policies in Brazil. *IDS Bulletin* 33:65–73.

Coelho, Vera Schattan P., Barbara Pozzoni, and Mariana Cifuentes Montoya. 2005. Participation and public policies in Brazil. In *The deliberative democracy handbook,* ed. John Gastil and Peter Levine, 174–84. San Francisco: Jossey-Bass.

Cohen, Joshua. 1989. Deliberation and democratic legitimacy. In *The good polity,* ed. Philip Pettit and Alan Hamlin, 17–34. New York: Basil Blackwell.

Converse, Philip E. 1964. The nature of belief systems in mass publics. In *Ideology and discontent,* ed. David E. Apter, 206–61. New York: Free Press.

Cook, Fay Lomax, Michael X. Delli Carpini, and Lawrence R. Jacobs. 2003. Who deliberates? Discursive capital in America. Paper presented at the annual meeting of the American Political Science Association, Philadelphia.

Craib, Ian. 1992. *Anthony Giddens.* London: Routledge.

Crosby, Ned. 1995. Citizen juries: One solution for difficult environmental questions. In *Fairness and competence in citizen participation: Evaluating models for environmental discourse,* ed. Ortwin Renn, Thomas Webler, and Peter Wiedemann, 157–74. Boston: Kluwer.

Crosby, Ned. 2003. *Healthy democracy: Bringing trustworthy information to the voters of America.* Minneapolis, MN: Beaver's Pond.

Crosby, Ned, and Doug Nethercutt. 2005. Citizens' juries: Creating a trustworthy voice of the people. In *The deliberative democracy handbook,* ed. John Gastil and Peter Levine, 111–19. San Francisco: Jossey-Bass.

Dahl, Robert A. 1989. *Democracy and its critics.* New Haven, CT: Yale University Press.

Dahl, Robert A. 1998. *On democracy.* New Haven, CT: Yale University Press.

Dahl, Robert. 1999. Can international organizations be democratic? In *Democracy's edges,* ed. Ian Shapiro and Casiano Hacker-Cordon, 19–36. New York: Cambridge University Press.

Dahlgren, Peter. 2002. In search of the talkative public: Media, deliberative democracy and civic culture. *Javnost The Public* 9:5–26.

Daugherty, Renee A., and Sue E. Williams. 2007. Applications of public deliberation: Themes emerging from twelve personal experiences emanating from National

Issues Forums Training. *Journal of Public Deliberation* 3. http://services.bepress
.com/jpd/vol3/iss1/art10 (accessed July 5, 2007).

DeConto, Jesse J. 2003. Planning board approves plan for Sagamore Creek conservation
land. *Portsmouth Herald*, May 16, 2003. http://www.seacoastonline.com/2003
news/05162003/news/28861.htm (accessed July 16, 2007).

Dees, Tom M. 2001. Juries: On the verge of extinction? A discussion of jury reform.
SMU Law Review 54:1755–812.

Delli Carpini, Michael X., and Scott Keeter. 1996. *What Americans know about politics
and why it matters*. New Haven, CT: Yale University Press.

Delli Carpini, Michael X., Fay Lomax Cook, and Lawrence R. Jacobs. 2004. Public deliberation, discursive participation, and citizen engagement: A review of the empirical literature. *Annual Review of Political Science* 7:315–44.

Denver, David, Gordon Hands, and Bill Jones. 1995. Fishkin and the deliberative opinion poll: Lessons from a study of the Granada 500 television program. *Political
Communication* 12:147–56.

de Tocqueville, Alexis. 1961. *Democracy in America*. New York: Schocken. (Originally
published 1835)

Devine, Dennis J., Laura D. Clayton, Benjamin B. Dunford, Rasmy Seying, and Jennifer
Pryce. 2001. Jury decision making: 45 years of empirical research on deliberating
groups. *Psychology, Public Policy and Law* 7:622–727.

Dewey, John. 1910. *How we think*. New York: Heath.

Domke, David, Mark D. Watts, Dhavan V. Fan, and David P. Shah. 1999. The politics of
conservative elites and the "liberal media" argument. *Journal of Communication*
49:35–58.

Dorroh, Jennifer. 2005. Eye on CBS: Network launches a blog to scrutinize its news
operation. *American Journalism Review* 27 (5): 14.

Drucker, Susan J., and Gary Gumpert. 1996. The regulation of public social life: Communication law revisited. *Communication Quarterly* 44:280–96.

Dryzek, John S. 1990. *Discursive democracy: Politics, policy, and political science*.
Cambridge: Cambridge University Press.

Dryzek, John S. 2000. *Deliberative democracy and beyond: Liberals, critics, and contesta-
tions*. New York: Oxford University Press.

Dryzek, John S. 2001. Legitimacy and economy in deliberative democracy. *Political
Theory* 29:651–69.

Dubois, P. L. 1984. Voting cues in nonpartisan trial court elections: A multivariate
assessment. *Law and Society Review* 18:395–436.

Dwyer, William L. 2002. *In the hands of the people*. New York: St. Martin's Press.

Dzur, Albert W. 2002. Public journalism and deliberative democracy. *Polity* 34:313–36.

Eakin, Beth A. 1975. An empirical study of the effect of leadership influence on
decision outcomes in different sized jury panels. *Kansas Journal of Sociology*
11:109–26.

Edelman, Murray. 1977. *Political language*. New York: Academic Press.

Edelman, Murray. 1988. *Constructing the political spectacle*. Chicago: University of
Chicago Press.

Eliasoph, Nina. 1996. Making a fragile public: A talk-centered study of citizenship and
power. *Sociological Theory* 14:262–89.

Eliasoph, Nina. 1998. *Avoiding politics: How Americans produce apathy in everyday life*.
Cambridge: Cambridge University Press.

Elkin, Stephen L. 2004. Thinking constitutionally: The problem of deliberative democracy. *Social Philosophy and Policy* 21:39–75.

Elster, Jon. 1998. *Deliberative democracy.* Cambridge: Cambridge University Press.

Elving, Ronald D. 1995. C-SPAN gets pushy. *Columbia Journalism Review* 34:38–42.

Eriksen, Erik Oddvar, and John Erik Fossom. eds. 2000. *Democracy in the European Union: Integration through deliberation?* New York: Routledge.

Erikson, Robert S., and Thomas R. Palfrey. 1998. Campaign spending and incumbency: An alternative simultaneous equations approach. *Journal of Politics* 60:355–73.

Ettema, James S. 2007. Journalism as reason-giving: Deliberative democracy, institutional accountability, and the news media's mission. *Political Communication* 24:143–60.

Etzioni, Amatai. 1993. *The spirit of community: The reinvention of American society.* New York: Crown.

Evans, Sara M., and Harry C. Boyte. 1992. *Free spaces: The sources of democratic change in America.* Chicago: University of Chicago Press.

Fagotto, Elena, and Archon Fung. 2006. *Embedded deliberation: Entrepreneurs, organizations, and public action.* Boston: Taubman Center for State and Local Government.

Fairchild, Amy L. 2004. Policies of inclusion: Immigrants, disease, dependency, and American immigration policy at the dawn and dusk of the 20th century. *American Journal of Public Health* 94:528–39.

Farhi, Paul. 2003. Everybody wins. *American Journalism Review* 25:32–36.

Farrell, David M. 2001. *Electoral systems: A comparative introduction.* New York: St. Martin's Press.

Fasulo, Linda. 2005. *An insider's guide to the UN.* New Haven, CT: Yale University Press.

Faux, Jeff. 2000. Do the "Seattle protestors" have a point? *International Economy* 14 (4): 42–47.

Filner, Matthew F. 2002. Grassroots harvest: Assessing the "post-ideology" of pragmatic communitarianism. *Polity* 35:311–23.

Finkel, Steven E. 1985. Reciprocal effects of participation and political efficacy: A panel analysis. *American Journal of Political Science* 29:891–913.

Fiorina, Morris P. 1981. *Retrospective voting in American national elections.* New Haven, CT: Yale University Press.

Fiorino, Daniel J. 1990. Citizen participation and environmental risk: A survey of institutional mechanisms. *Science, Technology, and Human Values* 15:226–43.

Fisher, Roger, and William Ury. 1981. *Getting to yes: Negotiating agreement without giving in.* Boston: Houghton Mifflin.

Fishkin, James S. 1988. The case for a national caucus: Taking democracy seriously. *Atlantic* (August): 16–18.

Fishkin, James S. 1991. *Democracy and deliberation: New directions for democratic reform.* New Haven, CT: Yale University Press.

Fishkin, James S. 1995. *The voice of the people.* New Haven, CT: Yale University Press.

Fishkin, James, and Cynthia Farrar. 2005. Deliberative polling: From experiment to community resource. In *The deliberative democracy handbook,* ed. John Gastil and Peter Levine, 68–79. San Francisco: Jossey-Bass.

Fishkin, James S., and Robert C. Luskin. 1999. Bringing deliberation to the democratic dialogue: The NIC and beyond. In *The poll with a human face: The National Issues Convention experiment in political communication,* ed. Maxwell McCombs and Amy Reynolds, 3–38. Mahwah, NJ: Lawrence Erlbaum.

Fletcher, Michael A. 1998. The color of campaign finance. *Washington Post National Weekly Edition,* September 28.

Foley, Michael W., and Bob Edwards. 1996. The paradox of civil society. *Journal of Democracy*, 7:38–52.

Forde, Susan, Michael Meadows, and Kerrie Foxwell. 2003. Experiencing radio: Training, education and the community radio sector. *Australian Studies in Journalism* 12:83–103.

Forgette, Richard, and Glenn Platt. 2005. Redistricting principles and incumbency protection in the U.S. Congress. *Political Geography* 24:934–51.

Freeman, Samuel. 2000. Deliberative democracy: A sympathetic comment. *Philosophy and Public Affairs* 29:371–418.

Galston, William A., and Peter Levine. 1998. America's civic condition: A glance at the evidence. In *Community works: The revival of civil society in America*, ed. E. J. Dionne, 30–36. Washington, DC: Brookings Institution.

Gamson, William A. 1992. *Talking politics*. Cambridge: Cambridge University Press.

Gans, Herbert J. 2007. Everyday news, newsworkers, and professional journalism. *Political Communication* 24:161–66.

Gastil, John. 1992. Undemocratic discourse: A review of theory and research on political discourse. *Discourse and Society* 4:469–500.

Gastil, John. 1993. *Democracy in small groups: Participation, decision-making, and communication*. Philadelphia, PA: New Society Publishers.

Gastil, John. 1994. A definition and illustration of democratic leadership. *Human Relations* 47:953–75.

Gastil, John. 2000. *By popular demand: Revitalizing representative democracy through deliberative elections*. Berkeley: University of California Press.

Gastil, John. 2004. Adult civic education through the National Issues Forums: Developing democratic habits and dispositions through public deliberation. *Adult Education Quarterly* 54:308–28.

Gastil, John, Laura Black, and Kara Moscovitz. Forthcoming. Group and individual differences in deliberative experience: A study of ideology, attitude change, and deliberation in small face-to-face groups. *Political Communication*.

Gastil, John, Stephanie Burkhalter, and Laura Black. 2007. Group deliberation in the courthouse: Predicting deliberation, participation, and satisfaction in municipal juries. *Small Group Research* 38:337–59.

Gastil, John, and Ned Crosby. 2003. Voters need more reliable information. *Seattle Post-Intelligencer*, November 6, 2003. http://seattlepi.nwsource.com/opinion/147013_uninformed06.html (accessed October 21, 2006).

Gastil, John, and Ned Crosby. 2006. Taking the initiative. *Seattle Times*, November 26, 2006. http://seattletimes.nwsource.com/cgi-bin/PrintStory.pl?document_id=2003448042&slug=sungastil26&date=20061126 (accessed online December 5, 2006).

Gastil, John, Eugene P. Deess, and Phil Weiser. 2002. Civic awakening in the jury room: A test of the connection between jury deliberation and political participation. *Journal of Politics* 64:585–95.

Gastil, John, Eugene P. Deess, Phil Weiser, and Jordan Larner. Forthcoming. Jury service and electoral participation: A strong test of the participation hypothesis. *Journal of Politics*.

Gastil, John, and James Price Dillard. 1999a. The aims, methods, and effects of deliberative civic education through the National Issues Forums. *Communication Education* 48:1–14.

Gastil, John, and James Price Dillard. 1999b. Increasing political sophistication through public deliberation. *Political Communication* 16:3–23.

Gastil, John, Daniel Kahan, and Donald Braman, D. 2005. The cultural resonance model: Integrating culture, ideology, partisanship, and knowledge in theories of political communication and public opinion. Paper presented at the annual conference of the National Communication Association, Boston.

Gastil, John, and William M. Keith. 2005. A nation that (sometimes) likes to talk: A brief history of public deliberation in the United States. In *The deliberative democracy handbook*, ed. John Gastil and Peter Levine, 3–19. San Francisco: Jossey-Bass.

Gastil, John, and Peter Levine. eds. 2005. *The deliberative democracy handbook*. San Francisco: Jossey-Bass.

Gastil, John, and Phil Weiser. 2006. Jury service as an invitation to citizenship: Assessing the civic value of institutionalized deliberation. *Policy Studies Journal* 34:605–27.

Gastil, Raymond. 2002. *Beyond the edge: New York's new waterfront*. Princeton, NJ: Princeton Architectural Press.

Gerber, Alan. 1998. Estimating the effect of campaign spending on senate election outcomes using instrumental variables. *American Political Science Review* 92:401–11.

Gergen, Kenneth J., Sheila McNamee, and Frank J. Barrett. 2001. Toward transformative dialogue. *International Journal of Public Administration* 24:679–707.

Giddens, Anthony. 1984. *The constitution of society*. Berkeley: University of California Press.

Glaberson, William. 2001. Juries, their powers under siege, find their role is being eroded. *New York Times*, March 2.

Glendon, Mary Ann. 1991. *Rights talk: The impoverishment of political discourse*. New York: Free Press.

Glendon, Michael J. 2003. Why the security council failed. *Foreign Affairs*. http://www.foreignaffairs.org/20030501faessay11217/michael-j-glennon/why-the-security-council-failed.html (accessed online October 24, 2006).

Goldberg, Bernard. 2003. *Bias: A CBS insider exposes how the media distort the news*. New York: HarperCollins.

Goldfarb, Jeffrey C. 1998. *Civility and subversion: The intellectual in democratic society*. New York: Cambridge University Press.

Goodin, Robert E. 2000. Democratic deliberation within. *Philosophy and Public Affairs* 29:81–109.

Goodin, Robert E. 2003. *Reflective democracy*. Oxford: Oxford University Press.

Goodin, Robert E., and Simon J. Niemeyer. 2003. When does deliberation begin? Internal reflection versus public discussion in deliberative democracy. *Political Studies* 51:627–49.

Gore, Al. 2007. *The assault on reason*. New York: Penguin Press.

Gould, Carol C. 2004. *Globalizing democracy and human rights*. New York: Cambridge University Press.

Gouran, Dennis S., & Hirokawa, Randy Y. (1996). Functional theory and communication in decision-making and problem-solving groups: An expanded view. In *Communication and group decision-making*, ed. Randy Y. Hirokawa and Marshall S. Poole, 55–80. 2nd ed. Thousand Oaks: Sage.

Green, Donald P., and Alan S. Gerber. 2004. *Get Out the Vote: How to increase voter turnout*. Washington, DC: Brookings Institution Press.

Green, Donald P., and Bradley Palmquist. 1994. How stable is party identification? *Political Behavior* 16:437–66.

Green, Donald P., and R. Shachar. 2000. Habit formation and political behaviour: Evidence of consuetude in voter turnout. *British Journal of Political Science* 30:561–73.

Greenwald, Marilyn, and Joseph Bernt. eds. 2000. *The big chill: Investigative reporting in the current media environment.* Ames: Iowa State University Press.

Grice, H. Paul. 1975. Logic and conversation. In *Speech acts,* ed. Peter Cole and Jerry Morgan, 41–58. New York: Academic Press.

Grossberg, Joshua. 2005. Carlson out: *Crossfire* canned at CNN. *E!Online,* January 6.

Gulati, Girish J., Marion R. Just, and Ann N. Crigler. 2004. News coverage of political campaigns. In *Handbook of political communication research,* ed. Lynda Lee Kaid, 237–56. Mahwah, NJ: Lawrence Erlbaum.

Gutmann, Amy and Dennis F. Thompson. 1996. *Democracy and disagreement.* Cambridge, MA: Harvard University Press.

Gutmann, Amy, and Dennis F. Thompson. 2004. *Why deliberative democracy?* Princeton, NJ: Princeton University Press.

Habermas, Jurgen. 1975. *Legitimation crisis.* Boston: Beacon Press.

Habermas, Jurgen. 1979. *Communication and the evolution of society.* Boston: Beacon Press.

Habermas, Jurgen. 1989. *The structural transformation of the public sphere.* Cambridge, MA: MIT Press.

Habermas, Jurgen. 2006. Does democracy still enjoy an epistemic dimension? *Communication Theory* 16:411–26.

Hallin, Daniel C. 1992. Sound bite news: Television coverage of elections, 1968–1988. *Journal of Communication* 42:5–23.

Halvorsen, Kathleen E. 2003. Assessing the effects of public participation. *Public Administration Review* 63:535–43.

Hans, Valerie P. 2000. *Business on trial: The civil jury and corporate responsibility.* New Haven, CT: Yale University Press.

Hans, Valerie P. 2002. U.S. jury reform: The active jury and the adversarial ideal. *Saint Louis University Public Law Review* 21:85–97.

Hans, Valerie P., and Neil Vidmar. 1986. *Judging the jury.* New York: Plenum.

Harrison, Elliott. 1928. *The process of group thinking.* New York: Association Press.

Hart, Roderick, and Sharon Jarvis. 1999. We the people: The contours of lay political discourse. In *The poll with a human face: The National Issues Convention experiment in political communication,* ed. Maxwell McCombs and Amy Reynolds, 59–84. Mahwah, NJ: Lawrence Erlbaum.

Hastie, Reid, and Nancy Pennington. 1996. The O.J. Simpson stories: Behavioral scientists' reflections on *The People of the State of California v. Orenthal James Simpson. University of Colorado Law Review* 67:958.

Hastie, Reid, Steven D. Penrod, and Nancy Pennington. 1983. *Inside the jury.* Cambridge, MA: Harvard University Press.

Hastie, Reid, David A. Schkade, and John W. Payne. 1998. A study of juror and jury judgments in civil cases: Deciding liability for punitive damages. *Law and Human Behavior* 22:287–314.

Hawley, Willis D. 1973. *Nonpartisan elections and the case for party politics.* New York: John Wiley & Sons.

Held, David. 1998. Democracy and globalization. In *Re-imagining political community: Studies in cosmopolitan democracy,* ed. Daniele Archibugi, 11–27. Palo Alto, CA: Stanford University Press.

Hendriks, Carolyn M. 2005. Consensus conferences and planning cells: Lay citizen deliberations. In *The deliberative democracy handbook,* ed. John Gastil and Peter Levine, 80–110. San Francisco: Jossey-Bass.

Herbst, Susan. 1993. *Numbered voices: How opinion polling has shaped American politics.* Chicago: University of Chicago Press.

Herbst, Susan. 1999. The cultivation of conversation. In *The poll with a human face: The National Issues Convention experiment in political communication,* ed. Maxwell McCombs and Amy Reynolds, 187–209. Mahwah, NJ: Lawrence Erlbaum.

Herman, Edward S., and Noam Chomsky. 1988. *Manufacturing consent: The political economy of the mass media.* New York: Pantheon.

Hibbing, John R., and Theiss-Morse, Elizabeth. 2002. *Stealth democracy: Americans' beliefs about how government should work.* Cambridge: Cambridge University Press.

Hilberg, Raul. 2003. *The destruction of the European Jews.* 3rd ed. New Haven, CT: Yale University Press.

Hing, Bill O. 2004. *Defining America through immigration policy.* Philadelphia: Temple University Press.

Hofstetter, C. Richard, Mark C. Donovan, Melville R. Klauber, Alexandra Cole, Carolyn J. Huie, and Toshiyuki Yuasa. 1994. Political talk radio: A stereotype reconsidered. *Political Research Quarterly* 47:467–79.

Hollander, Barry A. 1997. Fuel to the fire: Talk radio and the Gamson hypothesis. *Political Communication* 14:355–69.

Holt, Jim. 2006. Export this? *New York Times Magazine,* April 23.

Howarth, Richard B., and Matthew A. Wilson. 2006. A theoretical approach to deliberative valuation: Aggregation by mutual consent. *Land Economics* 82:1–16.

Huckfeldt, Robert, Paul E. Johnson, and John Sprague. 2004. *Political disagreement: The survival of diverse opinions within communication networks.* New York: Cambridge University Press.

Huckfeldt, Robert, Jeanette Morehouse Mendez, and Tracy Osborn. 2004. Disagreement, ambivalence, and engagement: The political consequences of heterogeneous networks. *Political Psychology* 25:65–95.

Huckfeldt, Robert, and John Sprague. 1995. *Citizens, politics, and social communication: Information and influence in an election campaign.* Cambridge: Cambridge University Press.

Isbell, Linda M., and Victor C. Ottati. 2002. The emotional voter: Effects of episodic affective reactions on candidate evaluation. In *The social psychology of politics,* ed. Victor C. Ottai, Victor C., Scott Tindale, John Edwards, Fred B. Bryant, Linda Health, Daniel C. O'Connell, Yolanda Suarez-Balzacar, and Emil J. Posavac, 55–74. New York: Kluwer.

Ivins, Molly. 2004. Clueless people love Bush: Studies show Bush supporters are misled on Bush policies and the news. *Common Dreams Newscenter,* October 27, 2004. http://www.commondreams.org/views04/1027-34.htm (accessed October 21, 2006).

Jackman, Robert W., and Ross A. Miller. 2004. *Before norms: Institutions and civic culture.* Ann Arbor: University of Michigan Press.

Jacobs, Lawrence R., Michael X. Delli-Carpini, and Faye Lomax Cook. 2004. How do Americans deliberate? Paper presented at the annual meeting of the Midwest Political Science Association, Chicago.

Jacobson, Gary C. 1993. The misallocation of resources in house campaigns. In *Congress reconsidered,* ed. Lawrence C. Dodd and Bruce I. Openheimer, 115–39. 5th ed. Washington, DC: Congressional Quarterly Press.

Jacobson, Gary C. 1997. *The politics of congressional elections.* 4th ed. New York: Longman.

Jacobson, Gary C., and Samuel Kernell. 1981. *Strategy and choice in congressional elections.* New Haven, CT: Yale University Press.

Jacoby, William G. 1991. Ideological identification and issue attitudes. *American Journal of Political Science* 35:178–205.

Jacoby, William G. 1995. The structure of ideological thinking in the American electorate. *American Journal of Political Science* 39:314–35.

Jamieson, Kathleen Hall. 1992. *Dirty politics: Deception, distraction, and democracy.* New York: Oxford University Press.

Jamieson, Kathleen Hall. 1996. *Packaging the presidency: A history and criticism of presidential campaign advertising.* New York: Oxford University Press.

Janis, Irving L. 1982. *Groupthink: Psychological studies of policy decision and fiascoes.* 2nd ed. Boston: Houghton Mifflin.

Jerome, Lee, and Bhavini Algarra. 2005. Debating debating: A reflection on the place of debate within secondary schools. *Curriculum Journal* 16:493–508.

Johnson, Thomas J., and Barbara K. Kaye. 2004. Wag the blog: How reliance on traditional media and the Internet influence credibility perceptions of weblogs among blog users. *Journalism and Mass Communication Quarterly* 81:622–42.

Jonakait, Randolph N. 2003. *The American jury system.* New Haven, CT: Yale University Press.

Jones, David A. 2004. Why Americans don't trust the media—A preliminary analysis. *Harvard International Journal of Press-Politics* 9:60–75.

Just, Marion, Rosalind Levine, and Kathleen Regan. 2002. Investigative journalism despite the odds: Watchdog reporting continues to decline. *Columbia Journalism Review* 41:102–103.

Kahan, Daniel, Paul Slovic, Don Braman, and John Gastil. 2006. Fear of democracy: A cultural evaluation of Sunstein on risk. *Harvard Law Review* 119:1071–109.

Kaid, Lynda Lee. 2004. *Handbook of political communication research.* Mahwah, NJ: Lawrence Erlbaum.

Kalven, Harry, and Hans Zeisel. 1966. *The American jury.* Boston: Little, Brown.

Kang, John M. 2004. The irrelevance of sincerity: Deliberative democracy in the Supreme Court. *Saint Louis University Law Review* 48:305–25.

Kapoor, Ilan. 2004. Deliberative democracy and the WTO. *Review of International Political Economy,* 11:522–41.

Kay, Alan F. 1998. *Locating consensus for democracy.* St. Augustine, FL: Americans Talk Issues Foundation.

Keane, John. 1984. *Public life and late capitalism.* Cambridge: Cambridge University Press.

Keith, Bruce E., David B. Magleby, Candice J. Nelson, Elizabeth Orr, Mark C. Westlye, and Raymond E. Wolfinger. 1992. *The myth of the independent voter.* Berkeley: University of California Press.

Kelshaw, Todd Spencer. 2003. Public meetings and public officials: Officeholders' accounts of participatory and deliberative democratic encounters with citizens. PhD diss., University of Washington.

Kettering Foundation. 1989. *The public's role in the policy process: A view from state and local policymakers.* Dayton, OH: Kettering Foundation.

Kim, Joohan, Robert O. Wyatt, and Elihu Katz. 1999. News, talk, opinion, participation: The part played by conversation in deliberative democracy. *Political Communication* 16:361–85.

Kirp, David L. 1992. Two cheers for the electronic town hall: Or Ross Perot, meet Alexis De Tocqueville. *The Responsive Community* 2 (4): 48–52.

Klein, Gary. 2001. When the news doesn't fit: The *New York Times* and Hitler's first two months in office, February/March 1933. *Journalism and Mass Communication Quarterly* 78:127–49.

Knock, Thomas J. 1995. *To end all wars: Woodrow Wilson and the quest for a new world order.* Princeton, NJ: Princeton University Press.

Kraig, Robert A. 2004. *Woodrow Wilson and the lost world of the oratorical statesman.* College Station: Texas A&M University Press.

Krueger, Brian S. 2002. Assessing the potential of Internet political participation in the United States: A resource approach. *American Politics Research* 30:476–98.

Kuklinski, James H., and Norman L. Hurley. 1996. It's a matter of interpretation. In *Political persuasion and attitude change,* ed. Diana C. Mutz, Paul M. Sniderman, and Richard A. Brody, 125–44. Ann Arbor: University of Michigan Press.

Lange, Lynda. 2002. *Feminist interpretations of Jean-Jacques Rousseau.* University Park, PA: Penn State Press.

Lau, Richard R., and Gerald M. Pomper. 2004. *Negative campaigning: An analysis of U.S. Senate elections.* Lanham, MD: Rowman & Littlefield.

League of Women Voters. 1997. *Charting the health of American democracy.* http://www. lwv.org/report.html (accessed July 16, 2007).

Lee, Eugene C. 1960. *The politics of nonpartisanship.* Berkeley: University of California Press.

Lee, Tien-Tsung. 2005. The liberal media myth revisited: An examination of factors influencing perceptions of media bias. *Journal of Broadcasting and Electronic Media* 49:43–64.

Leib, Ethan J. 2004. *Deliberative democracy in America: A proposal for a popular branch of government.* University Park, PA: Penn State Press.

Leigh, Lawrence J. 1984. A theory of jury trial advocacy. *Utah Law Review* 763–806.

Levi, Margaret, and David Olson. 2000. The battles in Seattle. *Politics and Society* 28:309–29.

Levine, Peter. 1990. *The new progressive era.* Lanham, MD: Rowman & Littlefield.

Levine, Peter, Archon Fung, and John Gastil. 2005. Future directions for public deliberation. In *The deliberative democracy handbook,* ed. John Gastil and Peter Levine, 271–88. San Francisco: Jossey-Bass.

Levine, Peter, and Rose Marie Nierras. 2007. Activists' views of deliberation. *Journal of Public Deliberation* 3. http://services.bepress.com/jpd/vol3/iss1/art4 (accessed July 26, 2007).

Lewis, Charles. 1998. *The buying of Congress.* New York: Avon Books.

Lipsitz, Keena, Christine Trost, and Matthew Grossmann. 2005. What voters want from political campaign communication. *Political Communication* 22:337–54.

Lukensmeyer, Carolyn J., Joe Goldman, and Steven Brigham. 2005. A town meeting for the twenty-first century. In *The deliberative democracy handbook,* ed. John Gastil and Peter Levine, 154–63. San Francisco: Jossey-Bass.

Lunt, Peter, and Paul Stenner. 2005. The Jerry Springer show as an emotional public sphere. *Media, Culture and Society,* 27:59–81.

Luskin, Robert C., James S. Fishkin, and Roger Jowell. 2002. Considered opinions: Deliberative polling in Britain. *British Journal of Political Science* 32:455–87.

Lyons, W. E., David Lowery, and Ruth DeHoog. 1993. *The politics of dissatisfaction: Citizens, services, and urban institutions.* Armonk, NY: M. E. Sharpe.

MacCoun, Robert J., & Kerr, Norbert L. 1988. Asymmetric influence in mock jury deliberation: Jurors' bias for leniency. *Journal of Personality and Social Psychology* 54:21–33.

MacMillan, Margaret. 2003. *Paris 1919: Six months that changed the world.* New York: Random House.

Macoubrie, Jane. 2003. Logical argument structures in decision-making. *Argumentation* 17:291–313.

Madison, James. n.d. *The Federalist,* No. 42. http://usinfo.state.gov/usa/infousa/facts/funddocs/fed/federa42.htm (accessed October 21, 2006).

Magleby, David B. 1984. *Direct legislation: Voting on ballot propositions in the United States.* Baltimore, MD: Johns Hopkins University Press.

Mahtesian, Charles. 1997. The politics of ugliness. *Governing Magazine* 10:18–22.

Makinson, Larry, and Joshua Goldstein. 1996. *Open secrets: The encyclopedia of congressional money and politics.* 4th ed. Washington, DC: Center for Responsive Politics.

Maltzman, Forrest, and Lee Sigelman. 1996. The politics of talk: Unconstrained floor time in the U.S. House of Representatives. *Journal of Politics* 58:819–30.

Mansbridge, Jane J. 1983. *Beyond adversary democracy.* Chicago: University of Chicago Press.

Mansbridge, Jane J. 1992. A deliberative perspective on neocorporatism. *Politics and Society* 20:493–505.

Mansbridge, Jane J., Janette Hartz-Karp, Matthew Amengual, and John Gastil. 2006. Norms of deliberation: An inductive study. *Journal of Public Deliberation* 2. http://services.bepress.com/jpd/vol2/iss1/art7 (accessed July 5, 2007).

Manzo, John F. 1996. Taking turns and taking sides: Opening scenes from two jury deliberations. *Social Psychology Quarterly* 59:107–25.

Mathews, David. 1994. *Politics for people: Finding a responsible public voice.* Chicago: University of Illinois Press.

Matsusaka, John G. 2004. *For the many or the few: The initiative, public policy, and American democracy.* Chicago: University of Chicago Press.

Mattson, Kevin. 1998. *Creating a democratic public: The struggle for urban participatory democracy during the progressive era.* University Park: Pennsylvania State University Press.

McAfee, Noelle, Robert McKenzie, and David Mathews. 1990. *Hard choices.* Dayton, OH: Kettering Foundation.

McBride, Cillian. 2005. Deliberative democracy and the politics of recognition. *Political Studies,* 53:497–515.

McCombs, Maxwell, and Amy Reynolds. eds. 1999. *The poll with a human face: The National Issues Convention experiment in political communication.* Mahwah, NJ: Lawrence Erlbaum.

McCombs, Maxwell, and Donald L. Shaw. 1972. The agenda-setting function of mass media. *Public Opinion Quarterly* 36:176–85.

McDevitt, Michael. 2003. In defense of autonomy: A critique of the public journalism critique. *Journal of Communication* 53:155–64.

McDevitt, Michael, Spiro Kiousis, and Karin Wahl-Jorgensen. 2003. Spiral of moderation: Opinion expression in computer-mediated discussion. *International Journal of Public Opinion Research* 15:454–70.

McKinley, Jesse. 2005. Admiration for a comedian who knew no limits. *New York Times,* December 13.

McLeod, Jack M., Katie Daily, Zhongshi Guo, William P. Eveland, Jan Bayer, Seungchan Yang, and Hsu Wang. 1996. Community integration, local media use, and democratic processes. *Communication Research* 23:179–209.

McLeod, Jack M., Dietram A. Scheufele, and Patricia Moy. 1999. Community, communication, and participation: The role of mass media and interpersonal discussion in local political participation. *Political Communication* 16:315–36.

Melville, Keith, Taylor L. Willingham, and John R. Dedrick. 2005. National Issues Forums: A network of communities. In *The deliberative democracy handbook,* ed. John Gastil and Peter Levine, 37–58. San Francisco: Jossey-Bass.

Mendelberg, Tali. 2002. The deliberative citizen: Theory and evidence. *Political Decision Making, Deliberation and Participation 6:* 151–93.

Mengual, Gloria F. 2003. *Portsmouth, N.H.: Where public dialogue is a hallmark of community life.* http://www.studycircles.org/en/Article.141.aspx (accessed October 23, 2006).

Merkle, Daniel M. 1996. The National Issues Convention deliberative poll. *Public Opinion Quarterly* 60:588–619.

Miller, Warren E., and J. Merrill Shanks. 1996. *The new American voter.* Cambridge, MA: Harvard University Press.

Mitzen, Jennifer. 2005. Reading Habermas in anarchy: Multilaterial diplomacy and global public spheres. *American Political Science Review* 99:401–17.

Mooney, Chris. 2005. *The Republican war on science.* New York: Basic Books.

Morrell, Michael E. 2005. Deliberation, democratic decision making and internal political efficacy. *Political Behavior* 27:49–69.

Moy, Patricia, David Domke, and Keith Stamm. 2001. The spiral of silence and public opinion on affirmative action. *Journalism and Mass Communication Quarterly* 78:7–25.

Moy, Patricia, and John Gastil. 2006. Discussion networks, media use, and deliberative conversation. *Political Communication* 23:443–460.

Moy, Patricia, and Michael Pfau. 2000. *With malice toward all: The media and public confidence in democratic institutions.* New York: Praeger.

Muhlberger, Peter and Lori Weber. 2006. Lessons from the Virtual Agora Project: The effects of agency, identity, information, and deliberation on political knowledge. *Journal of Public Deliberation* 2. http://services.bepress.com/jpd/vol2/iss1/art13 (accessed July 5, 2007).

Mutz, Diana C. 1998. *Impersonal influence: How perceptions of mass collectives affect political attitudes.* Cambridge: Cambridge University Press.

Mutz, Diana C. 2006. *Hearing the other side: Deliberative versus participatory democracy.* New York: Cambridge University Press.

Mutz, Diana C., and Paul S. Martin. 2001. Facilitating communication across lines of political difference: The role of mass media. *American Political Science Review* 95:97–114.

Mutz, Diana C., and Byron Reeves. 2005. The new videomalaise: Effects of televised incivility on political trust. *American Political Science Review* 99:1–15.

Nanz, Patrizia, and Jens Steffek. 2005. Assessing the democratic quality of deliberation in international governance: Criteria and research strategies. *Acta Politica* 40:368–83.

National Issues Forums. 1990. *For convenors and moderators: Organizing your first forum/study circle.* Dayton, OH: National Issues Forums Institute.

National Issues Forums. 1992. *National Issues Forums leadership handbook, 1991–1992.* Dayton, OH: National Issues Forums Institute.

Navarrette, Ruben. 2006. Commentary: Immigration hearings "cynical and cowardly." *CNN.com,* July 6, 2006. http://www.cnn.com/2006/US/07/06/navarrette.immigration (accessed October 21, 2006).

Newhagen, John E. 1994. Self-efficacy and call-in political television show use. *Communication Research* 21:366–79.

Newman, Andy. 1993. Is it opinion, or is it expertise? *American Journalism Review* 15 (March): 2, 12–13.

Nie, Norman H., Jane Junn, and Kenneth Stehlik-Barry. 1996. *Education and democratic citizenship in America.* Chicago: University of Chicago Press.

Nimmo, Dan, and James E. Combs. 1990. *Mediated political realities.* 2nd ed. New York: Longman.

Nino, Carlos Santiago. 1996. *The constitution of deliberative democracy.* New Haven, CT: Yale University Press.

Nishizawa, Mariko. 2005. Citizen deliberations on science and technology and their social environments: Case study on the Japanese consensus conference on GM crops. *Science and Public Policy* 32:479–89.

Noelle-Neumann, Elisabeth. 1991. The theory of public opinion: The concept of the spiral of silence. In *Communication Yearbook 14,* ed. James A. Anderson, 256–87. Newbury Park, CA: Sage.

Nye, Joseph S. 2001. Globalization's democratic deficit: How to make international institutions more accountable. *Foreign Affairs* 80 (4). http://www.foreignaffairs.org/2001/4.html (accessed June 21, 2007).

Ober, Josiah. 1989. *Mass and elite in democratic Athens: Rhetoric, ideology, and the power of the people.* Princeton, NJ: Princeton University Press.

Oldenburg, Ray. 1997. *The great good place: Cafes, coffee shops, community centers, beauty parlors, general stores, bars, hangouts, and how they get you through the day.* 2nd ed. New York: Marlowe.

Oliver, J. Eric, and Raymond E. Wolfinger. 1999. Jury aversion and voter registration. *American Political Science Review* 93:147–52.

Oliver, Leonard P. 1987. *Study circles.* Washington, DC: Seven Locks Press.

Orwell, George. 1956. *The Orwell reader.* New York: Harcourt Brace.

Ottati, Victor C., and Megan Deiger. 2002. Visual cues and the candidate evaluation process. In *The social psychology of politics,* ed. Victor C. Ottati, 75–87. New York: Kluwer.

Page, Benjamin I. 1996. *Who deliberates? Mass media in modern democracy.* Chicago: University of Chicago Press.

Page, Benjamin I. and Robert Y. Shapiro. 1992. *The Rational Public: Fifty Years of Trends in Americans' Policy Preferences.* Chicago: University of Chicago.

Parenti, Michael. 1995. *Democracy for the few.* 6th ed. New York: St. Martin's Press.

Park, Won-Woo. 1990. A review of research on groupthink. *Journal of Behavioral Decision Making* 3:229–45.

Parker, Walter C. 2003. *Teaching democracy: Unity and diversity in public life.* New York: Teachers College Press.

Parkinson, John. 2003. Legitimacy problems in deliberative democracy. *Political Studies* 51:180–96.

Passel, Jeffrey. 2004. *Mexican immigration to the US: The latest estimates.* Washington, DC: Migration Policy Institute.

Pearce, W. Barnett, and Stephen W. Littlejohn. 1997. *Moral conflict: When social worlds collide.* Thousand Oaks, CA: Sage.

Pein, Corey. 2005. Blog-gate. *Columbia Journalism Review* 43:30–35.

Perrin, Andrew J. 2005. Political microcultures: Linking civic life and democratic discourse. *Social Forces* 84:1049–82.

Peters, John Durham. 2001. *Speaking into the air: A history of the idea of communication.* Chicago: University of Chicago Press.

Pettus, Ann Burnett. 1990. The verdict is in: A study of jury decision making factors, moment of personal decision, and jury deliberations—From the juror's point of view. *Communication Quarterly* 38:83–97.

Petty, Richard E., and John T. Cacioppo. 1981. *Attitudes and persuasion: Classic and contemporary approaches.* Dubuque, IA: Brown and Benchmark.

Pfau, Michael, and Allan Louden. 1994. Effectiveness of adwatch formats in deflecting political attack ads. *Communication Research* 21:325–41.

Phelan, Jo, Bruce G. Link, Ann Stueve, and Robert E. Moore. 1995. Education, social liberalism, and economic conservatism: Attitudes toward homeless people. *American Sociological Review* 60:126–40.

Pollack, Mark A. 2003. Control mechanism or deliberative democracy? Two images of comitology. *Comparative Political Studies* 36:125–55.

Polletta, Francesca. 2002. *Freedom is an endless meeting: Democracy in American social movements.* Chicago: University of Chicago Press.

Potapchuk, William R., Cindy Carlson, and Joan Kennedy. 2005. Growing governance deliberatively: Lessons and inspiration from Hampton, Virginia. In *The deliberative democracy handbook,* ed. John Gastil and Peter Levine, 254–70. San Francisco: Jossey-Bass.

Powers v. Ohio, 499 U.S. 400, 407 (1991).

Price, Vincent, and Clarissa David. 2005. Talking about elections: A study of patterns in citizen deliberation online. Paper presented at the annual meeting of the International Communication Association, New York.

Putnam, Robert. 1993. *Making democracy work: Civic traditions in modern Italy.* Princeton, NJ: Princeton University Press.

Putnam, Robert D. 1995a. Bowling alone: America's declining social capital. *Journal of Democracy* 6 (1): 65–78.

Putnam, Robert D. 1995b. Tuning in, tuning out: The strange disappearance of social capital in America. *PS: Political Science and Politics* 28:664–83.

Putnam, Robert D. 2000. *Bowling alone: The collapse and revival of American community.* New York: Simon & Schuster.

Rakove, Jack N. 1996. *Original meanings: Politics and ideas in the making of the Constitution.* New York: Vintage Books.

Ratner, R. S. 2004a. British Columbia's Citizens' Assembly: The Learning Phase. *Canadian Parliamentary Review* 27:20–26.

Ratner, R. S. 2004b. The B.C. Citizens' Assembly: The public hearings and deliberations stage. *Canadian Parliamentary Review* 28:24–33.

Rawls, John. 1971. *A theory of justice.* Cambridge, MA: Harvard University Press.

Rawls, John. 1995. *Political liberalism.* New York: Columbia University Press.

Rawls, John. 1999. *The law of peoples.* Cambridge, MA: Harvard University Press.

Reich, Robert B. 1985. Public administration and public deliberation: An interpretive essay. *The Yale Law Journal* 94:1617–41.

Renn, Ortwin, Thomas Webler, Horst Rakel, Peter Dienel, and Branden Johnson. 1993. Public participation in decision making: A three-step procedure. *Policy Sciences* 26:189–214.

Reynolds, Amy. 1999. Local television coverage of the NIC. In *The poll with a human face: The National Issues Convention experiment in political communication,* ed. Maxwell McCombs and Amy Reynolds, 113–32. Mahwah, NJ: Lawrence Erlbaum.

Risse, Thomas, and Kathryn Sikkink. 1999. The socialization of international human rights norms into domestic practices: Introduction. In *The power of human rights: International norms and domestic change,* ed. Thomas Risse and Kathryn Sikkink, 1–38. New York: Cambridge University Press.

Robert, Henry M. 1990. *Robert's rules of order.* Glenview, IL: Scott, Foresman.

Rojas, Hernando, Dhavan V. Shah, Jaeho Cho, Michael Schmierbach, Heejo Keun, and Homero Gil-De-Zuniga. 2005. Media dialogue: Perceiving and addressing community problems. *Mass Communication and Society,* 8:93–110.

Rosen, Jay. 2001. *What are journalists for?* New Haven, CT: Yale University Press.

Rosen, Jay, and Davis Merritt. 1994. *Public journalism: Theory and practice.* Dayton, OH: Kettering Foundation.

Rosenau, James N. 1998. Governance and democracy in a globalizing world. In *Re-imagining political community: Studies in cosmopolitan democracy,* ed. Daniele Archibugi, David Held, and Martin Kohler, 28–57. Stanford, CA: Stanford University Press.

Rosenberg, Shawn W., Dana Ward, and Stephen Chilton. 1988. *Political reasoning and cognition: A Piagetian view.* Durham, NC: Duke University Press.

Rosendorff, B. Peter. 2005. Stability and rigidity: Politics and design of the WTO's dispute settlement procedure. *American Political Science Review* 99:389–400.

Rosenstone, Steven J., and John M. Hansen. 1993. *Mobilization, participation, and democracy in America.* New York: Macmillan.

Rostboll, Christian F. 2005. Preferences and paternalism—On freedom and deliberative democracy. *Political Theory* 33:370–96.

Rousseau, Jean-Jacques. 1950. *The social contract and discourses.* New York: E. Dutton. (Original work published 1762)

Ryan, Joal. 1998. "Seinfeld" goes directly to jail. *E!Online.* http://cache-origin.eonline .com/News/Items/0,1,3006,00.html (accessed June 21, 2007).

Ryfe, David Michael. 1999. Franklin Roosevelt and the fireside chats. *Journal of Communication* 49:80–103.

Ryfe, David Michael. 2002. The practice of deliberative democracy: A study of 16 deliberative organizations. *Political Communication* 19:359–77.

Ryfe, David Michael. 2005. Does deliberative democracy work? *Annual Review of Political Science* 8:49–71.

Ryfe, David M. 2006. Narrative and deliberation in small group forums. *Journal of Applied Communication Research* 34:72–93.

Ryfe, David M. 2007 Toward a sociology of deliberation. *Journal of Public Deliberation* 3. http://services.bepress.com/jpd/vol3/iss1/art3 (accessed July 26, 2007).

Salisbury, Robert H. 1986. Washington lobbyists: A collective portrait. In *Interest group politics,* ed. Allan J. Cigler and Burdett A. Loomis, 146–61. Washington, DC: Congressional Quarterly.

Samuels, Suzanne U. 2004. *First among friends: Interest groups, the U.S. Supreme Court, and the right to privacy.* Westport, CT: Praeger.

Sanders, Lynn M. 1997. Against deliberation. *Political Theory* 25:347–76.

Sandys, Marla, & Dillehay, Ronald C. 1995. First-ballot votes, predeliberation dispositions, and final verdicts in jury trials. *Law and Human Behavior* 19:175–95.

Scher, Richard K. 1997. *The modern political campaign: Mudslinging, bombast, and the vitality of American politics.* Armonk, NY: M. E. Sharpe.

Scheufele, Dietram A. 1999. Framing as a theory of media effects. *Journal of Communication* 49:103–22.

Scheufele, Dietram A., Bruce W. Hardy, Dominique Brossard, Israel S. Waismel-Manor, and Erik Nisbet. 2006. Democracy based on difference: Examining the links between structural heterogeneity, heterogeneity of discussion networks, and democratic citizenship. *Journal of Communication* 56:728–53.

Scheufele, Dietram A., and Patricia Moy. 2000. Twenty-five years of the spiral of silence: A conceptual review and empirical outlook. *International Journal of Public Opinion Research* 12:3–28.

Scheufele, Dietram A., James Shanahan, and Sei-Hill Kim. 2002. Who cares about local politics? Media influences on local political involvement, issue awareness, and attitude strength. *Journalism and Mass Communication Quarterly* 79:427–44.

Schkade, David, Cass R. Sunstein, and Reid Hastie. 2006. What happened on deliberation day? University of Chicago Law and Economics, Olin Working Paper No. 298. http://ssrn.com/abstract=911646 (accessed June 21, 2007).

Schmitt-Beck, Rudiger. 2004. Political communication effects: The impact of mass media and personal conversations on voting. In *Comparing Political Communication: Theories, Cases, and Challenges,* ed. Frank Esser and Barbara Pfetsch, 293–392. Cambridge: Cambridge University Press.

Schudson, Michael. 1997. Why conversation is not the soul of democracy. *Critical Studies in Mass Communication* 14:1–13.

Schudson, Michael. 1998. *The good citizen: A history of American civic life.* New York: Free Press.

Schudson, Michael. 2001. Politics as cultural practice. *Political Communication* 18:421–31.

Scully, Patrick L., and Martha L. McCoy. 2005. Study circles: Local deliberation as the cornerstone of deliberative democracy. In *The deliberative democracy handbook,* ed. John Gastil and Peter Levine, 199–212. San Francisco: Jossey-Bass.

Segall, Shlomi. 2005. Political participation as an engine of social solidarity: A skeptical view. *Political Studies* 53:362–78.

Shah, Dhavan V., Nojin Kwak, and R. Lance Holbert. 2001. "Connecting" and "disconnecting" with civic life: Patterns of Internet use and the production of social capital. *Political Communication* 18:141–62.

Shultz, Jim. 2002. *The democracy owner's manual: A practical guide to changing the world.* New Brunswick, NJ: Rutgers University Press.

Simon, Rita J. 1967. *The jury and the defense of insanity.* Boston: Little, Brown.

Sirianni, Carmen, and Lewis Friedland. 2001. *Civic innovation in America: Community empowerment, public policy, and the movement for civic renewal.* Berkeley: University of California Press.

Skocpol, Theda. 2003. *Diminished democracy: From membership to management in American civic life.* Norman: University of Oklahoma Press.

Skocpol, Theda, and Morris P. Fiorina. 1999. *Civic engagement in American democracy.* Washington, DC: Brookings Institution Press.

Smith, Robert C. 2003. Migrant membership as an instituted process: Transnationalization, the state and the extra-territorial conduct of Mexican politics. *International Migration Review* 37:297–343.

Smith, Tom A. 1999. The delegates' experience. In *The poll with a human face: The National Issues Convention experiment in political communication,* ed. Maxwell McCombs and Amy Reynolds, 39–58. Mahwah, NJ: Lawrence Erlbaum.

Sniderman, Paul M., Richard A. Brody, and Philip E. Tetlock. 1991. *Reasoning and choice: Explorations in political psychology.* Cambridge: Cambridge University Press.

Sprain, Leah, and John Gastil. 2007. What does it mean to deliberate? An interpretative account of the norms and rules of deliberation expressed by jurors. Unpublished manuscript prepared for the University of Washington, Seattle.

Stauber, John, and Sheldon Rampton. 1995. *Toxic sludge is good for you: Lies, damn lies and the public relations industry.* Monroe, ME: Common Courage.

Stavistsky, Alan G. 1994. The changing conception of localism in U.S. public radio. *Journal of Broadcasting and Electronic and Media* 38:19–33.

Street, Marc D. 1997. Groupthink: An examination of theoretical issues, implications, and future research suggestions. *Small Group Research* 28:72–93.

Strodtbeck, F. L., & Lipinski, R. M. (1985). Becoming first among equals: Moral considerations in jury foreman selection. *Journal of Personality and Social Psychology* 49:927–36.

Sturgis, Alice. 1988. *Standard code of parliamentary procedure.* 3rd ed. New York: McGraw-Hill.

Sturgis, Patrick, Caroline Roberts, and Nick Allum. 2005. A different take on the deliberative poll: Information, deliberation, and attitude constraint. *Public Opinion Quarterly* 69:30–65.

Sunstein, Cass R. 2002. The law of group polarization. *Journal of Political Philosophy* 10:175–95.

Surian, Luca. 1996. Are children with autism deaf to gricean maxims? *Cognitive Neuropsychiatry* 1:55–72.

Svoboda, Craig J. 1995. Retrospective voting in gubernatorial elections: 1982 and 1986. *Political Research Quarterly* 48:135–50.

Tarrance, V. Lance, Tarrance De Vries, and Donna L. Mosher. 1998. *Checked and balanced: How ticket-splitters are shaping the new balance of power in American politics.* Grand Rapids, MI: William B. Eerdmans.

Theiss-Morse, Elizabeth, and John R. Hibbing. 2005. Citizenship and civic engagement. *Annual Review of Political Science* 8:227–49.

Thompson, Michael, Richard J. Ellis, and Aaron Wildavsky. 1990. *Cultural theory.* Boulder, CO: Westview.

Thornton, Russell. 1987. *American Indian holocaust and survival: A population history since 1492.* Norman: University of Oklahoma Press.

Tilly, Charles. 2004. *Social movements, 1768–2004.* Boulder, CO: Paradigm Publishers.

Tonn, Mari B. 2005. Taking conversation, dialogue, and therapy public. *Rhetoric and Public Affairs* 8:405–30.

Townsend, Rebecca. 2006. Widening the circumference of scene: Local, politics, local metaphysics. *K.B. Journal* 3. http://kbjournal.org/townsend (accessed June 21, 2007).

Tracy, Karen, and Heidi Muller. 2001. Diagnosing a school board's interactional trouble: Theorizing problem formulating. *Communication Theory* 11:84–104.

Tuchman, Barbara. 1994. *The guns of August.* New York: Ballantine.

Uleman, Gerald F. 1996. The five hardest lessons from the O.J. trial. *Issues in Ethics* 7:1. http://www.scu.edu/ethics/publications/iie/v7n1/lessons.html (accessed October 21, 2006).

Underwood, Doug. 2001. Reporting and the push for market-oriented journalism: Media organizations as businesses. In *Mediated politics: Communication in the future of democracy,* ed. W. Lance Bennett and Robert M. Entman, 99–116. New York: Cambridge University Press.

Uslaner, Eric M. 2000. Is the Senate more civil than the House? In *Esteemed colleagues: Civility and deliberation in the U.S. Senate,* ed. Burdett A. Loomis, 33–55. Washington, DC: Brookings Institution Press.

Verba, Sidney, Kay L. Schlozman, and Henry E. Brady. 1995. *Voice and equality: Civic voluntarism in American politics.* Cambridge, MA: Harvard University Press.

Vidmar, Hans. 2000. A historical and comparative perspective on the common law jury. In *World jury systems,* ed. Hans Vidmar, 1–52. New York: Oxford University Press.

Walsh, Katherine Cramer. 2004. *Talking about politics: Informal groups and social identity in American life.* Chicago: University of Chicago Press.

Walsh, Katherine Cramer. 2007. *Talking about race: Community dialogues and the politics of difference.* Chicago: University of Chicago Press.

Walzer, Michael. 1991. The idea of civil society. *Dissent* 38:293–304.

Warren, Mark E. 1992. Democratic theory and self-transformation. *American Political Science Review* 86:8–23.

Warren, Mark, and Hilary Pearse. Forthcoming. *Designing democratic renewal.* New York: Cambridge University Press.

Watkins, Ralph. 1998. Report on an experiment in direct-mail distribution of the voters guide. Unpublished manuscript prepared for the League of Women Voters of Montgomery County, MD.

Wattenberg, Martin P. 1994. *The decline of American political parties, 1952–1992.* Cambridge, MA: Harvard University Press.

Watts, Mark D., David Domke, Dhavan V. Shah, and David P. Fan. 1999. Elite cues and media bias in presidential campaigns: Explaining public perceptions of a liberal press. *Communication Research* 26:144–75.

Weaver, David, Maxwell McCombs, and Donald L. Shaw. 2004. Agenda-setting research: Issues, attributes, and influences. In *Handbook of political communication research,* ed. Lynda Lee Kaid, 257–82. Mahwah, NJ: Lawrence Erlbaum.

Webler, Thomas, and Ortwin Renn. 1995. A brief primer on participation: Philosophy and practice. In *Fairness and competence in citizen participation: Evaluating models for environmental discourse,* ed. Ortwin Renn, Thomas Webler, and Peter Wiedemann. Boston: Kluwer.

Weiksner, G. Michael. 2005. E-ThePeople.Org: Large scale, ongoing deliberation. In *The deliberative democracy handbook,* ed. John Gastil and Peter Levine, 213–37. San Francisco: Jossey-Bass.

Weithman, Paul J. 1995. Contractualist liberalism and deliberative democracy. *Philosophy and Public Affairs,* 24:314–43.

Weithman, Paul J. 2005. Deliberative character. *Journal of Political Philosophy,* 13:263–83.

Wells, Chris, Justin Reedy, John Gastil, and Carolyn Lee. 2006. Deliberation during initiative elections: What (little) we know and why it (still) matters. Paper presented at the annual conference of the National Communication Association, San Antonio, TX.

Wildavsky, Aaron. 1987. Choosing preferences by constructing institutions: A cultural theory of preference formation. *American Political Science Review* 81:3–21.

Wildavsky, Aaron, and Mary Douglas. 1982. *Risk and culture: An essay on the selection of technological and environmental dangers.* Berkeley: University of California Press.

Williamson, Abigail, and Archon Fung. 2004. Public deliberation: Where are we and where can we go? *National Civic Review* 93 (4): 3–15.

Wilson, James Q. 1990. Interests and deliberation in the American republic, or, why James Madison would never have received the James Madison award. *PS: Political Science and Politics* 23:559–62.

Wiseman, Virginia, Gavin Mooney, Geoffrey Berry, & Kwok-Cho Tang. 2003. Involving the general public in priority setting: Experiences from Australia. *Social Science and Medicine* 56:1001–12.

Wodak, Ruth. 1989. The power of political jargon—A "Club 2" discussion. In *Language, power, and ideology,* ed. Ruth Wodak, 137–63. Amsterdam: John Benjamins.

Woodward, Bob, and Scott Armstrong. 1979. *The brethren: Inside the Supreme Court.* New York: Simon & Schuster.

Wyatt, Robert O., Elihu Katz, and Joohan Kim. 2000. Bridging the spheres: Political and personal conversation in public and private spaces. *Journal of Communication* 50:71–92.

Yankelovich, Daniel. 1991. *Coming to public judgment.* New York: Syracuse University Press.

Zaller, John R. 1992. *The nature and origins of mass opinion.* Cambridge: Cambridge University Press.

Zimmerman, Joseph. 1989. *The New England town meeting: Democracy in action.* Westport, CT: Praeger.

Zunes, Stephen. 2004. Implications of the U.S. reaction to the world court ruling against Israel's "separation barrier." *Middle East Policy* 11:73.

Index

About the Author

John Gastil is a professor in the Department of Communication at the University of Washington, where he specializes in political deliberation and group decision making. Prior to joining the University of Washington, he worked for three years at the University of New Mexico Institute for Public Policy, where he conducted public opinion survey research and convened citizen conferences. He received his communication PhD from the University of Wisconsin–Madison in 1994 and his BA in political science from Swarthmore College in 1989. Gastil is the coeditor, with Peter Levine, of *The Deliberative Democracy Handbook: Strategies for Effective Civic Engagement in the Twenty-First Century* (2005). This book brings together the experiences of activists, nonprofit organization leaders, and scholars to understand how the most promising and innovative methods of citizen deliberation can fit into existing political cultures and institutions. In 2000, Gastil's *By Popular Demand: Revitalizing Representative Democracy through Deliberative Elections* was published. This book built on his previous work by showing how small-group discussions can be integrated into the electoral process and public institutions. In 1993, his book *Democracy in Small Groups* came out, clarifying what it means for a group to be democratic and describing the obstacles groups face when trying to make decisions democratically. Gastil's scholarly articles have appeared in *Communication Theory, Harvard Law Review, Human Communication Research, Journal of Applied Social Psychology, Journal of Politics, Policy Studies Journal, Political Communication, Small Group Research*, and other journals.

77.5cm 30½ L

52.4cm 20 ⅝ 8

38.7cm 15¼ H